The
WPA Guide
to South Dakota

The WPA Guide to South Dakota

*Compiled and written
by the Federal Writers' Project
of the Works Progress Administration*

With an introduction by
JOHN E. MILLER

MINNESOTA HISTORICAL SOCIETY PRESS

www.mhspress.org

The Minnesota Historical Society Press is a member of the
Association of American University Presses.

Manufactured in Canada

10 9 8 7 6 5 4 3 2 1

∞ The paper used in this publication meets the minimum requirements of the American National Standard for Information Sciences—Permanence for Printed Library Materials, ANSI Z39.48-1984.

International Standard Book Number 0-87351-552-8 (paper)

Library of Congress Cataloging-in-Publication Data

South Dakota guide.
The WPA guide to South Dakota : the Federal Writers' Project guide to 1930s South Dakota / compiled by the Federal Writers' Project of the Works Progress Administration ; with an introduction by John E. Miller.
    p.   cm.
Includes bibliographical references and index.
Originally published: Pierre, S.D. : State Pub. Co., 1938. With new introd.
ISBN-13: 978-0-87351-552-8 (pbk. : alk. paper)
ISBN-10: 0-87351-552-8 (pbk. : alk. paper)
    1. South Dakota.
    2. South Dakota—Guidebooks.
    I. Miller, John E., 1945–
    II. South Dakota Federal Writers Project.
    III. Title.
F656.F45 2006
978.3—dc22   2006003521

CONTENTS

(Mile-by-Mile Description of the State's Highways)

A chart of
SOUTH DAKOTA
and points therein
FEDERAL WRITERS' PROJECT

INTRODUCTION

South Dakotans think of themselves as—and are considered by others to be—hard-working, optimistic, resourceful people. When blackbirds devoured the entire corn crop of the pioneer Ingalls family during territorial days, Caroline, the family matriarch, strove to make the best of it. As described in *Little Town on the Prairie* by her daughter Laura Ingalls Wilder, she fried up a batch of the birds for dinner, the whole family agreeing they made the tenderest, most delicious meat they had ever eaten. "There's no great loss without some small gain," Ma Ingalls benignly concluded.

Half a century later, as South Dakotans endured the greatest sustained natural and economic catastrophe they had ever experienced, they likewise coped as best they could. Already laid low by depressed agricultural prices and extensive bank failures during the supposedly prosperous twenties, South Dakota residents during the "dirty thirties" reeled under the twin calamities of drought and economic depression. At the economy's lowest point, farmland had lost three-fourths of its value, more than 34,000 farm mortgages had undergone foreclosure, more than two-quarters of the state's banks had failed, and thousands of businesses had closed their doors. In late 1934 the state had the highest percentage of residents on government relief (39 percent), and by the end of the thirties, so many tens of thousands of people had abandoned South Dakota that its population registered the largest percentage loss of any state during the decade (7.2 percent).

Out of this maelstrom of environmental, economic, and social upheaval emerged countless instances of bravery, tenacity, and resourcefulness. One of the unanticipated—but highly welcome—outcomes of the thirties was a series of state guidebooks designed to aid travelers navigating America's rapidly expanding road system and to provide basic information about the history, geography, economic resources, and social and cultural development of each state. Largely accidental in their inception, the books were the major accomplishment of the Federal Writers' Project (FWP), launched in the summer of 1935 as part of President Franklin D. Roosevelt's massive new federal relief program and one of the rapidly proliferating "alphabet soup" agencies of the early New Deal. Under relief administrator Harry Hopkins's direction, the Works Progress Administration (WPA) put 3.5 million Americans to work at its peak, but that count comprised only one-third of the pool of unemployed workers looking for jobs. While the program remained focused on industrial workers and service employees, government officials responded enthusiastically to suggestions that white-collar jobs, including positions for writers and for those in art, music, and theater, be provided, too. Federal One, as the program was dubbed, put more than 40,000 people to work at one time in those four areas, including more than 6,500 on the Federal Writers' Project.

Millions of Americans welcomed the WPA, including its arts projects, as money well spent, helping the destitute survive, preserving dignity and hope, and providing valuable results that benefited the entire society. From the beginning, however, critics objected to inefficiencies, wastefulness, and political machinations—both real and imagined—associated with government relief. In August 1938 the attacks took a somewhat different turn when Congressmen Martin Dies of Texas and J. Parnell Thomas of New Jersey, endeavoring to discredit Roosevelt and the New Deal, used their positions on the newly created House Committee on Un-American Activities to launch an attack on the federal writers' and theater projects for being riddled with Communists and fellow travelers. They and their supporters succeeded in killing the latter while greatly reducing federal support for and control over the other three arts programs.

In the meantime, however, the South Dakota branch of the FWP had turned out its state guide and was working on what emerged as more than a dozen publications, ranging in length from thirty to nearly seven hundred pages, on historical and other subjects, including homesteading in McPherson County, a vacation guide to Custer State Park, a Hamlin Garland Memorial, and legends of the Sioux (Dakota) Indians. The longest and most valuable of these products was a book on South Dakota place names, published in 1940.

The South Dakota unit's outstanding production—one of continuing value today—is, however, the book at hand, originally published as *A South Dakota Guide* in July 1938 with a print run of 4,000. Available for $2.00 in bookstores or from the state FWP office in Mitchell or the South Dakota Guide Commission office in Pierre, the books cost twice as much as the original publicity had estimated, but even at that price they were a rare bargain. Perhaps in imitation of Charles Beard's classic *An Economic Interpretation of the Constitution,* the guide did not claim to provide *the* account of the state's history or geography but rather presented *a* version that was the best its writers and editors could assemble under the constraints of time and available resources.

Whatever some people may have thought about "that man" in the White House or alleged New Deal "boondoggles," published reviews of the handsome 441-page volume were generally glowing: "a friendly host rather than a professional guide" (*Aberdeen American-News*); "should be a great help to tourists passing through the state" (*Huron Evening Huronite*); "such beautiful English that the reader becomes so interested that he reads on and on, finding no place where he wants to stop" (*Hartford Herald*). "How so tasty a dish came from a pot stirred by so many cooks, we don't know, but *A South Dakota Guide* kept us up nights—and not with indigestion," observed the *Rapid City Journal.* The *Sioux Falls Argus Leader* called it "really an interpretation of South Dakota, linking its history with present-day interests and aspirations." John T. Frederick, a professor of literature at Northwestern University, approvingly observed over a nationwide radio hookup that the authors had written of their state with appreciation and respect "without falling in the too familiar booster tone that condemns one's product by its obvious insincerity."

That willingness of the authors to value the state's heritage without being cloying or predictable draws us, more than half a century later, back to the book. Like other state volumes, the

South Dakota guide followed a standard format, dictated by a steady stream of memos and directives from the Washington office on what topics to cover and how to treat them and warning against the insertion of personal bias or interpretation into the text. Considerable room remained, however, for researchers and writers in each state to choose what to put in and what to leave out and what tone to adopt in treating the material. In Washington a major decision had been made at the outset regarding the general nature of the series. Katharine Kellock, chief editor of the tours section of the books, had lobbied hard to make them Baedekers, or European-model guidebooks. The United States had received its Baedeker treatment in 1893, followed by a revised version in 1909. FWP director Henry Alsberg wanted instead a book built around general essays treating broadly the central historical and cultural themes that defined the states.

Not surprisingly, a compromise completely satisfying to neither party emerged. Alsberg's office notified the states that each guide would consist of three parts: a set of unsigned introductory essays treating natural setting, history, government, transportation, labor and industry, folklore and folkways, recreation, architecture, literature, fine arts, and music; a shorter section on the larger towns and cities including information that could not be dealt with adequately in the tours section; and, the largest section, a series of tours covering the entire state and highlighting major historic sites and points of interest. Following national guidelines, the compilers of the South Dakota book had their tours progress from east to west (tours 1–8) and from north to south (tours 9–14), with a final one (number 15) running 35 miles along a railroad line in the Black Hills. Many tours also featured short side trips to places not too far off the main routes. In charge of coordinating the process was state FWP director Lisle Reese, a twenty-four-year-old former Aberdeen and Pierre newspaperman.

A South Dakota Guide differed from most of its counterparts both in devoting considerable attention to religious life in an introductory essay and including an essay on Indian life, and it also departed from standard procedure by omitting a section on music and the fine arts. More heavily agricultural and thinly populated than most states, South Dakota in the thirties was preeminently a place defined by its small towns and their rural environs, and it remains so today. For this reason rereading the book now, seven decades after it first appeared, is more than an exercise in nostalgia or historical memory. Much of what was written then continues to be true today. Patterns visible in the thirties remain discernable now, if in modified form. Much, of course, is different; if people living then could have been instantly transported to the present, they scarcely could have comprehended the enormous changes that have occurred in the meantime. One paragraph written in 1937, however, would hardly need modification at all, at least for many places in the state:

> Throughout South Dakota, a stranger will notice in the cities and along the highways a human familiarity like that of a small village. On the streets the resident speaks to nearly everyone, and calls by their first names half of those he meets. Visitors will often find themselves being greeted on the street by natives with whom they have had only the most casual contact. South Dakotans pride themselves on the number of their acquaintances over the State.

Current readers will enjoy *The WPA Guide to South Dakota,* first, as a companion and reference while traveling around the state, no doubt by automobile (passenger trains stopped running more than thirty years ago), and, second, as an inspiration to reflect upon what kind of people South Dakotans are, what kind of society they have become. Alfred Kazin, at the start of his writing career in the late 1930s, deemed the state guides collectively to be "an extraordinary contemporary epic." Out of their vast storehouse of facts "emerged an America unexampled in density and regional diversity." To Stephen Vincent Benet they were "the states themselves, talking."

In South Dakota that meant talk about the state's Indian heritage, immigrant folkways, traditional values, faith in education, architectural variants, changeable weather, diverse topography, agricultural plenitude, nascent industry, enjoyment of hunting and fishing and outdoor recreation, legends and folklore, and historical achievement. Wide variations, especially between the East

River and West River sections, their dividing line the Missouri River, were acknowledged. Only by traveling the highways from town to town could visitors comprehend the entirety of the state's unique culture. The fifteen tours laid out at the time identified the distinctions that set off one town from another, just as those same tours to a large extent do today. Tabor constituted a rural Bohemia; Baltic, a little Norway. Plankinton (not Mitchell, famed for its Corn Palace) rated as the site of the first grain festival. Yankton sported unusually wide (130-foot) streets; Java was noted for its girls' basketball teams. Selby was home to a man who almost every year built a houseboat and floated it downriver to New Orleans, spending the winter there and returning home to build another.

For all their differences, most of the towns shared similar experiences and were shaped by like forces. It was a trick for guide writers to highlight these without repeating themselves in the descriptions of town after town, so certain places became the sites where universal experiences were discussed. Canton provided the setting for a description of spring flooding in 1881, an 1885 prairie fire, and the famous blizzard of 1888. The Missouri River became the topic of discussion in the story on Wheeler, where Highway 18 crossed it. Rainmakers were associated with Westport. The distances between each town listed in the guide remain unchanged today. Population shifts between 1935 (taken from the mid-decade state census) and the present reflect the transformations that have occurred in the meantime, as most of the larger towns have grown or held steady, most of the smaller towns have lost population, and the ones in between have experienced a net loss or gain depending on circumstances.

History, geography, folklore, economics, religion, culture, social life, governmental institutions—these and more were grist for the guide's authors. There is a feast here for every taste. Read and enjoy.

JOHN E. MILLER

FOREWORD

A SOUTH DAKOTA GUIDE is one of the publications in the American Guide Series, written by members of the Federal Writers' Project of the Works Progress Administration. Designed primarily to give useful employment to needy unemployed writers and research workers, this project has gradually developed the ambitious objective of presenting to the American people a portrait of America,—its history, folklore, scenery, cultural backgrounds, social and economic trends, and racial factors. In one respect, at any rate, this undertaking is unique; it represents a far-flung effort at cooperative research and writing, drawing upon all the varied abilities of its personnel. All the workers contribute according to their talents; the field worker collects data in the field, the research worker burrows in libraries, the art and literary critics cover material relevant to their own specialties, architects describe notable historical buildings and monuments; and the final editing of copy as it flows in from all corners of a state is done by the more experienced authors in the central offices. The ultimate product, whatever its faults or merits represents a blend of the work of the entire personnel, aided by consultants, members of university faculties, specialists, officers of learned societies, oldest residents, who have volunteered their services everywhere most generously.

A great many books and brochures are being written for this series. As they appear in increasing numbers we hope the American public will come to appreciate more fully not only the unusual scope of this undertaking, but also the devotion shown by the workers, from the humblest field worker to the most accomplished editors engaged in the final rewrite. The Federal Writers' Project, directed by Henry G. Alsberg, is in the Division of Women's and Professional Projects under Ellen S. Woodward, Assistant Administrator.

HARRY L. HOPKINS,
Administrator.

PREFACE

The South Dakota volume in *The American Guide Series,* prepared by the Federal Writers' Project of the Works Progress Administration, represents a sincere attempt to describe briefly, faithfully, and as entertainingly as possible the varied background and contemporary life of the State. It was no easy task for the small staff, engaged in this work since the autumn of 1935, to gather information through research, interviews, and personal observation, and then select without bias from a huge mass of material the significant and interesting facts relating to this comparatively new State, one of the last ten to enter the Union, and still one of the most sparsely settled. This book is frankly only a beginning, a spur to further research and interpretation of life in South Dakota. A special effort has been made to illustrate the story attractively with old and new photographs and many original drawings.

South Dakota is extremely conscious of its newness as a State, of the fact that it offers one of the few remaining opportunities to see pioneer life. It is just as conscious of its great geologic age, vividly manifest in the Black Hills formations and the Badlands, one of the most picturesque and scientifically interesting eroded areas in the world. The three nicknames given the State in a sense describe it—the Sunshine, the Blizzard, and the Coyote State.

Perhaps its official name, Dakota, taken from the Sioux language and meaning "an alliance of friends," is equally characteristic. South Dakota believes in its State motto "Under God the People Rule"; it was the first State to introduce the initiative and referendum in State affairs, and it has one of the lowest illiteracy rates. Dwelling within its borders is one of the largest Indian populations in the country, descendants of the highly developed Sioux who chose their leaders, chief among them Sitting Bull, because of personal qualities rather than heredity.

The State Legislature of 1937 made possible the publication of *A South Dakota Guide* through an appropriation setting up a revolving fund under the supervision of the South Dakota Guide Commission.

The Federal Writers of South Dakota acknowledge with gratitude the valuable advice and assistance given by numerous consultants, specialists in the respective fields. Especially helpful were the South Dakota Historical Society, the University of South Dakota, South Dakota State College, the National Park Service, the United States Forestry Service, and the State Department of Agriculture.

In order to make corrections in future editions of the Guide, the editors will appreciate the reporting of any inaccuracies.

LISLE REESE, *State Director.*

HOW TO USE THE GUIDE

General Information contains practical information for the State as a whole; specific local information is given in the introduction to The Black Hills recreational area, and to each city and tour description.

The introductory essays are designed to give a composite, yet comprehensive, survey of the State's contemporary scene, natural setting, history, and social, economic and cultural development. Frequent cross-references are made to further information on these subjects elsewhere in the book, particularly in the Tour section; these are found by reference to the index. *A South Dakota Guide* is not only a practical travel book; it will also serve as a valuable reference book.

The guide is built on a framework of tour descriptions, written in general to follow the principal highways from East to West, or from North to South. They are easily followed, however, in the reverse direction. In many cases the highway descriptions are equally useful to travelers on railroads. Whenever railroads parallel the described highway the fact is stated in the tour heading.

As a matter of convenience, several of the towns in South Dakota are described separately in the Cities section.

The tour descriptions contain cross-references to other tours crossing or branching from the route described, and to pertinent material found elsewhere in the book.

Important routes, with terminals, are listed in the Contents and are indicated on the tour key map. Each tour description follows a single main route. Descriptions of routes branching from the main routes are in smaller type. The long route descriptions are divided into sections at important junctions.

Cumulative mileage is used on main and side tours, the mileage being counted from the beginning of each section or, on side tours, from the junction with the main route. The mileage notations will vary somewhat from future driven mileages because of an extensive road-building program in South Dakota which is eliminating curves and avoiding villages.

The list of descriptive titles of tours gives the nearest out-of-State cities on the routes, important South Dakota cities on them, and State and Federal highway numbers of routes.

Points of interest in each city are arranged in the order in which they can conveniently be visited, and the numbers correspond with those on city maps.

Standard abbreviations are used throughout.

GENERAL INFORMATION

(State map, showing highway routes, railroads and air lines, in pocket, inside of back cover.)

Railroads: Chicago & North Western ("North Western"); Chicago, Milwaukee, St. Paul & Pacific ("Milwaukee"); Chicago, Burlington & Quincy ("Burlington"); Chicago, St. Paul, Minneapolis & Omaha (CStP M&O); Chicago, Rock Island & Pacific ("Rock Island"); Great Northern (GN); Illinois Central (IC); Minneapolis & St. Louis (M&StL); Minneapolis, St. Paul & Sault Ste. Marie ("Soo Line"); Rapid City, Black Hills & Western ("Crouch Line"). Owing to the natural trend of migration, most of the important lines run E. and W.; one, the Milwaukee, is a transcontinental line.

Highways: 12, 212, 14, 16, 18, about evenly spaced, cross the State E. to W.; 77, 81, 281, 83, 85, cross it N. to S., principally in the eastern section. No inspection at State borders. State highway motor patrol, whose aim is helpful rather than punitive. State tax on gasoline, 4¢.

Motor Vehicle Laws (digest): No set speed limit, but motorists are required to drive so as "not to imperil the life or property of anyone." Towns and cities in general have their own speed limits, indicated by highway signs. No driver's license required and no age limit for drivers. Lights must be properly adjusted and dimmed on meeting another car. Brakes must be capable of stopping a car going 20 m.p.h. within 33 ft. Non-residents allowed 90 days before they are required to have a South Dakota license. Car license plates bear two numbers separated by a dash. The first number designates the county, in its alphabetical order. County numbers remain the same year after year.

Air Lines: Hanford Air lines (Omaha to Bismarck) stops at Sioux Falls, Huron, and Aberdeen. One plane a day in each direction.

Bus Lines: Thirty-nine bus lines in State, covering East-river country with network. One bus line connects Pierre with Black Hills latter region served by other lines.

Accommodations: First-class hotels in all larger cities and also tourist camps on outskirts. Better organized and more attractive tourist camps in recreational areas, Lake Region of the NE. and Black Hills in extreme W. While tourist camps in scenic regions are open only during summer, there are enough of them to take care of the crowds, even at height of season.

Precautions: Only one poisonous reptile in South Dakota—the rattlesnake. Practically confined to western portion of State. Not so prevalent even there as to constitute a menace. Out-of-state visitors might spend weeks here and never see one. Rattlers most likely to be found on dry, rocky hillsides. If possible, they always give warning by that strident buzz from which they take their name. If person is bitten, tourniquet should be applied above wound as soon as possible, then each fang mark criss-crossed to depth of a quarter inch and the blood sucked thoroughly from it. Poison ivy common in wooded sections. Recognizable by its dull, green-white flowers or fruit and trifoliate leaves. If poisoned by it, mix one ounce of tincture of iron with one-half ounce of alcohol and apply with camel's hair brush or tuft of cotton.

Recreational Areas: Chief recreational sections in Lake Region, Black Hills, and Badlands. (See Sports and Recreation.)

Big Game Hunting: Deer Season, Nov. 1-20 incl. Open only in Meade, Lawrence, Pennington, Custer and Fall River Counties. Limit: One deer having two or more points to one antler. Fee: Resident, $5; non-resident, $25. Elk season regulations prescribed annually by the State game and fish commission. Law provides that illegally used fishing and hunting equipment is subject to confiscation.

Upland Game Birds: Pheasants (most numerous in eastern section) found in larger numbers than other upland birds. Season usually in October or early November. Sometimes split season, first half in October, second half in November. (Bag limit and other regulations prescribed by commission.) Fee: Resident, $1; non-resident, $15. Uniformed officers empowered to stop automobiles on public highways for inspection and count of game.

Migratory Waterfowl: South Dakota law empowers commission to prescribe regulations in conformity with Federal regulations for taking ducks, geese, coot, rails, gallinules, snipes, and other migratory waterfowl.

Fishing Laws: Open season on trout (found principally in Black Hills), Apr. 1 to Sept. 30 incl.; crappies, pike, perch, pickerel, sunfish and bullheads, May 1 to last day of February. Bass, June 15 to last day of February, except in Big Stone Lake, Lake Traverse, and Lake Hendricks, where season opens May 29 and closes last day of February to conform with Minnesota laws. No size limit on game fish except trout (min. 8 in.), but every fish landed must be kept and counted in string limits. Limits: Black bass, pike and pickerel (or all or any combined), 8 per day, 16 total in possession; perch and bullheads, 50 per day, 100 total in possession; trout and bluegills, 25 per day, 50 total number in possession; all other varieties of protected fish, 15 per day, 30 total in possession.

Liquor Regulations: State has both "on sale" (by the drink) and "off sale" (by the package) system of dispensing intoxicating liquors. Municipal ownership of liquor stores permitted in towns and cities where election has been held deciding in favor of such ownership. Any city or town permitted to have both on sale and off sale license but not both on same premises. No sale on election days until after 5 o'clock. No sale on Sundays. Two kinds of beer licenses issued— one for 3.2% or less alcoholic content, and one for "high point" defined as "containing in excess of 3.2% and not more than 6% by weight." Possession of a bottle of liquor with seal broken in a public place subjects violator to minimum fine of $200 or 90 days in jail, or both.

SOUTH DAKOTA TODAY

VISITORS who come to South Dakota for the first time expecting to see near-naked Indians, gun-toting cowboys, and Calamity Janes will be disillusioned. Although there are as many Indians as there were a hundred years ago, when the early white adventurers found them living in their natural state, today they live peaceful and interesting lives, foreign to war whoops and breechclouts. There are cowboys, but not of the motion picture variety. Recurrence of such early hardships as drought and grasshoppers, with the addition of a new one, the dust storm, for a time arrested prosperity and progress, but it failed to discourage the tenacious people.

To know whence the South Dakotans came, and why, is to begin to understand them. When the land west of Minnesota—Dakota Territory until 1889—was thrown open to homestead settlement, school teachers, lawyers, farmers, merchants, and bright-eyed youths turned to the new country to stake their claims, their hopes, their lives. From eastern cities and long-established communities, from Yankee and old frontier families, these adventuring homesteaders brought with them to the Middle Border a deep-set cultural tradition and training, coupled with a determination to achieve economic independence.

The serious task of making a living in the undeveloped country occupied the minds and hands of its people, leaving little time for the enjoyment of esthetic pursuits. The soil was turned by men dripping sweat; store counters were worn smooth by calloused hands. In young South Dakota there were no operas, no symphonies, no dramas. When the corn was picked and the earth left to sleep for the winter, father unpacked his fiddle and uncle his harmonica, mother baked a cake and the children "buggied" to the

THE HUSKING BEE

neighbors with invitations—a husking bee tonight. To lively tunes learned "back East," a dance was started and the corn was husked. And so it has been with South Dakotans through the recent pioneering years: combining work with pleasure, making their own entertainment, and still keeping an appreciation of the finer arts.

Not always physically strong, these homesteaders were mentally alert and formed the bases of ambitious communities. Then came an influx of foreign groups, men of the soil—Germans, Swedes, Norwegians—strongly built and strong of will. The assimilation was fast, the Yankee pioneers and foreigners uniting in business and marriage. Today only 7 per cent of the State's population are foreign born.

All this has happened within a lifetime. Many of that famous homesteading cavalcade of the eighties are still living. They are the grey-haired weathered men and women who tell strangers of the county-seat fight and the blizzard of 1888. They love to recall their hardships, yet they keep their sons at home to run the farm or the store because "we've had mighty good crops, and they'll come again." That second generation makes the State of today. Whether in professions, business, politics, or the kitchen, South Dakotans want it known that their parents or themselves originated farther east, but that they themselves have lived here most of their lives. Now the third generation is taking root. While a period of drought has retarded immigration to the State, the exodus of young South Dakotans is also slight. The spirit of the pioneers lingers among them.

Although settled in comparatively recent times by men and women of eastern origin, South Dakota by no means lacks western color. In this State, as large as Indiana, New Hampshire, and South Carolina combined, there are wide variations in activity and scene. There is the broad, flat farming region, the rugged ranching country, the mountainous mining and recreational area, each having its own type of citizenry and culture. The widely differing regions divided by the Missouri River are known locally as East-river and West-river.

The eastern half of the State is a continuation of Iowa and Minnesota farm land, with the latter's recreational lake region duplicated in the northeastern section. In the James and Sioux River Valleys, the barns are large and well-stocked; radios and motor cars are as common as plows; and their owners are politically conservative and deeply religious. Diversified farming and cooperative societies have made for prosperous communities. Schools and churches are large and numerous. Here one will find small cities not unlike Oshkosh, Terre Haute, and Hackensack. Outside the long, narrow valley-lands, the farms are newer, smaller, and farther apart; the people are busy fighting the elements for a living. Dust storms raised havoc in this region of huge plowed fields without windbreaks.

Across the Missouri River the large fringe of the Middle West's rich farming region merges into the first long reaches of the western cattle and mining empire. While in eastern South Dakota, groves of trees around the farmhouses stand today as monuments to the homestead period in which ten acres of trees were planted and nursed to secure the land, farther west, beyond the Missouri River, abandoned shacks stand in dejected silence to give testimony of over-optimism and the unwise use of land. Here the legendary "wide open spaces" roll away as far as the eye can see. There is something about the vast expanse that appeals to strangers and holds the scattered inhabitants. In the northwest part of the State, the original pioneer ranchers still color the homestead tide that swept over the country in 1909 and 1910 and receded for the most

part in the years following. Today "honyock," or farming homesteader, a n d old-timer live peaceably side by side, and each has learned much from the other. The old-timer taught his neighbor the art of stock raising on the range, and the honyock convinced the old-timer that some forage crops could be raised and that it was not good economics to ship out a carload of cows and ship in a carload of condensed milk.

Although largely unfit for farming this region is being utilized for ranching with further potentialities undeveloped. In this range country inland prairie towns still retain their hitching posts and general stores.

Farther on in the Black Hills a current mining boom suggestive of the gold rush of 1876 gives an increased prosperity to towns clinging like swallow's nests to the mountainsides. T h e B l a c k Hills people, strangely worldwise though isolated, are in the midst of an artistic, scientific, and industrial awakening. To the visitor, the general knowledge of these native South Dakotans, so far

**WHERE OLD AND
NEW MEET**

removed from cities and culture, is puzzling. The explanation lies in the fact that, with spasmodic discoveries of valuable minerals, the Hills like a magnetized needle attract financiers, engineers, prospectors, gamblers, and entertainers from the world at large. Artists, writers, and sculptors come here for the color; scientists come to study the secrets of earth and air. From contacts with the famous and notorious, idealist and realist, great and near-great, these people have absorbed a cosmopolitan atmosphere. Whether in new tweeds or ragged packet, the man who is confronted by a visitor will probably be a composite of many men who have come this way before. He may seem at first a merchant, a rancher, or a prospector, then a woodsman or hunter; as the day wears on he may reflect the artist who stopped off the previous year to paint wild animal life, or the paleontologist who came to track down a triceratops. Next summer he may have also the characteristics of his recent visitor.

Throughout South Dakota, a stranger will notice in the cities and along the highways a human familiarity like that of a small village. On the streets the resident speaks to nearly everyone, and calls by their first names half of those he meets. Visitors will often find themselves being greeted on the street by natives with whom they have had only the most casual contact. South Dakotans pride themselves on the number of their acquaintances over the State.

While the transition from the "firsts" to the modern scene is reflected in nearly every town and city, it is more clearly marked in the West-river region. There an unpainted, frame, false-front store with its board sidewalk and porch stands alongside another building of brick, steel and concrete; wide-brimmed, tent-shaped hats and high-heeled boots are worn with cravats of Park Avenue style; grizzled prospectors pick the earth in the shadow of million-dollar gold mine shafts.

Culture, in the urban sense, has had to wait on the unhurried assimilation of external elements impinging on a society essentially pioneer in character. When Hamlin Garland wrote of the endless drudgery and loneliness of life on the prairie in "Main Traveled Roads" and "A Son of the Middle Border," his homesteading neighbors would have nothing to do with him or his books. It was fifty years before he was accepted as a native son. Meanwhile, South Dakota furnished settings and characters for many novels, among them Rolvaag's "Giants in the Earth," Stewart Edward White's "Gold" and "Claim Jumpers," and Rose Wilder Lane's "Let the Hurricane Roar." Today there is a serious effort to acquire culture. Farm families meet weekly in rural schools to discuss new books furnished by the State's free lending library; villages have active literary societies and imported lecturers; people in cities turn out en masse to band and orchestral concerts, to local and road-show dramas, operas and art exhibits. In nearly every town are libraries and historical museums, in which are proudly exhibited collections of Indian relics and those of pioneer days.

South Dakota has been, and still is, a pioneer State.

NATURAL SETTING

SOUTH DAKOTA is a rectangular tract of land, about 370 miles long by 210 wide, lying approximately in the geographical center of the North American Continent. It is about equidistant from the Atlantic and Pacific Oceans, and about midway between the North Pole and the Equator. It is bounded roughly on the north by the 46th and on the south by the 43rd parallels of latitude, on the west by the 104th meridian of longitude and on the east by Traverse and Big Stone Lakes, the 96th meridian, and the Big Sioux River. It embraces an area of 77,615 square miles, or nearly 50,000,000 acres of land, being larger than the combined areas of the New England States, and one and one-half times as large as England. It ranks fourteenth among the States of the Union in size. North Dakota lies along its northern border, Montana and Wyoming bound it on the west, Nebraska has a common boundary line with it to the south, and Iowa and Minnesota lie directly to the east.

TOPOGRAPHY

The Missouri River, which flows through the middle of the State from north to south, divides South Dakota roughly into two parts —East-river and West-river. The Missouri marks the western edge of the vast ice sheet that in prehistoric times covered the north central portion of the United States. In fact the Missouri was forced out of its original course, possibly the present James River valley, and in rounding the edges of the ice-sheet it cut the extremely narrow valley in which it now runs. When the ice receded, the river had already cut through the height of land in the southern part of the present State, and so could not return to its former course.

But while the ice-sheet had no effect on the West-river country, other than to define its eastern border, it had a literally transforming effect on the eastern half of the State. The ponderous mass of ice leveled off eminences and filled in valleys, and over all it spread a thick layer of glacial soil brought from every point along its route. This soil was deposited sometimes in large terminal and lateral moraines that are clearly defined today, and sometimes as a rich and fertile covering that needed only the stirring-plow of the settler to release its wonderful strength into corn and grains. But the ice had still another effect. From its receding face the James, the Vermillion, and the Big Sioux rivers flowed south to join the Missouri, through a rich and gently sloping plain left by retreating ice.

The northeast corner of the State, as abandoned by the ice-sheet, had very little slope and correspondingly poor drainage. The result is that this whole section is dotted with lakes and marshes. It is likely that in some places masses of ice were left buried when the ice-sheet retreated; and that when this buried ice melted it left lakes, ponds, or marshes, according to the depth of the depression. All this has resulted in making this region today a playground for the inhabitants of the eastern part of the State, and of sections of Minnesota and Iowa. Fish are plentiful in the lakes, which are stocked by the State fish hatcheries. The marshes abound with wild fowl that summer there, and afford excellent hunting in season.

Just south and west of the Lake Region lie the James and Sioux River Valleys, constituting perhaps the richest agricultural section of the State.

West of this region, the Missouri River flows between high bluffs for almost its entire course through the State. Its swift current is still cutting a channel, its present course being so new that it has not had time to make a wide valley for itself, as has the much smaller James River. The land bordering the river on both sides is a mixture of farm and ranch land, reaching westward to the semi-arid ranching country.

This section, lying just east and north of the Black Hills, is an area like no other part of the State—a region of buttes and badlands, semi-arid, thinly populated. In the southern part of it are the unique Badlands (*see Tours 6 and 6A*). To the north is a long and wide belt of "gumbo."

One more giant movement of Nature's forces, comparable in importance to the ice-sheet, was to affect profoundly the future State. In the extreme western end of what is now South Dakota, some internal convulsion of the earth caused a gigantic upheaval or upthrust and formed the Black Hills.

The lowest point in the State is in the northeast corner at Big Stone Lake, 965 feet above sea level. But the slope in this portion is very gradual. The James winds its lazy, snake-like way across the State with the dubious distinction of being "the longest unnavigable river in the world." West of the Missouri River, the story is quite different. At the extreme western border are the Black Hills, crowned by Harney Peak, a granite crag with an elevation of 7,244 feet, the highest point in the State and the highest point in the Nation east of the Rocky Mountains.

CLIMATE

South Dakota is known as "the Sunshine State"; the sun shines nearly every day of the year. Its climate is subject to extremes of heat and cold, but the high, dry character of the terrain makes this heat and cold less noticeable than in damp and muggy climates. The highest temperature ever recorded was 115°, and the lowest, 46° below zero. Such extremes, however, are rare. The average temperature for January, the coldest month, is 10° above zero; and the average for July, the hottest month, 71°. The year-round average is 44°.

The rainfall of the State varies from less than 15 inches in the extreme northwest corner to more than 25 in the southeast portion. In general it may be said that the rainfall increases as one goes eastward. The average for most of the West-river territory is from 15 to 20 inches; east of the river it is from 20 to 25. Average annual rainfall for the entire State is about 20 inches. Three-fourths of this occurs during the growing season, and this feature of the climate makes the crop production equal to that of many regions having a much higher annual precipitation. The rainfall, however, varies greatly from year to year, producing good crops one season with perhaps a complete crop failure the following year.

The last killing frosts rarely occur after May 10 and the first serious frosts of autumn do not come before September 15. The average growing season for the State is 135 days, but various sections show differences in this regard as they do in rainfall. The high plateau of the Black Hills has a growing season of less than 105 days. From this point the growing season lengthens as one crosses the State from northwest to southeast, till in the latter region it exceeds 145 days.

One feature of South Dakota's climate which has received wide publicity is the blizzard, a combination of snow and high wind. The violence and destructiveness of these storms can hardly be over-estimated, but their occurrence is very rare. The Great Blizzard of 1888, in which 112 people lost their lives, is the classic example of this type of storm. During the average winter there will be two or three storms of a somewhat similar nature, but not approaching this one in severity. The winter of 1935-6 was exceptional for its snow and long-continued period of intense cold. The average depth of snow is not nearly as great as that in the wooded areas of the North Central and Northeastern States, there being a much lighter precipitation. The wind does not allow the snow to lie on the level.

Dust storms and drought have played their part in the State's recent history. In the central and south central portions in 1934, dust-laden winds left freakish piles of granulated soil in ditches and along fences. Fences and farm machinery in the so-called "Dust Bowl" were frequently covered beneath drifts of shifting soil. In South Dakota, as in other States of this area, a period of drought is likely to be followed by occasional dust storms. Drought was combatted by the construction of dams, frequently with WPA labor; and the effects of dust storms are being overcome by soil erosion projects.

GEOLOGY

Ancient Black Hills: In order to realize the age of the region, one must first consider the Black Hills. They are the key to the geology of the whole State of South Dakota and much of the adjacent territory.

The Black Hills were ages old before the Rocky Mountains were uplifted. They existed long before the Alps, the Caucasus, the Pyrenees, the Apennines, and while the site of the Himalayas was still a marsh. All these great mountain ranges were still level land when the Black Hills first began to rise in a great dome 150 by 75 miles in extent.

This huge dome or batholith, somewhat like an overturned wash basin, gradually rose through several million years. It is not certain that the Hills are through rising yet. But, however long the process took, it accomplished an enormous task; all the rest of the strata, from the bottom to the top of the geological column were pushed aside out of the way of this rising knob. The deepest and oldest rocks are now the highest.

It will be noticed in the Black Hills that all the layers, or strata, of rock run at about the same level in concentric rings completely around the Hills—a streak of red here, a strip of yellow there. Nearly every stratum, except the softer and more easily weathered ones, forms more or less of a cliff, facing the central backbone of the Hills and sloping downward and outward toward the plains, the successive layers roughly resembling shingles on a roof. This pattern is repeated so that one entering the Black Hills traverses the following formations of shales, limestone, and sandstones: Lance, Fox Hills, Pierre, Niobrara, Carlile, Greenhorn, Granerous, Dakota, Fuson, Minnewasta, Lakota, Morrison, Unkpapa, Sundance, Spearfish, Minnekahta, Opeche, Minnelusa, Paha Sapa, Englewood, Whitewood, and Deadwood. The highest and innermost are the Algonkian schists and granite core. The slender pinnacles known as the Needles, worn by weathering and erosion, are remnants of this granite center or core.

Plains Section: From the eastern border of the State, between Watertown and Redfield, is found the Pierre formation, running westward to the James River. Here, running northeast from the southwest corner of the State, a long arm of the Niobrara, a whitish chalky material, extends to Redfield; this formation varies in width from 12 miles at Redfield to 72 miles east of Chamberlain. From Flandreau southward through Sioux Falls, covering parts of Moody, Minnehaha, McCook, and Hanson Counties, is an arm of the Sioux Falls quartzite, a hard flint-like rock used extensively as building material. West of these two formations, the Pierre stretches to the Black Hills uplift just east of Rapid City, covering about three-fifths of the whole State; it is bordered on the northwest by the Fox Hills formation from the point where the Missouri River enters the State to Belle Fourche. Its gray to bluish shade distinguishes it, and its gumbo clay properties in wet weather are notorious. In the extreme northwest corner of the State is the Lance formation, in which are the Hell Creek Beds.

PALEONTOLOGY

The Dinosaurs: Huge monsters wallowed along the shores of tropical swamps in western South Dakota more than forty million years ago, and skeletal remains of these long-extinct dinosaurs come to light each year through erosion and scientific excavation. During the Mesozoic era, or age of reptiles, the lumbering *triceratops,* resembling a combination of elephant and rhinoceros, waged mortal combat with the swift-moving, kangaroo-shaped *tyrannosaurus rex;* while perhaps the *brontosaurus,* largest of all prehistoric reptiles, watched the battle from aloft, his long neck rising 30 feet above the earth. Fossilized bones of the *brontosaurus*—he of the 15-ton body and 2-ounce brain—have been found in the area surrounding the Black Hills. In the so-called Hell Creek Beds, in the northwest corner of the State, expeditions from various museums have excavated many fine specimens; an almost perfect head of the great "frilled" dinosaur, *triceratops,* was obtained by the State School of Mines in 1927 in the region of the West Short Pine Hills, south of Camp Crook. Along White River and in the Badlands National Monument, many interesting fossils are found annually. Here are fossilized bones and teeth of the giant rhinoceros, *titanothere;* mountain sheep, *oroedon;* three-toed horse, *mesohippus;* tiny camel, *poebrotheium;* giant pig, *leptauchenia;* and saber-tooth tiger, *dinictis squalidens.* Snow, rains, and wind erode the surface clay, so that each spring new fossils are found protruding from the banks.

Marine Fossils: Most of the State is covered by the Pierre formation. It is a dark clay, gray-blue in color, and weathers to a yellow or light gray shade; in many localities where it emerges it is called gumbo. Scattered through the gumbo are thousands of iron-like clay concretions, containing fine fossil remains of marine creatures. The nautilus, a round, thin-edged, coiled fossil in the shape of a snail, is common; and ammonites of the same shape, but sometimes as much as 24 inches in diameter, have been dug up along the rivers in western South Dakota. A long jointed fossil known as the baculite, an ancient ancestor of the present devilfish, is also found. All of these marine fossils are especially prized because, on shaving off the soft shell, the scales show all the opalescent colors of the rainbow, and beneath that layer is a fine lace-like pattern. Oyster and clam shells, cup corals, and fishbones are also frequently found, along with imprints of ferns and sea lilies.

NATURAL RESOURCES

Minerals: Much of the rock of the Black Hills holds hidden fortunes, and prospectors who roam the hills hunting for gold, silver, and precious stones occasionally find veins of rich ore. One "mother lode," the Homestake, has yielded more than 300 million dollars' worth of gold; new mines are springing up throughout the Hills and old ones are being reopened. But the mineral resources of this mountain region are not confined to gold and silver. Feldspar is mined, crushed, and treated, until it finally reaches the home as the enamel on the bathtub or a white dish in the cupboard. Cassiterite, the ore of tin, tantalum, soda spar, and lithium are being put to commercial use in making such things as ordinary tin cans, gas mantels, lubricants, composition roofing, movie snowstorms, porcelain, steel alloys, and even lemonade.

The high yellow limestone cliff that rims the Black Hills, known as the Paha Sapa formation, is used in cement, as a filler in certain kinds of paper, for plaster, and even to clarify beet sugar juice. Manganese is also present in this formation, and is used for painting outdoor iron and other metal work. One of the strangest of minerals is bentonite, found in the Belle Fourche region. In its natural state it appears to be a bed of dried yellow clay; a foot underground it becomes wet, and still deeper it is like stiff butter. Just as it is found, it can be used as a soap that will wash off black sticky motor oil from one's hands; it has 96 commercial uses, including its employment in the manufacture of face powder and in the outside chocolate-coating of candy to prevent melting. Hidden in some small cavity in the heart of a chunk of beryl that has rested for millions of years locked in a dike of granite, there may be a glass-clear, deep-water green crystal—the emerald. Or perhaps a dirty grayish rock protruding from the ground may expose, when broken, a ledge of corundum, the second hardest mineral in the world; in this ledge may be also a transparent crystal of blood-red color—the ruby; or it may be, instead, a blue or straw-colored gem —a sapphire.

Forests: Although most of South Dakota is a plains region, there are three national forest areas. In the Black Hills are the Harney and Black Hills National Forests, covering 1,191,201 acres in South Dakota and containing an amount of timber estimated at 2,791,468,000 board feet, most of which is ponderosa pine. The annual growth of the timber is estimated by the United States Forestry Service as 50 million board feet, and the amount cut each year totals about 40 million board feet. The Custer National Forest is divided into four groups, all in Harding County—the Slim Buttes, Cave Hills, and the East and West Short Pines; no lumber operations are carried on in these reserves. To perpetuate the supply of timber in the Black Hills, stagnated stands of young trees are thinned and the defective, diseased, and weaker trees removed. After 35 years' growth, mature trees are cut to make room for a new growth. In addition to the stately ponderosa pine, there are lodgepole and limber pines, western white spruce, Rocky Mountain red cedar, ground juniper, aspen, cottonwood, balsam, poplar, birch, burr-oak, hackberry, ash, elm, willow, and ironwood.

Water Power: Potential water power flows through the center of South Dakota in the form of the turbulent Missouri River. Hydroelectric power proposals and surveys are often presented to city, State and Federal agencies for harnessing the power of the Missouri; but the problem of silt has not yet been solved.

An artesion basin underlies the central portion of the State, and water for farm and city use comes from this source. Nearly every farm in this region has an artesian well, with force enough to pipe water without pumps.

Land Conservation: Soil erosion, irrigation, and water-conservation programs have been undertaken in South Dakota by the Federal Government since 1933, to reclaim land struck by drought and dust storms. The Works Progress Administration alone formed 480 lakes by building large dams across creeks, and made 300 more stock-watering places. Some of the lakes, such as Richmond and Amsden, cover as much as a thousand acres. Dams have been built in every county of the State; and after the heavy snows of 1936-7, most of them were filled. In the areas affected by dust storms, those counties in the east-central and south-central portion of the State, soil-erosion projects were established to halt the shifting of dirt.

Irrigation is a new phase of conservation in South Dakota. An irrigation project near Belle Fourche shows the possibilities of the market gardening of fruits and vegetables, particularly sugar beets; and proposals have been made for large-scale irrigation projects along the Missouri River.

A program for retiring sub-marginal land from cultivation is also under way. The eastern third of the State is known to be best fitted for farming; westward the soil is not so suitable for agriculture, but the hay crop is a valuable one for cattle and sheep raising. In certain sections of the West-river country, tilled land is being purchased by the Government and leased for grazing purposes only.

FAUNA AND FLORA

Animal Life: The coyote is a native of South Dakota, and is the State university mascot and the State animal. At one time South Dakota was known as "the Coyote State." These animals are still quite numerous in western South Dakota, where it has been estimated by professional hunters that there is an average of one coyote to each square mile.

Until 75 years ago, great herds of buffalo roamed the plains and river breaks of South Dakota, but with the coming of white men they were slaughtered by the thousands and became nearly extinct. However, a herd of 350 buffalo is kept in Custer State Park, and the Wind Cave National Park game refuge has a herd.

Elk and deer are numerous in the Black Hills, both in and out of the game refuges. Beaver, porcupines, squirrels, raccoons, and bobcats are also found in the Black Hills. Antelope, jackrabbits, and prairie dogs are plentiful in the West-river section; the State maintains an antelope preserve in Harding County (*see Tour 2A*). Badgers, weasels, skunks, muskrats, jackrabbits, and gophers are numerous in the eastern section of the State, especially along creeks and lakes.

Bird Life: Nearly 300 species of birds are found in South Dakota, this large number being due mainly to the State's varied regions, such as mountains, forests, and prairies. The Missouri River is an important route of the north-south migration of waterfowl; and each spring and fall flocks follow this watercourse. In addition to ducks and geese, flocks of pelicans and occasional swans nest in the Lake Region; while herons, cranes, cormorants, sea gulls, and snipe are common. A waterfowl peculiar to the Black Hills is the water ouzel, which dives into the mountain streams and feeds and swims against the current.

Chinese pheasants, prairie chickens, and Hungarian partridges are plentiful in the eastern section of the State; and toward evening the highly colored ring-necked pheasants are seen as they come out to feed near the road.

In the eastern section of the State the meadowlark, with its cheery song, is the best known of South Dakota birds. The robin, red-winged and yellow-headed blackbirds, flicker, goldfinch, swallow, kingfisher, humming-bird, and brown thrush are the most common birds in the East-river section; in the Black Hills there are catbirds, bluebirds, wood thrushes, rock wrens, warblers, crossbills, wood peewees, and woodpeckers. Of the larger birds, bald and golden eagles are frequently seen west of the Missouri River, especially in the Badlands; magpies are common to the Black Hills and buttes sections; turkey buzzards and prairie hawks are seen in the cattle country; and barn, screech, great horned, and burrowing owls are found throughout the State.

Wild Flowers: The State flower is the pasque, a purplish, fur-petaled prairie blossom. that shows itself at Easter time on sunny hill sides. The pasque (also called crocus, mayflower, and anemone) is the first to bloom in the spring. Early in June, the pink wild rose and evening primrose blossom profusely in the fields. In the Lake Region are yellow and white lilies in the creeks; and pink beard-tongues, yellow and purple violets, buttercups, and blazing stars are found in grassy sheltered places. In the central part of the State, the wild orange geranium grows on the prairie, with an occasional black-eyed-susan, Mariposa lily, and prickly poppy. Native to the Missouri River "breaks" and westward is the soft wax-like gumbo lily, growing out of bare gumbo. In this region is the yucca plant, also called Spanish bayonet and soapweed, with its sharp spears and delicate white flowers blossoming on a tall spike. The cactus plant, common in western South Dakota, has waxy yellow flowers flecked with pink, which may brighten an entire hillside. In the Black Hills are scores of flower species, including the blue-flag or fleur-de-lis, yellow lady slipper, wood orchid, bluebell, larkspur, monkshood, woodland star, bog-violet, shooting star, baby's-breath, and forget-me-not. In autumn, the goldenrod and sunflower are common throughout the State.

Chokecherry, wild plum, gooseberry, and currant thickets are frequent in the eastern part of the State; and wild grapes, raspberries, and wild strawberries are found along creeks and lakes. Buffalo-berry bushes grow thickly in the "draws" of the western section.

There are also several noxious plants and weeds such as nettles, poison oak, and poison ivy; likewise barberry, creeping-Jennie, leafy spurge and dodder.

INDIANS AND INDIAN LIFE

LARGE areas of South Dakota are still Indian country. There are 26,500 Sioux, or Dakota, Indians and 9 reservations—the Pine Ridge, Rosebud, Cheyenne, Standing Rock, Crow Creek, Lower Brule, Yankton, Sisseton, and Flandreau. In remote sections of the Pine Ridge and Rosebud Reservations live bands of Sioux who cling to old customs, language, and crafts; in more populated regions the assimilation with whites has resulted in a strange group of people, red-haired and light-skinned, their Indian features dominating their evident foreign heritage. Bands of Indians in various stages of culture may be seen on the reservations; archaelogical remains of tribes who preceded the Sioux may be seen elsewhere in the State.

Mound Builders: Traces of a primitive people, presumably part of the great race of mound builders that at one time inhabited the Ohio valley, are found in eastern South Dakota. How long they lived here or what became of them is not known. They vanished, leaving only their burial mounds as evidence of their presence. These earth mounds, some round and others almost square-sided, are filled with bones and implements of this early race. From the artifacts, it appears that the mound builders knew little of agriculture and were mainly a carnivorous people. Their first craftsmanship was displayed in the making of weapons, which were gradually improved from crude, rough stones, through the stages of stone hatchets and knives, to those made of hammered metal. Their pottery shows some measure of ornamentation, chiefly in linear form. In one instance, in the investigation of a mound in Hutchinson County, an attempt at color decoration was found, pottery burned to darker shades. Personal ornaments in the form of beads were made from shells and bones. In the Brandon mounds, near Sioux Falls, shell beads were found made from the columnella or conch shells. The outstanding characteristic of the mound builders was their veneration of the dead. In the few mounds opened in South Dakota by archaeologists, the burials had been made in groups. The bodies were placed in varying positions—some lying straight or with flexed limbs, others in sitting postures—and they were covered with clay and rock. Above them other burials were made, the bodies covered with another stratum of soil, making a huge mound, erected with all the toil involved in the use of the rudest implements—the shoulder blade of an animal to dig with and a small basket to transport the earth.

Skeletal remains and artifacts from the mounds· are on display at the University of South Dakota Museum at Vermillion and in the Pettigrew Museum at Sioux Falls.

The mounds of this vanished race are found in South Dakota principally along the Big Sioux River and Big Stone Lake. Sites have been located in the following counties: Roberts, Grant, Deuel, Brookings, Moody, Minnehaha, Marshall,· Day, Codington, Kingsbury, McCook, Hutchinson, Clay, Yankton, Charles Mix, Brown, Spink, Jerauld, Davison, Lincoln and Faulk. More detailed descriptions of certain mound areas are given in other sections:

> City of Sioux Falls, Sherman Park, a small group of mounds well-preserved and accessible to visitors. (See SIOUX FALLS)
>
> The Brandon group 8 miles east of Sioux Falls between the Sioux and Split Rock Rivers, comprising 38 mounds. (See Tour 5.)
>
> Hartford Beach on Big Stone Lake, a large group situated in a stand of natural timber. (See Tour 2.)

Arikaras: The second known inhabitants of what is now South Dakota were the Arikara, or Ree, Indians. Closely related to the Pawnee Indians of Nebraska, the Arikaras came up the Missouri River early in the seventeenth century. From Yankton northward they built large villages, planted gardens of beans, corn, squash, and tobacco, and hunted buffalo along the Missouri to supplement their vegetable diet. Increasing in numbers, they built other villages, always tending northward. The Arikaras occupied the river banks unmolested until 1750, then for 40 years they were engaged in war with the invading Teton Sioux who drove them up the Missouri and into virtual extinction. It was near Mobridge that the Lewis and Clark Expedition of 1804 found the pursued Arikaras, who were friendly and eager to trade.

The Arikara villages were made up of from 10 to 50 dirt lodges, circular, with rounded tops. The frame for the huts was made of poles set in the ground, around which sod was banked. At the height of a man's head the poles were bowed toward the center. Covered with skins, dry grass, and dirt the dwelling was warm in winter and cool in summer. A hole left in the side formed the door, with a buffalo hide to cover it, and niches around the interior of the walls, with robes hung in front, formed the sleeping cubicles. The size of the lodges varied, some accommodating as many as three families. Beside each dwelling were refuse heaps with pieces of pottery, arrowheads, and scrapers which have since been helpful in studying Arikara culture. In the center of the village would be a large council lodge. The villages, usually facing the river, were protected by trenches on the other three sides. Village sites are identified along the Missouri River by the circles made by the lodge walls and the rubbish heaps. An excellent collection of Arikara pottery is housed in the Soldiers' and Sailors' Memorial building at Pierre.

Nearly all of the Arikara village sites are difficult to reach by car. Among the more accessible are:

Crow Creek site, east side of Missouri River where creek enters. Traces of deep trench with redoubts may be seen. (See Tour 4-A.)

De Grey site, 18 miles east of Pierre, State 34, one-half mile west of De Grey on Grandle and Bowman farms. Series of sites may be seen by careful examination.

Fort Pierre site, high terrace 9 miles north of Fort Pierre just outside buffalo pasture. Bluff gradually being washed away into Missouri. (See Tour 4.)

Fort Sully site, across dry creek from abandoned Fort Sully, 23 miles northwest of Pierre. Circles and rubbish heaps visible. (See Tour 4.)

Lewis and Clark site, west bank of Missouri and on both sides of Elk Creek. Located 6 miles east of Wakpala. (See Tour 2.)

Mobridge site, east side Missouri near Milwaukee Railroad bridge, 1½ miles north of Mobridge. This is a Mandan Indian village site. (See Tour 2.)

Mitchell site, on south shore of Lake Mitchell, with rings visible and mounds to west. (See MITCHELL.)

The Sioux: The Sioux, or Dakota, Indians, who had resided in Wisconsin and Minnesota, were forced out on to the prairies by the more numerous Ojibways when the latter were given firearms by the French. The Sioux were a nomadic people, following their food supply, principally buffalo, and ranging westward to the Missouri River. Here they found the Arikaras and promptly attacked them. The Sioux were a virile race, splendid specimens physically. They were unusually mobile with their herds of ponies, and accurate marksmen with bow and arrow.

Taking the country for themselves, Sioux bands spread from the lake region of what is now northeastern South Dakota, south to Yankton and westward to the Black Hills. Then the Sioux began encountering occasional white men—trappers and fur traders. In 1775 Pierre Dorion, a fur trader, married an Indian woman and made his home in the Sioux country near the present site of Yankton. Explorers and missionaries followed and found hospitable entertainment. Trading posts were established and, with the coming of the steamboat, trade multiplied between the Indians and whites; white blood was fused with that of the Indian, and the Indians adopted the white man's dress.

During the War of 1812, the Sioux, friendly with the British through long association with the English fur companies on the upper Missouri, joined forces against the Americans. With the treaty of Ghent, signed Dec. 24, 1814, the Indian tribes were left to make their own terms with the United States. Governor William Clark, who had met the Sioux during the Lewis and Clark expedition in 1804-06, called a great council of Indians from the Upper Missouri and Mississippi at the confluence of the two rivers, July 19, 1815. All the Sioux tribes came in full regalia. Separate treaties were made with the Sioux of the Lakes, one having been handed down through the family of Walking Buffalo. The document, yellowed with age and worn with much folding, is still in the possession of South Dakota Indians. The thumbprints of the several Indian chiefs were in blood. The treaty (see accompanying picture) reads as follows:

> A Treaty of Peace and Friendship made and concluded between William Clark, Vivian Edwards and Auguste Chouteau, Commissioners Plenipotentiary of the United States of America, on the part and behalf of the said States of the one part; and the undersigned Chiefs and Warriors of the Sioux of the Lakes on the part and behalf of their Tribe, of the other part.

The parties being desirous of reestablishing Peace and Friendship between the United States and the said Tribe; and of being placed in all things and in every respect on the same footing upon which they stood before the late war between the United States and Great Britain, have agreed to the following Articles.

Art. Ist   Every injury or act of hostility committed by one or either of the contracting parties against the other, shall be mutually forgiven and forgot.

Art. IInd   There shall be perpetual Peace and Friendship between all the citizens of the United States of America, and all the individuals composing the said Tribe of the Lakes, and all the friendly relations that existed between them before the war shall be and the same are hereby renewed.

Art. IIIrd   The undersigned Chiefs and Warriors for themselves and their said Tribe, do hereby acknowledge themselves and their aforesaid Tribe to be under the protection of the United States, and of no other nation, power or sovereign whatsoever.

In witness whereof the said William Clark, Vivian Edwards, and Auguste Choteau, Commissioners aforesaid, and the Chiefs and Warriors of the aforesaid Tribes have hereunto subscribed their names and affixed their seals this nineteenth day of July in the year of our Lord one thousand eight hundred and fifteen and of the Independence of the United States the Fortieth.

Done at Portage des Siouxs   Wm. Clark (Seal)
in the presence of
R. Wash, Sec'y to the Commission   Vivian Edwards (Seal)

John Miller	(Louis Decouagne Auguste Chouteau
Col. 3rd Inft.	(Louis Dorian
A. Paul C. I. of the C.	(John A. Cameron
Edw. Hall Lt. late	(Jacques Mette
28th Inft.	(John Hay
J. B. Clark	(Ta-tan-ga-manie
Adjt. 3rd Inft.	(The Walking Buffalo X (Seal)
Manuel Lisa, Agt.	(Hai-san-nee—The Horn X (Seal)
Thomas Forsyth, I. Agt.	(A-am-pa-ha—The Speaker X (Seal)
Jno. W. Johnson, U. S. L.	(Na-ree-sa-ga-ta
& I. Agent	(
Marin Blondeaux, land Agt.	(Hai-bo-haa
	(The Branching Horn X (Seal)

In 1862 the bands in Minnesota had a desperate war with the whites. Scouts and soldiers forced the Indians back across the Minnesota border, broke up their villages, and herded them into encampments near forts. The names of these old army posts cling to spots along the Missouri River, where all signs of established life have vanished and grass grows again on upland prairie benches. Among the.forts were: Fort Randall, Fort Lookout, Fort Thompson, Fort George, Fort Pierre, Fort Sully and Fort Bennett. The only permanent one, Fort Sisseton, has been restored. (*See Tour 1A.*)

Some of the most dramatic events in western Indian warfare occurred after the treaty of 1867 in which the Sioux agreed to retire to reservations before 1876. Reservations were established in 1868, and the Sioux were moved into these confines at the same time that homesteaders were moving into the open land of Dakota Territory after the Civil War. The discovery of gold in the Black Hills led to a rush of prospectors and settlers, protected by the U. S. Army, thus violating the treaty. The Sioux, in defence of their rights, were led in an uprising by a talented strategist—Red Cloud, chief of the Oglala Sioux. In a series of swift campaigns he forced the U. S. Army to abandon its forts and roads north of the treaty line, and to close the Bozeman Trail. This is almost the only occasion in American history where an Indian leader, fighting U. S. regular soldiers on equal terms, defeated them and procured his own demands. Red Cloud retired to a reservation in South Dakota to live peacefully. His brilliant achievement was preliminary to the encounter on the Little Big Horn where Gen. George A. Custer's foolhardy advance led to the "massacre" in 1876. Twelve years later, land allotments were made each individual Indian and attempts were made to establish them on farms. Then in 1890 the Messiah War broke out, climaxed by the last warfare between the Indians and whites at Wounded Knee when about two hundred Indians were killed by soldiers.

After the homesteaders' invasion, other stockmen and farmers came into the reservation, buying and leasing land. In 1934 considerable reservation land was designated as sub-marginal, repurchased by the Government from bankrupt whites, and turned back to the Indians.

Tribal Organizations: Thirteen recognized tribes of the Sioux Nation now live within the borders of this State. Each tribe claimed descent from a common family whose exploits were exalted in legend and song; each tribe was held together by a set of tribal fetishes and common taboos. These tribal divisions still remain. If Pete High Elk from one tribe marries into another division and makes his home on his wife's land amongst her tribe, he will be spoken of as an outsider after years of residence there.

When Indian reservations were established in 1870, the groupings closely followed recognized tribal divisions of the Sioux Nation. Today these tribes are living in largest numbers in the following localities.

1. Mdewakanton—(Mday-wah-kan-ton) "Mystery Lake village" located at Flandreau.
2. Wahpekute—(Wah-pay-koo-tay) "Shooters among the leaves (of deciduous trees)." Combined with Mdewakanton.
3. Wahpeton—(Wah-pay-ton) "Village among the leaves (of deciduous trees)." Sisseton Reservation.
4. Sisiton—(See-see-ton) "Marsh village." Sisseton reservation.
5. Yankton—(Ee-angk-ton) "End village." This tribe is closely related to the Yanktonais tribe. Yankton Reservation.
6. Yanktonais—(Ee-angk-ton-aye) "Little-end village." Upper Yanktonai—Standing Rock Reservation. Lower Yanktonai —(Hunkpatina) Crow Creek Reservation.
   Teton—(Tee-ton) "Dwellers on the prairie." The largest division of the Sioux. There were seven divisions of this tribe.
7. Sicangu—(Si-chang-hu) "Burned thighs." Also called Brule. Rosebud Reservation. Lower Brule Reservation.
8. Itazipco—(Ee-tah-zip-cho) "Without a bow." Also called Sansarc. Cheyenne Reservation.
9. Sihasapa—(See-hah-sah-pah) "Black feet." Cheyenne River and Standing Rock Reservation. (Not to be confused with tribe in Montana which is not of Siouan stock.)
10. Miniconjou—(Miniikanyedan wojupi) (Mnee-ko-jou) "Those who plant beside the stream."
11. Oohenonpa—(O-o-hay-non-pah) "Two boilings," called "Two Kettles," Cheyenne Reservation.
12. Oglala—(O-glah-la) "To scatter one's own." Pine Ridge Reservation.
13. Hunkpapa—(Hung-kpah-pah) "End of the circle." Standing Rock Reservation.

Within each tribe were numerous bands; these were firmly knit family groups who lived together in winter villages and had economic and social interdependence. Each band was led by a headman and the name of this leader became the name of the band. When the Indian social structure came to grips with military rule in the Dakota Territory in the 1860's, the headman's name was translated into English. This became the final name of the band as marked down in the Government records. There is the Drifting Goose Band in the Yanktonais tribe and the Red Cloud Band of the Oglalas, named for the chief who led the war in 1866. He-Dog on the Rosebud Reservation and the Iron Nation Post Office on Lower Brule Reservation mark the spots where these headmen camped with their kinfolk about them. The names of the bands may be found in the current conversation of the people, and traceable, too, are the personal traits and the family characteristics of a band.

Chiefs: Those who come to find chiefs on the reservations of South Dakota will find them as numerous as colonels in Kentucky. In old days the wisest headmen formed the chief tribal council and these were called "chiefs." None of them was given arbitrary power in the council, where the vote of the majority ruled. Rather these chiefs were fathers to their bands; their duties were to study the welfare of their people, to counsel wisely after deliberation, and to set examples of bravery and generosity. But for years the "chiefs" have been named by the white men for either economic or sentimental reasons. When the white trader or soldier came into Indian country he picked out the leader most amenable to his interests and by favors and gifts marked him out and called him "Chief." At fairs and shows and during visits to Washington, the "chiefs" come into their own. At home they are "on a par" with the rest and are called "Tom," "Charlie" or "Joe."

Family Life: During the past century the old pattern of home life disintegrated, with only a few customs remaining. A hundred years ago the men's work was to protect the home, provide materials for food and clothing, make bows, arrows, and household implements, and supervise political activities. The first two occupations, war and the hunt, kept the young men busy; the others, craftwork and the holding of councils, were left to the elders.

Three generations formed the family unit and each generation had its appointed and accepted tasks. The women's work was the preparation and care of the food, including the drying of meat, wild fruits, vegetables, rice and herbs; gardening, which meant raising squaw corn and drying it; storing and transporting all the food; making clothes and tepees from the hides of buffalo by dressing the skins and decorating them. The care of the young children and the instruction and protection of the young girls fell to grandmothers. Children gathered wood and carried water; the boys hunted small game, the girls sewed on hides and learned to decorate them with porcupine quills and beads. For the children there was always understanding sympathy, affection, and respect.

When wars, hunting, and fur trading passed, the Indians moved into log cabins and small frame houses. The men took up meager farming and stock raising, without enthusiasm for work that kept

them alone in the fields all day. During this period, payments under treaties and from sale of lands, together with regular money
from land rents, came to the Indians in large sums of fairly even
distribution. It was money from these sources and rations of food
from the Government which supported family life for fifty years.
For this half-century the cost of children to the family group was
practically nothing, because the children were at Government or
mission boarding schools where everything was provided without
direct payment by the parents.

When payments became rare and leasing dropped off, when
drought and mismanagement made it difficult to raise a crop, the
standard of simple living adopted in 1870-80 began to go down.
Shortly after the close of the World War the Indians of South
Dakota entered into a pitiable struggle for existence. They bartered
their household goods and sold their heirlooms; their houses fell
into disrepair and dilapidation. The men worked as day laborers
at whatever small jobs the agency superintendent or the neighboring farmers could provide; the women picked wild fruit and bartered it in nearby towns. After their jobs failed, came poverty,
want, then Government relief. On the work projects, designed for
ten or twenty men, the social element came back, and with its revival came pleasure in work. Now with the return of children to
the home and with regular work for men and women, there is a
marked revival of the old spirit of industry and community living.

Arts and Crafts: Through the years of transition the Sioux satisfied his need for adornment by decorating all kinds of useful objects. The preparation of materials for art work as well as the execution of each piece took days of work; creative art filled the leisure hours. The Indian's sense of limitless time and his devotion
to a task until it was completed made him undertake large pieces of
fine design and patiently work out every technique needed to produce a thing of beauty. He excelled in geometrical design made interesting by a combination of bright colors. His pictorial represen-
tations of events are sparing in the use of line; in pictorial art the
Sioux does not excel but he has left interesting records of his way
of living pictured on tepees and saddle blankets.

Early decorations were made on hide with porcupine quills,
colored with native dyes. Symbols were worked on tepees, clothing,
saddle blankets, baby cases, and tobacco bags.

Examples of this earliest art can be seen in the Pettigrew Museum in Sioux Falls, in the Memorial Building in Pierre, in the

SIOUX SYMBOLS

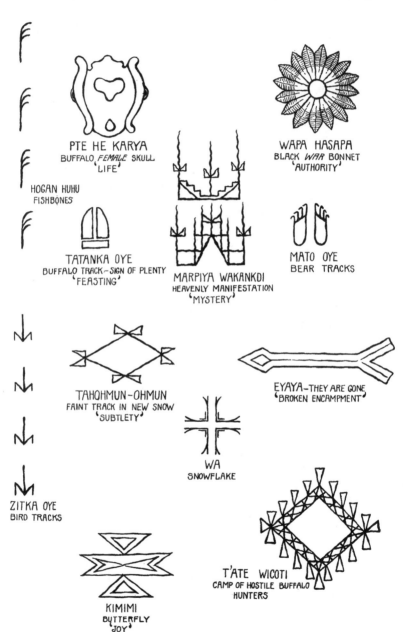

PTE HE KARYA
BUFFALO *FEMALE* SKULL
'LIFE'

WAPA HASAPA
BLACK *WAR* BONNET
'AUTHORITY'

HOGAN HUHU
FISHBONES

TATANKA OYE
BUFFALO TRACK - SIGN OF PLENTY
'FEASTING'

MARPIYA WAKANKDI
HEAVENLY MANIFESTATION
'MYSTERY'

MATO OYE
BEAR TRACKS

TAHOHMUN-OHMUN
FAINT TRACK IN NEW SNOW
'SUBTLETY'

EYAYA - THEY ARE GONE
'BROKEN ENCAMPMENT'

WA
SNOWFLAKE

ZITKA OYE
BIRD TRACKS

T'ATE WICOTI
CAMP OF HOSTILE BUFFALO
HUNTERS

KIMIMI
BUTTERFLY
'JOY'

John Anderson collection in Rapid City, and in collections on display at Indian agencies and schools. The only buffalo hide tipi on exhibit in South Dakota is in the Pettigrew Museum; the only "bull boat" (hide) is in the Memorial Building in Pierre.

When the fur trader came bringing beads, the medium of decoration changed. Beads in place of porcupine quills were used in later designs and pictures. Beaded moccasins are made on every Sioux reservation today and worn by many members of the tribe. This skill is being passed on to the younger generation; but a knowledge of the technique of quill work is dying because quills were flattened between the teeth of the workers and eventually the teeth were worn down. The younger Indians will not subject their teeth to this punishment.

The younger people are, however, learning from the old men the art of carving. Pipe stems, ceremonial bowls, and bows and arrows were rudely carved before knives came to the Indians. With a good knife in his hand the Indian man grew skillful, and worked long hours decorating pipestone and wood. This craft has brought money to the Indians in recent years and is being worked at steadily by a number of present-day craftsmen.

Craft work is opening up in several reservation centers; Indian dolls, beaded belts, souvenirs, and excellent reproductions of old pieces are being made. The Indian people draw, paint, carve, and bead for fun—arts and crafts are a great resource in their leisure time and an economic asset, as well as an expression of their appreciation of beauty.

Legends and Songs: Legends and songs of the Sioux were repeated through so many generations that all the people came to know them well. As soon as white men came among the Indians they devised a phonetic writing of the Dakota language and wrote down legends and songs. Because of their meter and rhythm the songs have been easier to preserve in the original form than the legends. The story-teller varies the wording with each re-telling.

Wanagi Wacipi Olowan	Song of the Spirit-Dance (Mother)
Ina, hekuye,	Mother, oh come back,
Ina, hekuye,	Mother, oh come back,
Misunkala Seya-ya omani	Little brother calls as he
Misunkala Seya-ya omani	seeks thee, weeping.
Ina, hekuye,	Mother, oh come back,
Ina, hekuye.	Mother, oh come back.

Reservations: To see Sioux Indian life, one may visit the various reservations on the following tours:

Sisseton Reservation ....Tours Nos. 1 and 10
Standing Rock Reservation ....Tour No. 2
Cheyenne Reservation ....Tour No. 3
Crow Creek Reservation ....Tour No. 4A
Lower Brule Reservation ....Tour No. 4A
Pine Ridge Reservation ....Tour No. 7
Rosebud Reservation ....Tour No. 7
Yankton Reservation ....Tour No. 8
Flandreau Reservation ....Tour No. 9

HISTORY

THE State of South Dakota derived its name from Dakota Territory, which in turn was named for the Dakota Indians, who were the inhabitants of this region when the first white explorers came. Dakota means "allied" or "many in one." From a loose confederation of Indian tribes came the connotation of an "alliance of brothers." The name of the Indian nation became that of the new Territory; and when the Territory was divided in 1889, the resulting States were called North and South Dakota respectively

Although South Dakota belongs to that group of States more recently admitted to the Union, it has a history reaching back to Colonial days. Thirty-three years before the declaration of Independence was signed, white men stood on the banks of the Missouri within the present confines of this State and left indisputable evidence of their presence.

Although never glimpsed by white men, the first known inhabitants of South Dakota have been identified as the so-called Mound Builders, who occupied roughly the eastern third of the present State. Of the tribes with which the white men came in contact, the first were the Arikara or Ree Indians, who lived in villages along the Missouri River. The Sioux, driven from the upper Mississippi valley by the Ojibways, in turn drove the Rees from the present State by keeping the buffalo at a distance from the river and by harrassing the river villages until, about the year 1800, the Rees finally left the region and retreated up-river into what is now North Dakota.

Early Exploration: There is some question as to who was the first white man to enter the boundaries of the present State. It is fairly well established that the Spanish explorer, Coronado, came as far north as the River Platte in 1540, but there is no evidence that he visited what is now South Dakota. Le Sueur, the French trapper and trader, wintered near the site of Mankato, Minn., in 1699; and he afterward furnished material for a geography of the upper Mississippi, including what is now eastern South Dakota. But there is no direct proof that he entered the present State.

The first indisputable visit of white men to this region was that of the Verendrye brothers in 1743. On March 30 of that year they climbed a "gumbo" hill above the present site of Fort Pierre, and took possession of the country in the name of the King of France; and in proof of this, they buried an inscribed lead plate and raised a cairn of stones over it. This plate lay undiscovered for 170 years (*see Tour 4*).

In 1775 Pierre Dorion, who afterward guided the Lewis and Clark Expedition, settled among the Yankton Sioux on the lower James River and married one of their women. He thus became the first white resident of the State. In 1794 a school teacher, Jean Baptiste Trudeau, came up from St. Louis with 10 men to engage in trade on the upper Missouri River, and he built the "Pawnee House" under the chalk cliffs in what is now Charles Mix County (*see Tour 17*). This was the first house erected in the State. That same year Jacques d'Eglise pushed up the river as far as the Ree villages at the mouth of Grand River; and in 1796 Registre Loisel built a fortified trading post on Cedar Island, just above Big Bend in present Hughes County.

On March 9-10, 1804, at St. Louis, the Louisiana Purchase was formally transferred to the American Government. On the afternoon of May 14, the Lewis and Clark Expedition set out up the Missouri River. The purpose of this expedition, sent out by the Federal Government, was to discover the shortest feasible water route to the Pacific Coast, to gauge the trade possibilities of the region through which they passed, and to make treaties of friendship with the various Indian tribes. On August 22, at Elk Point, the expedition made its first encampment in what is now South Dakota. On August 27 it arrived at the mouth of the James River. Learning that there was a large Indian encampment near by, the leaders invited the Indians to a feast and a council. This lasted several days, in the course of which Lewis took a new-born Indian babe, wrapped him in an American flag, and prophesied that he would become a distinguished leader and a great friend to the Americans. Both these prophecies were fulfilled, for this was

Struck-by-the-Ree, who was afterward instrumental in saving the white settlement at Yankton.

On September 8 the party reached the "Pawnee House," and on the 22nd the Loisel Post on Cedar Island. On September 24 it arrived at the mouth of the Bad River, where some trouble developed with a band of Teton Sioux under Black Buffalo. At the mouth of the Cheyenne the expedition encountered a French trader who said he had spent the previous winter up the Cheyenne River, near the Black Hills. On October 8 the party reached the Ree villages at the mouth of Grand River, where it was entertained for several days. From that point it passed out of present South Dakota.

Two years later, almost to the day, the expedition crossed the present South Dakota line on its return trip from the Coast. It again visited the Rees on Grand River, but passed by the Teton Sioux at the present site of Fort Pierre. After stopping briefly with the Yankton Sioux, the party set off for St. Louis, arriving there in September. The guides for the trip had been Charbonneau and his wife, Sacacawea (*see Tour 2*).

On the return trip, Lewis and Clark had persuaded Big White, a Mandan chief, to accompany them, and later they took him to Washington. They had agreed to give him safe conduct back to his own country; so in the spring of 1807 he was assigned a place with a party of traders (under Pierre Chouteau) and soldiers bound for the upper Missouri. All went well until they reached the Ree village at the mouth of Grand River. Here the Indians suddenly turned hostile; there was fighting and three soldiers were killed. This was the first armed conflict between soldiers and Indians on what is now South Dakota soil. The expedition was abandoned, and the party returned to St. Louis.

The Fur Trade: In the spring of 1811, Walter Price Hunt, leader of the so-called Astorians and an agent of John Jacob Astor, the leading fur merchant of the day, set out with a party up the Missouri on his way overland to establish a trading post at the mouth of the Columbia River. About the same time, Manuel Lisa, fearing Hunt's rivalry in the fur trade, left St. Louis in pursuit. Lisa, born in New Orleans of Spanish parentage, was one of the leading fur traders of St. Louis. He had done much work in cultivating the goodwill of the Missouri River Indians, and he did not like the idea of an outside trader or company reaping the fruits of his labor. In the vicinity of Springfield, Hunt was overtaken by a messenger from Lisa, who proposed that he wait for him so that they might travel together for mutual protection. Hunt replied that he would, but he had no intention of doing so and pushed on with all speed. He met Black Buffalo and his Sioux, but on convincing them that he did not seek trade on the Missouri he was allowed to proceed. Just above Big Bend, Manuel Lisa overtook Hunt, and for a while there were strained relations. However, when they arrived at the Ree villages and each saw that the other was not interfering with his purposes, they came to a friendly agreement.

They stayed at the Ree village many days. Hunt bought horses of the Indians, who promptly raided the herds of neighboring tribes when they ran short of animals with which to supply his needs. Lisa traded out his goods and returned south. Hunt set out straight west up Grand River and on the way traversed the present upper tier of counties—the first white man to pass through this part of the present State.

At the outbreak of the War of 1812, Capt. William Clark, formerly of the Lewis and Clark Expedition and now superintendent of Indian Affairs for Louisiana Territory, raised $11,000 on his own responsibility and sent Manuel Lisa up the Missouri with a large outfit of goods to trade with the Sioux and keep them friendly to the American Government. Clark appointed Lisa a sub-agent for the Sioux of the Missouri valley. Lisa first built Fort Manuel (1812) near the present North Dakota line; and when the Indians destroyed this fort, he moved south and built another at Big Bend. Through cunning strategy he caused the defection of the Mississippi Sioux from the British cause, kept the Dakota Sioux friendly, and contributed in no small measure to the final outcome of the war and the retention of American sovereignty in the West.

After a temporary set-back on account of the War of 1812, the fur trade revived; and in 1823 Gen. William Ashley, Lieutenant Governor of Missouri Territory, organized a trading party and set out up the Missouri River. He reached the Ree village at the mouth of Grand River in safety, and traded with the inhabitants for several days. But the night before he and his party were to leave over the Grand River route, they were treacherously attacked by the Rees, a number of them were killed, and the rest were forced to retreat down the river. The Rees were later punished by a detachment of the United States Army under Col. Henry Leavenworth, commanding officer of the district, and they left the State, retreating up-river into what is now North Dakota (*see Tour 2*).

In 1817 a French-Indian trader named Joseph La Framboise established a trading post at the junction of Bad River with the Missouri. This became the first permanent white settlement within the present border of the State. In 1822 it was rebuilt as Fort Tecumseh; and in 1832 it was again rebuilt and named Fort Pierre Choteau, which was afterward shortened to the present Fort Pierre.

OLD FORT PIERRE

In 1831 the first steamboat on the upper Missouri, the *Yellowstone*, ascended the river to Fort Pierre, and a new era dawned in the fur trade. A journey that formerly required a whole season could now be accomplished in a few weeks. The following year Pierre Choteau took a steamboat up to the mouth of the Yellowstone. The revived impetus which this gave to the fur trade lasted till the Civil War. By that time the buffalo herds were becoming smaller, and the supply of other furs had greatly lessened. The Civil War, with its disruption of trade and its frontier Indian troubles, practically ended the fur trade in this region.

First Agricultural Settlement: Up to this time trade and settlement had been confined to the Missouri River and had been related to the traffic in furs. But in 1857 it became apparent that Minnesota would be admitted as a State without the eastern portion of future South Dakota, which it then included as a Territory. Therefore far-seeing men in Minnesota Territory and Iowa formed land companies with the idea of getting control of desirable sites for settlement, which might be sold at advanced prices when the influx of settlers began. The Dakotah Land Company was formed by Gov. Medary of Minnesota Territory and a party was sent to establish a settlement at the site of Sioux Falls. But when the settlers arrived, they found the falls themselves in the possession of the Western Town Company of Dubuque, Iowa. However, the newcomers appropriated for themselves the power available above the falls, and the two groups cooperated in perfect harmony. Settlements were also made at other nearby points including Flandreau and Medary. By the organization of the Territory of Nebraska, May 30, 1854, and the State of Minnesota, May 11, 1858, a great tract of country lying to the north and west was left without legal name or existence. So the settlers on the eastern fringe of what is now South Dakota, in their eagerness to obtain government and recognition, resorted to political strategy of a most unusual character. In order to set up a Territorial government and to give an impression of substantial numbers, the 30 or 40 inhabitants of Sioux Falls split up into groups of three or four and set out in different directions; and whenever they stopped to rest their teams, they set up election precincts, appointed one another judges and clerks of election, and proceeded to vote themselves, their relatives, and even their distant friends. The total vote was quite respectable in volume, if not in quality. Shortly after this, the "rump" Legislature thus chosen convened and elected a Governor and one or two State officers, including a Delegate to Congress. That body, however, refused to recognize him. In 1859 the settlers again held an election, choosing a new Legislature and a Governor and Delegate. But again Congress failed to set up a Territory.

By the treaty of Traverse des Sioux in 1851, the Indians ceded to the United States all lands east of the Big Sioux River in present South Dakota. On July 10, 1859, the Indians tacitly accepted a treaty by which the land between the Big Sioux and Missouri Rivers was opened for settlement. Having previously refused to vacate this territory they were told by the tactful new Indian agent that a feast was being prepared for them in their new home, Yankton Reservation, which had been set aside for them farther west. Thereupon they followed along the river bank, while the agent's steamer forged upstream. A great crowd had been waiting on the Nebraska side of the river; and as soon as the Indians had left for the reservation, the settlers poured across. They took up farms and established the townsites of Bon Homme, Yankton, and Vermillion. This region thus became the first permanent agricultural settlement of the State.

The people of Bon Homme erected the first schoolhouse within the State in 1860. It was built of logs and had a dirt floor. Ten pupils attended during a school term of three months. South Dakota's first church, of the Presbyterian denomination, was established at Vermillion in 1860.

Territorial Days: There are two quite remarkable points about South Dakota's history. The first is the very small population it had when it became a Territory, and the second is the large population it acquired before it became a State. One of the last official acts of President Buchanan was to sign the bill creating Dakota Territory, which consisted of the present States of North and South Dakota and those portions of Montana and Wyoming lying east of the ridge of the Rocky Mountains. The act was signed on March 2, 1861. At this time there were only 2,402 white inhabitants of this vast region. One of the first official acts of President Lincoln was to appoint his family physician, Dr. William Jayne of Springfield, as the first Territorial Governor. The latter selected Yankton as the temporary capital, and called an election for the choice of a Legislature and a Delegate to Congress. The *Weekly Dakotan,* which still survives as the *Press and Dakotan,* was established June 6, 1861. Pursuant to the proclamation, the first Legislature, nicknamed "The Pony Congress" on account of its small size in comparison with the National Congress, convened on St. Patrick's Day 1862 with 9 members of the council and 13 of the house. After a strenuous contest, Yankton was chosen permanent capital of the Territory. The Legislature was in session two months.

South Dakota took little active part in the Civil War. Although a company of militia was raised by the State and tendered to the President, it was deemed advisable to keep the unit in South Dakota for use in possible Indian hostilities. In 1862 occurred the War of the Outbreak, when the Santee Sioux in Minnesota rose and massacred the whites. Though most of the fighting took place outside the State, two men were killed in a hayfield near Sioux Falls, and Gov. Jayne immediately sent soldiers to remove the inhabitants of that place to safety at Yankton. The Indians pillaged and burned the deserted settlement, and it was several years before any further attempt at settlement was made, although Fort Dakota was built there in 1865. In the same year a great council with the Indians held at old Fort Sully officially ended the War of the Outbreak.

This was was no sooner settled than the Red Cloud War began. The Government had determined to open a new road to the gold fields recently discovered in Montana. It proposed to survey a road from Fort Snelling west, and from the California Trail north from Laramie through the Powder River valley. Red Cloud, chief of the Oglala Sioux, saw that this would mean the ruin of the last buffalo ranges left to his people, and he therefore resisted the survey. As he was debating the proposal with white leaders, Red Cloud saw a company of soldiers approaching. "What are these men for?" he asked. He was told that they were troops sent to guard the proposed road. Red Cloud held aloft the rifle that was in his hand and said "In this and in the Great Spirit I put my trust!" Whereupon he and his followers immediately withdrew from the council.

Notwithstanding, the survey was undertaken with the protection of the military. A company of 80 of these was ambushed by Red Cloud and massacred. A council was thereupon held to which Red Cloud sent representatives. He demanded the abandonment of the forts which had been established in the Powder River country. Although this was agreed to, Red Cloud refused to come in and sign the treaty until the abandonment had actually been carried out. According to the terms of the treaty, all the land between the Big Horn Mountains on the west, the Platte River on the south, and the Missouri River on the east and north was to be reserved to the Indians as a permanent hunting ground. No white man was to be allowed in that region except on business connected with the Indians. Furthermore, this treaty could not be altered without the consent of three-fourths of the Indian braves affected.

In 1865 occurred the first of several serious grasshopper infestations, commonly referred to as "plagues." They have been a sporadic menace to agriculture ever since that time, a particularly severe visitation occurring in 1877.

The first railroad entered the State in 1871, a short stub of the Winona & St. Peter Railroad, operating only as far as Gary just within the State line. The following year, the Chicago, Milwaukee, St. Paul & Pacific built into the State through Elk Point and reached Yankton in 1873, when the panic of that year put a temporary end to railroad building.

Discovery of Gold: In 1874 occurred the most important single event in South Dakota's history—the discovery of gold in the Black Hills by a military expedition under Gen. George A. Custer. The first find occurred near the present town of Custer on August 2, 1874, and the discoverers were Horatio N. Ross and William McKay, prospectors with the expedition. Word of the discovery was immediately sent to St. Paul. On October 6 the so-called Gordon Party left Sioux City for the Black Hills. The group numbered 28 persons, among whom was Annie D. Tallant, who thereby became the first white woman to enter the Hills. After a trip lasting three months and entailing much suffering, the party arrived at Custer and built a stockade in which it spent the rest of the winter. A reproduction of this stockade may be seen near Custer today (*see Tour 5*). But early in the spring the military arrived, put the members of the party under arrest and took them to Fort Laramie, since it was contrary to the treaty for whites to be in the Hills.

In the fall of 1875 the Sioux were summoned to meet at Red Cloud's agency and arrange for the leasing of the Black Hills to the whites. The plan was that the whites should be allowed to extract the gold and other precious metals and then abandon the territory to the Indians again. But it was soon evident that no agreement could be reached and less than the required three-fourths of the braves were present; so the council broke up without accomplishing anything. Immediately after this the military, realizing the futility of doing otherwise withdrew all opposition to the entry of whites into the Hills. Gold seekers poured in and in the winter of 1875-6 there were several thousand men in the vicinity of Custer.

In the late fall of 1875, John B. Pearson of Yankton discovered rich placer diggings in the northern Hills between the present cities of Lead and Deadwood. When news of this "strike" reached Custer, it depopulated that place almost in a day, leaving fewer than 100 people in the town. In the summer of 1876 there were more than 25,000 people in Deadwood Gulch. At that time they had no legal government, since they were squatters on Indian land; but they maintained a kind of rough justice of their own, after the manner of mining communities. The town of Deadwood was laid out that summer, along both sides of the single trail up the gulch. In the same year gold was discovered at the head of Gold Run Gulch, on the site of the present city of Lead, and that prosperous mining town was born.

The discovery of gold in the Black Hills was important not only to South Dakota but to the country at large. For Black Friday of September 1873 had plunged a large part of the country into bankruptcy; and this was the first ray of light that heralded the coming of a brighter day. Both in its actual and its psychological effect, it was instrumental in bringing about recovery from the panic.

The battle of the Little Big Horn in which Custer and his command were annihilated, occurred in June 1876. Following this, Gen. Crook, who had been unable to take an active part in the battle of the Little Big Horn, was on his way from Fort Abraham Lincoln to protect the settlers, when he unexpectedly encountered a band of Indians in the Slim Buttes of what is now Harding County. Thereupon followed the Battle of Slim Buttes (*see Tour 2A*). It was on Sept. 8, 1876, that the advance guard, under Maj. Anson Mills, contacted a small band of Indians in Reva Gap of the Buttes. He held them off until night, when he was reinforced by Gen. Crook and the main body of the troops. But the Indians also received reinforcements during the night from portions of Crazy Horse's band. The Battle of Slim Buttes was fought all the following day. At the conclusion of it three whites had been killed, two soldiers and a scout, and a dozen or more of the Indians. Several of the latter were also taken prisoner. The battle resulted in more or less of a stalemate but the Indians withdrew during the ensuing night. The following morning Gen. Crook burned what was left of the Indian village and buried his own dead, causing the entire command to tramp over their graves as they broke camp.

In the fall of 1876, a peace commission visited the various reservations and obtained the signatures of the Indian leaders to a new treaty ceding the Black Hills to the whites. The Indians claimed later that they were merely ceding mineral rights, as they had been asked to do before, and that the treaty did not have the requisite three-fourths of the signatures. However, a regular and legal government was now established for the whites in the Black Hills region.

Following the discovery of gold in the Black Hills came the great boom period of the Dakotas. People came for gold, but many of them remained to take up farms. Two railroads, the North Western and the Milwaukee, built their lines halfway across the State, arriving at the Missouri River by 1880—at Pierre and Chamberlain respectively. Beyond this they could not go, for the West-river region, with the exception of the Black Hills, was still Indian country. People poured into the eastern part of the State, and within five years Brookings, Madison, Mitchell, Huron, Pierre,Watertown, Redfield, Aberdeen, Webster, and Milbank had become important towns. Rivalry between various communities was keen, especially with regard to the location of county seats. In one instance, the militia had to be called out to preserve the county records.

Commerce west of the Missouri River was carried on by stage-coach and ox train. There were main trails leading into the Hills from Pierre, Chamberlain, Sidney, Neb., Cheyenne, Wyo., and Bismarck, N. Dak. But the coming of the railroads to the Missouri meant the end of the steamboats. Thereafter they survived on the upper Missouri only as ferries at the principal crossings, until the building of the State bridges many years later.

The winter of 1880 was a memorable one for this region. The snow fell heavily in a blizzard in October, and did not disappear until the following spring. Train service was interrupted and the roads were practically impassable. In the resultant thaw in the spring, a great amount of damage was done, especially on the lower Missouri in the southeastern corner of the State.

The Fight for Statehood: When Dakota Territory was created in 1861, it included what is now North and South Dakota, much of what is now Montana and most of present Wyoming. But with the creation of Montana Territory in 1864 and Wyoming Territory in 1868, Dakota Territory was reduced to the present size of the "Sister States."

As early as 1872 there was some agitation for the division of Dakota Territory into two equal parts as at present; but nothing came of it. In 1879, however, an attempt was made to buy the school lands of the State at a low figure; and through the influence of the superintendent of public instruction, Gen. William H. H. Beadle, it was determined to combine the fight for the division of the Territory with a demand that no school lands should be sold for less than $10 an acre. A convention of citizens was held at Canton in June 1882, and a committee was appointed to further both these ends. The committee carried the matter to the Legislature the following winter and the latter passed a bill calling for a constitutional convention. This bill, however, was vetoed by Gov. Nehemiah G. Ordway. The executive committee thereupon called a delegate convention to meet at Huron in June 1883. Every county in South Dakota was represented by its strongest men. An ordinance was passed providing for a constitutional convention to be held in Sioux Falls on September 4. In the meantime delegates to the convention were elected. At the appointed time they met in Sioux Falls and drew up a constitution, in which was inserted the $10 school-land provision. This constitution was submitted to the people at the November election, and was adopted almost unanimously. A committee was appointed to present it to Congress, together with a petition for Statehood; but Congress did not see fit to act.

The next Legislature provided by law for a new constitutional convention to be held in Sioux Falls in September 1885. The constitution framed by this convention again with a $10 minimum clause was ratified once more by the people at the November election; and a complete set of State officers together with a Legislature and Congressman were elected at the same time. The Legislature elected two United States Senators and these men and the Governor carried a petition to Congress. But the National Administration was at this time Democratic and the leaders did not favor a plan that would be sure to introduce four new Republican Senators to cut down the Democratic majority. They favored the admission of the whole Territory as one State and the National Administration brought pressure to bear to the same end. But every time the question came to a test vote the people of the Territory voted overwhelmingly for division.

In 1888 the Republican National Convention made the admission of the two States a campaign issue. The Republicans prevailed in the fall elections and the Congress then in session yielded to the inevitable and passed the enabling act on Valentine's Day 1889. It was approved on Washington's Birthday. A new constitutional convention met in Sioux Falls on July 4 with power only to amend and resubmit the constitution of 1885. At a special election on October 1 this document was approved; and on November 2, 1889, the long fight was ended and proclamations were issued by President Cleveland admitting North and South Dakota to the Union. At the time of its admission, the State of South Dakota had a population of more than 300,000.

An interesting method was employed in preparing the proclamation for the Chief Executive's signature. The President desired to give neither State priority, but to admit both as "Sister States." Before the Presidential signatures were attached, therefore, the two proclamations were placed on the President's desk with the texts covered and only the lines for the signature showing. As a further precaution, after the signatures had been attached, the documents were thoroughly shuffled by another person. This made it impossible to tell which State was admitted first. It can only be said that the two Dakotas are the thirty-ninth and fortieth States. As a matter of courtesy, when it is necessary to rank the States,

South Dakota yields to North Dakota, which has a prior position in alphabetical order.

Immediately after entering upon Statehood, South Dakota experienced its last Indian trouble—the Messiah War. A Nevada Piute Indian named Wovoka claimed to have had a vision following an eclipse of the sun in 1889. From this he evolved a religion which was a curious mixture of Christianity and Indian religious thought. The gist of it was that he, as the Messiah, had come to drive out the whites, restore the land to the Indians, and bring back the buffalo. This was to be accomplished by means of a religious dance called the "Ghost Dance," during which the dancers wore a "ghost" shirt, which was supposed to render them immune to the white men's bullets. The dancing craze spread till it was inflaming the Indians to a dangerous degree. Sitting Bull was killed resisting arrest on the eve of setting out for the Ghost Dance with his band; and orders were given for the arrest of Big Foot's band, which was also on its way to join the dancers. The band was overtaken and apparently submitted to arrest; but during the night they escaped into the Badlands. A young captain named John J. Pershing was among the troops maneuvering to isolate Big Foot, although he was not present at the ensuing battle. The morning following its escape, Big Foot's band was overtaken on Wounded Knee Creek. Again they surrendered and the soldiers began to disarm them. This angered the Indians and they were further inflamed by a medicine man named Yellow Bird who, speaking in the Sioux tongue, exhorted them to resist and reminded them that they were wearing the bullet-proof ghost shirts. Finally, as a soldier pulled aside an Indian's blanket to see whether he was armed, another Indian fired at the soldiers and was joined at once by all the rest of the Indians. The soldiers immediately fired in return and at point-blank range the carnage was frightful. Then the Hotchkiss guns of the artillery raked the Indian village, setting fire to the tipis and killing women and children indiscriminately. The superior arms of the soldiers and their artillery could have but one result. Only a few of the Indians escaped to the hills and the draws, and the soldiers cut down those whom they could overtake, women as well as men, leaving their bodies scattered for a distance of two miles. The Wounded Knee massacre—for it was that, rather than a battle—resulted in the death of nearly 200 Indians, men, women, and children, and some 60 soldiers. It was caused by the use of green troops, led by inexperienced officers. Shortly after this, Gen. Nelson A. Miles arrived, restored order, and composed the last of the serious differences between the whites and Indians.

The first Legislature of Dakota Territory made provision for a Territorial university; but it was not until twenty years later that the university became an accomplished fact. The story goes that after Pierre had won the capital, Sioux Falls had the next choice of State institutions, and chose the penitentiary; then Vermillion had to take what was left, and got the university. The University of South Dakota was established at Vermillion in 1882 through the enterprise of the citizens and the people of the county. In 1883 the State College of Agriculture and Mechanic Arts was founded at Brookings.

The Capital Fight: The question of the location of the Territorial and later of the State capital was one that agitated the people for years. Although Yankton had won the honor in 1861, the fact that it was in one corner of the vast Territory led to agitation for removal of the capital to some more central location. Finally, in 1882, the Legislature appointed a capital commission to select a permanent site. They chose Bismarck, largely because of the inability of South Dakotans to agree upon a site themselves. Although many subsequent attempts were made to remove the Territorial capital from Bismarck, they were unsuccessful for the same reason.

The constitutional convention of 1885 submitted the selection of a capital to popular vote, and Huron won. The enabling act of 1889 again required that the people should designate a temporary capital. This brought on a hard-fought struggle in the summer of 1889, with Pierre, Huron, Watertown, Sioux Falls, Mitchell, and Chamberlain as contestants. Pierre won by a large margin. Under the constitution, the permanent capital was to be selected at the election of 1890. This time Pierre and Huron were the only contestants. Pierre again won by a large majority.

Despite this decisive outcome, agitation still continued for the removal of the capital to some other city. In the Legislature of 1901, the other candidates agreed to abide by the result of a caucus, and Mitchell won. An attempt was made to submit a constitutional amendment, but a filibuster blocked this. At the session of 1903, the caucus plan was again adopted and again Mitchell won. The Legislature passed the submitting resolution by a large majority in both houses. During the next two years a strenuous campaign was waged. It became a contest between the State's two principal railway systems. The Milwaukee backed Mitchell and the North Western, Pierre. At first the railroads gave influential citizens throughout the State passes to visit their respective candidates for capital. Finally the situation developed to a point where the railroads felt obliged to transport free anyone who wished to visit either of these cities; and in the summer of 1904 they carried upwards of one hundred thousand people to the rival cities, a mass movement unprecedented in the history of the State. The election resulted in a victory for Pierre by about 18,000 majority. The Legislature of 1905 made provision for a permanent capitol building, which was dedicated in 1910.

During the Spanish-American War, South Dakota raised and equipped a regiment for service. It went to the Philippines, participated in the hardest fighting in many battles, and won great distinction, several of its members receiving the highest military award, the Congressional Medal of Honor; and on its return it was reviewed by President McKinley at Aberdeen.

In the year 1907, the Milwaukee and the North Western railroads continued their lines from Chamberlain and Pierre, respectively, through to the Black Hills at Rapid City. Earlier, about 1890, the North Western and the Burlington had built their lines to Deadwood from their Nebraska terminals—the Burlington through the heart of the Hills and the North Western up their eastern edge. At the same time, the Milwaukee extended its main line west from Aberdeen to Lemmon.

State Enterprises: During the period from 1915 to 1925, the State engaged in a number of experimental ventures into business and finance. Some of these the State administered directly and some it controlled. The first of these ventures was the State Bank Guaranty Law of 1915. Under the provisions of this act, the State undertook to administer a fund, contributed pro rata by the banks, to liquidate closed banks and thus protect the depositors. This plan worked satisfactorily during prosperous times, and the first few banks which failed were liquidated promptly. But with the coming of the depression the financial strain proved too great, the fund was soon exhausted, and the law fell into abeyance.

In 1917 the Rural Credits constitutional amendment became effective. This provided a means whereby landowners could borrow money directly from the State, from funds secured by the sale of interest-bearing bonds. As in the case of the Bank Guaranty law, the plan proved effective during normal times. But the depression caused many farmers to default on their payments, a large amount of land reverted to the State, and in 1936 more than 1½ million acres, representing about 5,700 separate tracts, were in the hands of the State; while more than 60 million dollars in bonded indebtedness and interest remain. The debt is gradually being liquidated by a diversion of a portion of the gasoline and other taxes.

Another State venture was the purchase in 1919 of a coal mine at Haynes, N. Dak., for $200,000. The vein of coal pinched out, and the mine was sold in April 1936 for $5,500, which was insufficient to pay outstanding obligations against the property. In the winter of 1933-4, the State opened a strip coal mine at Firesteel, S. Dak. (*see Tour 2A*), but this work was halted when it was discovered that coal could be purchased elsewhere for less than it could be mined at the State project.

A method whereby farmers could receive the benefits of hail insurance was the objective of another State-promoted venture. The act provided that every farm should be automatically covered; and if the beneficiary did not wish protection, he was obliged to file an application for exemption. Although farmers in the areas subject to hail storms reaped benefits, the fact that the average farmer did not wish to carry this insurance led to the repeal of the law.

Another State-owned enterprise is the cement plant, located at Rapid City (*see Tour 4*). Since 1925 the plant has virtually monopolized the cement business of the State, because of the high quality of its product and the low cost of production, the latter being due to the presence of all the necessary ingredients within a small area. More than a million dollars in profits have been turned into the State treasury by the plant since 1925. The original indebtedness amounted to about $1,200,000. The business has been under the direction of a five-man commission.

Gov. William H. McMaster rose to Nation-wide prominence in 1924 when, announcing that the oil companies were charging too much for gasoline, he ordered the State to engage in the gasoline business. The result was that motor fuel prices dropped sharply. The public praised the step, and a little later McMaster rode into the United States Senate on a wave of popularity. The act was later declared unconstitutional.

The State has much progressive legislation on its books. In 1899 South Dakota became the first State to provide by statute for the initiative and referendum; but these laws have not proved as effective as was expected, since it has proved difficult to overcome public apathy with regard to any particular issue.

The Last Twenty Years: South Dakota's contribution to the World War was not made as a State. Her population was too sparse to make up even a single division, so her recruits were scattered among various commands. The State ranked high, however, in the per capita purchase of Liberty Bonds, and it did its part in Red Cross and other war-time activities.

An interesting feature of South Dakota's participation in the war was that in the first selective draft recruits from this State ranked highest in point of health in the United States. The rejection of recruits for physical defects was less than 20 per cent in South Dakota, as against an average of more than 29 per cent for the country at large, and a rejection of four out of ten candidates in certain States.

In 1919 the citizens of Yankton decided that they must have a bridge across the Missouri at that point. The money was partly raised by a bond issue. An excellent bridge was built, at a cost of 1¼ million dollars. To raise money for payments on the bonds, a toll is charged.

At about the same time the State decided to erect a number of bridges across the Missouri River, to unite the two halves of the State more closely. All vehicular communication between them up to that time had been by ferry. Five bridges were erected, at a total cost of more than two million dollars. The bridges were located, from north to south, at Mobridge, Forest City, Pierre, Chamberlain, and Wheeler. The money was secured by means of a legislative appropriation and a small tax levy.

In the summer of 1927, the State for the first time had the honor of providing the summer home of a President of the United States. President Coolidge occupied the State Game Lodge in Custer Park (*see Tour 5*) for the season, and maintained business offices in the high school at Rapid City.

The Federal order in 1933, increasing the price of gold at United States mints from $20.67 to $35 an ounce, by changing the dollar's gold content brought a revival of mining activity in the Black Hills, the renewed operation of many mines that had been closed as unprofitable, and, for the first time in many years, a revival of placer mining. While no outstanding "strikes" occurred, it developed that placer mining could be made to yield a fair day's wage and that was important at a time when jobs were scarce. This renewed mining activity in the Black Hills region still persists (1937).

In July 1934 occurred the first stratosphere flight from the Stratosphere Bowl, 12 miles west of Rapid City (*see Tour 5*). This and the succeeding flight were sponsored by the National Geographic Society and the U. S. Army Air Corps. The 1934 flight did not succeed in breaking the record, although the balloon, Explorer I, attained a height of over 60,000 feet. At this point the fabric began to rip and the descent was begun. The flight ended near Holdredge, Neb., when the balloonists were forced to resort to their parachutes to save their lives.

In the early summer of 1935 a second attempt to penetrate the stratosphere was made; but an hour before the time scheduled for the take-off, the already inflated balloon burst at the top and the charge of helium escaped. Nothing daunted, the sponsors of the flight repaired the balloon, Explorer II, and on Armistice Day, 1935, their efforts were crowned with complete success; for on that day the greatest balloon ever made by man reached the greatest heights ever attained by man. The giant bag arose to a height of 72,395 feet, remaining in the air eight hours. The descent was as felicitous as the rise and the balloon made a perfect "egg-shell" landing near White Lake, S. Dak., 240 miles southeast of the rock-walled starting point. Capt. Albert W. Stevens commanded the flight and Capt. Orvil A. Anderson was the pilot.

INDUSTRY AND LABOR

South Dakota, with few large cities and a thinly-scattered population, is preeminently an agricultural State, but mining, manufacturing, and lumbering are also important in various sections. Although 14th in size among the States of the Union, it ranks only 36th in population (692,849 in 1930). The entire State contains but 5,000 more people than the city of Pittsburgh, Pa. In 1935 the State contained 18,000 fewer people than it had five years previously.

In 1929 South Dakota had a per capita wealth of roughly $5,-000, the third highest in the United States. Although this wealth lies largely in livestock and agricultural products, in 1933 there were 348 manufacturing establishments in the State employing 4,731 persons with products valued at $46,265,812. The total mineral production in 1934 was valued at $19,173,000 and the value of the gold alone in 1935 was $19,853,057. South Dakota is also one of the leading States in the production of mica, tin, feldspar, and lithium products, and stone, gravel, sand, and cement are other leading products. Large deposits of lignite coal have been found in the northwestern part of the State but as yet they remain inaccessible to transportation. The forested areas include 1,067,745 acres of National forests and 77,482 acres of State forests, while the 478,000 acres of water surface make South Dakota 18th in that respect. Among other developments, there were, by 1936, nine hydroelectric plants producing 19,853 horsepower and about 75,000 acres of land under irrigation.

On the other hand the value of the crops, livestock, and livestock products marketed in 1935 reached $100,838,000, while in 1929 it was $242,797,000. Dairy products alone in 1933 were valued at 16 million dollars. The State in 1935 had more than 1½ million cattle, more than 1½ million sheep (of which over 100,000 were in one county) and more than half a million hogs. The wool clip in 1935 was just short of 10 million pounds. In the same year the farm population numbered 358,204 and the 83,303 farms with their buildings had a total value in excess of 1¼ billion dollars.

Serious labor troubles are rare in South Dakota, with only 16 strikes recorded between 1920 and 1935, of which but two or three were important. There were two strikes in 1934 and three in 1935. The problem of migratory labor has lessened in recent years. Where formerly hundreds, if not thousands, of transients "bummed" their way on freight trains to the harvest fields, now the combines and the small threshing machines have done away with the necessity for large crews, and farmers "change work" with one another.

Misfortune, in the form of drought, grasshoppers and dust storms, has plagued South Dakota for the past several years, during which time Federal aid was a tremendous boon to both business and agriculture. Government-supplied employment on permanent improvements, such as water conservation, soil erosion projects, roads, and public buildings, was the biggest factor in South Dakota's battle against the lean years.

STATE GOVERNMENT

According to the State constitution, a candidate for nomination as Governor must receive at least 35 percent of the votes cast by his party in the primary; otherwise the nominee is decided on by a caucus, which quite often has nominated some candidate other than the one receiving the highest number of votes. The salary of the Governor, $3,000 a year, is the lowest paid to any State Executive in the Union.

The State has a bicameral Legislature, reduced in 1937 to 75 representatives and 35 senators, elected every two years. They convene at Pierre on the first Monday after the first Tuesday in January of odd-numbered years, for a limited session of 60 days. Special sessions have been rare.

Legislators draw a salary of $5 per day for not more than 60 days, and travel allowance of 10 cents a mile from their homes to Pierre and return. They also draw an expense allowance of not more than $200.

South Dakota has five judges in its supreme court. Originally there were three, but the number was increased in 1909 by an act of the Legislature. The judges are elected every six years by a vote of the entire State, and vacancies are filled by appointment by the Governor. The court has both original and appellate jurisdiction, although most of its cases are appellate. The only appeal from its decisions is to the United States Supreme Court. Salary of the judges is $3,000 a year, with an $1,800 annual allowance for expenses.

Twelve circuit judges, elected by districts every four years, preside over the tribunals that hear most of the civil and criminal cases arising in the State. They have original jurisdiction over all cases except those of probate, city ordinance, and Federal character. The salary of circuit judges is $2,500 a year.

The trend of South Dakota's finances is toward a decrease in bonded indebtedness. In 1927 the percapita net bonded indebtedness was approximately $88.66 and by 1936 it had been reduced to $63.56. This included Rural Credit bonds which in 1936 constituted 91.8% of the total net bonded indebtedness while contributing only 16.1% of the total amount in the interest and sinking funds. Outside of the Rural Credits, the bonded indebtedness of South Dakota is almost negligible.

The total revenue available for the State in 1936 was $21,646,-494.06, of which practically 23% was Federal aid. The total expenditures were $12,923,444.55, 59.9% for expenses in departments under appointive officers (three-fourths of which was for highway construction), 14.6% for educational institutions, 11.4% for State enterprises, 8.6% for penal and charitable institutions, and the rest for miscellaneous operations.

AGRICULTURE

THE process of transformation from raw and unfinished prairie lands to a relatively developed countryside began in 1857 in the extreme southeastern corner of the State, and the last raw land was opened for settlement as late as 1910 in the opposite section, in the counties of Harding, Perkins, and Butte. During this period of agricultural and commercial expansion, there was a modest but determined growth in education, social welfare, and the fine arts, so that today economic and social development keep abreast in South Dakota.

With nearly one half the soil in its virgin state, untouched by the plow, the agriculture of South Dakota might be considered still in the infant stage of development. However, scanty moisture in the western half precludes the practicability of its successful utilization as a farming country without the aid of irrigation.

In the western half, crops that mature quickly, require little moisture, and supply a large quantity of forage are the most popular. This section, in the main, is still devoted chiefly to stock raising. In some cases, large yields of wheat, oats, barley, and other small grains during wet seasons enable farmers to cling to their holdings during lean years.

Prairie grasses are still the chief source of stock feed, with crops raised as a side line to supplement the native rations. The West-river region began as a stock country, and after being engulfed for a decade by a tide of homesteaders who came, were conquered by the elements, and left, the land reverted to its earlier uses.

Progress of farming in the State has been necessarily slow. Indian troubles disrupted the first settlements and caused their abandonment; the Civil War halted advancement; and it required a long time for Eastern farmers to adapt themselves to the drier prairies. Drought and grasshoppers sent many scurrying back East. Gradually, however, they learned to change their methods, and eventually the prairie became checkered with farm plots. The lack of railroads was another handicap, and it was not until the attainment of statehood that much thought was given to settling as far west as the Missouri River.

After the extension of the railroads into the important farming areas, progress was more rapid. Then a few years ago it became evident that too much non-productive land had been broken. Many large wheat areas could not be properly cared for after the first two or three seasons, and the land gradually reverted to sod, with a great loss for those who had attempted to farm it.

Stock feeding is becoming more important each year. Baby beeves picked up on the range are fattened in eastern South Dakota feed lots and shipped to market when between 12 and 18 months old. Poultry raising brings the State an income two and one half times that obtained from gold, although South Dakota ranks second among the gold-producing States. Creameries dot the State, especially in the eastern part, and small flour mills are found wherever water power or other factors render them profitable.

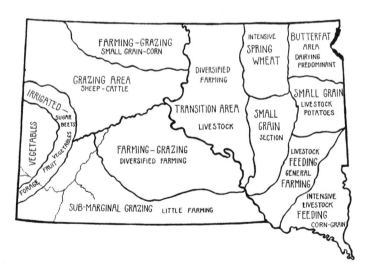

A glance at the agricultural map of South Dakota reveals several kinds of farming, each peculiar to a certain section. Whereas, Iowa, for example, is noted for its corn and hog production, it would be difficult to name any predominating crop in South Dakota. A tour across the State from east to west gives a cross section of wide variety in farming methods—a variety enforced mainly by differences in rainfall, soil textures, and topography.

Near the eastern border, farm scenes are similar to those in Iowa or Minnesota. Silos, windmills, tree-sequestered farm houses with sturdy buildings, dairy herds grazing in green pastures, fields of corn, small grain and forage crops checkering the landscape, all enter into the composite picture of eastern South Dakota's farming area, where crop failures are the exception and diversified agriculture insures the farmer an income from several sources. Here farms are smaller than farther west, but the yield per acre is greater. From this region come vegetables and various kinds of fruit in abundance. Potatoes raised in the east central area are shipped west, where tuber yields are small and often uncertain.

Westward from this region, a progressive change in the nature of the country is evident. Farmhouses are less and less pretentious, groves of trees are only occasionally visible, pastures are not so luxuriant, lakes are no longer seen. Farming still predominates, and eastern characteristics gradually give way to those of the West. For miles the land has been level; now it is slightly rolling, often broken. Creeks and "draws" that, in the eastern section, appear to wander aimlessly through the prairie, now take a more positive course, leading eventually to the Missouri, the Mississippi, and the Gulf.

Undulating, treeless prairies, gumbo hills rising like sharp irregular steps from deep river bottoms, herds of cattle grazing on slopes of creeks and draws, occasional farms breaking the monotony of tablelands—these are characteristic of the semiarid part of the State known as the Missouri River range section.

Never classed as a farming area, chiefly because of scanty moisture, unsuitable soil, or unfavorable topography, this region is virtually dependent on stock raising. On the eastern margin are farms with fairly pretentious buildings, although they are generally attached to land units comprising several quarter-sections. More land is necessary to produce a livelihood here because the yield is unusually small. Westward, the interval between farms becomes greater and there is an increasing amount of grassland, unbroken and often ungrazed.

The eastern plateau ends in an abrupt downward plunge past rugged and frequently almost grassless hills to the broad productive bottoms of the Missouri River. Here attempts are made at farming, the most successful crop being alfalfa or other forage growths. Timber, matted with dense underbrush, thickly fringes the banks on either side—an indication of what is possible, given sufficient moisture, on lands more distant from the stream. From the flat expanses of river bottom, fences mount toward higher ground, where the hills are dotted with grazing cattle, shut out by barbed wire from the hay meadows below.

The prairie country on the west side of the river is in striking contrast to that of the valley. For miles not a house is visible, and only a fence here and there in the distance indicates that human life is somewhere near. The country is rolling, and only occasionally does a farm plot break the line of the grassy prairie. The summit of each succeeding ridge presents nothing but the view of another ridge, until a divide is reached. From this latter point, small ranch houses can be seen, tucked away in creek bottoms, where "draws" and gullies converge to permit trees and greener grass to grow. It is typical stock country, the animals depending on native grasses rather than on forage furnished by tilled crops.

Less than 30 years ago, this same prairie was dotted with the shacks of homesteaders who came only to leave as soon as the land became theirs or when adversity overtook them. The few who remained, living mostly along dry creeks or near springs, gradually managed to acquire large herds of cattle or sheep and to wrest a living from the ruthless prairie. This prairie is still the cattleman's paradise; but today he owns or rents his land; yesterday it belonged to anyone or to no one.

But it is not all sparsely settled. Above the gumbo soil on higher tableland a great difference is noted. Though the moisture is no heavier, the soil is better. Black sandy loam, capable of resisting considerable drought, has kept the farmers on the land. In normal years they raise fair crops; in dry years they raise something, perhaps only forage, but they stay on and are contented, for life is not as pressing as it is farther east and the temptation to move to town is less. Many farms in this area are well improved, with small groves of trees adding a touch of beauty to the level expanses. The same kinds of crops are raised as in the eastern section, but the yield is smaller.

Farther on, below the rim of the tableland, there is again rolling prairie, resembling a huge rumpled blanket, each undulating section no different from the rest. In the distance mud buttes, badlands, and rocky knolls appear, the beginning of the buttes and Badlands section. Except for the sharply broken surface, with many deep "draws" and creeks, the country is similar to the Missouri River range section and the Black Hills is still the realm of the rancher, with cattle predominant over other livestock. Where farming is attempted, it is usually for the purpose of supplying feed for stock. Forage crops—alfalfa, clover, and cane—are preferred. Persons who have broken ground with the intention of depending on "dirt farming" for a living have learned to their sorrow that it is impracticable that eventually they must relinquish their holdings to those engaged in pursuits better adapted to the land and climate.

If the traveler approaches the Black Hills from the northeast, his route bisects South Dakota's irrigated area—a little country by itself, where rich green foliage appears suddenly in sharp contrast to the dun prairies surrounding it. To one ignorant of the existence of the artificial water supply, it resembles a veritable oasis covering thousands of acres. Sugar beets, utilized both for sugar and for stock feed in the vicinity where they are raised, are the important crop. Alfalfa, too, grows phenomenally well under irrigation, and seed from this section is shipped to distant States and even to foreign countries.

The Black Hills rise suddenly from the surrounding grassland. Large-scale farming is no longer in evidence, and there are no broad fields of corn or small grain. Only in the fertile valleys, where at best the farmer or gardener is cramped for space, are there any cultivated plots. Here garden vegetables, principally head lettuce and potatoes, the latter of unusual hardiness, are raised for market. An exception is the famous Spearfish Valley, long noted for its output of apples and other fruit as well as garden truck, raised under irrigation. Every year thousands of bushels of apples and vegetables find their way to outside markets.

The four years of relentless drought, from 1933 to 1936, accompanied by grasshopper hordes and dust storms, left in their wake parched fields and discouraged farmers, and paralyzed every source of farm income in most of the State. Ushered in by the famous and devastating "black blizzard" of November 1933, the dust storm scourge, something new to Dakota prairies, swept much of the top soil from hundreds of farms. Dirt from the fields was deposited like brown snowdrifts along fences.

With no income, farmers were unable to pay taxes or provide a meager living for destitute families without Federal help. The southeastern section of the State suffered least, but residents of the grazing area, through lack of feed and water, were forced to sell their stock. Several years of good crops will be necessary to effect recovery from the searing heat and lack of rains during the past few years.

Thousands of well improved farms, especially in the eastern part of the State, bear testimony to the fact that drought is the excep-tion rather than the rule. Even in the western section, where pre-cipitation rarely reaches 18 inches during an entire year, comfort-able homes have been made possible through the combination of farming and ranching.

Although latest crop estimates for 1937, based on conditions September 1, are below normal, they point to the second largest yield in the last five years and indicate that agricultural recovery is on the way.

A total production of 48,902,000 bushels of corn is predicted compared with the 1936 yield of only 8,446,000 and the 1928-32 five year average of 78,447,000 bushels. Durum wheat production is expected to total 3,906,000 bushels in 1937 as compared with but 700,000 bushels in 1936 and the five year pre-drought average of 12,607,000 bushels. The yield of oats is forecast at 37,474,000 bushels, with a production in 1936 of 12,710,000 bushels and a five year average of 59,033,000 bushels. Barley is expected to yield a total of 22,982,000 bushels while the 1936 production was 8,977,000 and the 1928-32 average was 34,277,000. Rye in 1937 will yield one of the largest crops on record in South Dakota with the total production estimated at 6,108,000 bushels, as compared with 1,608,-000 bushels in 1936 and the 1928-32 average of 4,072,000 bushels.

Among the minor crops, flax should produce 252,000 bushels in 1937 as compared with 132,000 in 1936 and the five year average of 2,170,000, the total yield of potatoes is estimated at 1,708,000 bushels as compared with 783,000 bushels in 1936 and the five year average of 3,971,000 bushels, and the forecast for all tame hay produced in 1937 is 768,000 tons as compared with 582,000 tons in 1936 and the 1928-32 average of 1,126,000 tons. More than half of this tame hay, 442,000 tons, will be alfalfa, while in 1936 294,000

tons of alfalfa were produced and the five year average was 813,-
000 tons. The wild hay production is estimated at 1,036,000 tons for
1937 while the 1936 yield was 424,000 tons and the five year average was 1,218,000 tons. The production of all hay combined for
1937 will be approximately 1,804,000 tons, compared with 1,006,-
000 in 1936 and an average of 2,344,000 tons during the 1928-32
period.

Cattle raising in South Dakota is carried on under three general
systems. Two of these, dairying and the feeding of beef cattle, are
practiced mainly east of the Missouri River. Since dairying is carried on much the same everywhere, there is no need of describing
it in detail. In the feeding of beef for market, young steers are
purchased from the range country to the west of the river and fed
intensively for a short period on the surplus corn of the eastern
and southeastern sections; after which they are shipped the comparatively short distance to Midwestern markets.

The third system, the range raising of cattle, is necessarily confined to the range sections of the West-river country. The 20 years
from 1880 to 1900 were the halcyon days of the big cattle outfits,
with thousands of stock run under a single brand, frequently with
absentee ownership. Little or no provision was made for winter
feeding of such vast numbers, and cattle raising under such conditions was a gamble. If the winter was an open one, the stock came
through in fine shape; if it were severe, the ranges were cleaned.

But with the turn of the century, the prosperous days of the big
outfits came to an end. There were probably many factors contributing to this, but the chief was perhaps the "nester." Some cow-
hand with the makings of a good stockman, becoming tired of
working for someone else, would start up for himself. He knew
all the favorable ranch locations on his range, and would file on a
piece of land with shelter and water; if possible, some hay bottoms.
There he would build up his herd—some say at the expense of
outfits so large that all their unbranded stock could not be rounded
up.

But the reign of the "nester" was short. Just as he had driven
out the big outfits, so the homesteaders drove him out, or at least
curtailed his activities. As the wave of homesteading swept over the
land, shacks, dugouts, and sod shanties appeared overnight on every quarter-section. The homesteaders for the most part had little
knowledge of farming and none of ranching, but they had an ex-

SQUATTER'S CLAIM

aggerated idea of the value of the grass. The "nester" now became the cattleman, could not meet their terms and survive. Some sold out, some were cut down, some made arrangements with the more reasonable homesteaders. Those who survived made good, for the homestead wave receded—not so rapidly as it rose, but just as surely. Today in the West-river country there are cattle ranches of varying size, with a small nucleus of deeded land as the core, with a larger body of homestead and State land, surrounding it, and always with a fringe for which the cattleman pays neither rental nor tax.

In South Dakota sheep are raised either on farm plots or in range flocks. The farm flock may be found anywhere in the State. It numbers all the way from one "bum" lamb to two or three hundred head of sheep. If carried on as an adjunct to farming, it is profitable, like raising chickens or milch cows. The range flock, on the other hand, averaging from 1,500 to 1,800 head, usually represents the total investment of its owner and his whole means of livelihood.

It is axiomatic to say that sheep raising on the range can be carried on only in a natural range country. Certain conditions must be present before sheep can be raised in large numbers, and the first is an abundance of grazing space. The three northwestern counties meet this requirement, having the lowest population density in the State.

The second requisite is cheap land. In the northwestern corner of the State this condition also exists. The land there may be leased from the government and from private individuals at a minimum of six cents an acre a year, the rental varying in different counties. Another requisite for range sheep-raising is feed and shelter. This region has an abundance of natural grasses of various kinds, including buffalo, wheat, blue-stem, and sand grasses. Grass in this region cures on the ground in July and August and, unlike the grasses in moist climates, is as nutritious in winter as it is when first cut and stacked. Shelter is found along creeks and draws, and it is in these places that stockmen usually build their ranch houses and sheds and feed their flocks during the winter.

The final requisite is water supply, at least during the summer months. Sheep, like horses, will eat snow in the absence of water and survive, whereas cattle must have water, winter and summer. This particular region has a number of streams that run the year around, and others that at least have waterholes along their courses. The result is that this northwestern corner of the State, an area of roughly 100 miles square, supports an enormous number of sheep. Harding County alone, for example, showed a production of more than 68,000 spring lambs in 1931. Butte and Perkins counties also produce many sheep by the range method, but few others employ this system.

Different sections of the country find different breeds of sheep best suited to their purposes. In the range section of South Dakota, almost the only breed found is the Rambouillet. It is a dual purpose sheep, valuable both for wool and lambs. The range wool in South Dakota ranks with the best, comparing favorably with the high grade wool of the Montana ranges.

With the acknowledgement among most farmers that the best way to sell grain is "on the hoof," hog raising in South Dakota, as elsewhere, is complemented by the production of corn and other grains. This is true especially in the eastern section, where alfalfa and clover fields furnish pastures to supplement the corn ration. Western South Dakota ranchers and farmers usually raise some hogs, but not with the care and attention to scientific formulas that characterize those in the eastern section.

Poland-China, Duroc-Jersey, and Hampshire breeds have been the mainstay of the farmers of the State, Hampshire being more popular in the West-river country because of its hardiness and ability to rustle for its living. It is the leading type of bacon hog raised in the State.

Although seldom raised exclusively, poultry, principally chickens and turkeys, are raised on nearly every farm where diversified agriculture is practiced. Poultry and egg houses buy the products from farmers and ship them to Eastern markets.

This brief general picture of South Dakota shows a State with wide diversification in farm crops and methods, each section peculiar to itself. Farmers are learning, after years of uncertain fumbling, that particular areas are adaptable to particular crops and products, and that the land is generous to those who observe this rule, unsympathetic and unyielding to those who do not.

EDUCATION AND RELIGION

EDUCATION

The early settlers of South Dakota believed no community was complete until a school had been built and a teacher engaged. The first school building was erected by public subscription in Bon Homme County in 1860; the second was built at Vermillion by Company A., U. S. Cavalry, in 1862.

In the same year William Jayne, first Governor of Dakota Territory, signed the original law establishing a school code and a common school District. In 1864 Gov. Newton Edmunds appointed James S. Foster as first superintendent of Public Instruction. It proved to be a happy choice, for this educator, grounded in the school of Horace Mann, through three successive terms laid the foundation of the present school system of the State. By 1870 there were 83 schools in the State, with approximately 1800 children in attendance.

The school district system was originally modeled after that of New England. Later the township system was introduced, with one school board having control of all schools within the township. The two systems have existed side by side since that early day, and later legislation was enacted to permit communities to change at will from one form to the other.

The decade 1870-80 was marked by the installation of the first course of study, the enactment of much school legislation, and the raising of the qualifications for the office of county superintendent. In this time the enrollment in schools increased to more than 13,000, with 464 teachers employed.

The years 1880-90 saw a complete recodification of school laws. Courses of study were revised and United States history, temperance, physiology, and hygiene were added to the curriculum. From 1890-05 the important developments were the advent of the first grade teaching certificate, the strengthening of the compulsory education laws, and the advocacy of uniform textbooks and consolidated schools. The period from 1906-16 saw the establishment of the State Certificate, the raising of teacher requirements and the founding of consolidated schools.

The period of greatest expansion was from 1917-1929. During this time 80 per cent of the rural schools of the State were built, State aid was made available for rural schools, free textbooks were provided and $6,500 was appropriated for a State-wide educational

LOG SCHOOLHOUSE, VERMILLION

survey. In 1919 a revision of elementary and secondary school courses was completed. In 1926 the peak of teaching salaries was reached, the high salaries attracting a better qualified class of teachers.

Since 1929 economic conditions have forced many changes, including drastic reduction in teaching salaries, amounting to more than 50 per cent in many cases. The school laws were recodified in 1931. In 1933 the Legislature enacted a Gross Income Tax and assigned 50 per cent of it to public education. In 1935 it replaced this measure with a Sales and Net Income Tax, apportioning 32 per cent of it to the schools. This, together with the income from school lands (*see above*) and local taxes, forms the present basis of school support. At present (1937) there are between 1,500 and

1,800 teachers, with more than 50,000 pupils in attendance. So much for the system of common schools; but the founders of the State felt the need of something more.

To provide further educational facilities for the youth of this new frontier, the first Territorial legislature, at its first meeting at Yankton in 1862, passed a measure to create a university of Dakota Territory. The act provided for a board of 18 regents with authority to appoint teachers, form courses of study, fix tuition, and grant degrees. The legislature was given power to determine salaries. But it was not until 20 years later that the university buildings were actually started.

As the State developed, and its agricultural, commercial, and industrial activities expanded, its school system expanded also. The interests of the State became more clearly defined, and the types of educational institutions needed became more evident. To meet these recognized needs, there are now in the State, in addition to the grade and high schools, twelve institutions of higher education, seven of them State-supported and five privately supported. W. H. H. Beadle, Superintendent of Public Instruction from 1879 to 1885, was greatly interested in the common schools of the State, and in the problem of supplying teachers for them. As a result, during the next few years normal schools were established at Madison, Spearfish, Springfield, and Aberdeen.

The first institution of higher learning in South Dakota was established by the Congregational Church in 1881 at Yankton. It is known as Yankton College. The University of South Dakota was founded at Vermillion in the following year, 1882, through the aid of the people of the town and county. At present the university consists of seven colleges and schools of higher education and offers courses leading to the following degrees: Bachelor of Arts, of Science, of Science in Business Administration, of Law, of Fine Arts in Music, Dramatic Art, Painting, Public School Music, and Public School Art; Master of Arts, Master of Music; and Doctor of Philosophy. There is also a university high school.

Many members of the faculty are known as the authors of textbooks and other scholarly publications, or for their contributions to scientific research. The university has granted more than 3,000 degrees. Among its more distinguished graduates is an internationally recognized scientist, Ernest O. Lawrence, who has done outstanding research in the structure of atoms.

Since its founding in 1883, the State College of Agriculture and Mechanic Arts at Brookings had had a wide influence in the advancement of South Dakota, both through the activities of its graduates and through scientific service rendered. The work of this institution falls into five major divisions: agriculture, engineering, pharmacy, home economics, and general science.

It is only natural in an agricultural State such as South Dakota that major emphasis should be given to this subject in a State educational institution. The four-year college course provides instruction in agronomy, animal husbandry, dairy husbandry, horticulture, agricultural engineering, veterinary medicine, poultry raising, entomology-zoology, and farm economics. In addition, students are given broad training in English, mathematics, chemistry, biology, modern languages, history, and political science.

One of the greatest services State College performs for the farmers is the continuous research carried on through its experiment station farm at Brookings and the substations at Highmore, Cottonwood, Vivian, and Eureka. Here crops are tested for adaptability to soil and climate; feeding and breeding experiments are carried on for all classes of animals; fruit varieties are originated and tested; and destructive plant diseases and insects are studied to develop methods of control and eradication.

One of the potent forces in carrying to the people the information derived from these experiments is the agricultural extension service, with its corps of specialists, county agents, and home demonstration agents in the field.

The first of the teachers' colleges, Eastern State Normal School, was opened at Madison in 1883, and in the same year, Sioux Falls College was founded at Sioux Falls by the Baptist Church. In 1884 the Episcopal Church established, at Sioux Falls also, a special school for girls, known as All Saints' School. The following year, 1885, witnessed the founding of two more major educational institutions: Dakota Wesleyan University, a Methodist school, at Mitchell, and the Black Hills Teachers College at Spearfish.

The State School of Mines at Rapid City, established in 1887, is ideally situated among the Black Hills. The great variety of minerals, ores, and rock formations; the streams available for experiments in light, power, and irrigation; the nearby manufacturing plants; the forests, and the fossil-bearing Badlands—all these give to the School of Mines scientific and engineering advantages such as few other technical institutions possess.

Major attention is given to the study and teaching of chemistry, metallurgy, mineralogy, geology, mining, milling, engineering, mathematics, mechanics, and draftsmanship. The student enrollment at the School of Mines increased approximately 300 per cent from 1919 to 1931, reaching a maximum of 392 for the year 1930-1.

Lutheran Normal at Sioux Falls and Augustana College at Canton were founded in 1889, but have since been united as Augustana College at Sioux Falls. Southern Normal was established by the State at Springfield in 1895. In 1902, the Northern Normal and Industrial School, later changed to Northern State Teachers College, was started at Aberdeen and soon became one of the Northwest's largest teacher-training schools.

In 1898 the Presbyterian University, founded at Pierre in 1883, was moved to Huron and became known as Huron College.

Today there are some 4,487 rural schools with an enrollment of about 55,738 pupils, 82 consolidated high schools, and about 319 four-year accredited high schools. In addition to the classical and traditional high school courses, agriculture, manual training, home economics, and commercial courses are taught.

The most recent development in the high school curriculum is illustrated by the introduction into the Aberdeen High School of what is known as a "cooperative placement course," leading to a vocational diploma. This course is designed especially for those students who are not planning to go to college. Students are placed in the vocation of their choice, spending 20 hours a week in the shop or business establishment and learning through practical experience. Among trades offered to the students are those of printer, stenographer, baker, cook, woodworker, dressmaker, salesman, mechanic, radio worker, plumber, cleaner and presser, journalist, and electrician.

Among the educational institutions of more recent development are Wessington Springs Junior College established in 1923; and Freeman Junior College established in 1927.

Special schools to care for the afflicted and abnormal members of the State's citizen body include the State School and Home for the Feeble-Minded at Redfield, the School for the Blind at Gary, the School for the Deaf at Sioux Falls, and the South Dakota Training School at Plankinton.

RELIGION

Among the earliest explorers of the region which is now South Dakota were the Jesuit missionaries, who worked among the Indians, converting many to the Christian faith. Rev. Thomas S. Williams and Rev. Stephen R. Riggs, with their wives, were the first Protestant missionaries to make their homes among the Indians in this region. In 1840 Dr. Riggs made a journey to Fort Pierre and while there conducted a religious service, the first Protestant service conducted in what is now South Dakota.

Working together, Williams and Riggs translated the Bible, *The Pilgrim's Progress,* several hymn books, and other literature into the Eastern Sioux language. Dr. Riggs was the author of a valuable Dakota-English dictionary, giving the Sioux words and their English equivalents.

The work of the early Catholic missionaries was confined at first to the wandering bands of the Sioux, rather than in settled missions. The first mass in the State was held on the James River in Bennett County in 1842 by Father A. Ravoux. On the same trip he visited the French-Canadian trappers and their families at Fort Pierre. In 1848 Father De Smet made the first of many visits to the Dakota Sioux. He visited the Badlands of the White River on this trip and found a band of Sioux there. He returned in 1851 and many times thereafter until 1866. The first Catholic Church was erected at Jefferson in 1867.

The earliest Protestant religious movement in Dakota Territory (including what is now the States of North and South Dakota) was begun by Baptists in 1852, when they established a mission at Walhalla for the evangelization of the Indians. Its leaders were Elijah Terry and James Tanner.

In the southern half of Dakota Territory, the missionaries came with the pioneers to the earliest settlements, especially those at Yankton, Vermillion, Elk Point, and Bon Homme. They risked the dangers of frontier life in their desire to preach the gospel to those who, with them, were laying the foundation of a new State and endeavoring to shape its character and destiny.

In January 1860 Rev. Charles D. Martin, a missionary connected with the Presbyterian Church, reached Yankton and preached the first sermon to a congregation of white people in Dakota Territory. The congregation was large and enthusiastic. His text was, "Who so despiseth the Word shall be destroyed; but he that feareth the commandment shall be rewarded" (Proverbs 13:11). He preached from an upturned whiskey barrel, the only available substitute for a pulpit.

Rev. Martin seems to have been familiarly called "Father Martin," and to have come at that time from Dakota City, Neb., a distance of about 70 miles. In October 1860, he solemnized the first marriage recorded after Dakota Territory was opened for settlement, that of Miss Robinson to Mr. Jacob Deuel.

One incident of early days reveals the attitude of many of the rougher pioneers in what is now western South Dakota. It is related that an Easterner, visiting Fort Pierre, asked, "Does the stage to the Black Hills run on Sunday?" A man from Deadwood, who happened to be going on the same stage, replied, "Stranger, there ain't no Sunday west of the Missouri River and no God west of the Cheyenne. If a man dies west of the Missouri, they don't bury him; and if he dies west of the Cheyenne, the coyotes won't eat him."

Two other figures of importance in the religious development of South Dakota were Rev. J. W. Cook, an Episcopal minister, who located at Greenwood in 1870, and Jedediah Smith, a young minister of the Methodist Episcopal Church who is said to have been the first person to perform a public act of worship within the confines of the State of South Dakota.

The heterogeneous nature of the population of the State has resulted in the establishment and growth of numerous religious organizations. The Norwegians, Swedes, and Germans brought with them Lutheran doctrines and ideas and established their Lutheran churches; the Irish, French, and Germans established Catholic organizations. Other groups with varying religious doctrines organized themselves in like manner.

Today nearly all common religious faiths are represented in South Dakota. The 1936 census report shows the Lutherans to be the largest in membership, with a total of 165,836; the Catholics second, with 114,941; the Methodists third, with 78,767; the Congregationalists fourth, with 35,700; the Presbyterians fifth, with 32,000; the Baptists sixth, with 21,193; and the Episcopalians seventh, with 12,233. Besides these leading groups there are the Reformed churches with 11,539 members; the Christian church, with 7,301; the Evangelical, with 11,539; the Mennonites, with 4,289, and yet other smaller organizations. Generally three or four denominations are represented even in the smaller communities—most often the Catholic and Lutheran and, in addition, the Congregational, Presbyterian, or Baptist.

Most of these denominations have their young people's organizations and meetings. Summer institutes for young men and women are held annually by the Methodist, Congregationalist, Baptist, and Presbyterian groups. Most of the groups meet in the Black Hills in the latter part of June and the early part of July, in their various church camps.

TRANSPORTATION

SOUTH DAKOTA has the framework of an adequate transportation system. The northeast and southwest corners of the State are cut by transcontinental railroads Two lines traverse the State from east to west, and other lines run north and south through the eastern and Black Hills regions. Ten Federal highways cross South Dakota, five from north to south, and five from east to west. An air line serves the eastern section.

The State's first highway was the Missouri River, which flows south through the approximate center of the State and then curves out of it at the southeast corner. Up this broad highway, in the early days of the white man's settlement, came the explorer and the trader, the trapper and the priest. They came by canoe, by boat, by barge, and finally by steamer. When the first farms fringed the eastern border of the State, the covered wagon and the ox team brought the settlers in from Iowa and Minnesota, and the agricultural frontier was pushed slowly westward.

Gold was discovered in the Black Hills and immigration swept the State. Railroads that had just touched the eastern border sprang into life and leaped halfway across the State. The Chicago & North Western stopped on the river at Pierre, and the Chicago, Milwaukee, St. Paul & Pacific at Chamberlain. Farther than that they could not go, because beyond was Indian country. But gold lay 250 miles to the west. Long winding bull trains began to thread their way from Pierre westward, from Sidney and Cheyenne northward, from Bismarck southwestward to the Black Hills.

Oxen, however, were too slow for passengers, so the stagecoach was added to the crowded thoroughfare, and the still swifter pony express carried the mail. Boats, competing with the railroads, carried the heavy freight up the broad Missouri from Yankton and Sioux City, and unloaded at Chamberlain and Fort Pierre. Ten years later, the Chicago, Burlington & Quincy and the North Western came from the south into the Hills, and the bull trains vanished.

The first railroad to enter the State was the Winona & St. Peter, afterward part of the North Western system. In 1871 this railroad was built as far as Lake Kampeska, but for seven years it was operated only to Gary, just within the State lines. In 1872 the Dakota Southern, afterward acquired by the Milwaukee, built into the State from the south, through Elk Point to Vermillion. In 1878 the Worthington & Sioux Falls Line was built, connecting Sioux Falls with Sioux City. Thus prior to 1880 there were short stubs of railroad projecting into the State at three points.

The discovery of gold in the Hills brought in the Great Boom period, and with it the building of railroads. In the year 1880 both the Milwaukee and the North Western extended their lines to the Missouri. The same year the Milwaukee began to build its transcontinental line across the northern border counties of the State.

The eighties saw much railroad building. In 1884 the Minneapolis & St. Louis began building lines in South Dakota, eventually to reach half across the State; and in the same year the Chicago, Rock Island & Pacific entered Watertown from the southeast. In 1886 the North Western built north from its Nebraska lines to skirt the eastern and northern borders of the Black Hills, putting an end to the picturesque old trails, from Sidney, Neb., from Cheyenne, Wyo., from Bismarck, N. Dak., and from Fort Pierre. In 1887 the Great Northern built one of its two lines reaching into the State from the northeast, and the Illinois Central reached Sioux Falls. The following year the Burlington built across the extreme southwestern corner of the State, and three years later extended a branch line up through the center of the Hills to Deadwood. This compelled the North Western also to build up into the Hills from its terminus at Whitewood.

The depression of the early 1890's put an end to railroad building in the State for a time. It was not until 1902 that the Sault St. Marie built a short line into the Lake Region in the northeast. In 1906 the Rapid City, Black Hills & Western constructed a scenic line up Rapid Canyon for 35 miles. In 1907 the North Western and the Milwaukee extended their lines from the Missouri River to the Black Hills, and the railroad picture was practically complete.

The railroad history of the State is unique in many respects. The transcontinental lines do not traverse the central part of the State. Pierre, the capital city, is served by a line of the North Western ending in the Black Hills. The reason is twofold. The Indian reservation to the west blocked railroad building till the first decade of this century, and the Black Hills furnished a natural barrier, becoming a terminus in themselves.

There has been a marked rivalry between the North Western and the Milwaukee systems. Both built their roads to the Missouri River in the same year, and both completed their lines to the Hills at the same time; but the rivalry did not stop there. In the first five years of the present century, when the question of a permanent site for the capital was still being agitated, the North Western backed Pierre, and the Milwaukee backed Mitchell.

The Black Hills Region, with its wealth of scenic and historic features, is served by the North Western, the Burlington, and the Milwaukee. While, due to the difficulties of the terrain, the railroads do not approach the more impressive areas, they connect at convenient points with adequate bus services. One of the railroads, the Burlington, conducts its own motor tour of the Hills. The Badlands are skirted on the south by the Milwaukee. The Lake Region is touched by practically every line that enters the State.

In the early years of the present century the coming of the automobile brought the demand for good roads, and with the roads came cars of higher speeds, necessitating still better roads—a prairie trail, a dirt grade, a graveled highway, and now the beginnings of a hard-surfaced highway system.

The State highway department was not organized until 1918. Its first improved road project was between Watertown and the Codington county line to the east, a distance of 13.2 miles. Of the 6,000 miles in the State highway system today, only 326 are unimproved. Of the remainder, 550 miles are graded dirt roads, 4,216 are graveled, 645 are bituminous-surfaced, and 247 are concrete. In 1937, U. S. 16 was hardsurfaced almost across the State. The transition from gravel to hardsurfacing will be made on other routes as fast as funds will allow.

The first regular air service was established in South Dakota in 1928, from Rapid City through Pierre and Huron to Watertown. This service however was later discontinued and the only line operating in the State at present is the Hanford Air Lines between

Bismarck N. Dak., and Kansas City, Mo. This line enters the State opposite Sioux City, passes through Sioux Falls, Huron, and Aberdeen and leaves the State a little to the northwest of Aberdeen. Regular stops are made at landing fields in Aberdeen, Huron, Sioux Falls and Sioux City. Besides this route, the Hanford Air Lines has a shorter line connecting Sioux Falls with St. Paul and Minneapolis, which leaves the State just east of Sioux Falls.

Although the Missouri River has played an important part in the history of the State and formed its first great highway, there is no commercial traffic on its waters within the confines of the State today.

ARCHITECTURE

ALTHOUGH no type of architecture is peculiar to South Dakota, there are wide variations within the State, owing to the character of the country. Materials and styles differ in the farming, ranching and mountainous sections, each showing influences brought from surrounding regions, coupled with the utilization of the earth, timber, and stone at hand.

First the Arikara Indian went to the river banks to build his hut of sticks and mud, inside of which were living quarters for his several wives, children, and horses. Then came the Sioux Indian with his portable tent of buffalo hide, well-tanned and stretched on poles. When the first white settlers began pouring into the new country, they laboriously built log houses where trees were available; but as most of the State was treeless, the earth was made to serve as the building material. These pioneers who came to file claims on the virgin prairie found that by hitching their oxen to a plow, it was comparatively simple to loosen furrows which could be cut into blocks five or six inches thick, a foot wide and two or three feet long. The dirt was so interwoven with the strong roots of prairie grass that the chunks were solid enough to be carried easily and laid, brick-fashion, into place. Damp dirt was used to fill in crevices and around the windows, which were usually high and small. Roofs often were made of limbs, brush and hay with a covering of dirt; usually, however, cheap slab lumber covered the sod shanties. In the late 1870's and for a few years the land seekers were content to live in their drab, squat sod houses while they proved up their claims; those people became known as Soddies.

That was more than a half-century ago, but on the Indian reservations, particularly the Pine Ridge and Rosebud, sod houses are still being occupied by white families as well as Indians, and it will be some time before the complete transition to modern homes will be effected. Today there is a revival of interest in utilizing the prairie soil as building material. The use of rammed earth is being proved practical as well as economical through experiments at South Dakota State College, and its use in small towns and on the farms is gaining favor again. Dirt with a high content of sand is placed in molds and compressed, simple tire jacks often being used in the operation. Rammed earth walls afford excellent insulation, holding the heat in winter and keeping it out in summer; the mottled soil has a lovely natural color and the walls increase in strength with age. Such structures are conveniently used for chicken houses and livestock barns.

Along the rivers and in the Black Hills logs were the most available building material in the eighties when much of this frontier area was young. Rivers were banked with large cottonwood trees and the soft wood was hewn square, notched at the ends, and chinked with clay. The use of logs was not confined to home-building; in fact, the first schoolhouse in the State was made of logs in Bon Homme County in 1860, and many business establishments combined logs with "store" lumber to save money. When the Black Hills were suddenly populated during the gold rush of 1876, log buildings were put together as simply and quickly as possible. Ponderosa pine logs were peeled, notched a few inches from the end, laid up and chinked with either plaster or slabs; exceptions, however, where the logs were carefully hewn and notched so that the ends were flush at the corners, still stand while the others have fallen to disrepair. An old cabin in Custer which was built in 1874 shows the intricate system of notching logs, and the axe marks where the log was evened give indication of the tedious labor expended by the pioneers (*see illustration*). Stone fireplaces in those days were held together with mud instead of cement; an example of such a fire place, still in good condition, is in the cabin on the floor of Stratosphere Bowl (*see Tour 5, Section b*).

Log cabins are still popular in the Black Hills. There along creeks and under crags an almost endless number of cabins are built attractively of native pine logs. But the style has been adapted to a new taste and expression; from the rectangular, hand-hewn, one-story cabin, the home-builders have evolved bungalows and huge, rambling residences of stained, peeled logs, with stone foundations and trim.

The character of the wind-swept plains country, coupled with the background of homesteading groups, resulted in some peculiar designs in the eastern section of the State. Most of the pioneers, both in town and country, built square, four-room, frame houses, which invariably were painted white; then as the family and income grew, an addition was tacked on the house, or a second story built. Since then have come the second and third generations, adding a porch or sun parlor to meet their increased demands. Into the north-central section of the State, around Eureka (*see Tour 1*), came families to homestead from Eastern Europe. Economical and practical, these Germans who had previously emigrated to Russia constructed long, low, frame buildings combining the house, granary and barn. By dividing the building into three sections—the first for the family, second for the grain and third for the livestock—wall space and heat were conserved. Such houses still stand, but the families have grown and prospered and the customs have changed so that the original practice is no longer observed. One of the features of early residences in South Dakota was the cupola perched on top of many houses. Because of the frequent snowstorms that often reach blizzard proportions, combined with the lack of landmarks on the flat prairie, the cupola, like the Old North Church, was used to hang lanterns in so that members of the family, neighbors and strangers could find their way on stormy nights. The extreme weather has had its effect on architecture. Windows and doors facing north are avoided, especially in the open country where icy wintry blasts seem to penetrate even the sideboards. And protection in summer against the bright sun is acquired by means of wide porches and awnings.

Borrowing their designs from more easterly States, there was a strong predilection during the nineties for frills and fringes carved out of wood around windows and porches. This was the "scroll-saw" period and townsmen and farmers alike had curlicues dropping from the eaves and around porch pillars. Houses long deserted in ghost towns of the State may have sideboards flapping in the wind, but the slightly askew wooden lacework still reflects that gay period.

The use of native materials in public buildings is prevalent; in fact, the State owns and operates a cement plant (*see Tour 4*), there are several quarries of granite and sandstone, and the Black Hills yield quantities of lumber. A new trend is shown in the Black Hills where Federal agencies are constructing buildings from rock taken, virtually, from their own back yards. Such is the modern-styled Sylvan Lake Hotel high on a granite cliff overlooking the lake and facing towering Harney Peak. Begun in 1936 by the State, it is an inhabitable continuation of the gray, moss-covered rock cliff, looking as natural in its surroundings as if it had grown there (*see Tour 14*). Limestone was hauled across the road to build the new Black Hills Airport near Spearfish (*see Tour 4, Section b*), and the rough-edged, yellow stone buildings make an attractive landmark. In Custer State Park, uncut boulders with moss intact have been rolled up to form a rambling museum, and in several Black Hills cities native stone is being utilized for public buildings. While the trend in the Black Hills is to make public buildings blend with the natural scene, cities in other sections of the State have coupled economy with local pride and rolled boulders, residue of the glacial period, off nearby hills, and cut and chipped them to make business and monumental buildings. In Pierre, for instance, the county courthouse, a new, attractive structure, was built of colorful reddish-gray flecked rocks from the hillsides, costing only the trouble of moving; sandstone from Hot Springs is used for trim. More of this easily cut sandstone is found in the State Soldiers' and Sailors' Memorial Hall where it is used exclusively for exterior and interior, its soft texture allowing effective carvings.

The plan for the State Capitol was taken from that of the National Capitol, and the stone imported from Indiana. Most of the county courthouses, built in the early 1900's, have copper domes long weathered black; the wings of the buildings which were patterned after the State Capitol were of such abbreviated proportions that the desired effect was lost; examples of this type are at Webster (*see Tour 3*), Brookings (*see Tour 4*), and Onida (*see Tour 12*). The newer courthouses, however, are modern in design, usually with an addition on the roof, looking like a penthouse but used as a jail; of the newer type, courthouses at Ipswich (*see Tour 2*), Redfield (*see Tour 3*), Pierre (*see Tour 4*), Mitchell (*see Tour 5*) and Rapid City (*see Tour 5*) are examples.

The trend toward combining local materials with a rambling design where building space is plentiful was followed in the new Governor's Mansion at Pierre. The building has two large wings, one at the front and one at the rear so that it forms a modified letter-Z. Native lumber, brick, and cement were used exclusively, and the fireplaces were made of petrified wood from the Badlands.

In Sioux Falls, the State's largest city, many of the buildings are of a durable pink rock, quarried barely outside the city limits. The county courthouse, with its church-like spire, and a new million-dollar high school, two stories high and covering a block are examples of the use of native stone. There are no skyscrapers in South Dakota; the highest building is the 11-story Alex Johnson Hotel in Rapid City. With so much space available, buildings of more than four stories are few in all the cities of the State.

In the large towns and cities the style of the architecture is lost in a maze of variations. A Dutch Colonial house is neighbor to a California bungalow; public buildings are patterned after those in older States. The college campuses have buildings of many styles and materials.

Small prairie towns almost invariably present the picture of a high, black-bowled water tower, three or four tall, red grain elevators lined up along the railroad, a few one-story brick buildings on Main Street, false-front and unpainted stores on the side streets, spired churches—one brick and others wood—a large imposing brick schoolhouse, located proudly on the highest rise of ground, and four out of five houses painted white with open porches in front and coal sheds at the rear. The false-front, frame store buildings, many of which have second-story porches protruding over board sidewalks, are still found in most towns of western South Dakota. The so called false-front buildings are those with fronts extended squarely upward beyond the ridge of the roof, giving the effect of an extra story. (*See illustration.*)

White farmhouses and large red barns which splotch the South Dakota plains are as characteristic of the entire Middle West. It is an established axiom that architectural priority is given the barn in preference to the house. Out in this farming country, the hip-roof barns are huge, and the chicken coops, hog barn, granary, garage and outhouses are grouped together to break the wind in winter. Unlike surrounding grain belt States, there are few silos; but windmills dot the prairie.

Unlike the farm buildings which are almost always built on the highest rise of ground available, the ranches in the western part of the State are located in draws, and out of the wind. The cattle ranches are distinguished from farms by the usually unpainted, rambling house, low barn, bunkhouse and corrals. Every first-rate ranch has at least two corrals; one is round, the other square, each made of poles and posts. The round corral has a stout snubbing post in the center of it, and is used in roping and branding horses and cattle; the square corral is for confinement purposes and serves also as an adjunct to the round corral. Few buildings are needed for a ranch, as only saddle horses and a few work horses and cows are kept in the barn, and the feed is piled in stacks out of doors. A sheep ranch differs from a cattle ranch with regard to the style of barns and corrals. A sheep shed is about 100 by 30 feet, has a high board fence which extends south from the west side, and a wire fence completes the rectangular corral with the shed and board fence furnishing shelter against the northwest winds. Many of the old cattle and sheep ranch houses are made of logs; they are apt to follow a certain type—long and low. The building, of heavy cottonwood, cedar or pine logs hauled from a distance, is the width of one room with the length governed only by the number of rooms required. To save on materials the eaves begin little higher than a man's head, the roof slopes only slightly, and the windows are set low. In a long house of several connecting rooms, there are usually two outside doors, both on the south side. The main door leads into an entry which connects with the large kitchen, the most important and most-used room on the ranch. As a ranch prospers, a new frame house is built and the old log house is relegated to storehouse purposes, or becomes the bunkhouse. The new home is usually square and painted the ubiquitous white with green trimmings.

Attempts are being made to evolve a type of architecture to fit the prairie sites of this plains region. The U. S. Indian Service, in constructing hospitals at Sisseton, Wagner and Rapid City, designed rambling, one-story stucco buildings with large windows and roof gardens. The Rural Rehabilitation Corporation in planning houses for farming communities featured five-room cottages made of pine boards, 10 inches wide, running up and down, rows of windows to the south and east, and a storage tank for water in the attic to provide plumbing facilities. Simplicity rules in the design of new buildings and the material used is that at hand.

Except for the engineering feat of blasting and drilling out the features of four Presidents on Mount Rushmore (*see Tour 5B*), the erection of impressive monuments must await sufficient time and funds in South Dakota. Large boulders, with bronze tablets, mark most of the historic landmarks, awaiting the time when suitable monuments, replicas and restorations can be made.

FOLKLORE AND FOLKWAYS

Origin of Folkways: When large groups of people migrate from one country to another, they tend to take with them and perpetuate in the new country the language, customs, and traditions of the old. They retain their group identity and are slow to assimilate with their new fellow countrymen. An example of this is the twice-transplanted German-Russians. Originally German they migrated to Russia where they remained for several generations. From there many of them migrated once more to the plains of North and South Dakota and settled in large groups. But in spite of their double migration, they still retain their racial purity, a partial use of their language, and many of their old world characteristics and customs. Conversely, when people migrate as individuals and scatter out in the new country, they tend to assimilate quickly. They forget their childhood language and lose their racial identity. In South Dakota the principal groups retaining their folkways are the Finns, the Scandinavians, and the Russian-Germans. It goes without saying that the largest body of people within the State having their own peculiar customs and ways of living are the Indians, but they are dealt with in a separate article in the present volume.

The Finns have the reputation of being somewhat clannish, and State statistics of racial strains show that they tend to settle in large colonies, more so than any of the other racial elements. They show a persistent attachment to their native tongue, which is unlike any other North European language and very difficult to understand or acquire. With them Finnish is the universal language of the home. While the children learn English in school and speak it without accent, at home they use the language of their elders. Finns are likely to take the same side on questions of public policy, and to vote as a unit.

One trait of the Finns is their exceeding fondness for coffee. In a Finnish household the coffee pot is literally never off the stove. When a guest enters a Finnish home, he is immediately offered a cup of coffee; and even in the absence of guests, the family is likely to drink coffee at least once between each two meals. The Finns also use skis to a greater extent than the Scandinavians and their skis are somewhat different in shape and appearance.

Probably the most characteristic custom existing among the Finns today is their system of bathhouses—"Finlander hells," as they are popularly known. These bathhouses are detached buildings of sod, stone, or any other convenient material, built as nearly airtight as possible. There will not be a bathhouse for every house but perhaps two or three to a community. On a set day a fire is built in the bathhouse under a flat rock or rocks, and when the rocks have been thoroughly heated, the fire is raked outside the building and as many as wish to bathe, or as many as the hut will hold, enter with pails of water and close the door tight. Water is then poured on the heated rocks, and immediately the place is filled with steam. The amount of steam can be accurately regulated by the amount of water thrown on the rocks. The Finns, through practice, can endure a great amount of the hot vapor, but others would be well-advised to proceed with caution. Since rocks hold heat for some time, those who have bathed give their places to others until all have had their turn. Sometimes the baths are prepared for men and sometimes for the women and girls, since the whole community follows this custom. The Finns are very hospitable in inviting those not of their race to avail themselves of these baths and, although in principle a Turkish bath, it is an experience not often to be met with in such a setting.

The Scandinavians, while not so clannish as the Finns, have a strong feeling of racial solidarity. This is more true of the Swedes and Danes than of the Norwegians. The racial tables show that the Danes, more than the other two, tend to settle in large colonies. The Swedes and Norwegians are scattered generally throughout the State. But all these races have certain characteristics in common, among them a fondness for coffee. It is a Scandinavian custom to have a lunch in the middle of the forenoon and again in the middle of the afternoon, consisting of coffee and cookies or cake. The men come to the house, if they are working nearby; but if at a distance the women take the lunch out to them in the field.

On Easter Sunday the men stage a contest to see who can eat

the greatest number of eggs. The Norwegians celebrate their independence day on the 17th of May with games, sports, and community picnics.

Another Scandinavian characteristic is their fondness for the cooking of the homeland. In Beaver Valley near Sioux Falls and in many other Swedish communities there is still to be found the *smorgasbord,* an array of "appetizers" of all sorts, often forming the evening meal. The Scandinavian fondness for fish is proverbial, and of the many varieties *ludefisk* or *lutefisk,* cod cured in lye, seems to be the favorite. The *ludefisk* season extends roughly from the first day of November until after the Christmas holidays. At Storla, south of Woonsocket, there is a huge annual *ludefisk* dinner, to which people come from all that part of the State. In addition, almost every Scandinavian church in the eastern part of the State has its annual *ludefisk* feast.

Perhaps the most strongly-marked community in the State is the Mennonite colony at Rockford. It is a religious group, held together by ties of both faith and race, since it is a segment of the Russian-German immigration. The Mennonites have certain customs which tend to set them apart from their neighbors. The men never shave after they marry. Previous to that they live in large dormitories with others of their kind. Both men and women wear a dress sober in the extreme, eschewing the use of bright colors and jewelry. The sect does not believe in the use of liquor or tobacco in any form, nor in shows, dances or other light amusements. All property is held in common, and anyone voluntarily withdrawing from or marrying outside of the sect loses all his financial interest in the community. For the rest, these people are frugal, industrious, peaceable (their strong pacifist belief has been the principal cause of their world-wide wanderings), and inclined to settle their difficulties among themselves. They are good neighbors and welcome visitors to their community, but have a strong aversion to having their pictures taken. They prefer to have their own schools, since their children's difference in dress from the other pupils sometimes subjects them to petty annoyance.

In the northern section of Aberdeen is a large community of so-called Russian-Germans. Although they are to a very large extent Americanized, their houses, painted in many brilliant hues, still show an old world influence, as does the use of their native language in the home and of head kerchiefs by the older women.

Folklore: In a State not yet fifty years old and with a population drawn from a dozen States and as many foreign countries, it is obvious that there cannot be any one body of folklore common to the various groups. As men gather around the campfire or before the bar, the grizzled prospector dreams of hidden gold and future wealth; the leathery-faced rancher harks back to the days of the sheep and cattle wars; and the lumberjack recalls the tales of Paul Bunyan that he heard in the Minnesota and Michigan woods. The largest and most authentic body of folklore in the State is of course the great storehouse of Indian legends, accounting for the phenomena of Nature, the path of life which the Indian treads, and even the origin of the Indian himself. But first listen to the lumberjack as he tells of the origin of the Black Hills, according to the best traditions of Paul Bunyan mythology, in the story of *The Mountain That Stood On Its Head.**

According to this tale, Paul Bunyan, the mightiest of all logging bosses, came to the Dakotas to log off the strangest of all forests, on the Mountain That Stood On Its Head. Paul had just obtained the help of Hels Helsen,. the Big Swede, whom Paul christened Bull of the Woods and appointed him his foreman. As long as the logging operations were confined to the ground beneath the mountain, the industrious but unimaginative Hels managed the work successfully, leaving Paul Bunyan free to do the book work he detested but which had to be done by someone.

Now the Mountain That Stood On Its Head rested on its peak instead of its base and its slopes flared outward from the bottom, shadowing the ground beneath; and on its slopes the trees grew head-downward with their tops pointing to the earth. The rim, or base, of the mountain was two miles above the plain and on top of this base was another plain, covered with the finest standing timber and one hundred and twenty-seven miles in circumference. There were High Springs in the center forming Lofty River, which tumbled from the rim two miles to the plain beneath in a mighty cataract called Niagara, a name which was later given to a little waterfall along the Canadian border.

Now when the trees beneath the five-mile slope of the inverted mountain had all been logged off, the Big Swede began to have trouble with his loggers. He insisted that they should go on logging the inverted slope just as they would an ordinary one—in

(*Paul Bunyan, by James Stevens, 1925.)

other words that they should stand on their heads, supported by wire cables that ran from tree to tree. But while doing this all the dirt and sawdust fell into their mouths and eyes instead of to the ground and the blood ran to their heads and altogether the conditions were so unusual that they returned exhausted from each day's labors. So each day found the work going more slowly until finally there was only one tree cut per man for each seventy-two hours of work. But while the unimaginative Swede was being bested, Paul Bunyan was working out his own solution of the problem.

One morning when Bunyan awoke he found that none of the loggers was starting for the woods. He inquired the reason of the Big Swede and that taciturn individual made a speech of unaccustomed length:

"Sye forgot tal you, Bunyan, but aye goin' move dar camp. No use to try har no moore noo aye tank. Logger can' stan' on head mooch lonker har. Aye don' tank so, Bunyan. We move new yob noo."

Paul Bunyan was enraged both at the Big Swede's assumption of authority and his familiar form of address. Raising his voice in a shout that tumbled the loggers from their bunks, he ordered them to follow him to the Mountain That Stood On Its Head. On his shoulder was a double-barrelled shotgun that he had fabricated for the job, the barrels of which he used later as smokestacks for his first sawmill. In his belt were cartridges loaded with vast amounts of powder and with sheets of steel two feet square. Arrived at the base of the mountain, actually its peak, he took aim along its inverted slopes and pulled both triggers. A thousand pine trees were sheared off and dropped straight to the ground, their tops sticking in the earth and their bare trunks waving helplessly in the air. All day the mighty Paul cleared the slopes of trees and at evening a new forest stood beneath the inverted cone, promising easy work for the loggers on the following morning.

But next day Paul saw the Big Swede going alone to the inverted mountain. With Paul Bunyan in hot pursuit the Bull of the Woods clambered up the shelving slope, crawled over the rim and began tearing up the standing pine with his bare hands. Enraged at this independent logging system, Paul took a flying leap at the rim but missed his hold and took considerable of the edge with him in his fall. A second leap and he gained the upper plain and lay there resting before what he knew would be the battle of his career. The Big Swede came toward him.

All day that epic battle raged. The sound of the blows struck could not be told from thunder and the stamping of the giants made the earth tremble till the frightened loggers crawled into their bunks and stayed there. Whenever the contestants neared the edge, great masses of earth would crumble off and fall to the plain below. Whole acres of standing pine were flattened as one or the other of the fighters felled his opponent with a mighty blow. All that day and all that night the battle raged and finally at sunrise the next morning there came a shock that overturned every bunkhouse. Shortly afterward Paul Bunyan appeared, carrying on his shoulder the vanquished Bull of the Woods.

"You're going to be a good foreman now, Hels Helsen!"
"Aye tank so, Mr. Bunyan."
"You *know* so, Hels Helsen."
"Yah, Mr. Bunyan."

But the Mountain That Stood On Its Head was no more. That titanic struggle had demolished it and spread it out over the plain. Only a few heaps of blood-darkened dust remained, a series of mounds that are called the Black Hills today.

Gold: What magic there is in that four-letter word! How many men has it sent into the frozen Arctic and the burning African wastes. Men in all ages have lived for it, fought for it, died for it. Perhaps as much or even more sudden wealth has come from oil, but there is not the same glamour about it that clings to gold. It was gold that filled the Black Hills with tens of thousands of people drawn from all parts of the country and that gave to the State an impetus which still is felt. And now that the various "strikes" have been made, the placer deposits worked out, and gold mining has passed from the individual to the industrial phase there linger tales of the early days—of mysterious mines that no one but the owner ever saw, of gold dust cached in large quantities, to remain forever lost because of the sudden death of the man who took it from the earth, of gold taken in hold-ups of treasure caches, hastily concealed and never reclaimed. All these tales are a "second crop" in any gold country. They represent the hopes of those who know that gold in its virgin state is no longer to be had. But where buried treasure exists, anyone may hope to find it, even a child; hence the appeal is universal. Many of these legends are current in the Black Hills, and there is a tale of buried gold along the banks of the Missouri at Pierre, and some in the Lake Region of the northeast.

Sioux Legends: One of the important contributions of the Sioux Indian is a body of legends that have furnished inspiration to many of our American poets besides Longfellow. The following legend of *The Red-Eyed Quail* might find its counterpart in the Bre'r Rabbit stories of Uncle Remus.

Once upon a time a lone traveler was making his way across the plains. He had traveled many days and was becoming tired and hungry. Suddenly he saw in the distance a beautiful lake. He made up his mind that this would be a nice place to rest and procure some food. As he approached the lake he saw a large group of ducks, geese, prairie chickens and quail feeding and resting at the edge of the water. The sight of the birds increased his hunger, but he had to determine just how he could approach them without scaring them away. So he sat down and thought for some time. Finally he spread out his blanket and filled it with sticks until he had a large bundle. Throwing it on his back, he went on his way hoping that his plan would work. Suddenly the birds saw him and asked where he might be going and what he was carrying in the bundle. He told them that it contained songs that he was taking to his people. The birds all became interested and asked him to stop and sing them some of his songs, so that they might dance. He told them that he would have to put up a tent and that they would all have to go inside with him and dance as he sang. They all agreed.

So he used his blanket and put up a tent and they all went inside. Then he told them that they must close their eyes and dance in a circle around him and the first one that opened them would have red eyes. The birds agreed to this and the dance began. The traveler sang as loud as he could and as a large goose came within his reach, he seized it, twisted its neck ,and pushed it under him and waited for another to come near. As he repeated his trick, a quail opened its eyes and seeing what was going on, shouted to the rest to flee. And this is said to be the reason why quails have red eyes.

Hexism: There is a difference between the harmless little super-stitions which we all pretend to accept and a belief in witchcraft and magic that may influence the deluded person to commit acts of folly and even violence. Most persons think that a belief in witchcraft has not existed in this country since early New England days, but the superstition still persists. In some parts of the State today there is a belief in hexes or hexism as the following stories from the vicinity of Sioux Falls illustrate.

About thirty years ago a man and his son were returning home one night with a team and wagon after doing their trading in a nearby town. All of a sudden, for no apparent reason, the team stopped. It was a dark night, but suddenly there was a shower of falling stars. Looking about him as best he could, the man decided that this was the place where the evil spirits had often manifested their power. He knew that this power must be concentrated in some particular object and he got out to see what it was. He found it. One of the wheels, instead of the regulation twelve spokes, had a thirteenth, made of bone and gleaming white. With a heavy ax that he had in the wagon he smashed the bone spoke and immediately the team was released from the spell and the wagon moved. The next day it was found that a certain woman, suspected of being a witch, had suffered a broken leg and refused to say how she received it.

Another story concerns a man who had been ill for some time, under the care of a nurse. Finally his wife suspected that he was being bewitched. She investigated and found that the feathers in his pillow were bunched in such a manner as to assume the forms of birds, rats, and other small animals. She took the pillows and all the rest of the bedding out into the yard and burned them. The man immediately recovered, but the nurse, presumably a witch, suffered burns.

There are certain beliefs, principally theories about weather, that are prevalent in the range sections of the State. One of the commonest is that if the horses and cattle grow long winter hair early in the fall, it is a sign that there will be a hard winter. An early flight of migratory birds is said to have a similar meaning. An early flight north in the spring is taken to be a sign of an early spring. Sundogs are said to be a sign of approaching cold weather. A bright aurora borealis, one reaching high towards the zenith, is said to be a sign of approaching storm. One of the commonest beliefs is that ninety days after a fog there will be a rain. When horses run and play or when small birds swoop in flocks without apparent reason, it is said a storm is approaching.

Language of the West: Every trade and profession has its own nomenclature but the language of the West is distinctive in many ways. Farm, cattle ranch, sheep ranch, and mining camp each speaks its own vernacular. The following are some of the terms employed in these various fields of work.

On the Farm.

BANG-BOARD: a wide board rising above the side of the wagon, against which the ears of corn are thrown as they are tossed into the wagon.

BREAKING: to turn virgin prairie.

BUNDLE PITCHER: one who pitches bundles from the field into the rack and from the rack into the separator.

FANNING MILL: a contrivance for blowing the dust and chaff out of seed grain.

HOUNDS: the braces that hold the wagon tongue steady.

LISTING: plowing a field with trench-like furrows to conserve moisture.

NIGGER WOOL: a grass with tough fibrous roots that resist decay.

ROUGHAGE: forage crops.

SNAPPING: picking corn without removing the husks.

SUMMER FALLOW: to let a field lie idle for one year to absorb moisture.

WAGON HAMMER: an iron pin that holds the evener to the tongue.

With the Prospectors.

CLEAN-UPS: final separation of gold from dirt.

DISCOVERY: the place of finding the vein, or "pay."

GRUB STAKE: to provide the prospector with food in return for a half interest in what he discovers.

A LOCATON: a mining claim.

LODE: a lead or vein of ore.

PLACER (Pronounced plasser) MINING: the washing of gold from sand deposits, either through hand panning or the use of hydraulic machinery.

SOURDOUGH: refers to the prospector himself, from his weakness for sourdough biscuits.

STRIKE: hitting pay dirt.

In the Cow Country.

BRUSH UP: used of cattle, to hide out in the brush.

BUNCH-QUITTER: an animal that voluntarily quits the herd.

CAYUSE: an Indian pony.

CLOSE SEAT: steady and firm seat in the saddle.

DALLY: to wind the rope around the saddle horn.

DOGIE (pronounced with long "o") : a young steer two or three years old; formerly used of cattle shipped in from the South.

FALL-BACK. a horse which deliberately falls backward with his rider.

FENCE-CRAWLER: a breachy animal that cannot be held in a fence.

FREE MARTIN: female of mixed twins, unlikely to calve.

HAYBURNER: a horse of little value.

KYACK: saddle.

LONG YEARLING: an animal, a horse or cow, several months older than a year and not yet two.

NIGHT HAWK: the man who watches the horse herd at night.

OUTLAW: a horse that cannot be broken.

PELTER: an old horse.

PILOT OR POINTER: rider preceding the herd to show the way.

PITCHING: same as bucking.

POINT RIDERS: horsemen on each side of the herd near the front to point the herd in the right direction.

POKE: a wooden collar to restrain the fence-crawler.

SEEING DAYLIGHT: the rider leaving his seat so that daylight appears between him and the saddle.

SLICK-EAR: an animal that has not had its ears notched or split.

SPRINGER: a cow heavy with calf.

SUNFISHER: a bucking horse which twists in the air, first to one side and then to the other.

SWAPPING ENDS: a horse making a half-circle in the air.

SWING KICKERS: horseman on each side, back of the point men, to swing the main body of the herd.

TO TAIL UP: to raise weak cattle by the tail.

TRAIL HERD: cattle cut out and ready to be driven to the railroad.

WHITE FACE: a Hereford.

In Sheep Country.

BEDGROUND: the spot back of the wagon where the sheep bed every night.

BLACK-FACES: any one of several shire breeds.

TO BOG DOWN: used of a band of sheep that bunch up and refuse to move.

BRAND: in the case of sheep, a mark stamped with paint on the wool.

BUM: a lamb raised by hand.

TO BUM A LAMB: to take it away from its mother and raise it by hand.

CAMP TENDER: the man who keeps the herder in supplies and moves the wagon; or, an old ewe who picks up scraps around the wagon.

CUT-BACK: a lamb or ewe that is rejected on account of size or condition.

TO DOCK: to earmark, amputate tail and castrate lambs.

A DRAG: an individual sheep too weak to keep up with the bunch.

THE DRAG: the rear end of a moving band of sheep.

DROP BUNCH: the ewes which have not lambed yet.

DRY BUNCH: the ewes which will not lamb in a given year.

EARMARK: to notch or split the ears to indicate age.

TO FLAG A BUNCH: to place scarecrows about it to scare away coyotes.

LAMBER: one of a crew assisting at lambing time.

LAMB-LICKER: derisive term for lamber.

THE LEAD: the fore end of a moving band of sheep.

MARKER: usually a black sheep, but may be any unusual one used in checking up on possible lost sheep.

PEEWEE: a late or stunted lamb.

SHEEP HOOK: a long pole with a steel hook to catch a sheep by the leg.

SKINNY: an old ewe.

STONE JOHNNY: a monument of piled rocks, usually erected by a sheepherder.

WETHER: castrated male sheep.

WOOL-BLIND: a sheep with wool grown over its eyes, shutting out its sight.

WOOL TRAMPER: one who tramps fleeces into wool sacks.

WRANGLER: one who moves small bunches of ewes and lambs; or, one who fills and empties pens for shearers.

General Terms.

BREAKS: rough or broken country along the present or former course of a stream; caused by erosion of softer soil.

BUTTE: abrupt hill rising from comparatively level country.

CHINOOK: warm wind in winter from the southwest, causing snow to vanish very quickly.

CUT-BANK: a perpendicular bank of earth, originally cut by running water, but may be any distance from existing stream bed.

COULEE: a canyon with steep sides.

DRAW: any swale or depression down which water drains or "draws"

GALLOPING GOOSE: a gas propelled, combined express and passenger railroad car, distinguished by striped front.

GUMBO: extremely sticky black clay, known geologically as Pierre clay.

HARDPAN: extremely hard clay, impervious to water and almost impossible to till.

HONYOCK: slang term for homesteader.

MUD BUTTE: a butte of pure clay and gumbo, devoid of vegetation and rising abruptly from the plain.

PROVE UP: to submit proof to the Government that the law governing homesteading has been complied with.

SQUAW SIDE OF A HORSE: right side, due to squaw's preference for mounting from that side.

RECREATION

POSSESSING a wide and diversified range of recreational opportunities, South Dakota with its many lakes and rivers, its forests, mountains and plains, affords all-year amusement for the average sportsman.

Noted for its pheasant hunting (two million birds have been shot in a single season), the State also offers excellent pass shooting for waterfowl and mountain big-game hunting. There is every kind of fresh-water fishing—trout in mountain creeks, pike, bass, and other game fish in the lakes, and catfish in the Missouri and tributary rivers.

HUNTING

Big Game. Every fall deer and elk hunting draw hundreds of sportsmen to the Black Hills. It is not uncommon, during open season, to see an automobile rolling slowly through town, the carcass of a deer lashed to the running board, while townsmen gaze with envy at the coveted prize.

Because each year outlaw bull elk and numerous cows escape from Custer State Park and make damaging forays into neighboring ranches, the game department deems it wise to allow an open season, rather than simply slaughtering the meat for sale.

Pheasants. Climatic conditions, natural haunts, and good feeding grounds have brought South Dakota pheasants, Chinese ring-necks, a reputation of superiority. Every fall sportsmen invade the hunting grounds, often bagging a million birds in a single season. Hunters come from distant States, often as far away as Texas, to indulge in a week or two of shooting. Pheasants are plentiful in most counties east of the Missouri River, increasing in numbers toward the eastern border.

Grouse. These once plentiful birds almost disappeared some years ago, but closed seasons and other methods of protection have restored their numbers to a large extent. Unlike the pheasant, grouse are most abundant in the counties west of the Missouri River. Open seasons are generally set in late September. Ruffed grouse, or "fool hens," are confined mostly to the Black Hills. Their lack of fear of human beings makes them rather easy to kill.

Ducks and Geese. With many natural haunts—lakes, marshes, favorable shelter where food is abundant—northeastern South Dakota is a favorite halting place for hordes of ducks that remain to propagate their families in sheltered spots, and for transient birds that stop to feed on wild rice, wild celery, or duck potato before continuing their long flight southward.

Numerous duck passes—the most noted of which is Hedtke Pass near Webster—between long chains of lakes provide hidden vantage points for hunters, who lie in wait for the fast-moving waterfowl on their way from one body of water to another. Boats and blinds are both popular with duck hunters. Many cottages and lodges are situated near the lakes, where every fall sportsmen spend several weeks hunting and fishing.

Among the better known habitats for ducks in the Lake Region are Rush Lake and Kettle Lakes and the chain known as Waubay Lakes.

Because the goose likes both water and food within easy reach along its route on the long flight southward, the Missouri River range section, that extends across the State from north to south, is a favorable hunting strip for sportsmen waiting to ambush the waterfowl that "honk high of night."

Snakes and Prairie Dogs. Despite the fact that residents of distant States often consider South Dakota a land alive with rattlesnakes, this species is fast disappearing and casualties from the State's only venomous snake are negligible.

It is an unwritten law that persons living in infested areas should spare no effort in killing a rattler, whenever one is found. Rattlers are found mostly in the western half of the State and along the slopes of the Missouri River.

Sitting on its haunches, its active little tail jerking with each saucy yip it directs at any person who passes through its village, and at the same time warning its neighbors, the prairie dog, another inhabitant of the drier section, is able to defy the hunter who considers himself skillful with a rifle. Few marksmen have been able to capture or kill any number of these prolific little pests, for almost ·invariably they dart down into their burrows before the huntsman is within shooting range.

FISHING

Mountain Trout. In the Black Hills three varieties of trout—rainbow, Loch Leven and brook—in numerous well stocked streams furnish opportunities for the angler to match his skill against the elusive fish that frequent the cold mountain waters. While there are other kinds of fish in the Black Hills region trout is the principal variety; it is found in every creek of appreciable size.

Lake Fish. In the northeastern part of the State, where ducks abound in the fall, Nature has provided one of her most picturesque playgrounds, the Lake Region. Bordering the northeastern line of South Dakota are the twin lakes of Traverse and Big Stone. Big Stone Lake's setting is one of the most beautiful in the entire State. Black bass, as well as wall-eyed pike, northern pike, crappies, and other pan-fish are plentiful here.

Watertown is the center of an extensive Lake region, the chief of the group being Lake Kampeska, long noted as a summer resort and amusement center. Other important fishing and pleasure centers include Lake Andes, Lake Preston, Buffalo and Four-Mile Lakes, and Blue Dog Lake. Probably the most popular fishing resorts in the State are at Pickerel Lake and Enemy Swim, both north of Waubay. All of these and many others have ample fishing facilities, and at most of them cabins may be rented.

River Fish. Of all river fish, the catfish is the most sought after as a delicacy. Every year the Missouri River and its tributaries give up thousands of pounds of this delicious fish. The catfish of the tributaries, however, are of smaller size than those found in the "Big Muddy." Among other varieties commonly found are crappies, bullheads, sunfish, and wall-eyed pike. (for hunting and fishing regulations, see *GENERAL INFORMATION.*)

SUMMER SPORTS AND ATTRACTIONS

Rodeos. The tide of homesteaders that sounded the death knell of the open range glory of the large cattle outfits 25 years ago also put an end to a unique pioneer figure—the cowboy. Suddenly swept from the free prairie life he had been used to, the cowboy, except in scattered sections, was forced to accept what little remained of his once colorful existence.

As an outgrowth of demands for a reenactment of spectacles and scenes from a day that is past, fragments of the old West have been salvaged through annual rodeos (pronounced "ro'-dee-os" in South Dakota) in which young men and women who have learned their skill from a past generation compete. The Black Hills Round-up held annually in July at Belle Fourche is well worth seeing.

Numerous rodeos are staged during the summer, many of these being incorporated in annual celebrations in connection with county fairs. The majority of them take place in the section west of the Missouri River where traces of ranching days still are in evidence.

Hiking and Riding Trails. Camps and outdoor clubs have been established in response to the demand of multitudes of pleasure seekers who throng the Black Hills each summer. The camps are situated in spots where there are trout streams, lakes and bridle paths. Harney Peak, accessible alike to the hiker and horseman, should not be missed because of the panoramic view of the entire Black Hills area to be had from the mountain's granite peak.

Swimming. The Lake Region offers the foremost attraction but hardly a section of the State is without swimming facilities of some description since many towns have built artificial lakes or swimming pools with the aid of Federal funds.

Golf and Tennis. Drawing as many as 200 players from all parts of the State, the South Dakota Amateur Tournament, held during the latter part of June, is the major golf event each year. The South Dakota Open Tournament, which anyone may enter, is held at the same time.

On Labor Day Aberdeen holds the Dakota open meet in which players from North and South Dakota and Minnesota may compete. This popular event draws an average of 100 entrants and comes as a climax at the end of the season.

Golfing fever is not confined to the larger cities. Most small towns have courses, and even in the Black Hills, where hazards are numerous, golfing is popular.

Tennis is the only minor sport that has gained much recognition on college and high school campuses. It has been played to some extent since the State was admitted into the Union in 1889. The year's chief event is the open State championship tournament held in Sioux Falls the third week in July.

Horseshoe Pitching and Corn Husking. These two farm sports are popular in South Dakota. Attracting thousands of people, a State corn husking contest and occasional national contests are held in the eastern part of the State each year. Horseshoe pitching courts are found on nearly every farm and contests are held at county fairs and celebrations.

Other Sports. There is only one professional baseball organization, the Nebraska League, in South Dakota. Teams in the South Dakota Association of Amateur Baseball Leagues play Sunday baseball, the winners of each circuit meeting annually in a State tournament early in September.

Football, basketball, and track athletics comprise part of the extra-curricular activities on most collgee and high school campuses. The State College and University, traditional rivals in all sports, are members of the North Central Conference. Other colleges and universities are members of a State conference.

WINTER SPORTS AND ATTRACTIONS

Ice-Skating and Ice-Boating. With the growing popularity of hockey in the State, more attention is being given to skating rinks and ponds. At Lake Kampeska ice-boating has proved an exciting addition to other winter sports. The northeastern section of the State with its many lakes takes the lead in available skating and boating places.

Skiing. Taking advantage of long and steep hills in rough areas of the State ski enthusiasts enjoy two or three months of Norway's famous sport each winter. Chiefly because of natural advantages, the Black Hills and the Lake Region have become most favored for skiing activities. The Sioux Valley Ski Club sponsors one of South Dakota's greatest sporting events—the Sioux Valley Ski Tournament at Canton, which is the scene of the national championship meet about once in five years.

CITIES

IF you are a person who believes that it takes more than 35,000 inhabitants to constitute a city, then South Dakota has only large towns. West of the Mississippi River, it is said that towns become cities early in life. In South Dakota, the term "cities" often applies to those municipalities which were optimistically platted fifty or sixty years ago to become metropolises, and sufficient time has not yet passed for them to do so. Some of the prospective cities have become quite "citified," as much so as larger and older places in the East; others have become ghost towns, but they still carry names such as Crook City, Central City, or Silver City.

There were several cities which could not be conveniently described in the Tours section on account of the amount of historical matter and the number of points of interest. The seven largest—Sioux Falls, Aberdeen, Rapid City, Mitchell, Watertown, Huron and Lead, augmented by Pierre and Deadwood, are described here. It is no reflection on any city, nor its Chamber of Commerce, if it is not included in this section; other large towns will be found in the Tours section.

Population is given in accordance with the 1935 State census. If early-day anecdotes do not always agree with those you have heard or read, it is because the sources—reference files and pioneers themselves—also differ. Short tours to points of interest on the outskirts of some of the cities have been arranged.

ABERDEEN

(Map of Aberdeen in back pocket)

Railroad Stations: C. M. St. P. & P., Main St. & Railroad Ave.; G. N., Main St. & Railroad Ave.; C. & N. W., Pennsylvania St. & 2nd Ave. S.; M. & St. L., Main St. at 11th Ave. S. **Airports:** Municipal Airport on US 12 2½ miles E. of Main St. Taxi fare 75c, for 1 to 3 persons. Time 10 min. **Bus Lines:** Bus station, Main St. & 6th Ave. S. for Greyhound and Swanson Bus Lines. **Taxis:** Rates: 25c for 1 to 12 blocks; 35c, 12 to 17 blocks; 10c per extra passenger in both zones; 3 to 5 passengers to same destination any part of city, 50c. **City Bus Service:** Bus service to principal parts of city, fare 10c.

Traffic Regulations: Standard traffic regulations prevail. U turns prohibited on Main St. No left turns on Main St. when stop and go signs in service. Double parking forbidden. Speed limit, 15 m. p. h. **Parking Lots:** Municipal parking lot on Lincoln St. at 1st Ave. S.

Street Order and Numbering: Main St. divides city into E. and W. sections while Milwaukee RR. is dividing line between N. and S. street numbering. Streets to W. of Main St. numbered from 1 upward. E. of Main St. names prevail. Both street and avenue numbering run in even hundreds, first block E. of Main St. or W. being designated with numbers from 2 to 100, the following blocks run in even hundreds.

Accommodations: Four hotels; seven tourist camps.

Information Service: Aberdeen Civic Association on US 12 one-half block E. of Main St. during tourist season, May 15 to Oct. 1. For balance of year information may be secured by calling the Aberdeen Civic Association, 115 S. Main St.

Theaters: Two movie houses present occasional road shows. Five movie houses. The auditorium of Northern State Teacher's College, 12th Ave. S. & Jay St., used for most musical events.

Recreation: Aberdeen baseball park, State St. & 14th Ave. S. **Swimming:** YMCA pool, YMCA building, Lincoln St. at 5th Ave S. Bathing beaches, Wylie Park and Moccasin Creek; lifeguard protection during season. **Tennis:** Clay-surfaced tennis courts at Melgaard Park, State St. & 17th Ave. S. **(open to visitors). Golf:** Hyde Park, extreme W. end of 8th Ave. N., public 18-hole course available to visitors; green fees 15c per round. **Shooting Club:** Shooting club of closed membership welcomes visitors to shoots at County Fair grounds; hunting of pheasants, ducks, and geese in season.

Annual Events: Ludefisk public dinners during winter season.

In Aberdeen (1,229 alt., 16,725 pop.) every one of the thousands of trees has been planted by hand, thus achieving a degree of forestation on a treeless prairie not surpassed by many cities on forest sites. Pioneer builders of the city were largely from wooded areas in the Eastern States, and this gave them the urge to plant trees in large numbers.

Aberdeen, second largest city in South Dakota, is situated in the fertile James River Valley, the site once a part of the ancient Lake Dakota, with a slope so gentle that drainage can be attained only by careful engineering of street levels. There is an air of financial, commercial, and political importance about the city not often found in urban communities of similar size in the more populous sections of the Nation. The fact that it is the largest city between Minneapolis, Minn., and Butte, Mont., a distance of more than 1,000 miles, accounts for its local importance.

While some manufacturing is carried on, a recognition as a commercial center is substantially built upon distribution of manufactured goods. Its retail territory extends in a rough circle approximately 100 miles in diameter; its wholesale activities cover much of the State, as well as parts of North Dakota and Montana. The four railroads employ the greatest number of workers in the city, with wholesale distributors second.

In architecture, city planning, schools, and social life, the city is typical of the Midwest. There is little difference in the dress of residents of Aberdeen and those of cities farther east. A mixed population of native American stock from the Eastern and Central States, together with Russian-German and Scandinavian immigrants, has built the city on a firm foundation. Evidence of the foreign element are the annual "Ludefisk" public dinners given by Scandinavian church groups and the German dinners sponsored by groups of German birth and descent. The German-Russian influence is still seen in the picturesque wedding dinners in the tradition of the homeland on such occasions.

The so-called German-Russian section on the northeast side of the city, about six blocks from the Milwaukee tracks and east of Main about the same distance, was settled almost exclusively by immigrants from southern Russia. Their forbears emigrated from Alsace-Lorraine during the Napoleonic Wars of 1808-10 to the lowlands of the Dneister River at the invitation of Duke Richelieu, French Royalist refugee, then serving as governor of Odessa. Although they lived in Russia for two generations or more before emigrating to the United States, they preserved their language, traditions and racial purity. They settled in Aberdeen beginning in 1884 and many of the immigrants still reside here. The neighborhood has lost most of its foreign atmosphere, but many houses are painted in bright, contrasting colors, front yards are planted to vegetables and flowers, and the older women still wear silk head shawls and flowing skirts. The older people use their native language, but the tongue is restricted almost entirely to the home. The typical old style wedding, with feasting and merry-making for two and three days is sometimes celebrated.

It is probable that no white man crossed the site of Aberdeen before the coming of the government surveyors in the closing years of the 1870's. Military trails and the routes of voyageurs and trappers were to the east and west, following the James River on the east and the Missouri to the west. Perhaps the first actual settler, on the site was Freidrich Fenske, a part of whose homestead was on the original city plat.

First to consider the site as a future city was a party of 12 who drove overland from Watertown in the spring of 1880. In the party were the Rice Brothers and Charles Boyden. The party chose a spot where the survey of the Chicago, Milwaukee, St. Paul & Pacific Railway crossed the Chicago & North Western, two miles south of the center of the present city. A store was built there, a post office established and the new town was named Grand Crossing.

Later in the summer, Charles H. Prior, immigration agent for the Milwaukee R. R., had the present site of the city platted. By July 6, 1881, the Milwaukee ran its first train into the city, named Aberdeen in honor of Aberdeen, Scotland, the native city of Alexander Mitchell, then general manager of the Milwaukee.

It was soon evident that Aberdeen, and not Grand Crossing, was to be the future city so the store erected by Rice Brothers and Boyden at the latter place was moved into Aberdeen. Here, John Firey occupied it as a drug store, one of the first in the new town. The building, now the Lacey Drug store, was still standing at Main St. & First Ave. S. in 1937.

Characteristic of the men whose leadership was to build Aberdeen into the second city of the State was Major Samuel H. Jumper, who arrived ahead of the rails to act as agent for Prior, the owner of the town site. He is said to have preceded his party on foot in order to be the first to sleep on the town site.

The settlers were largely young men who sought new homes and intended to build a new community. Wisconsin, Michigan, Illinois, Minnesota, and Iowa contributed the majority of the new settlers. There were almost no soldiers of fortune, no adventurers, nor any of the Wild West bad man type.

Almost the entire population was young, a circumstance well-illustrated by an anecdote. When Gen. Nelson A. Miles passed through the city in the eighties, he was feted and driven through the streets lined with people to greet him. Seated beside him was Mayor S. H. Jumper. Turning to Jumper the general said, "Where are the old men, Mr. Mayor?" "We have no old men, General," was the answer.

The city was incorporated in May 1882. A special charter was passed by the Legislature in 1883 providing for an aldermanic form of government, which continued until 1911 when electors decreed a change to the commission form.

With the coming of the Great Northern Railway in 1886, another spoke in the railroad wheel centering in Aberdeen was formed.

Shortly before the World War, Aberdeen gained considerable notoriety for its Home Guards. In the fall of 1916 the I. W. W. (Industrial Workers of the World) established headquarters in Aberdeen. Within a few weeks five murders and several damaging fires were attributed to the I. W. W., so young Aberdeen business and professional men organized the Home Guards, raiding the headquarters of the I. W. W. and ordering all members to stay outside the city limits. The I. W. W. in retaliation put a boycott on South Dakota in an attempt to hamper harvesting operations, but local clerks and business men turned out to help the farmers and the crops were harvested.

The city's ambition to become an industrial as well as a distributing center was thwarted largely by lack of a suitable water supply. The deep-flow artesian water used until 1935 was extremely hard. Water impounded by a large dam in Willow Creek northwest of the city and treated in a modern filtration and softening plant, provides an ample supply, with future needs assured by the damming of adjacent streams.

Two men who resided in Aberdeen during its formative years have gained literary recognition. One was Hamlin Garland, author of *Main Traveled Roads, A Son of the Middle Border, A Daughter of the Middle Border, Afternoon Neighbors,* and many other books. Pioneer residents recall the persons who were prototypes of characters immortalized in his novels (*see Tour 11*). L. Frank Baum, author of a series of children's stories known as the Oz books, lived in Aberdeen as a youth. His principal book, *The Wizard of Oz,* had a phenomenal run in New York as a stage play.

Among native Aberdeen artists is Frances Crammer Green-men, who has done portraits of Mary Pickford, Ella Wheeler Wilcox, and others. Frank Ashford of the Rondell community and Aberdeen has done portraits of President Calvin Coolidge, Senator Peter Norbeck, Dr. Frank Crane, and many persons of State prominence.

POINTS OF INTEREST

1. The SITE OF THE DRUG STORE in *Main Traveled Roads* by Hamlin Garland is at the corner of Main St. and First Ave. S. E., across from the Alonzo Ward Hotel. In this frame building the drug store clerk who "chased a crony with a squirt pump" worked for John Firey, Aberdeen pioneer.

2. NATIONAL GUARD ARMORY, 116 Third Ave. S.W., was built in 1936-37 by the Works Progress Administration. The National Guard units quartered here were preceded by Co. L, 4th S. Dak. Infantry, but neither Co. L nor the Guard ever had a home of their own. The armory upon its completion became the home of Battery A, 147th Field Artillery, and a Headquarters Battery, also of the 147th Field Artillery.

3. ALEXANDER MITCHELL LIBRARY, cor. Lincoln St. and Sixth Ave., was established two years after the founding of Aberdeen, when 150 citizens subscribed $2 each and loaned 100 volumes. The first library was housed with the telephone exchange. Since then, the library has acquired 25,000 volumes. It has a circulation of 190,000 volumes annually.

4. The buildings of NORTHERN STATE TEACHERS COLLEGE, cor. 12th Ave. and Jay St., form a quadrangle. On the E. side are Spafford Hall, the Administration Building, and the Mechanic Arts Building; on the S. is Central Hall, to the W. women's dormitories, Graham, and Lincoln Halls.

The campus is landscaped with spacious lawns, flowers, and trees. East of the buildings is Johnson athletic field and grandstand, and the power plant. An open air amphitheatre in which spring pageants and plays are presented, a greenhouse, and hockey rink are to the south.

Offering the only four-year normal course in the State, Northern State has an annual enrollment of from 600 to 1,000 students. The school was founded in 1902 and accepted graduates of the eighth grade for instruction as teachers in rural and urban schools of the State. Only in the last few years has high school graduation been necessary for entrance to the college. The students receive practical teaching experience in the Aberdeen rural and small town schools.

Gypsy Day, in mid-October, is the annual homecoming celebration, when students don the garb and habits of gypsies and revel throughout the day and evening.

The FATHER ROBERT HAIRE MONUMENT, on the campus, was erected in honor of the pioneer priest of South Dakota. Father Haire came to Dakota Territory in 1880 and built a sod church by his own efforts near Columbia. He founded St. Luke's hospital in Aberdeen, was a member of the State Board of Regents and was active in the move to place the initiative and referendum law on the statute books of the State.

5. A reproduction of the LONGFELLOW HOUSE is at cor. of N. Main St. and 12th Ave. The yellow frame house, with its green shutters and white trim, was built from a copy of the original plans of Longfellow's home in Cambridge Mass., by W. D. Swain, an early resident. The interior is also designed in the manner of the original.

6. ST. LUKE'S HOSPITAL, State St. and Third Ave. S., is considered one of the finest hospitals in the State. The new 4-story fireproof building was constructed in 1920 by the Presentation Sisters, who established the first hospital in 1900 and now use the adjoining building as an academy.

7. THE CITY BASEBALL PARK, State St. and 14th Ave. S., accommodates State and National amateur baseball tournaments. The park was sponsored by the city in 1936 and built by the WPA. The City League plays its schedule three evenings a week, and games are played each Sunday during the summer.

8. MELGAARD PARK, State St. at S. edge of city, is a recreational city park comprising the tree claim of Andrew Melgaard, pioneer, whose statue is in the horseshoe flower bed. The figure is cast in bronze and is the work of Alice Letting Siems, Chicago. The park has a band shell where the municipal band presents weekly concerts. It also has tennis courts, a playground, a picnic area, and tourist camp.

TOUR 1—*2 m.*

L. from Main St. on 12th Ave. N.

9. HYDE PARK GOLF COURSE (*public; nominal green fees*) is an 18-hole course with built up hazards.

10. THE ABERDEEN COUNTRY CLUB has an 18-hole course with natural hazards, a clubhouse and polo field. The club sponsors the Dakota Open Golf Tournament each Labor Day, a 72-hole medal contest, in which players from North and South Dakota compete.

R. from Country Club on gravel road.

11. WYLIE PARK, 2 m., has an artificial lake and bathing beach (small admission charge). The lake is called Minne-eho, or Water Behold. The park consists of 25 acres, part of which is a zoo with buffalo, deer, elk, bears, coyotes, foxes, monkeys, eagles, pheasants, and waterfowl. There is an excellent public golf course on the grounds and a dancing pavilion.

DEADWOOD

Deadwood (4,630 alt., 3,662 pop.), historic mining town of gold rush days, has a most unusual location. No one who has stood on the rocky ledge of Mt. Moriah cemetery and looked down at the substantial little city in the gulch can ever forget the sight of this compact small community where the closely set pine trees vie with dwelling houses for possession of the steep slopes on either side. Deadwood is a town of one main street, the narrow bottom of the gulch having no room for more; and that one street is needed for the business section. So the houses must climb the steep sides of the gulch on either hand and the roads that lead to them form so many terraces. Where the gulch divides toward the upper end of town, the buildings follow both valleys, the business houses below and the residences above; while at the lower end of town, the valley becomes so narrow that the road itself is forced to leave the stream and wind its way up the almost perpendicular hillside. Above the famous Mt. Moriah cemetery, with its graves of Wild Bill and Calamity Jane, tower the glistening pinnacles of the White Rocks, from which, northward, can be seen the gleaming line of the Slim Buttes, 100 miles away.

Every year the "Days of '76" celebration draws aside the curtain of the years that would dim the memory of hard-bitten men drawn by the lure of gold from the far corners of the world to the wilderness that was Deadwood. For a brief time during the month of August there are festivities that may invoke the ghosts of those whose glasses clinked in the old Green Front Saloon to the strain of a prospector's fiddle. The program is keyed to recall the easy abandon with which gold dust and nuggets were "swapped" for liquor and other camp entertainment. The swinging doors, painted front and wooden sidewalks of the old saloon have disappeared but the memory of the pack mules with bulging saddle-bags, of men and women, loud with energy and hope, lives anew through "Days of '76."

Each morning of the celebration, over the paved highway, which follows the same course that the first placer miners picked out through the gulch, there winds a mile-long historical parade. Ox teams, covered wagons, stage coaches, sidesaddle girls, a prospector with his pack mules, Sioux Indians in native dress, Preacher Smith killed by the Indians, Calamity Jane, Poker Alice, Wild Bill Hickok, and Jack McCall who shot him in the back, march up Main Street. Wild Bill is shot; in the evening his murderer, Jack McCall, is tried by a miners' rump court and acquitted. The night life of the mining camp is revived. There are gay dance hall girls, and a carnival. In the Bucket o' Blood, the Deadwood of '76 is rebuilt. There are saloons where games of chance, faro, poker, and roulette wheels may be found. And after the "Days of '76" are over, Deadwood reassumes her sober mask.

But it is only a mask, for Deadwood of the present is the same mining town of '76 for all its modern trappings. Because the business of Deadwood always was and always will be—gold. And gold never loses its glamour or fascination, nor the things with which it is so richly and closely associated.

Deadwood still has her saloons and dance halls which operate under the name of "night clubs." And glasses still ring and cards continue to slide across tables for a price, whether that price be gold dust or crisp bills and silver dollars. But Calamity Jane, she who carried her gun on her hip and bought drinks for the boys, might be a bit disgusted with the feminine antics of her modern sisters; certainly she would have scoffed at the conventional chains that curtail their freedom over the streets of the old gulch. The general social life of Deadwood swings around its night clubs. Some of these, known at one time the country over as rough mining resorts, are now the essence of polish and propriety. But Deadwood grew up with glitter, and it cannot quite put away its past.

Deadwood's prosperity rests on a very substantial basis, due to various factors. To begin with, it is the seat of Lawrence County, which contains three cities, rich farming land, irrigated orchards, and valuable mining properties. Then it has a Nation-wide fame and is a magnet for every tourist who enters the Black Hills. In fact it would be unthinkable to leave the Hills without seeing historic Deadwood. In the third place, it shares in the prosperity of its larger neighbor, Lead. And lastly it has the reputation all through that region of being a liberal, more or less "wide open" town, a reputation it has held from the beginning and still holds. It has, it is true, spasms of virtue at times, but, like many another penitent, it finds it difficult to hold to the narrow way.' As long as its guests do not infringe upon the rights of others, they are welcome to avail themselves of those pleasures which Deadwood so freely offers.

Such is Deadwood, the most famous town not only in the Hills but in the State; for people all over the country have heard of this little town of thirty-six hundred inhabitants in the northern Hills. The reason for this lies in Deadwood's history, both true and false. Thousands of boys have read millions of words about Deadwood Dick's adventures and Deadwood itself has always been synonymous with adventure, with the old frontier, and with gold.

In 1874 Custer's expedition discovered gold on French Creek, near where Custer stands. At once various parties set out for the Hills, but many were turned back by the soldiers since this was at that time Indian country. But in the fall of 1875 the Government, after a fruitless parley with the Indians, no longer offered any objections to the entry of white gold seekers and the latter poured into the Hills from every direction in the turbid flood which only a gold rush knows. Most of them went to the southern Hills, where gold had first been discovered. But late that same fall John B. Pearson of Yankton penetrated the northern Hills and discovered rich placer diggings in Deadwood Gulch. That winter the snow was very deep, with little communication, and perhaps Pearson kept the good news to himself. At any rate it was March of the next year before word of the rich gold strike got out. At this time Custer was said to have a population of 7,000. When word of the strike in Deadwood Gulch reached it, the town was depopulated almost overnight. It is said that less than 100 people remained. There was a mass movement northward through the Hills and Deadwood was born, taking its name from the gulch in which it lay, which in turn was named for the dead timber of some forgotten fire.

There were 25,000 people up and down that narrow gulch before the end of the summer and the new town had to meet their needs. It would probably be impossible to overdraw the glamour of those early Deadwood days and that first summer in particular. There were the usual accompaniments of a gold strike—saloons, dance halls, brothels, and gambling houses. There was an unusually colorful assemblage of individuals, even for that time and place. Wild Bill, Calamity Jane, and Preacher Smith walked the streets, together with an assortment of men who were glad to be there because their presence was undesired elsewhere. The most momentous happening of that summer, and indeed of all Deadwood's history was the shooting of Wild Bill (*see Motor Tour 2*). Next in importance perhaps came the killing of Preacher Smith by the Indians while on his way to Crook City (*see Tour 4*). Of the three most noted personages of that summer, two died in their prime and the third, Calamity Jane, out-lived her environment. (*see Motor Tour 2*).

In the early years of Deadwood's prosperity profits were high, and gold plentiful. Each miner carried his buckskin sack filled with gold dust, which he squandered recklessly. One big miner scattered the contents of his gold sack on the streets to see the people scramble for it. Flour cost $60 per 100 pounds, wages were from $5 to $7 a day, while mine owners made small fortunes in a short time.

By the year 1879 the town had outgrown the canyon and had already started climbing the mountainsides of Deadwood and Whitewood gulches. On the night of September 25th, a fire which originated in a bakery on Sherman Street spread to a hardware store next to it. In the latter was stored a great deal of black powder which exploded, sending cinders all over the wooden buildings of the little gulch. Having no water system, miners and merchants alike stood helpless and watched their town burn. But in spite of the fact that it lay hundreds of miles by wagon road from its nearest base of supplies, the town was soon rebuilt.

During the winter of 1883 the snowfall had been unusually heavy and had melted but little; then followed warm rains, swelling Whitewood and Deadwood Creeks until the town was flooded and much damage done. Strong retaining walls have since been built on Deadwood Creek, harnessing the stream, black with mill tailings, to its course through the heart of the city.

As with all boom mining towns, Deadwood's greatest glory was in her first years. When the placer diggings became exhausted, many miners left. A new gold strike in Lead, which was later absorbed by the Homestake Mining Co., attracted still other inhabitants of the older town (*see LEAD*). But in 1887, with a silver boom in the nearby towns of Carbonate and Galena, Deadwood experienced a rejuvenation. In like manner, in 1894, when the price of silver declined, Deadwood slumped in population to a total of 1600. Later a smelter was built and the Golden Reward erected its plant and reduction works in the town. A cyanide plant was conconstructed for the Rossiter Mill. These activities brought about a revival of prosperity for a time. But this came to an end with the strike of 1909, which closed all the plants, and only the Golden Reward reopened.

Deadwood shared in post-war prosperity and since then has progressed steadily and rapidly. This is particularly true of the years, 1934-37, for Deadwood's prosperity is closely linked with that of its larger neighbor, Lead, only 3 miles away and with a population of almost 8,000. When the United States went off the gold standard in 1934, the price of gold rose substantially and this brought such prosperity to the Homestake that, in addition to the high wages that it habitually paid, it gave bonuses to its employees twice a year. This has brought a boom period to Lead, which in turn has found its reflection in Deadwood business conditions.

POINTS OF INTEREST

1. The ADAMS MEMORIAL HALL MUSEUM, cor. of Sherman and Deadwood Sts. (*open weekdays 10:00 a. m.—9:30 p. m., Sun. 2-6 p. m.; free*), is one of the outstanding features of the city of Deadwood. For many years it had been the hope and dream of some of the far-seeing citizens of the Black Hills to establish a place of safety for the fast disappearing records and relics of the early days. The gathering of such mementos is laying a foundation for a complete history of the struggles of the early pioneers.

To Fred D. Gramlich of Deadwood goes the credit for originating the idea of a museum, but it was W. E. Adams who realized this dream. He was a pioneer, and in memory of his family and of the pioneers who together with himself had helped to make the city of Deadwood the flourishing community that it is, he gave the

Adams Memorial Hall. This Memorial forms a link between the pioneer life of more than half a century ago and the Deadwood of today. The Hall was dedicated October 4, 1930.

The most important exhibits in the Adams Memorial Hall are: A book containing the laws and rules that the Gordon Party (*see Tour 5*), laid down in writing on February 23, 1875; the Theon Stone, which was found by Louis and Ivan Theon at the base of Lookout Mountain and is the only record of six Missourians, who, otherwise unknown, left the first authentic record of white men in the Hills, dating the stone 1834; a saddle and a pair of boots which President Theodore Roosevelt used on his ranch at Medora, N. Dak., and later gave to Captain Seth Bullock in October 1908; a saddle used by Quincy Turner, a cowpuncher, when he came with the first trail herd from Texas into the Black Hills; the first locomotive in the Black Hills, which arrived in August 1879 by bull team from Bismarck, N. Dak.; more than 100 shotguns and rifles dating from the pioneer period to the present day, also ox yokes, grain cradles, sluice boxes, rockers, broadaxes, bear traps, gold scales, and spinning wheels, which were all brought in during the early days; a collection of Indian saddles belonging to High Bearers, Two Moons, and Plenty Coups (High Bearers and Two Moons were in the Custer fight); a letter from the Messiah, a Piute Indian, Wovoka, who had emissaries among the Sioux and spread the religious rite of the ghost dance (*see Tour 7*); original marriage certificate of the only couple married by Preacher Smith while he was in Deadwood; and a most complete collection of early photographs of Deadwood and the Black Hills.

2. At the lower end of Main Street is that area which in early Deadwood days was known as CHINATOWN. At one time included in Deadwood's population was a considerable element of Chinese. They rapidly assumed the dress and manners of Americans. Chinatown extended from what is now the North Western depot to Mumford's garage.

Besides their usual occupations as laundrymen and restaurant keepers, there were merchants and doctors who conformed to the American fashions in all except their "cues," to which they religiously clung. The women and girls adhered to the native costumes. The Chinese had their own place of worship which they called the Joss House.

Most of the Chinese came under contract, which stipulated that their bodies be sent back to China. After six or seven years, allowing sufficient time for decomposition, a Chinese undertaker would go to the cemetery, disinter the bodies, separate the bones, wrapping each in a newspaper and muslin with proper labels, and place the package of bones in a small zinc-lined box 10 x 14 x 22 inches, which was sealed and shipped to San Francisco where with 1,700 or 1,800 more it would be sent to the Orient.

Mrs. Wong was the last Chinese woman to rear a family in Deadwood. An opium pipe which belonged to her is on display at the Adams Memorial Hall. Also on display at the Museum is a picture of the Chinese Hose Team of America which won the Great Hub and Hub Race in Deadwood on July 4, 1888. There is also a picture of the Chinese Sunday School class and some of the teachers. There are very few Chinese in Deadwood today, but this part of the city is called Chinatown.

3. The site of the old GREEN FRONT, the most famous brothel of the Deadwood of early days, and one of the most notorious in the entire West, extended from what is now 591 to 601 Main St. It was in existence from the early days of Deadwood until 1911.

4. At 613 Main St. is the site of the GEM THEATRE, probably the first and only legitimate theatre of the eighties in this western land of cowboys, miners, and gamblers. It was known as having excellent stock companies at that early day.

5. At 620 Main St., was the famous old NO. 10 SALOON, where Wild Bill Hickok was shot by Jack McCall (*see Motor Tour 2*). McCall ran across the street and hid in an old barn which was next to a pool hall.

TOUR 1—3.7 m.

W. from Main St. on Shine St.

6. BLACK HILLS NATIONAL FOREST (entrance at 1 *m.*) covers practically the entire northern Hills area, as the Harney National Forest covers the southern portion. (*See BLACK HILLS RECREATIONAL AREA.*) At some points along this road the mountain side slopes away from the highway at a very sharp angle and careful driving is necessary.

7. ROOSEVELT MONUMENT is at the summit of Mt. Roosevelt (5,676 alt.). This circular tower is 35 ft. high, set in a solid base, the whole being built of native diorite found on the hill

where the memorial stands. A bronze tablet placed on the monument bears the following inscription:

In Memory Of
Theodore Roosevelt
"The American"

The idea of a monument was conceived by Captain Seth Bullock (*see Motor Tour 2*), an intimate friend of Theodore Roosevelt, and was carried out by the Society of Black Hills Pioneers in 1919, when the memorial tower was erected; and the mountain, formerly known as Sheep Mountain, was dedicated to the former President of the United States.

From the summit of Mt. Roosevelt it is possible to see four States, North Dakota, South Dakota, Wyoming, and Montana; and in the foreground to the south and west are the Black Hills and to the north and east rolling plains.

TOUR 2—0.9 m.

S. from Sherman St. on Van Buren Ave.

WHITEWOOD CREEK, once a crystal-clear, tumbling mountain stream, now a dirty leaden color, literally a flow of liquid mud, caused by the tailings from the Homestake mine at Lead, flows through the center of Deadwood. It is said that this one small stream carries down 4 million tons of tailings annually to the Belle Fourche River. The stream leaves the Hills in a continuous series of rapids with a flow too swift to deposit mud at any point within the Hills; and it remains turgid and heavy with mud all the way to the Belle Fourche. Livestock will drink the water along the lower reaches; but no animal life is possible in it.

8. MT. MORIAH or "BOOT HILL" CEMETERY is visited annually by thousands of tourists, curious to see the graves of four famous Western characters, Wild Bill, Calamity Jane, Preacher Smith, and Seth Bullock. Of these, easily the most famous was Wild Bill, or as he was christened, James Butler Hickok, "the Prince of Pistoleers," one of the handsomest men on the frontier, and admittedly the quickest and best shot on the turbulent border in its most turbulent days. Born in Illinois, he was fired with a determination to emulate the career of his hero, Kit Carson; and going out to the frontier while still a boy, he became successively a freighter, hunter and trapper, stage driver and station-tender, and soldier and scout in the Union Army, penetrating the Confederate

lines three times in disguise. After the Civil War he was a scout on the plains for various units of the United States Army, then an actor (a poor one it must be admitted), and finally marshal of one after another of the roughest towns of the old West and the entire country. It was the last-named activity that brought him his greatest fame. As one after another of the Kansas towns became the head of steel and consequently the shipping point for the herds of wild Texas cattle driven up from the South by equally wild cow-hands, these cow towns became the Mecca for gamblers, prostitutes, and bad men who congregate wherever money is freely spent. It was the business of the town marshal to protect the merchants and law-abiding citizens and it was usually necessary to remove permanently from society the worst of the bad men in order to accomplish this. Wild Bill is generally credited with having killed 27 men, although he himself would never discuss the subject. It was this reputation of his as a law-enforcement officer that led directly to his killing. Although he came to Deadwood to make a stake for the bride he had just taken, the lawless element of the town feared that he would be appointed marshal and put an end to their activities. They therefore bribed a weak character, Jack McCall, to assassinate Wild Bill, promising him $300 to accomplish the deed and filling him up with cheap whiskey to give him courage. Wild Bill was indulging in his favorite pastime of a friendly game of cards in the old No. 10 saloon. For the second time in his career, he was sitting with his back to an open door. Jack McCall walked in, shot him through the back of the head, and rushed from the place, only to be captured shortly afterward. Wild Bill's dead hand held aces and eights, and from that time on this has been known in the West as "the dead man's hand." Jack McCall was tried before a packed jury and acquitted. He later went to Custer and Cheyenne and bragged of the killing, but was arrested by a United States Marshal in Cheyenne and taken to Yankton for trial before the District Court. His plea of "double jeopardy" was disregarded on the ground that the miner's court had no jurisdiction; and he was convicted, sentenced, and hanged. Although Wild Bill was technically a killer, he killed only in self-defense or in the line of duty as a peace officer. His grave in Mt. Moriah is surrounded by an iron fence and marked by a red sandstone, life-sized statue of dubious artistic merit which has suffered considerably from vandalism.

In the adjoining enclosure is the grave of another famous character of early Deadwood, Calamity Jane, or Martha Jane (Canary)

Burke. Born at or near La Salle, Ill., May 1, 1852, she drifted west with her family and at an early age was left an orphan. She became a hanger-on of construction camps, bull trains, army expeditions, and gold camps; and according to some accounts she served at times as an army scout or mail carrier. She dressed by preference in men's attire, frequently a suit of fringed buckskin, and few persons ever saw her in women's apparel. She was credited with a vocabulary of extraordinary breadth and richness, even for a time and place that was not entirely lacking in self-expression. There exists the widest divergence both in the accounts of her life and estimates of her character. Time has made of her a legendary figure and the different accounts of how she gained her sobriquet, "Calamity Jane," are none of them very authentic. Although she had been a wanderer up to the time she reached Deadwood in 1876 at the height of the gold rush, she seemed to find that region to her liking, for she made it more or less her home for the rest of her life. She took trips to Montana and to the East, and for awhile was a midway attraction at the Pan-American Exposition in Buffalo. But always she returned to the Hills, and there passed away in a boarding house at Terry, Aug. 1, 1903, almost twenty-seven years to the day after the shooting of her friend, Wild Bill. In accordance with her last wish she was buried beside him. Her funeral is said to have been the largest ever held in Deadwood and South Dakota remembers her colorful career rather than her human frailties.

A short distance up the hill from the graves of these two is another lifesize red sandstone statue marking the last resting place of another pioneer, Preacher Smith (*see Tour 4*).

Somewhat apart from the other graves, on a slight elevation, is the grave of Seth Bullock. Originally a cowboy with the big outfits, he organized Theodore Roosevelt's Rough Riders and was immediately appointed captain. After Roosevelt became President, he appointed his old companion-at-arms United States Marshal for South Dakota, a position which he held for many years. He also served as first sheriff of Lawrence County and was the first Forest Supervisor of the Black Hills forests. Before he died he asked to be buried where his grave would be in sight of the monument erected to his hero, Theodore Roosevelt. That request was the reason for locating the grave where it is.

POINTS OF INTEREST IN ENVIRONS

Cabin and Grave of Deadwood Dick 2.3 m.; Preacher Smith Monument, 3.3 m., (*see Tour 4*).

HURON

Railroad Stations: The Chicago & North Western R. R., Dakota Ave. and Second St., and the Great Northern R. R., Dakota Ave. and First St. **Bus Lines:** The Swanson, Jackrabbit, Mitchell and the Pierre lines depots at Marvin Hughitt Hotel, Corner Dakota Ave. S. and 4th St. and Royal Hotel, Wisconsin Ave. S.W. and 3rd. **Airport:** Hanford Line and Watertown and Rapid City lines, Municipal Airport 2 mi. N. on Dakota Ave. **Taxi Service:** City limit fare 35c.

Accommodations: Two hotels; tourist camps.

Information Bureau: Chamber of Commerce office at 28 3rd St. S.W. (second floor).

Theaters: Three motion picture houses.

Athletics: Baseball Park, N.E. Huron; College Field, S.W. **Golf:** Public links N. on State 37, Country Club N. 1 m. **Tennis:** Public courts, Oregon St. between 5th and 6th Sts.

Street Order and Numbering: Street numbering begins at C & NW R.R. tracks, numbering N. and S. on all avenues. All other streets begin numbering E. and W. from Dakota Ave. Dakota Ave. and 3rd St. center of business district.

Annual Events: South Dakota State Fair, held Sept. 10, or later (5 days). Pow Wow Day—October (last week in month, 1 day). Public Scandinavian ludefisk suppers during fall and winter.

Huron (1,288 alt., 11,753 pop.) is situated on the west bank of the James River in the center of a broad, level prairie region that spreads, fan-wise, in all directions. As the hub for the numerous small towns that lie within the confines of a mythical wheel, Huron draws trade from a large agricultural area. Good highways, airlines, railroads, and hotels have combined with the city's location near the State's center of population to make it popular as a convention city as well as the home of the State Fair.

Largely dependent upon agricultural and allied pursuits—dairying, poultry raising, grain, and livestock farming—the city also has industries to process the farm products, including a meat packing company and brewery.

Huron has always been known for its strong labor organizations. There are 23 trade and labor unions in this small city, and they maintain the Huron Central Labor Union Hall for their activities. The first labor organization was the Brotherhood of Locomotive Firemen whose charter, issued July 13, 1883, was signed by Eugene V. Debs, one-time candidate for president of the United States on the Socialist ticket.

Called an "overgrown country town" in 1910, Huron has lost many of the characteristics of a small town. Up-to-date structures have replaced the old frame buildings in the business section, and a new courthouse, city hall, school buildings, and airport show the recent progress.

Although named for an Indian tribe, Huron was born to the accompaniment of squeaking wagon wheels, humming hay mowers, and locomotive bells. The history of the present site of Huron, dates back to 1879 when John Cain, among others, staked out a claim on the east bank of the James River. Shortly afterwards a party of surveyors of the Chicago & North Western Railroad arrived and camped near there. At the direction of Marvin Hughitt, general manager of the line, the west bank of the river was selected as division headquarters of the railroad. This was in reality the first step toward bringing the city of Huron into existence. The railroad company through its subsidiary the Western Town and Lot Company gained title to 880 acres of land on which final entry was made in September 11, 1879. The railroad company built depots, a roundhouse, shops and offices covering a building space of 38,000 feet. Either Mr. Hughitt or someone in the Chicago office of the railroad gave the new town its name.

Huron was a busy place in the summer of 1880, with building operations going on and settlers coming in to seek land. Perhaps it was for this reason that the first July 4th celebration was staged in Huron a day late. The event was none the less important. Journalism, like the new town, was informal—yet personally vital. Following is an example of it, as carried in the columns of a newspaper on July 6, 1880, reporting the belated celebration:

"The grand success of Huron's first celebration of the Nation's birthday is the general topic of conversation among her citizens, and the occasion of their mutual congratulations.

"At the first indication of the rising sun on the morning of the 5th, he was greeted by the National salute and an extra gun for Huron, fired under the supervision of M. Chase. Pistols, shotguns and firecrackers made music in the air until afternoon, when a crowd assembled to witness a game of baseball on a ground which had been prepared near the city. Two nines were selected by Messrs. Fairbanks and Parkhurst, and play was commenced with Lon Hartis as umpire and A. L. Church as scorer. Before the nine innings were played, the last bat in Huron was broken and the game could not be finished.

"Shortly before sundown two running races took place over a course west of Wright's Hotel, one of which was won by Williams' gray mare and the other by a horse belonging to a young man in Wright's employ."

The dry summer and hard winter of 1880-81 retarded the growth of the town, but a boom began the next year as settlers continued to stake claims nearby and require implements, household necessities, and entertainment. The War Department installed a signal station in this prairie town in 1881; it has since become important as a weather bureau for the State. Cutting hay on Huron's present busiest thoroughfare—Dakota Avenue—took place in 1885 when Hollard Wheeler, pioneer druggist, mowed the foot-tall grass in front of his store to improve appearances. The present brick structure that houses the Wheeler Drug Store had just been built when "haying time" began on the street.

In the late eighties, crop failures, coupled with a period of depression, again temporarily checked the growth of the city. As times picked up, Huron was selected as the site for the State Fair in 1904. Following the World War came another period of growth as headquarters for oil, utility, and wholesale companies were established in Huron. From 1933 to 1935 drought and dust storms ravaged the crops in the rural regions surrounding Huron, and crippled the sources of income. This area, which was more affected than any other in the eastern half of the State, was the scene of soil conservation and shelter belt work, and in 1937 lakes and streams were again filled.

Huron has a city manager who is the sole administrative officer.

POINTS OF INTEREST

1. THE SOUTH DAKOTA STATE FAIR GROUNDS, on 3rd St. bet. Nevada and Indiana Sts., (*Adm.: Adults, 25c, children under 12, free.*) comprises 150 acres where the State Fair is held the second week in September. There are spacious barns and pavilions for housing livestock and poultry exhibits, a large glass building called Machinery Hall, a main exhibit building, a zoo, a large grandstand, and a half-mile racetrack, besides numerous hot dog, peanut and popcorn vendors' stands and the usual cheap "midway attractions."

A plot of ground, conveniently located and enclosed to afford police protection, is set aside by the State Board of Agriculture for the exclusive use of families desiring to camp while attending the

Fair. No charge is made and parties may bring their own tents or rent one on the grounds. Maintained on the grounds as additional service for visitors are an express office, post office, rest cottage for women and children, check rooms, dining halls, telephone and telegraph offices.

2. HURON COLLEGE, on Illinois Ave., 7th and 19th Sts., was founded at Pierre in 1883 by Harlan Page Carson as Pierre University. Soon afterwards, 1898, it was moved to Huron and established as a Presbyterian college, starting with three students. Today it comprises one main building—Ralph Vorhees Hall—a girls' dormitory and a large gymnasium and auditorium, all set deep on a broad, well-landscaped campus. For many years students from Oriental countries—China, Korea and Japan—have attended Huron College. This is largely due to the efforts of George Shannon McCune, former president, who spent much of his life in the Far East. The college is developing the group system of studies and a correlation between high school and college work. It has added all the pre-requisite courses in engineering, medicine, dentistry, journalism, and law.

3. LAMPE MARKET, cor. Dakota Ave. and 4th St., is an example of the idea of the "vertical trust" in commerce, the inclusion of all the processing steps in the converting of raw material to the finished product within the confines of a single organization, with consequent elimination of profit-taking on the various steps of manufacture and marketing. The Lampe Market raises its own meat on its 900-acre farm, kills it, packs it, and markets it.

The Lampe Market was first opened by Albert Lampe, Sr., in 1887. A native of Wernigerode, Germany, he came to Huron in 1882. Improvements in the plants were made in 1907, and the market was enlarged to accommodate increased business. The improvements were of such a character as to cause the market to be described in the newspapers of that day as "the best market in the Northwest." Twenty years later, in 1927, the present market was opened.

On request the visitor is shown "behind the scenes" where there are large ranges for delicatessen cooking, ovens for bakery goods, and the meat department where sausage, bacon, ham, and lard are prepared. The basement is a complete packing plant with exception of the slaughter house and fertilizer department. There also are thousands of square ft. of cold storage rooms.

4. CHIC SALE HOUSE, 643 Illinois Ave., S.W., was the boy-hood home of "Chic" Sale, as he was known to the theatrical and literary world, but whose real name was Charles Partlon Sale. He was born in Huron in 1884, the son of Dr. Frank O. and Lillie B. Sale who came to Huron in 1882. "Chic" spent the first 11 years of his life in the new prairie town and attended the school on the present site of the Huron High School. The publication of *The Specialist* was "Chic" Sale's debut into the literary field and it became the "mirth of a nation," over a million copies being sold. This was followed by *The Champion Cornhusker* and *I Tell You Why*.

5. AIRPORT: The W. W. Howes Municipal Airport joins the city on the north, and includes 120 acres of land, a hangar, admini-stration building, and repair shop. The airport was named for W. W. Howes of Huron, assistant Postmaster General (1933-   ), and was built with the aid of the Works Progress Administration. All the buildings are substantially constructed of hand-cut native stone and all have cement floors. The hangar is 108 ft. long, 94 ft. wide, and has a 19 ft. ceiling.

The administration building, west of the hangar, has two stories, a full basement, and an observation lookout on the roof from which the activities of the airport are directed. The offices, waiting rooms, and lunchroom occupy the ground floor.

LEAD

Railroad Stations: Bus connections with Chicago, Burlington & Quincy at Pluma, 1.5 m.; bus connection with Chicago & North Western at Deadwood, 3 m. **Bus Station:** Highland Hotel. Deadwood-Lead bus line and Black Hills Transportation Co. **Airport:** Black Hills Airport, 14 m. N. on US 85; no scheduled service.

Traffic Regulations: Main St. stop street, with severe penalties for violation. No U turn on Main St. within city limits. Parking only flat to curb. No double parking.

Information Service: Highland Hotel.

Accommodations: One hotel, 2 tourist camps.

Theater: One motion picture house.

Athletics: Grier Park, southwestern section of town. **Golf:** Country Club, 10 miles SW. of town on Rochford road. **Swimming:** Recreation Building. **Library:** Recreation Building.

Annual Event: Labor Day celebration and sports at Grier Park.

Lead (pronounced Leed, 5,320 alt., 7,847 pop.), is the seat of the Homestake, the largest gold mine in the United States, and one of the largest in the world. Lead takes its name from the famous Homestake "lead," meaning lode or vein, which has yielded over $300,000,000 worth of gold and in 1937 is still producing at the rate of more than $15,000,000 a year. Lead is the Homestake and the Homestake is Lead; the two are inseparable.

The contrast in the physical appearance of Lead and Deadwood, three miles apart, is remarkable. While the latter is packed into the bottom of the gulch, Lead, at the head of Gold Run Gulch, is spread out, a mile high, over the tops of the surrounding hills. The two towns have one feature in common, the almost total lack of level ground. But Lead is the hillier of the two. The porch of one residence is often on a level with the roof of the one in front of it.

Lead is what might be called a town on the move, for with shafts and tunnels undermining the city, large areas are in danger of subsiding and have been cleared of buildings. On top of the highest hill in Lead a new residence section has sprung up, where the underground workings are not likely to undermine it. Because of cave-ins and shifting earth, together with the prosperity of the city, there are few old buildings in Lead and no high ones.

The upper end of Main Street apparently leads into the sky, while the lower end drops steeply into the canyon of Gold Run Gulch on its way to Deadwood. On one side of Main Street rises the tall and silver-colored slenderness of the Ross and Ellison shafts and on the other side is the yawning chasm of the Open Cut, the most striking single physical feature of the City of Lead.

Unlike most mining towns, Lead has no night life. Night clubs and taverns are forbidden and presumably Deadwood reaps a rich harvest from this ruling. In Lead, the overall is a high badge of respectability, and a dinner pail the most common accompaniment of "the man in the street." An old car is a curiosity in Lead, while new cars are to be seen on every hand.

The foreign element of Lead is diverse, the population being divided among 18 nationalities. Seventy percent of the inhabitants, however, are native born. The population is stable, because Homestake jobs are obtained with difficulty and held tenaciously.

Practically all the land in Lead is owned by the Homestake, but any employe may build on a site and occupy it rent-free, as long as it is not needed for mining purposes.

The Homestake operates its own hospital and medical department, free to employees and their families; also a large club building free to both employees and the public. Sanitary, well-appointed dressing rooms with shower baths are available for the men coming off-shift.

It was when the late winter snows began to melt in 1876 that Thomas E. Carey, a mining pioneer, left his claim in Deadwood Gulch, crossed over the divide to Gold Run Creek in search of gold, and, finding the swollen stream and surrounding soil rich with the precious yellow metal, staked his claim and sent word of his discovery to Deadwood Gulch.

On July 14, 1876, the first town lot was recorded, Lot 1, Block 1, at 100 Mill and Pine Streets. The first meeting of miners to organize Lead City was held July 26, 1876. On Feb. 28, 1877, the Black Hills area was ceded by the Indians to the United States, and on Sept. 21, 1877, the first mineral applicatoin to the Land Office was made.

A few weeks subsequent to the founding of Lead, the town of Washington was laid out not far from it by a different set of locators. The two towns had a separate existence for a number of years; but Washington finally became an addition to Lead.

In this same year, 1877, the first gold-bearing quartz from the site of the present city was treated and recovered by the Manuel

Brothers, Mose and Fred. To test their finds, the Manuel brothers hauled 4,000 tons of quartz to Whitewood Creek. They built a rude home-made crushing mill called an "arrastra" (a Mexican term), and the ore yielded so richly that the fame of Lead spread to all parts of the country. Promoters and big-time prospectors became vitally interested and from Alaska down the western coast to Mexico traveled the news that gold lay in the Black Hills. From all parts of the United States came the gold seekers, showmen, adventurers, and seasoned miners. So it was that George Hearst, Lloyd Tevis, and J. B. Haggin, members of a San Francisco syndicate, sent Samuel McMaster, a mining engineer, to Deadwood early in 1877 to report on silver mines there. But gold was god of the Hills at that time, so McMaster recommended the purchase of two claims, the Homestake and the Golden Star in Gold Run Canyon; and they were bought. The Homestake Mining Company was incorporated in 1877 in San Francisco, and under the guidance of that company Lead grew into a city.

During the summer of 1877, several quartz custom mills were built in Lead. The first, built for the Racine Mining and Milling Co., near the former site of the North Western passenger depot, consisted of 10 stamps. It was soon afterward enlarged to 20 stamps and proved satisfactory. The rate for treating ore was $10 per ton.

The Racine Mill was followed by the Enos Mill, built by C. H. Enos & Co., which purchased Harney's interest in the Homestake. Soon after the Thompson, the Gwin, the Smith and Pringle, the Marshman, the White, and the Costello, and several other mills were built. All these treated ore for the Homestake and Golden Star. The latter companies, despite the heavy milling tolls, paid the owners well.

In early days a small stream called Gold Run ran through Lead and down to Pluma where it was lost in Whitewood Creek. Today no stream is to be seen in Lead until a point below the Homestake regrinding plant. Much of the water that now runs down Gold Run Gulch is from Spearfish Creek and is piped by the Homestake Company over a rise of hundreds of feet to Lead.

In a new mining camp today, the first thing built is a hotel or boarding house. This, however, was not so with Lead. The Lead miners lived in cabins until the spring of 1877. In June of that year, four hotels were built.

The first dance in Lead City was held on the night of July 4, 1877, in the second frame building, known as Jentes Corner. There were but seven women present, the total feminine population of Lead at that time.

A little log cabin was the city's pioneer school in the year 1877. It was a tuition school.

In 1879 the first hospital, a log cabin, was erected. At first a physician was selected, satisfactory to both employees and the management, to render aid to employees and their families. In 1906 the company took charge of the department and the service was extended to include general medical, surgical, and obstetrical cases, free of charge to all employees of the Homestake and their families. A two-story frame building was erected in 1889 and the present hospital was completed in 1925, a three-story brick structure, modern and completely equipped.

Lead became a municipality in 1890. The city grew, wards were added, and eight councilmen selected to assist the mayor. The superfluous "City" was dropped and the town has since been known as Lead.

On the morning of March 8, 1900, occurred the most disastrous fire in the history of the city. It destroyed a quarter of a million dollars' worth of property. The fire burned the entire business section of Lead and a part of the residence section also. The wind sent clouds of sparks whirling across Bleeker Street to the frame buildings which lined Pine and Mill Streets, threatening the Hearst store and the Star Mill of the Homestake Mining Co. After hours of hard work the fire was stopped in its course up Mill Street. With the aid of dynamite it was kept from spreading to the mills.

On March 25, 1907, between 4 and 5 o'clock in the morning, the timber stoping on the 500-ft. level of the Homestake Mine caught fire. The air pipes, through which water was run in case of fire, had been removed on this level. An attempt was made to put the fire out with two hoses, each having 200-lbs. pressure. Pipes were laid to carry water and men were doing good work with them, when the stope began to cave in behind them and this method had to be abandoned.

Steam was next tried. The drift was tightly closed, and this took many days. Steam was then turned in for 7½ days. The gases were by this time so strong that all work had to be stopped except at the extreme north end. After the steam was turned off the fire was still raging, and the rock in the vicinity was at a temperature of about 1500 degrees F.

As a last resort it was decided to flood the mine and on April 18th the water was allowed to fill the lower workings instead of draining off as usual. This, too, proved inadequate and therefore two tunnels were built and a small stream was turned through them. During 23 days these tunnels carried 19 million cubic feet of water into the mine.

After the fire had been smothered by this means, the task of "unwatering" began. This required the removal of over 300 million gallons of water. The machinery in the mine was rusted but was soon made usable, while the mine itself needed but few repairs to put it in working condition again. The blow to the community was only temporary. In a very short time, owing to the resources of the company and the energy and devotion of the men, Lead's usual prosperity was restored.

Owing to world conditions the price of gold increased from $20.67 per ounce in 1933 to $34.00 per ounce in January 1934, and by reason of the Gold Act of 1934 the price was fixed at $35.00 per ounce. This brought immense prosperity to gold producing regions. Wages went up in the gold mines, business was stimulated, and the mines made greatly increased profits; and, in the case of the Homestake, this prosperity was shared with the men in the shape of increased wages and semi-annual bonuses. In 1936 each employee received a $50 bonus in June and $100 at Christmas.

POINTS OF INTEREST

1. The HOMESTAKE MINE, Main St. bet. Mill St. and E. city limits, consists of two parts, the underground workings, or the mine proper, and the hoists, mills, and plants above ground. For a number of years it has not been the policy of the company to allow the casual visitor underground. The students of the South Dakota State School of Mines (*see RAPID CITY*) are taken through the underground workings as a part of their course of study. The Homestake furnishes guide service (*fee 50c.*) to conduct tourists to all parts of the surface plants of the company. The revenue thus derived is paid to the H. A. A., the local charitable organization. The group that is being taken through begins at the mine shaft, where the ore is taken from the ground, and follows

it through all its processes until the useless "tailings," or pulverized ore from which all gold has been extracted, are sent down Gold Run Gulch to Whitewood Creek.

The Homestake employs both the mercury and cyanide processes in extracting gold from ore. When the ore arrives at the mouth of the shaft, it is hauled to the stamp mill. Here, amid a din that renders even shouted conversation impossible, huge stamps reduce the ore to fine proportions. It is then ground in rod mills and mercury is added. The mercury unites with the free gold and the resulting amalgam is collected in amalgamators. The mercury is later driven off by heat and recovered and the gold remains. The residue of the ore is then reground till it is as fine as flour and leached in huge vats or in filter presses by a weak cyanide solution. The cyanide dissolves what little gold remains and forms a chemical combination with it. The bottoms of these vats are composed of canvas, through which the cyanide and gold filter and are drained off. This compound is chemically treated, the cyanide driven off and recovered, and the gold remains. The residue in the vats, now free of all but the faintest trace of gold, is washed into Gold Run Gulch to find its way, via Whitewood Creek, to the Belle Fourche River. So thorough is this process and so adapted to the handling of ore in vast bulk that treatment costs are low and over 95 percent of the gold in the ore is recovered. The average yield of the ores treated is one-third of an ounce per ton.

An idea of the enormous investment necessary to produce gold on a large scale can be had from a view of the surface workings. The new ROSS SHAFT, whose silver-colored top may be seen rising above and behind the highest hill in Lead was recently completed at a cost of $2,000,000. Other construction in recent years includes a new power plant, a new compressor plant, and extensions to mill and cyanide plant. In all over $5,000,000 has been expended. A new shaft, equally as expensive as the Ross, is projected (1937) and will soon be built. The total depth of the Ross Shaft is now 4,100 feet. It will ultimately reach 5,200 ft. The new shaft will go still deeper. The output of the mine is, at normal gold prices, $6,000,000 a year. The men employed number between 2 and 3 thousand, and miners' wages are $6 per day.

2. The OPEN CUT is best viewed from the S. end of Mill Street near the Ross shaft. It is an immense gash in the earth where first there was an open pit mine, out of which enormous riches were taken in the early days, and where later the under-

ground workings of the mine caused the surface to cave in and add still further to the immense cavity. The Open Cut changed the whole topography of Lead. As it kept increasing in size and depth, the rest of the city retreated respectfully before it.

North Mill St. was at one time the leading business street of Lead, boasting the largest buildings in the city and most of the business activity. Formerly about 5 blocks long, now only one block remains and there are no buildings on it. The rest of the street has dropped into the Open Cut. But even then the Open Cut was not satisfied. In advance of its yawning cavity, the lower end of the new Main Street became unsafe. Its buildings were condemned, including the abandoned North Western depot, and business retreated W. along the sloping thoroughfare. Today the lower end of Main St. is denuded of buildings and next to this vacant space stand those which have been abandoned but are not yet torn down. The upper end of Main St., however, which is the present business center, stands on land which will not be subject to caving, and the same is true of the newest residence section on the hill above. But in the pavement of lower Main St. from time to time new cracks appear; and portions of the street have sunk several feet below their former level.

3. GRIER PARK, named in honor of T. J. Grier, a former superintendent of the Homestake Mine, is at the west end of Main St. and joins the city on the south. It is one of the highest hills in Lead and comprises 13 acres. In it are swings and other playground equipment, a large pavilion for dances and meetings, and what is probably one of the most unusual baseball diamonds in the world. Well over a mile high, it was built by the Homestake at a cost of $50,000 by blasting off two sharp peaks. Only by such means as this could level ground be obtained anywhere in Lead. One side of the diamond slopes sharply toward the city while the other drops into a canyon a thousand feet below. Ground rules had to be established. If the ball goes over teh precipice between such and such a point, it is good for so many bases. Otherwise, every ball struck out of the immediate field would be good for a home run. Visiting teams usually are affected somewhat by the unaccustomed altitude, but this does not account entirely for the athletic successes of the husky sons of the miners. Only with the facilities provided by this field is the Lead High School enabled to compete with other schools in baseball, football, and track events.

Grier Park is also the scene of an annual Labor Day celebration, consisting of various sports and contests. Formerly the feature of the celebration was a series of turtle races. Every Homestake employee bet on a turtle decided by lot. The race was run off in a number of heats, until the winner was determined. The turtles were numbered and released in the center of a large ring and left to their own devices. The first turtle to cross the circle at any point was the winner of that heat. A more fair (and a more uncertain) race could hardly be devised. It was more of a gamble even than the "wild horse race" of the rodeo. The proceeds of the Turtle Day Races, minus the prizes that went to the winners, were devoted to the welfare of Homestake employees.

4. The RECREATION BUILDING, on the south side of Main Street, is a clubhouse built by the Homestake for the use of its employees. On the ground floor is a large room with chairs, tables, and periodicals, a place for general visiting. On the second floor is the FREE LIBRARY, established in 1894 and today ranking with the best in the State. In the basement are bowling alleys, for the use of both men and women, and a swimming pool. All these are free to employees. There is also in the building a motion picture auditorium.

5. In the basement of CHRIST CHURCH (EPISCOPAL) on the south side of upper Main Street is a FREE KINDERGARTEN, established in 1900 by Mrs. Phoebe Hearst, mother of William Randolph Hearst.

MITCHELL

Railroad Stations: Chicago, Milwaukee, St. Paul and Pacific R. R., S. end of Main St.; Chicago and North Western R. R., Main St. and Eighth Ave. **Bus Station:** Red Ball, Custer Highway, Interlake, Palace City and Intercity Lines, Union depot, 114 S. Main St. **Airport:** No regular lines, municipal airport, 3 m. N. on State 37. **Taxis:** 25c upward.

Traffic Regulations: No double parking, and parking limitations where marked. **Parking Spaces:** Free parking spaces N. Main St. and Fourth Ave W.; 200-block E. Second Ave.

Accommodations: Two first class hotels; several cabin camps.

Tourist Information Service: Chamber of Commerce, 203 First Ave. W.

Theaters and Motion Picture Houses: Local productions and road shows at Corn Palace; three motion picture houses.

Athletics: Municipal field, night baseball games, E. Ninth Ave. and Fourth St. **Swimming:** Lake Mitchell. **Golf:** Lakeview Municipal Golf Course, Lake Mitchell, 25c greens fee; Country Club, 1½ m. E. on US 16, admission by invitation.

Annual Event: Corn Palace festival, last week in September.

Mitchell (1,312 alt., 12,834 pop.) is situated in the James River Valley and is widely known for its Corn Palace, the only one of its kind in the world, where the city each year stages a six-day festival as a climax to the harvest season. The town's location in a diversified farming region has made it an important trade center. The principal industries are meat and poultry packing, butter and cheese making, and livestock and grain shipping; tons of frozen eggs are shipped to eastern markets annually.

Following the trend of architecture begun in the nineties, most of the long main street has brick structures, although several of the old wooden buildings remain. Mitchell, lacking in natural recreational areas, was one of the first plains cities to create a large artificial lake to supply its demands.

A piece of driftwood and an engineer's farsightedness were the factors responsible for Mitchell's location. In the late seventies a town called Firesteel was started on a creek about two miles from the present site of Mitchell and early residents hoped the village would be permanent. But in 1879 the Chicago, Milwaukee & St. Paul R. R. sent an engineer to locate a town site. In examining the ground near Firesteel the engineer picked up a piece of driftwood, "This will never do for a town," he declared emphatically. "Where water has been it may come again." The report convinced the railroad company and Mitchell was platted. Although Firesteel residents laughed at the engineer's deductions at the time, two years later a flood completely inundated what remained of the town. However, 32 residents had moved meantime to the new town which had been named for the railroad's president, Alexander Mitchell.

The disastrous blizzard of 1880 left the town stranded for 16 weeks without a train and virtually no communication from the outside world. Church services continued regularly, however, in a hall used also for dances and parties. During services one Sunday, after the trains had been blocked for weeks, a man walked into the hall engrossed in reading a letter. Believing the long belated train had arrived with welcome mail, the congregation, one by one, slipped out until only one person, a woman, remained. No sermon could compete with a letter from home.

Unlike most frontier prairie towns, Mitchell's first residents included many college graduates. The reason was that the Government in 1880 opened a land office and employed only college-trained help. Some were married but among them were 15 eligible young bachelors. The group organized a dramatic club, and gave as its outstanding production "East Lynne." As stage properties were often lacking, audiences were implored to use their imagination. Until 1881 there was but one meeting place for all types of gatherings—a hall over a saloon on Main Street. Here public dances, private parties, and religious services were held, the seats consisting of plank boards supported by beer kegs. When prospects of the town's growth prompted the erection of permanent church buildings, the first was the Presbyterian Church, in 1881.

The city was chartered in 1883 and the prevailing mayor-council form of government was adopted. In 1892 the Corn Palace was started and the town developed without further fanfare.

POINTS OF INTEREST

1. CORN PALACE, Main St. and Sixth Ave. (*open weekdays, free; Corn Palace week, admission $1*), was conceived in 1892 to advertise the principal products of the locality. The Corn Palace each year attracts thousands of visitors from all parts of South Dakota and adjoining States.

There is a wide contrast between the frame building with its many turrets and towers that housed the first Corn Palace crowds in the

"Gay Nineties" and the spacious modern structure erected in 1921 at a cost of $300,000 with a capacity of 5,000.

Its exterior and interior are decorated with corn, 2 to 3 thousand bushels being used each year, and some 40 tons of other grains in bundle form. Flax, oats, millet, proso, and cane are all combined to picture a different theme each year. Designs are changed from time to time. One year, for example, in portraying local tradition, an interior panel showed an Indian chief beside his prairie tipi, buffalo meat roasting over the fire, while with misgivings he pointed toward the next panel, the sod shanty of a settler. Next came a house and barn of the nineties, followed by a large field with stacks of grain and finally a modern farmstead. Two large exterior panels, 14 x 35 feet, supplemented by smaller ones, depict other scenes. Ten separate shades of corn are used in imparting a lifelike appearance to the scenes, many of the colors having been developed for specific use near Mitchell. When unprecedented drought ruined crops in most parts of the State in 1936, boughs of evergreen trees from the Black Hills were employed as a substitute for the regular materials to aid in carrying out the scheme of the design.

Many nationally known bands have played in the Corn Palace, while among its visitors have been numerous prominent men, including Theodore Roosevelt, William J. Bryan, William H. Taft, and Franklin D. Roosevelt. Throughout the year the Corn Palace is used for educational and recreational events.

2. DAKOTA WESLEYAN UNIVERSITY, S. Sanborn at McCabe St., began in 1885 with the erection of Merrill Hall, which was destroyed 3 years later by a fire that took the lives of four students. Constructed of Sioux Falls granite, the present group of buildings is set in a picturesque 20-acre campus.

Noted for its extensive department of music Dakota Wesleyan's *a capella choir* of more than 50 trained voices tours the State and presents concerts each year. The institution is also noted for its dramatics, featured by the Prairie Players of 40 members.

3. TWO HACKBERRY TREES more than 50 years old stand on the corner of 4th Ave. and Rowley St. When mere twigs they were brought to Mitchell in a satchel and planted in the yard where they now stand. They are still growing, despite their age and the adverse weather conditions of recent years.

4. FARM MARKET, W. 4th Ave., is operated wholly by farm women. Every Wednesday and Saturday women offer for sale all

kinds of homebaked goods in addition to fresh farm produce and dressed poultry.

5. MUSEUM, 203 First Ave., W. (*open daily; free*), has an excellent collection of artifacts excavated from the Arikara Indian Village near Lake Mitchell, including a large pottery bowl and various implements of war. Sioux Indian trinkets, mounted birds and animals, and agricultural exhibits are displayed. The museum is sponsored by the Lions Club, and a curator is furnished by the Works Progress Administration.

TOUR 1—2.2 m.

N. from 6th Ave. on Main St.

6. LAKE MITCHELL, Main St. and Lakeshore Drive, was formed by damming Firesteel Creek and impounding the water in the creek bed. The city planned, financed and constructed the dam and spillway as a park improvement. It is popular in summer for fishing, boating and swimming.

L. from Main St. on Lakeshore Drive

7. In GRACELAND CEMETERY, L. of the Road, is the ISRAEL GREENE MONUMENT, a large, red stone marker bearing the coat of arms of the Greene family—Nathaniel Greene of Revolutionary War fame and Israel Greene who captured John Brown at Harpers' Ferry in 1859 while a lieutenant under Gen. Robert E. Lee. When the Civil War was over, Israel Greene came to Mitchell as a surveyor, living there the rest of his life.

8. An OUTDOOR AMPHITHEATRE is situated in a natural depression beside the lake on the west bank, and has a heavy green turf which is used in summer for city band concerts (*free*) and entertainments.

9. ARIKARA INDIAN VILLAGE SITE, marked by a large sign (R.) (*see Indians and Indian Life*), includes several acres of concentric rings, 10 to 20 feet in diameter, indicating where mud huts stood sometime prior to 1700. Pieces of broken pottery and flint scrapers are still found in remains of rubbish heaps on the grounds. A double defense trench forms the NW. boundary of the village.

POINTS OF INTEREST IN ENVIRONS

Rockport Hutterite Colony, 18 m. (*see Tour 5, Section a*).

PIERRE

(Map of Pierre and Vicniity in back pocket)

Railroad Station: Chicago & North Western R.R., Pierre Street and Pleasant Drive.

Bus Station: Red Ball, Pioneer, and Pierre-Winner lines, Union Bus Depot, US 14 and Capitol Ave. **Airport:** Walter J. Smith Airport, 3½ miles N. **Taxis:** Flat rate 50c for 1 or 4 passengers.

Traffic Regulations: Turns may be made either right or left at intersections. No U turns on Pierre Street. Drive through Statehouse grounds is one-way.

Accommodations: Three hotels and five tourist camps.

Tourist Information Service: Chamber of Commerce Bureau, lobby of St. Charles Hotel.

Theaters: Two motion picture houses.

Athletics: Hyde Park Stadium, Capitol Ave. opposite Capitol Lake. **Polo Field:** Near polo barns, N.W. at city limits. **Golf:** Country Club, 9-hole course half-mile N.E. of the Statehouse. Green fees. **Swimming:** Free pool, city park near St. Mary's Hospital. Indoor pool, Locke Hotel. **Riding:** Horses for hire at Polo Barns, N.W. at city limits, and at Tyler Ranch 3 m. E. and ¼ m. S. Rates, 50c per hour. **Tennis:** Public courts opposite Statehouse.

PIERRE, (pronounced "peer," 1,442 alt., 4,013 pop.), second smallest capital city in the Nation, is in the approximate geographical center of South Dakota and North America, and stands where the East-river farming section of the State merges with the West-river ranching country. At this natural and geographical "transitionary" point lies Pierre, neither eastern nor western. Here the West-River rancher with his typical broad-brimmed hat, dark shirt and high-heeled boots rubs elbows with the East-river farmer, the business man, and the Government official, giving a dual character to the town.

Pierre is spread out along the broad Missouri River, with rock and yucca-covered gumbo buttes bordering the town to the north and east. In the center of town on a plateau is the State Capitol, its dome dominating the landscape. Part of the town is on a rise of ground between the river bottoms and the buttes; the reason for Pierre being so spread out is the result of rivalry between early land promoters. Owners of land "on the hill," the section of town north of the railroad tracks, battled the owners "on the flat." Each sought to encourage expansion their way, but the town insisted on growing up between the two sections. Today the many-windowed Hyde Home stands lonesome guard on the northern fringe of the city, and pretentious homes of eastern capitalists are grouped at the extreme city limits to the east and south.

In spite of years of progress and development, Pierre remains a frontier town in many respects. Progress, with its backbone of brick and steel; has made substantial headway, but a walk through the business district, where modern brick stores have as neighbors squatty, false-front frame buildings, emphasizes the old-new compromise.

Pierre claims to be the only city on the Missouri River owning its entire stretch of waterfront, which it has converted into parks. The city also owns and operates its own light and power plant, natural gas business, water system, liquor store, auditorium, tourist camp, swimming pool, and a recreational park at Farm Island.

Although much of the city's revenue is furnished by State and Federal pay-rolls, the basic source of its prosperity is the livestock industry. A self-curing buffalo grass makes grazing profitable are, for the most part, in either of two groups: those who hold State or Federal positions, and those who have permanent homes and businesses. The first group is migratory, changing with each administration; the other consists of early settlers, their grown children, and business and professional men who have been attracted by the steady incomes. The social life is centered around the State and political balls. There are numerous social clubs and those for recreation such as country clubs, polo and riding clubs, and skeet shooting organizations.

The town received its name when J. D. and Anson Hilger of Bismarck consigned a shipment of lumber and household goods down the river in 1880 to "Pierre, on the east side of the river, opposite Ft. Pierre." At that time Pierre was simply a ferry landing for the bustling town of Fort Pierre across the river (*see Tour 4*). Upon the arrival of the Hilger barge, Napoleon Duchneau and two other ferrymen paid a social visit while the brothers had gone off seeking a likely-looking homestead claim. A three-gallon keg of whiskey was discovered among the boxes, and a jamboree was staged in the absence of the owners, after which the ravine was promptly called Whiskey Gulch. The incident in Whiskey Gulch, north of the present railroad bridge, typified the spirit of the early eighties, as whiskey and guns were staple articles of trade and figured in many land deals and purchases of food and clothing. Joseph Kirley, who with Duchneau ran the ferry, paved the way for the

first railroad by trading his squatter claim along the river to the Chicago & North Western railroad for a double-barreled shotgun. Before the first train arrived in 1880, the little town was recognized as a convenient stopping-off place when making the long stagecoach or ox-train trip to the Black Hills. And with the coming of the railroad, Pierre became the mecca for bull-whackers, soldiers, gamblers, prospectors, ranchers, settlers, and notorious outlaws. With persons of every description contributing to Pierre's prosperity in the early eighties, law and order battled with turmoil and confusion. A severe blizzard marooned the town from the world for five months, while pent-up emotions of outlaws found release in riotous plundering of limited supplies. Citizens formed the Pierre Vigilantes, rounded up the desperadoes, and sent them down the river.

In 1881-82 the town boomed as the surrounding country was settled and Pierre became the center of a large trading area as well as the terminus of the railroad. Nearly $1,000,000 were spent in one year as the rival land promoters fought tooth and nail for choice building lots, speculating as to where the railroad would build its bridge across the Missouri. Mostly unpainted and with protecting porch-effect roofs extending over board walks, Pierre was a thriving frontier town when incorporated in 1883.

After losing to Bismarck in 1883 for the Dakota Territorial capital, Pierre set out to be the State capital and won in 1889 when South Dakota was admitted to the Union. Once possessing the distinction, Pierre had to fight to keep it. A bitter struggle developed when Mitchell tried to wrest the seat of government from Pierre. The railroads serving the two towns got into the thick of the battle. Thousands jammed Pierre and Mitchell on free railroad passes; hotels and rooming houses were packed. When the smoke cleared away after the 1904 election Pierre settled down to a well earned rest, still the Capital City.

In 1907 the North Western railroad extended its line west to Rapid City. This, with the opening of the Sioux Indian lands west of the river, increased Pierre's business. It was not until 1927, however, that a highway bridge connected Pierre with the ranching country. Three years of drought 1934-36, while making inroads into the prosperity of most South Dakota cities, affected Pierre only slightly in comparison, the large government payrolls acting as a financial stabilizer.

POINTS OF INTEREST

1. The STATE CAPITOL, Capitol Ave. E. (*open weekdays 8 to 5; guide on first floor*) was begun in 1907 and occupied in 1910. It was constructed at a cost of $1,000,000 under the supervision of State. Engineer Samuel H. Lea. O. H. Olson **was the** architect. By 1931 the needs of the State demanded more office space, and an annex was added to the north side of the building at a cost of $250,000, doubling the office capacity.

Although the design suggests the Capitol at Washington with its central rotunda flanked by legislative wings, it is in no sense a copy of the older structure. The corridor of the first floor runs the entire length of the building, the walls of which are decorated with portraits of personages notable in the history of the State.

The lower portion of the building is constructed of sandstone; the walls above are of Bedford limestone. Native granite steps in front and door cases add trimming. A broad marble staircase leads to the main floor above which rises the 165 ft. dome. Around the walls of the rotunda are four allegorical paintings by Edward Simons, each with a feminine figure representing respectively the family, mining, agriculture, and the livestock industry.

The first suite of rooms on the south side of the west wing is for the use of the governor. A painting by Edwin H. Blashfield, called the "Spirit of the West" is in the main reception room.

At the head of the staircase leading to the legislative floor is a painting by Edward Simons representing the beginning of State commerce—a white man bargaining with an Indian for a pelt. In the wing to the west is the Senate Chamber, and to the east is the House Chamber.

The FREE TRAVELING LIBRARY is housed in the annex. The library furnishes books to readers and clubs in small towns and rural communities.

East of the Capitol is picturesque CAPITOL LAKE, resembling a large sunken pool in a vast, well-kept lawn. The lake, fed by warm artesian well water, is the home of numerous wild waterfowl that remain summer and winter. Bordering the western shore is an attractive rock garden, featured by three ponds, called the red, white, and blue ponds because of the three colors of water lilies, one color in each pond. A footpath of glistening white quartz, bordered by vari-shaped pieces of petrified wood, leads to the ponds in which trout, catfish, pickerel, pike, bullheads, and other kinds of fish are kept during the summer. Across the lake is the GOVERNOR'S RESIDENCE, a rambling white house built of native lumber, brick and stone with the aid of the Works Progress Administration in 1936.

2. MEMORIAL HALL, opposite the Statehouse on Capitol Ave. (*open weekdays 8 to 5; offices of State Historical Society on main floor*), is dedicated to South Dakota soldiers and sailors who lost their lives in the World War and houses the State Historical Society, Department of History, and State Museum. The cornerstone was laid in 1930 and the building was occupied in 1932.

Constructed of Hot Springs, S. Dak., sandstone, the building is stately and of classic design. Six large Ionic columns support the temple-like entrance; an elaborate frieze borders the top of the building, forming a sharp contrast to the pale sandstone walls. Windows are at the first story only, the second being served by skylights. Steps of Milbank granite lead to the entrance. The architects were Hugill and Blatherwick of Sioux Falls, S. Dak.

In the curve of the retaining wall is a large rock in which is visible the imprint of a human hand, believed to have been chiseled there with a sharp rock by an Indian.

The sandstone interior of Memorial Hall is carried out in the same classical manner as the exterior. A broken column, symbolic of the lives given in battle, stands with a girdle of four burning torches at the top of the first eight steps of the stairway to the second floor. In the background is a memorial window of cathedral glass, beneath which is a bronze tablet inscribed "In Flanders Fields." Each of the three side walls of the lobby has a carved stone slab bearing the symbols of the divisions with which South Dakota troops were identified.

In the Museum is the lead plate planted by the Verendrye expedition in 1743, claiming the land for France. It was found on a hill overlooking Fort Pierre in 1913 and represents the first authentic record of the presence of white men within the present confines of the State. (*See HISTORY.*)

Among the museum exhibits are sand crystals, collected in southwestern South Dakota, one of the two places in the world where they are found.

3. INDIAN MUSEUM, on the second floor of the Memorial Building, includes the Mary C. Collins and DeLorme W. Robinson

collections. The former shows Sitting Bull's relics—his sacred buffalo head, flutes, medicine bag, and peace pipe. Tomahawks with human hair streamers are displayed. Other exhibits include a gun collection, a World War display, mounted animals, a case of skulls of historical characters, and relics of early days in Dakota Territory.

4. HISTORICAL LIBRARY, in the right wing of Memorial Hall, has 7,500 volumes, in addition to many manuscripts and documents of historical importance. This library is a depository for official documents of the State and Federal Governments. The State Historical Society attempts to obtain everything in print pertaining to South Dakota, or written by present or former South Dakotans; and it is considered to be the best collection of such material in existence. Many of its possessions, especially pamphlets and records, are the originals.

5. HUGHES COUNTY COURTHOUSE, Capitol Ave. and Pierre St., is a modern, four-story building with brick walls faced with native granite boulders gathered from the hillsides near Pierre. It is trimmed with Hot Springs sandstone, the entrances carved by Joseph Auer. A stone slab from the first building marked "1883 Hughes County Courthouse," is built into the wall on the first floor.

6. FEDERAL BUILDING, cor. Capitol Ave. and Huron St., was built in 1906 of Bedford limestone and houses the post office on the main floor. The U. S. Land Office for South Dakota, Bureau of Public Roads and Federal Court occupy the second floor.

7. RIVERSIDE PARK, extending from the highway bridge to Belleview St., has a swimming pool (*open daily except Mon. in summer, and every evening; free*), municipal tourist camp and picnic grounds. In 1928 Mayor John Hipple obtained the first Federal permit of its kind—allowing the use of old automobile bodies to make dikes and keep the Missouri River's current from eating away the shoreline, reclaiming and enlarging the strip of parking along its banks.

8. THE THREE SISTERS, Missouri Ave. and Crow St., were originally three, now survived by two, towering cottonwoods in Riverside Park. They are believed to mark the spot where a ship loaded with bullion sank in the 1860's. The legend connected with them has several times caused excavations and shaft drilling for

the lost gold. The story is that a ship carrying gold from the mines in Montana came down the Missouri River with its precious cargo years before settlement was begun on the site of Pierre. The ship sank in the treacherous river near where three large trees stood close together. A search was made for the Three Sisters along the river bank, and these trees were believed to be the ones mentioned in the ship's dispatches. In 1922 a company was organized and a shaft sunk, but neither gold nor ship was found. The shaft, sunk in solid ground where the shifting river used to flow, can still be seen, covered with boards.

Pioneers recall having seen Indian bodies in these trees, in accordance with their custom of disposing of the dead high above ground.

10. The HYDE HOUSE, Grand Ave. at Eighth St., was built by Charles L. Hyde as a residence in 1890 with the hope that the town would soon grow north and west around it. However, it stands alone as an expensive sentinel of the boom days, its white cupola overlooking the river breaks. It was donated for an orphanage in 1936.

11. The EAKIN HOME, 1178 Erskine St. (*private*), was erected by an eastern capitalist in the eighties, and marks the extreme edge of Pierre to the east; but when it was built the town was expected to grow in that direction.

12. ST. MARY'S HOSPITAL, E. Dakota Ave., was founded in 1889, when five Benedictine Sisters with a capital of $50 arrived in Pierre with the intention of founding a school. Shortly after their arrival, Dr. D. W. Robinson persuaded them to found a hospital instead. The Sisters expended their little capital in furnishing one room of an abandoned hotel; and as their funds slowly increased, they furnished the remaining rooms, one after another. The original building, which adjoins the modern structure on the west, was thus slowly remodeled from a hotel to a hospital. It now serves as the nurses' home.

TOUR 1—4.8 m.

E. from Capitol Ave. on Lewis and Clark Road.

13. The PIERRE INDIAN SCHOOL (R), (*open; adm. free; liquor prohibited*) is a Federal institution with several large buildings, occupying 300 acres of land along the Missouri River. Here some 250 Indian boys and girls live and engage in agriculture, livestock raising, domestic science, music, and athletics, in addition to

their academic subjects. Music plays an important part in the school's curriculum, most interesting of all being the endeavor to perpetuate the old Indian songs and dances. Dormitories house the boys and girls who attend the school, some of whom remain the year around. The institution was secured for the city by Charles H. Burke of Pierre while Commissioner of Indian Affairs at Washington, and one of the buildings bears his name.

The students, for the most part, are young orphaned children or those coming from broken homes. Observation of the children about the campus reveals a striking variation in racial characteristics. Some of the youths are from homes of full-blood parents, some show partial Indian traits, while many, through intermarriage of their forebears with the whites, have lost every semblance of their Indian heritage, there being some children with blond or reddish hair.

Before reaching the campus proper the road passes a sunken garden (L) and recreation grounds. The gymnasium-auditorium is directly ahead as the road turns R. in a tour of the grounds. It is near the gymnasium that the bones of three Indians were unearthed in 1934 during road-building operations. Following the road west the last building in the group is an Episcopal chapel built by the Indian students. For a continued circle about the grounds, turn L. east of the chapel and continue, ultimately returning to the campus entrance. On the way are the power plant, dining room, machine shop, barns, and two dormitories. The largest dormitory, Morgan Hall, was destroyed by fire during the summer of 1936, resulting in a loss of nearly $100,000.

14. GRANITE BOULDERS (L), studding abruptly-rising hills, give an impression of utter wasteland, land unfit even for grazing. But these boulders are useful for building purposes and are the only ones of their kind found west of St. Cloud, Minn., a fact lending credence to the belief that a glacier transported them from that distant point to their present location.

R. from Lewis and Clark Road on Farm Island Road.

15. TYLER HORSE RANCH raises polo ponies. One of the Pierre polo teams which annually plays at Ft. Snelling, Minneapolis, and other cities, practices here.

16. The SITE OF OLD FORT SULLY, marked by a monument L. of road, is called Old Fort Sully to distinguish it from another of the same name, 30 miles north of Pierre, which replaced the

first one (*see Tour 4*). Old Fort Sully was built in 1863 amid the unrest caused by Indian disturbances during the Civil War. Named for Gen. Alfred Sully, the fort was never a garrison, but was merely headquarters for troops stationed in the vicinity. The structure was more or less temporary with none of the substantial buildings of its successor.

17. FARM ISLAND, a public city park in the Missouri River, is a heavily-timbered stretch of land 3 miles long, connected with the mainland by a dam. It is popular as a recreation point and for its picknicking facilities. So named because in the early days soldiers of Fort Pierre and fur traders used it for farming purposes, the island now has little resemblance to the sandy, brush-covered strip on which a party of the Lewis and Clark expedition hunted deer and elk in 1804. CCC boys, working with the U. S. Forestry Service, have constructed shelter cabins, lodges for Boy Scouts and Girl Scouts, a community building, roads, and still other buildings. There is a nursery for the growth of seedlings of more than a dozen varieties of trees that are transplanted in the Shelterbelt area.

The dam connecting the island with the mainland was built by CCC boys, who accomplished what many engineers thought impossible—the taming of the impetuous surging waters of the river. Thirty-five thousand cubic yards of earth and rock were required to dam this arm of the stream. When finished, it created a still body of water, named Hipple Lake, in honor of Mayor John Hipple of Pierre, who was an energetic force in promoting Farm Island improvements.

The island is a sanctuary for birds, and hunting is prohibited. Besides song-birds, many pheasants are finding this a refuge from the hunters' guns. There are numerous varieties of wild flowers on the island—among them gumbo lilies, wild roses, and morning glories. Visitors are forbidden to pick wild flowers or wild fruit—buffalo berries, grapes, chokecherries, and plums.

There are various routes on the island. Probably the most scenic of them is SHORELINE DRIVE, the first road (R) after reaching the island. This drive winds near the shore through a thickly wooded section composed mostly of cedar. On the way are several picnic spots (L).

By taking the first road L. after emerging from the thick timber on Shoreline Drive, a new BOY SCOUT CABIN is reached (L) and just beyond, on the same side of the road, is the CCC Camp, which houses more than 150 boys who have done most of the work in beautifying the island. In bearing to the right the road passes over a sandy course with picnic grounds and a new shelter cabin of native stone and logs from the Black Hills.

A GIRL SCOUT CABIN AND CAMP (R) is in front of the NURSERY GROUNDS of the Shelterbelt program. Here hundreds of trees comprising a dozen different varieties are grown through irrigation and later shipped to be transplanted along the Shelterbelt strip.

Beyond the Girl Scout Camp is the LEWIS AND CLARK MONUMENT, erected in memory of the hunting party's visit to the island in 1804.

Right from the monument is an OLD CABIN, built so long ago that no one in the vicinity knows when or why it was placed there; and L. is a new community building. The road follows Hipple Lake to the entrance.

RAPID CITY

(Map of Rapid City in back pocket)

Railroad Stations: C. & N. W., Rapid St. between 8th and 9th; C. M. St. P. & P., 7th and Omaha Sts.; R. C. B. H. & W., Rapid and 8th Sts. **Bus Stations:** Black Hills Transportation Co. Good connections with other bus lines and trains. Black Hills tours arranged. **Taxis:** Black Hills Transportation Co., 25c city, 5c charge additional passengers and baggage, or 10c per m. country; Yellow Cab, 25c per m., country charge 10c per m.

Traffic Regulations: Limited parking time restriction, main business area, no charge.

Accommodations: Three hotels, numerous apartment-hotels, boarding houses, tourist camps. Wide range of rates.

Information Service: Rapid City Chamber of Commerce, Harney Hotel.

Motion Picture Houses: Three first-class motion picture houses.

Swimming: Canyon Lake; Canyon Lake beach W. on St. Joe St. to Baken Park, turn L. and follow Canyon Lake road. **Golf:** Rapid City Country Club, SW. of Canyon Lake. **Tennis Courts:** City recreation center, E. Main St.

Rapid City (3,231 alt., 11,346 pop.) derives its name from Rapid Creek on which it is built. Situated in the foothills at the mouth of Rapid Canyon, where the river enters the broad expanse of prairie that extends east almost 200 miles to the Missouri River, Rapid City forms the link between the northern and southern hills of South Dakota's Black Hills.

The city is spread over a flat, lying in a natural gateway to the purple-hued mountains which rise to the west. Winding through the middle of town is the tortuous channel of Rapid Creek, and during the summer barefoot boys and hip-booted men line its banks just off Main Street. The streets, laid out with a pocket compass, are broad, and only one tall building breaks the even skyline. As the town expands, it is growing along the river up Rapid Canyon where the city has built an artificial lake and a large municipal park.

During the summer months Rapid City residents retreat into the mountains during the evenings and holidays to fish and rest. The tourist traffic swells the population in summer, and craft shops displaying native pottery, Indian curios and stone or mineral decorations have sprung up. During the heyday of ranching, saddle making was one of the most important industries in Rapid City, but a cement plant, lumber mill, packing plant, flour mill and creameries have become the leading industries.

That its centralized location and comparative accessibility would some day make this the distributing center of a great portion of the State west of the Missouri River was the vision of a group of disheartened prospectors had over a campfire on the outskirts of the present site of the town on February 23, 1876. Out of that conversation the town was born; for two days later four leaders of the little party, Sam Scott, John R. Brennen, John W. Allen, and James Carney, all of whom had been in nearby mining camps, realizing they were better suited for this work, began to lay out the new city.

Settlers immediately began to erect log houses and to consider how they could persuade business enterprises to locate there. Word reached the embryo city that a man from Bismarck was entering the Black Hills with a sawmill. A committee at once set out to meet him and induce him to set up his mill near Rapid City. Other men coming into the Hills with stocks of merchandise were persuaded to stop at Rapid City.

White settlement in this Indian territory would violate treaties signed by the Indians and the United States Government. So the latter declared all white persons in the Hills to be trespassers, ordered them to leave, and stationed guards on all trails to stop further immigration. The Indians, realizing that the white men were trying to usurp their last domain, began to use extreme measures as a right of self-preservation.

Still immigrants sifted through. Guards were placed on the trails from Sidney, Neb., Pierre, S. Dak., Cheyenne, Wyo., and Bismarck, N. Dak. The Indians lurked along the trails and the outskirts of the settlement to kill helpless travelers. By summer food and ammunition were getting scarce. Hundreds of discouraged settlers began to leave.

On August 23 Rapid City had 200 residents. The Indians were becoming bolder. The next day four white men were killed west of town. A freighter between Deadwood and Pierre stopped at Rapid City on the morning of the 25th. Citizens borrowed his team and wagon to get the bodies of the men killed the day before. They returned at noon with the bodies and found wagons loaded and lined up ready to start for Pierre with most of the population.

That afternoon a roll call was taken and only 19 men and one woman remained. The following morning the residents were notified by a traveler from Hill City of another death. The situation by this time was serious enough to cause another vote, to discuss whether or not the rest should follow the migration to Pierre. They voted to "stick it out" and work was immediately started on a blockhouse for protection. The new structure, 30 feet square and two stories high, was built at the present junction of Rapid and Fifth Sts. A well was dug and preparations were made for stubborn resistance.

The month that followed put the pioneers to an extreme test. Indians appeared every day, and none of the settlers dared leave even to hunt or fish. Guards were stationed day and night. Food and ammunition became extremely scarce. When hope was almost abandoned a small party arrived from Ft. Pierre with the news that the Government had withdrawn its blockade. Residents took new courage and attention was at once turned toward developing Rapid City.

The largest factor in that development was probably transportation. Stages from Ft. Pierre and Sidney, Neb., served the new town and gradually its favorable location brought results. At first dubbed the "Hay Camp" by the mining interests in the Hills, Rapid City carried this title for several years.

The first railroad to enter Rapid City was the Fremont, Elkhorn & Missouri River, from Gordon, Neb. July 4, 1886, was the day set for the first passenger train to arrive. As the train pulled into the station, a faked stagecoach hold-up was enacted in sight of the passengers and the throng that had congregated to see the first train come in. The holdup was a joke for the "bandits," but a serious episode for passengers on the stage. Dr. Pierce, driver of the stage, had previously arranged with nine other men to rob the passengers as he drove a four-horse team up to the depot just as the train pulled in. He had persuaded 10 or 12 unsuspecting young men who were generally well supplied with cash to ride with him on the stage to the depot. As the stage pulled up to the depot one "outlaw" grabbed the lead team and "buckled" it, so that further progress was impossible. The other "desperadoes" with six-shooters in their hands ordered the passengers out, lined them up, and took their cash, turning them all free after the job was completed. That afternoon and evening the former "desperadoes" were busy treating everybody, especially the innocent passengers.

The Government established a post office in Rapid City, April 18, 1877, and all mail for the Black Hills came through this office. Soon after this followed the establishment of the first newspaper, the first edition of which was published by Joseph and Alice Gossage Jan. 5, 1878, and called *The Black Hills Journal*. On Feb. 2, 1886, it was made a daily.

In 1907 Rapid City was the goal of two great railroad systems— the Chicago & North Western and the Chicago, Milwaukee, St. Paul & Pacific. In an effort to reach the Black Hills first, both companies started construction at the Missouri River and at Rapid City. The North Western's golden spike was driven near Philip, and the first train arrived from Ft. Pierre July 10, 1907. The Milwaukee drove its golden spike July 18, and the first train from Chicago reached Rapid City on July 20.

One of the enterprises that has kept the business men of Rapid City interested from an early day is the railroad up Rapid Canyon (*see Tour 15*). Some travelers have declared that it has more bridges, more curves, and more beautiful scenery for its 31.6 miles than a like distance on any other railroad in North America.

In 1904, after financial difficulties and reorganization, the road was completed to Mystic and the first train made the trip in 1906. In June 1907 a seven-inch cloudburst washed the track from the grade in most places and left only two out of 113 bridges strong enough to support an engine. The loss was too great for the company and it was turned over to receivership a second time. When the company reorganized again in 1909 the line was given its present name, the Rapid City, Black Hills & Western RR. When in 1920 the price of old iron reached an almost fabulous figure, many of the investors wished to sell the road as junk; but the suggestion aroused Rapid City residents who organized a company with local capital, took over the majority of the stock and bonds, and enabled the road to continue operation.

In 1922 Rapid City adopted the city manager form of government with nine commissioners. The city manager is the administrative and executive head of the city.

During President Coolidge's visit to the Black Hills in 1927, the high school building on Columbus St. was used by him and his staff as the SUMMER WHITE HOUSE OFFICE, the President driving back and forth each day from the Summer White House at the State Game Lodge (*see Tour 5*).

POINTS OF INTEREST

1. SOUTH DAKOTA SCHOOL OF MINES, State 79, E. St. Joe St., was established by law in 1885. During the earlier period of its history the institution was largely devoted to the teaching of mining and metallurgical engineering and the study of the mineral resources of western South Dakota. As the demand for training in engineering subjects developed, the curriculum of the School of Mines was gradually expanded. And although the original name, the South Dakota School of Mines, has been retained, the school has in reality become a college of engineering.

The geological situation of the School of Mines offers unexcelled advantages for the study of engineering. Teaching activities are not confined to the campus, but full use is made of the splendid field and laboratory facilities of the entire Black Hills. The rare minerals in the vicinity of Keystone, the cement plant and several quarries and lime kilns near Rapid City, the sugar plant at Belle Fourche, and various steam and hydroelectric plants are easily reached from the school.

2. SCHOOL OF MINES MUSEUM, Administration Building, first floor (R) (*guide during summer months; free*), has been an important feature of Rapid City for more than 45 years. The museum is not merely a collection of curiosities. There are relief maps, ores from other famous mining regions and minerals from many places. Fossilized skeletons found in South Dakota, particularly in the Big Badlands, collected, prepared, and mounted by members of the School of Mines, are among the most interesting and valuable features of the exhibit.

The paleontology exhibit contains in profusion fossilized remains of various types of life long since extinct, namely: The ancestral camel, rhinoceros, the saber-tooth tiger, three-toed horse, giant pigs, a deer no larger than a rabbit, a mother oreodon with unborn twins and many other fossils of animals that lived in the Badlands millions of years ago.

Several years ago some workmen while blasting rocks in a quarry near Rapid City uncovered in a line of cleavage in the rock the perfect imprint of a fish 10 inches long and this is on display in the museum.

3. ALEX JOHNSON HOTEL, cor. 6th and St. Joe Sts., is the tallest and most elaborately furnished privately-owned building in

the State. It was completed in 1928. This 11-story building of early English design is the first one to be seen on approaching the city. Indian pictures and decorations are displayed throughout. In the banquet hall hangs an oil painting of Alex Johnson by John Doctoroff, a Russian artist.

On the top floor is a roof garden, a display of Black Hills minerals and the studio of radio station KOBH. In the solarium at the top of the building sun baths through helio glass with ultra-violet rays are available. From this vantage point there is also an excellent view of the city, the distant Badlands and the immediate Black Hills.

4. HALLEY PARK, W. Blvd. at Main and St. Joe Sts., consists of a triangle of about three acres. American elm trees surround the entire park, with spruce forming the background of a rose arbor. There is also a series of rose beds arranged in formal designs, each containing 35 different varieties. Several varieties of unusual trees are scattered about the park. A central lily pond with numerous varieties of water plants is surrounded by the perennial garden with its 25 different types of long-lived plants.

At the extreme W. end is the OLDEST CABIN built in Rapid City, a squat, cozy-looking structure, built in 1876 near its present site. Beside the door is a stone with the inscription:

> I was built in the olden, golden days,
> When this was an unknown land;
> My timbers were hewn by a pioneer,
> With his rifle near at hand.
> I stand as a relic of "Seventy-Six,"
> Our nation's centennial year
> That all may see as they enter the Hills,
> The home of a pioneer.

5. A HORSE CAR, St. Joe St. and West Blvd., is a reminder of early-day transportation in Rapid City. It was the only one operated on the mile track, which for 20 years constituted the city's transportation system. Back and forth the car was dragged by one horse.

The street car was a source of enjoyment to cowboys when they came to town. A story is told of one cowboy who, desiring to celebrate and entertain his friends, chartered the car for the day for $10, driving the horse through the streets amid shouts and shots from his friends. By mid-afternoon the company manager stopped

ONE-HORSE STREET CAR

the hilarious party and offered to refund the money if the cowboy would give back the car.

Another incident, recorded in the Daily Journal of June 14, 1900, tells of the settlement of a strike between the company and the help. The story reads: "The company agrees to recognize the union but the old wages of 'six bits per day' shall stand and the help 'eats themselves'!" The track was torn up about 1907.

6. CITY MUSEUM, St. Joseph St. and West Blvd. (*open daily; free*), was built of uncut limestone with WPA aid in 1937. It houses the INDIAN COLLECTION of John A. Anderson who began collecting Indian material on the Rosebud Reservation in 1893. In the collection are 65 peace and ceremonial pipes, formerly owned by leading chiefs of the Sioux Nation, and beaded wearing-apparel, aprons, dresses, tobacco-pouches, chaps, vests, moccasins, belts, saddle blankets, papoose carriers, and a Masonic apron finished in 1914 after one and a half years in the making. A calf hide, once used as an Indian calendar, records the history of the tribe dating back to the early part of the 1700's. The years were recorded by winters and the most important event of each is illustrated.

7. "M" HILL, E. end of St. Joe St., bears a stone and cement letter "M" 112 feet high, 67 feet wide on the hillside. In 1911 the

students of the South Dakota School of Mines began building the letter with freshman labor on "M Day," annual homecoming event. It will be finished in 1942. Each fall freshmen are compelled to relay sand and gravel in 30 pound sacks up the steepest slope, then each boy is required to carry 15 gallons of water up the longest side, followed by a relay of 35 sacks of cement, while upper classmen urge them on.

TOUR 1—2 m.

W. from Quincy St. on Skyline Drive.

8. HANGMAN'S TREE, on Hangman's Hill, is the setting of a true tale of the early days of Rapid City. On June 21, 1887, the sheriff was notified that his services were required north of town. He called for volunteers and 10 men responded. After an absence of about two hours the posse returned with three strange men and five horses that bore the Sidney Stage Company's brand of "LV." There was no jail and while the sheriff was deliberating where to hold the men for investigation a crowd gathered. One of the witnesses heard the youngest but largest of the three remark: "If they had not caught us asleep, they would never have taken us." He talked continuously, while the older men said nothing. A witness identified the "LV" brand.

The prisoners were put in a granary and armed guards stationed outside. Shortly after the prisoners were lodged in the granary, the Deadwood stage arrived with the superintendent of the Crook City barn. He immediately identified the horses as the ones taken from their barn the night before. Considerable interest was manifested that night over the affair and around the post office spectators heard the phrase, "Whiskey drinks are free tonight, Stage Company's treat," passing from mouth to ear.

The next morning the attention of citizens was drawn to a tree on a high hill just west of town, where the bodies of three men were visible hanging limply from the limbs. A coroner's inquest was held that morning with about 50 men present, and the witness heard the testimony of the guards. "Hung at midnight by unknown parties," was the verdict signed by Roscoe Burleight, coroner. The original tree has long since disappeared, but one that stood close by it has been preserved in a casement of stone and cement to commemorate the first sentence meted out locally to criminals for so serious an offense as horse stealing.

HANGMAN'S HILL

The story is that during the night the three prisoners were placed on two horses with their hands tied and ropes dangling from their necks. The right arm of one and the left arm of the other of the two men that rode the one horse were tied together. In this state the horses were led up the hill to the big pine tree that had limbs extending far out in opposite directions, just high enough to let the horses and men pass under. A horse was led on either side and when the riders were just beneath the limbs the horses were stopped, the ropes thrown over the limbs, and made fast. Those details being attended to, the horses were led away and back down the hill, leaving the men to atone for their crime.

9. DINOSAUR PARK (*open*) has five life-sized prehistoric reptiles modeled in cement on the hillside. The reptiles are believed to have inhabited this region more than 40,000,000 years ago dur

ing the Mesozoic era. The idea of the park was conceived by Dr. C. C. O'Harra, late president of the State School of Mines and nationally known authority on geology and paleontology. Sponsored by Rapid City, the park was built with Works Progress Administration aid. The monstrous prehistoric creatures represented are the Triceratops, Tyrannosaurus rex, Brontosaurus, Stegosaurus and Trachodon. E. A. Sullivan, Rapid City Attorney and sculptor, was the designer; Dr. Barnum Brown, curator of the American Museum of Natural History, served as consultant. Fossils of these reptiles have been found in the Black Hills and Badlands regions of South Dakota; footprints of the Tyrannosaurus rex were found two miles N. of the park on the same range of hills and removed to Dinosaur Park.

At the right are the lumbering TRICERATOPS and TYRANNOSAURUS REX waging combat. The Triceratops, with features resembling the present-day rhinocerous and elephant, was a land reptile with heavy scales on its back; as reproduced it is 27 ft. long and 11 ft. high, with 40-in. horns. A head of this reptile was found in the Badlands 40 miles SE., and is on exhibit at the School of Mines Museum. The Tyrannosaurus rex, resembling a kangaroo, was the only carnivorous reptile of the group; swift-moving on its large hind legs, it probably roared through the swamps in pursuit of small animals. It had from 64 to 70 teeth, some of them six inches long. The figure has been reproduced 35 ft. long and 16 ft. high with a head 41 in. long. The BRONTOSAURUS, center, was the largest of prehistoric reptiles, and this reproduction is larger than any previous. However, there is no exaggeration, since it is reproduced exactly to the measurements of fossils in the American Museum of Natural History. This amphibian lived in the water, weighed about 15 tons, had a 2-ounce brain and a smooth skin. It was a peaceful reptile and was preyed upon by smaller animals. As reproduced it is 80 ft. long and 28 ft. high, and can be seen for 35 miles. The STEGOSAURUS (L) was a smaller reptile with large dermal plates protruding from its back, and from four to eight horns on its tail for protection. Comparatively little is known about this peculiar looking reptile which has been reproduced 11 ft. long and 7 ft. high. The TRACHODON, known as the "Duck Bill," had some features of both a duck and a kangaroo. It was a herbivorous reptile with web feet and a large bill; the reproduction is 17 ft. high and 33 ft. long.

SIOUX FALLS

(Map of Sioux Falls in back pocket)

Railroad Stations: Chicago, St. Paul, Minneapolis & Omaha Ry., 421 E. 8th St.; Great Northern Ry., 519 E. 8th St.; Chicago, Rock Island & Pacific Ry., 201 E. 10th St.; Illinois Central Ry., 304 E. 8th St.; Chicago, Milwaukee, St. Paul & Pacific Ry., 5th St. and Phillips Ave.

Bus Stations: Interstate Bus Co. operating: Interstate Transit Co., Jack Rabbit Lines, Southwestern Stages, Haley Transit Co., Ben's Bus Lines, Springfield-Sioux Falls Lines, S. Main Ave. and 11th St.; Palace City Lines directly across from Main Station. **Airport:** New airport established N. of city in 1937. **Taxis:** Fares—Minimum 25c for 15 blocks, 5c additional for every 5 blocks. **City Bus Lines:** The Sioux Transit Co.; Fares: single 10c, 4 for 25c.

Traffic Regulations: Speed limit 20 m. p. h., except as indicated by signs. On all intersections with stop and go signs, left inside turn used.

Parking Lots: Free parking places: Foot of 9th St. ½ block E. of Phillips Ave.; and N. W. corner of 7th St. and Dakota Ave.

Accommodations: Several hotels; tourist camps.

Information Service: Sioux Falls Chamber of Commerce, 131 S. Phillips Ave.

Theaters and Motion Picture Houses: Civic Theater in season at YMCA and Coliseum. Special shows, opera companies, local productions, occasional road shows at Coliseum. Six motion picture houses.

Athletics: Sioux Falls College; Augustana College; E. Side Ball Park; W. Side Ball Park. **Swimming:** Free Municipal Pools: Drake Springs, Covell Lake, Sherman Park. Pools for small children: McKennan Park, E. Side Park. **Golf:** Minnehaha Country Club, 18 holes, by invitation. Elmwood Park Golf Course, municipal, 18 holes, 50c. **Riding:** Three riding academies: West Sioux Falls, East Side and South Side.

Street Order and Numbering: Avenues N. and S., Streets E. and W.; Phillips Ave. is the dividing line between E. and W. for numbering and 9th St. for N. and S. Phillips Ave. and Main Ave. are the principal shopping districts.

Annual Events: Flower Show in June; Made in South Dakota Show, spring.

Sioux Falls (1,422 alt., 33,644 pop.), named for the falls of the Big Sioux River, is the largest city in South Dakota and the most important industrial and distributing center in the State.

The natural beauty of the site upon which Sioux Falls is built contrasts with the rather monotonous undulating plains of the surrounding country. The river often designated by early-day chroni-

clers as "The Thick-Wooded River" but called "Wakpa-Ipaktan,"
the winding river, by the Sioux Indians, meanders in the form of a
gigantic S through the center of the city. The business section follows the river flats from which the residential districts rise up the
gradual slopes to the level of the surrounding plains. On the steep
hill to the north is the State Penitentiary, its sturdy red and white
stone walls dominating the landscape except for the twin spires of
St. Joseph's Cathedral which loom infinitely graceful against the
sky to the west. Although a dam built for power purposes has
marred the original beauty of the falls, in springtime the swollen
river tumbles and roars over a series of cascades. The upheaval of
red quartzite in the rock-banked river is picturesque, for the stone
has worn smooth and taken on orange, pink and purple hues to
contrast with the blue-green river and its white foam.

The unusual coloring of the quartzite gives the town an individuality, for practically the whole of the city is underlaid by great
deposits of this durable building material which outcrops in many
places within the city limits; a number of business buildings, government edifices, churches, schools and residences are constructed
of this stone.

Sioux Falls resembles a century-old Eastern city more than one
of Western flavor so commonly associated with South Dakota—the
great trees that shade residential streets, the stately colleges, the
numerous churches, the well-kept parks, and the attractive lawns
and gardens.

The fertility of the surrounding prairie is the main reason for
the existence and rapid growth of Sioux Falls. Products of the soil
are manufactured and livestock processed; in turn the city has become a trading center for a large area and a distributing point.
Trucks and freight trains make a steady trek to huge warehouses,
stockyards and manufacturing concerns. This commerce is the life
of the town, and Sioux Falls is called the clearing house of a
prairie State.

The history of the white man in this region begins when Jean
Nicollet was sent by the Government of Canada in 1839 to treat
with several tribes of Indians. He published a sketch of his travels
in the Northwest, wherein he gave a description of the falls of the
Big Sioux River. A copy of this sketch found its way into the
hands of Dr. George M. Staples of Dubuque, Iowa, who was so
impressed by the natural advantages of the location that in 1865
he organized the Western Town Company of Dubuque, which the

same year sent a party to take up land near the falls for a town site. They followed the east bank of the river from Sioux City and took undisturbed possession of the location. A legend that a band of Indians forced the white men to retrace their steps just as they came to the point on Penitentiary Hill where the falls are visible has been proved erroneous.

Speculation in lands and town sites was at high pitch and in the winter of 1856-7 the Dakota Land Company was chartered by an act of the Legislature of Minnesota Territory. The same act established the city of Sioux Falls. Representatives of this company also occupied land in the vicinity of the falls, and erected a log house, naming their settlement Sioux Falls City.

The population of Sioux Falls numbered at that time five persons, and although they were representatives of rival companies, they lived together in peace and harmony, fearing only their common enemy, the Sioux. They were not troubled, however, until late in July, when the Indians threatened the extermination of all the settlements on the Big Sioux River. The new settlers discreetly withdrew, leaving the Sioux Valley once more deserted by white men, but not for long.

On August 27, 1857, a party of men sent by the Western Town Company arrived in Sioux Falls after a ten days' trip from Sioux City. They brought by ox-team machinery for a sawmill and a large stock of provisions. The sawmill was built, and also a stone house and a store. Several of the party then went back to Sioux City, leaving only six men in the settlement until the middle of October, when the Dakota Land Company sent seven men to look after their interests in the settlement.

The settlers passed a fairly comfortable winter in three new dwelling houses. During the spring of 1858 a number of other settlers came, some taking land in the upper part of the Sioux Valley, among them the first white woman who came to the Territory to settle, a Mrs. Goodwin, who came early in May with her husband.

In 1858 hostile Indians found the thirty-five settlers well fortified and left without molesting them. The white men did not know, however, that the enemy had gone, and remained close within their sod fort until they almost starved to death.

The initiative and the determination of the settlers is well shown by the two outstanding happenings of the year 1858. First, there was the acquisition of an old Smith printing press from St. Paul,

Minn., a veteran machine that had seen long service and had already a colorful past of perilous travels through the wilderness, having come from Dubuque, Iowa, to Lancaster, Wis., before being hauled to St. Paul. On July 2, 1859, *The Democrat,* the first Sioux Falls newspaper, appeared. Secondly, there were the proceedings that took place in September 1858, when the 30 or 40 persons who made up the population held in a most original manner an election to select members of a Territorial Legislature. The situation of the settlers was a peculiar one, with the admission of Minnesota as a State, since that part of the present Dakotas lying east of the Missouri and the White River had no legal name or existence. On the morning of the election, the whole population divided into parties of three or four, appointed each other judges and clerks of election and then started out with their teams in whatever direction pleased their fancy. Every few miles they rested their horses and established an election precinct on that spot. With all the dignity that the occasion deserved, the members of the party cast their votes, and being determined to succeed in their high ambition to impress the Federal authorities with their numbers, they thought it only fair to cast also the votes of all their relatives and friends, being convinced that these absent ones, if they knew of the high purpose of the actual voters, would without doubt be favorable to the plan. The total balloting reached the hundreds; and soon afterward the Legislature convened and a Governor and a speaker were chosen.

In April 1862, Company A., Dakota Cavalry, was organized and a detachment stationed at the Falls. In August an Indian uprising occurred. On the 25th Judge J. B. Amidon and his son were killed about a mile north of Sioux Falls while making hay. A party of Indians appeared on the bluffs northwest of the falls the next day but did not attack.

The settlers were alarmed and when two days later some messengers brought news of massacres on the frontier in Minnesota, and also orders from the Governor for the soldiers to proceed to Yankton and bring the settlers with them, the village was abandoned. The Indians then destroyed everything, setting fire to the buildings and throwing the old Smith press into the river. They carried the type away with them, however, and used the bits of metal for making inlaid decorations on the pipes carved from the celebrated pipestone, sung by Longfellow. Pieces of the old press were retrieved years later and are now in the Pettigrew Museum. A monument on the Sioux Falls College Campus marks the still visible ruts of the old trail that the fugitives followed to Yankton.

For nearly three years the Sioux Valley remained almost deserted. On May 1, 1865, a military post, Fort Dakota, was established in rambling log and stone barracks built on what is now Phillips Ave., between Seventh and Eighth Streets, and occupied by a company of soldiers on a military reservation five miles square, including the present site of the city. The sutler's store at the fort was the forerunner of the mercantile establishments of Sioux Falls.

Gradually the settlers returned, newcomers from the East joined them, and the town was established. In 1868 Minnehaha County was reorganized and the next year the hamlet of Sioux Falls had again reached a population equal to that of eleven years before.

In 1870 the military reservation was vacated and the land preempted by settlers and for the next three years the development of the valley stimulated the growth of the town, until in the fall of 1873 a census showed 593 inhabitants.

A scourge of grasshoppers the following year proved a calamity of such proportions that many people left the country and it took until 1876 for the struggling little town to regain 600 inhabitants.

In 1868 the first postmaster was appointed, and the office was kept in barracks, back rooms, stores, and like places, until in 1884 it was given permanent quarters. The city was the first in the Territory to have free carrier delivery.

In 1871 the first steps were taken towards the organization of a church. The first public school was taught in 1873 and a year later the first school building was erected, one teacher being sufficient. Fifteen years after the first venture, a second newspaper was established in Sioux Falls and from that time the city was never without one.

A grist mill built in 1873 proved to be the first successful attempt to use the power of the falls. The first shipment of stone took place in 1878 when the first railroad came in, and in 1881 the village trustees had lampposts erected for street lighting by kerosene.

The rigor of the climate added to the hardships of the pioneers, the winter of 1880-81 being the most noted for its severity. Snow fell in October and did not disappear until late the following spring. Railroads ceased operating; mail came only at rare intervals by sled; and corn, wheat, hay, and railroad ties were used for fuel. High water the following spring destroyed many buildings.

Because the laws governing divorce required only a short stay in the State to establish residence, Sioux Falls in the late 1890's and the first decade of the new century shone with the doubtful glory that has since been transferred to Reno, Nev. During that period Bob Fitzsimmons' wife came to seek a divorce from the heavyweight champion, who was deeply in love with her. He pleaded his case so insistently that she relented. Elated, Bob set out to celebrate, not at saloons, but at a blacksmith shop where he forged horseshoes and distributed them among the crowd of admirers gathered around him. The floor of the old shop was worn and the supporting timbers rotten. Without warning the floor gave way and the entire group, together with the anvil and forge of live coals, crashed through to the basement. One boy was painfully burned, but no one else was hurt. The child was the son of a poor man and the next day Bob staged a benefit performance at a theater. A large crowd swelled the receipts; Bob gave the boy $250 and the rest of the money to the Children's Home.

With the disappearance of frontier ways, Sioux Falls began early to be satisfactorily governed and policed. The advancement of the city has never been of the spasmodic variety that has characterized so many Western communities. Since 1876 the development has been continuous, keeping pace with that of the rich farm land of the surrounding region.

POINTS OF INTEREST

1. CITY HALL, 9th St. and Dakota Ave., a modern building, designed by Harold Spitznagel, Sioux Falls architect, was opened in 1937. For more than a quarter-century Sioux Falls' officials occupied a wooden, barrack-like structure. In 1934 the old building was torn down and replaced by this modern three-story structure. The exterior is constructed of buff-colored brick with limestone copings, limestone and black aluminum spandrels, carved plaques and rainbow granite trim. The interior is finished in gray Kentucky marble. Palmer Eide, Sioux Falls artist, designed the carved ornaments on the exterior walls, and Edwin Boyd Johnson, Chicago, painted the three symbolic panels in the City Commissioners' room.

2. The CARNEGIE FREE PUBLIC LIBRARY, 10th St. and Dakota Ave. (*open weekdays 10-9; Sun. 2-6*), is constructed of Sioux Falls quartzite. Begun with 100 volumes by the Ladies Club in 1879, the library now contains about 37,000 volumes, including the J. W. Tuthill collection of history and biography, the Bishop O'Gorman collection of Catholic books, among them several first editions, and the Glidden collection of books of art. The oil

paintings of Frank Hutchins and a comprehensive collection of government pamphlets are among the exhibits.

3. MASONIC LIBRARY, 415 S. Main Ave., (*open 8:30—4 daily, except Sat. and Sun.*), was begun in 1924 by George Pettigrew, grand secretary of the State Masonic organizaiton. The library lists between 25,000 and 30,000 volumes including a chronological record of the proceedings of the Masonic Lodges in all the States of the Union. At the west end is a small museum, one large show case being filled with trophies from various Masonic group meetings. One feature is a stained glass window which was in the stair room at the Columbia Exposition in Chicago. A reproduction of King Solomon's temple, delicately carved, with decorative beads worked out in Mosaic pattern is also in the library museum.

4. The MANCHESTER BISCUIT COMPANY, 205 E. 6th St. (*open weekdays 10 to 3, adm. free*), is the largest factory in Sioux Falls and employs 400 people. Intricate machines transform endless belts of dough into varied assortments of appetizing crackers, cookies and wafers. L. D. Manchester started with a one-man establishment and delivered his products on a bicycle. Organized in 1900, the Manchester Biscuit Company grew rapidly and in 1915 the present six-story building of Sioux Falls granite was completed. Since then branches have been established in many large cities of the Middle West.

5. WASHINGTON HIGH SCHOOL, between Main and Dakota Aves., and 11th and 12th Sts., known as the "million dollar high school," was constructed of native pink quartzite stone, with the north wing trim and column portico of a black quartzite so rare that it has been occasionally dismantled and exhibited at expositions. The gymnasium has a seating capacity of 6,000 persons.

6. The COLISEUM and ANNEX, N. Main Ave. and 5th St. a brick building of simple neo-classic architecture, provides the city with an auditorium a block long, a half-block wide and two stories high. the seating capacity of the Coliseum proper is about 7,000. A large variety of entertainments is included in the amusement program including road shows, opera companies, a flower show, automobile shows, the Made in South Dakota Exposition, recitals, athletic events and college activities.

7. PETTIGREW MUSEUM, N. Duluth and 8th St. (*Adm. free; weekdays 10:30—12; 1:30—5; Wed. 7—9 p. m.; Sun. 2—4 p. m.*) was formerly the private residence of U. S. Senator R. F.

Pettigrew and was given to the city in 1928. Constructed of native stone it is designed in Romanesque style. Speciments of polished petrified wood form part of the wall near the north entrance. The museum contains a collection of Indian relics, among them a Sioux Council tipi made from the hides of seven buffalo, set up with poles exactly as the squaws erected similar shelters long ago. Wampum and tomahawks, bead work, war bonnets and peace pipes fill many glass cases. There is also on display one of the famous "ghost shirts" worn in the Battle of Wounded Knee. The shirt was believed to be impervious to the white men's bullets; but the lead slugs crashed through the fabric notwithstanding.

Among the numerous other exhibits are guns, knives, and the brutal hand-forged manacles used in early days. A large collection of mounted birds, snakes, and animals found in South Dakota is worthy of note.

8. MINNEHAHA COUNTY COURTHOUSE, Main Ave. and 6th St., was built in 1890 of Sioux Falls quartzite and is a good example of the Richardson Romanesque style of architecture. The square tower is especially distinctive and gives the building a medieval aspect that contrasts pleasingly with the modern business buildings of the downtown district. Murals in the building were painted in 1916 by O. G. Running, a local artist. The scenes depicted are early historical views of Sioux Falls, and incidents in the life of the pioneers.

9. ALL SAINTS' SCHOOL (Episcopal), Philips and Dakota Ave., is a resident and day school for girls. The buildings, constructed of native stone, are surrounded by shade trees.

10. CALVARY CATHEDRAL (Episcopal), cor. Main Ave. and 13th St., was completed in 1889 as a memorial to Charlotte Augusta Astor whose husband, John Jacob Astor, donated funds for its construction. This handsome building of native stone, French Gothic in design, stands in contrast to the first church in Minnehaha County, the Calvary Episcopal Church erected in 1872 at the northwest corner of Main Ave. and 9th St., and since then dismantled.

A cross made of jasper similar to that used in Conrad's Glorious Choir in Canterbury Cathedral, England, was placed upon the altar of Calvary Cathedral by Bishop William Hare, known throughout the State as the "Apostle to the Sioux" and the founder of the Episcopal Church in South Dakota.

Another cross, imbedded in the floor a few feet in front of the altar, is formed of about 15 small stones taken from the foundation of St. Augustine Abbey, the oldest church in Britain. Every king, queen, and Archbishop of England, from the time of William the Conqueror to George VI, has stepped on or over the stones from which the fragments forming the small cross were taken.

11. ST. JOSEPH CATHEDRAL, (Catholic), Duluth Ave. and 5th St., was opened Dec. 8, 1918. The building is one of the most imposing edifices in the State. Of modified Romanesque and French Renaissance styles of architecture, it is designed with an Italian Basilican plan. The two spires are original with the architect, Masquerry. The nave is shorter and wider than in early cathedrals, bringing a large congregation within hearing distance of the pulpit. Huge transept arches, of Renaissance design, rising to a height of 50 feet, are among the most impressive features of the interior. The exterior of the building is entirely of white Bedford Limestone.

12. TERRACE PARK, at Covell Lake near 1st St. and Menlo Ave., has 52 acres of woodland and is the home of the locally well known Japanese gardens. Covell Lake which provides swimming facilities, is a small, natural, spring-fed lake, occupying a depression in the granite bed. The Community House in the park was originally a private residence. The park is noted for its distinctive quartzite terraces. There are facilities for tennis, swimming, and other sports; benches and tables are provided for picnics.

13. TOWER PARK, N. Main Ave. and McClellan St., derives its name from the large water tower, in the highlands of the city and affords a panoramic view of Sioux Falls, especially to the S. and E.

14. STATE PENITENTIARY, Main Ave. and Walnut St. on US 77 (*open by permission only*), is a somber fortress built of red Sioux Falls quartzite with white stone trim. The Penitentiary was established in 1881, most of the improvements and additions being erected by the prisoners, even to the huge wall that has made escape almost impossible. At intervals along the wall are towers in which guards keep constant watch, with a miniature arsenal beside them.

There is no death penalty in South Dakota and no death house in the penitentiary. The only punishment dealt to unruly prisoners is confinement in solitary cells.

Behind the red granite walls a twine plant works a day and night shift, employing about 120 men during the day and 100 at night. The twine is sold to the farmers of this State and others. Manila rope is also produced and the license plate plant manufactures all automobile, truck and compensation plates used in South Dakota. A farm of about 1,200 acres is worked in connection with the institution. The buildings are modern and much of the stock, notably the cattle, is thoroughbred.

Despite the formidable barriers, there have been two serious breaks in the history of the prison. On Aug. 17, 1922, three convicts escaped. One was killed and the others recaptured. In March 1936 two convicts, aided by an outsider, kidnaped the warden, Eugene Reiley, and won an hour's liberty. In the fight that ensued, the warden, a convict, and a civilian were killed and three persons were wounded.

15. MORRELL PACKING PLANT, Weber Ave. and Rice St. (*free tours, one hour, weekdays 10 and 1:30*), from a small beginning in 1909, has developed into a great meat packing plant with a daily capacity of 5,000 hogs and 500 cattle. As many as 1,700 men and women are employed at the peak. Engines burning natural gas piped from far-away Texas, furnish power for the refrigerators, and for the chilling of the storage rooms where thousands of carcasses of prime beef hang in orderly rows.

16. SEENEY ISLAND AND SIOUX FALLS, in the River S. W. of the John Morrell & Company plant, is a spot where the falls of the Big Sioux River can be seen, their beauty now somewhat marred by blasting that was neccessary in the construction of the power dam. During high water the violent, tumultuous rapids foam and roar over the many bold crags of quartzite.

17. McKENNAN HOSPITAL, 21st St. E. and S. 7th Ave., was established in 1912 and has a capacity of 95 beds and 18 bassinets. The institution, which is under the direction of the Presentation Sisters, has a nursing school with an average enrollment of 50 students.

18. McKENNAN PARK, 21 St. bet. 2nd and 4th Aves., includes a 20-acre tract of which seven acres are wooded. It is provided with tennis courts, and has a swimming pool for children. The band shell provides facilities for regular concerts, and a greenhouse and rock garden enhance the beauty of the park.

19. SIOUX VALLEY HOSPITAL, 1123 Euclid Ave., while easy to reach from the central section of the city, is removed from the

noise of heavy traffic. The Sioux Valley Association, organized in 1894, erected this modern building at a cost of $400,000 in 1930. There are 100 beds and 25 bassinets. A nursing school is maintained with an average enrollment of 70 student nurses.

20. SIOUX FALLS COLLEGE, 22nd St. and Prairie Ave., has buildings of Sioux Falls quartzite, and is of modified Gothic design. This college is the successor of the first Baptist school in South Dakota, which was established in 1883. Professional and two-year normal courses are offered, as well as extra-curricular activities.

21. AUGUSTANA COLLEGE, at extreme S. end of Prairie Ave., with buildings of Tudor Gothic, is the largest denominational school in South Dakota, with all regular courses and extra-curricular activities offered. It moved four times before becoming permanently located in Sioux Falls. While the prime purpose of the institution was to provide opportunity for imparting Lutheran teachings and to perpetuate the Norse language, non-Lutheran students are welcomed. In addition to the regular academic course, there is a School of Music that offers a four-year course leading to the degree of Bachelor of Music. The Augustana College Choir and the Augustana Symphony Orchestra have attained wide recognition.

22. THE SOUTH DAKOTA SCHOOL FOR THE DEAF, end of 8th St. E., was founded in 1880 in a frame structure. In 1883 substantial stone buildings of Tudor Gothic design, were erected.

The institution is maintained by the State for the purpose of providing individual instruction and special training for the deaf. In addition to intensive instruction and standard school courses, the girls are taught domestic science and needlecraft, and the boys dairying, manual training, and printing. Athletics are encouraged and the boys basketball teams compete with the high schools in the district. The boys are so trained that they notice simple signals and interchange gestures quickly. Spectators are unaware of the fact that the players are in any way handicapped.

23. The MINNEHAHA COUNTRY CLUB, W. 22nd St., and Harvard Ave., has an improved 18-hole golf course, the hazards of which test the ability of the most seasoned player. The Sioux River crosses the fairways 10 times, and numerous trees on the first nine holes and the hilly nature of the second nine add to the river hazard. A spacious clubhouse, containing all the necessary facili-

ties for recreation, and a large picnic ground are also features of the Club.

24. SHERMAN PARK AND MOUNDS, W. from 18th St. and Minnesota Ave., comprise 205 acres of tree-covered land, set aside in 1900 and developed as a park for picnics and recreation. It is also a game preserve. There are tourist cabins along the banks of the Sioux River, which winds through the park. The water, retained by a low dam, forms a pleasant swimming pool; bathhouses are provided and driveways are built into the Country Club golf course. There remain five well-preserved mounds along the crest of the ridge E. of the end of the old streetcar line. Other mounds are on a hill S. and E. of 26th St., but since this land has been plowed for many years it is impossible to identify the location of more than four of them.

In 1911 several mounds with human skeletons, the bones of a pony and a dog, and many small trinkets—pottery, rings from a bridle, and horseshoes bearing the letters "US"—were unearthed. The nature of the relics indicates that the burial was by the Sioux Indians and at a comparatively recent date. Artifacts unearthed point to a much earlier age, when the original mound builders existed.

The Indian village was on the Country Club golf course. The settlement, situated near the river and not far from the burial ground, covered about 10 acres. Fireplaces and rock circles which probably served as anchorage for tipis have been found on the village site. Excavation has also revealed a number of stone implements with fragments of pottery and crushed buffalo bones. All were found a foot or more below the surface, an indication of their antiquity.

25. ELMWOOD PARK, N. Harvard Ave. at Walnut St. in W. Sioux Falls, is the home of the local Izaak Walton League, with a fish and bait-casting pool, frequently used and interesting to visit. There are also an 18-hole golf course, a baseball diamond, and tourist cabins.

POINTS OF INTEREST IN ENVIRONS

Wall Lake, recreation center, 12 m., Brandon Mounds, Indian burial ground, picturesque scenery, 19 m. (*see Tour 5A.*); Sioux Valley Ski Slide, scene of annual ski jumping meets, 24 m. (*see Tour 7*); the Dells, beautiful scenery and unique formation 20 m. (*see Tour 9*).

WATERTOWN

Railroad Stations: Chicago and North Western R.R., 122 N. Maple St.; Rock Island and Minneapolis and St. Louis R.R., 168 N. Broadway; Great Northern R.R., SW. edge of city. **Bus Station:** Greyhound Lines, Jackrabbit and Swanson Lines, 22 N. Maple St. **Airport:** Hanford Airlines, Municipal airport, 3 m. from city on Kampeska Road. **Taxis:** 25c within city limits, 5c per extra person. **City Bus Lines:** Regular 30 minute schedule all parts of city, fare 10c.

Traffic Regulations: Inside left turns at intersections. 90 minute parking limit.

Accommodations: Three first-class hotels; several tourist cabin camps. Municipal tourist park N. on State 20 from Kemp Ave.

Tourist Information Service: Chamber of Commerce, Midland Nat'l. Life Insurance Building, Kemp Ave. and Broadway.

Theaters and Motion Picture Houses: One theater, local productions and occasional road shows; three motion picture houses.

Athletics: City ball park, Lake Kampeska; baseball field, S. Broadway and Eighth Ave. W.; diamond ball field, Sixth St. and Fourth Ave. SE. **Swimming:** Lake Kampeska, 3 m. west. **Tennis:** Kemp Ave. and 12th St.; S. Broadway between Fourth and Fifth Aves. S.W. **Golf:** Municipal Golf Course, Lake Kampeska, 3 m. W., 9 holes, reasonable greens fees; Watertown Country Club, 18 holes, Lake Kampeska, admission by invitation.

Annual Events: Roaring Gulch, June; Carn Aqua, late July or August; Play Day, September.

Watertown (1,750 alt., 10,246 pop.) is an agricultural and recreational center on the Big Sioux River near Lake Kampeska. The sandy loam of the Coteau Des Prairie (hills of the prairie) makes the area surrounding Watertown an intensive farming region, especially for potato growing. With a large lake so close at hand, the town draws a heavy trade from vacationists during summer and in the fall is headquarters for pheasant and duck hunters from adjoining States.

Watertown residents spend most of their spare time at Lake Kampeska, and a varied program of sports—ice boating, skating, fishing, swimming, sailing and golfing—goes on during the year.

Unlike most mid-western towns, Watertown has no long Main Street, but a concentrated business section. Almost treeless when founded, it has 300 shaded residential blocks.

When J. C. B. Harris of Yankton arrived at Lake Kampeska in 1873, he found mile after mile of rolling prairie with the lake alone breaking the monotonous landscape. The lake had always been a landmark for the Indians who computed distances from its shores; its clear waters were sought by the red men, since few springs were to be found in the region. After returning to Yankton, Harris obtained homestead rights to land about a mile east of the lake's outlet. In 1874 James P. Werner settled at the outlet, and homestead colonies were chartered along the lake. Colonies were organized in the East "sight-unseen," and a village called Kampeska City was started; but a grasshopper invasion during the fall of 1874 destroyed the crops and the colony dissolved.

Harris returned in 1876 and found two other settlers, Ben Lovejoy and O. S. Jewell, on the west bank of the Big Sioux, where Watertown is now situated. Lovejoy had hauled rough boards, shingles and tarpaper from Marshall, Minn., and built the first frame house in the vicinity. The spring of 1878 witnessed an influx of homeseekers as the Winona and St. Peter Railroad extended its line to the new town. The county was organized and named for Rev. G. S. Codington, a member of the Dakota Territorial legislature. A violent dispute broke out over the selection of the county seat and the railroad, wanting it at the terminus of the line, offered free transportation excursions from nearby villages. Crowds gathered to vote on the question, and Watertown was selected. After the ballots were counted, railroad officials decided to christen the town Waterville. But John and Oscar Kemp after considerable argument persuaded officials to designate the town Watertown in honor of their former home in New York State.

Colonel Jacoby platted the town Sept. 1, 1878. The first sign of spring in 1879 brought many newcomers to Watertown, some seeking homesteads, others business opportunities. The drug store of O. H. Tarbell was moved by oxen from its location in Kampeska City at the outlet of the lake to where the present establishment of Williamson and Tarbell stands immediately south of the First National Bank Building. During the early days a prairie fire, originating from a blacksmith forge in a shop where the Elks building is situated, razed almost the entire town, which then consisted of three stores and scattered homes.

Progress in building the new town went on as rapidly as men could be obtained, 100 carpenters working at the time of the snow blockade of 1878. During this time rail transportation was at a standstill. Ten feet, six inches of snow on the level, completely covered dwellings and made travel by foot impossible. Food and fuel supplies were meager. For flour, wheat was ground by hand in coffee mills. During the extreme weather residents burned railroad ties of the extension from the town to the outlet. The trestle bridge across the river was also torn down to provide fuel.

During the next two years the town's progress was rapid. In 1884 two railway lines were added, and the first edition of the present *Daily Public Opinion* was published in 1889.

In 1892 the Sisseton Reservation, north of Watertown, was opened for homesteading and day after day long lines of men and women stood at the door of the Land Office in Watertown to register. The opening of the reservation was a great aid to the settlement of the surrounding country, since 1,500 avid land-seekers were on hand awaiting the starter's gun at noon of April 15.

POINTS OF INTEREST

1. MELLETTE HOME, 5th St. and 5th Ave. N.W., was the residence of Arthur C. Mellette, last Governor of Dakota Territory and first Governor of this State. Governor Mellette was appointed to the Territorial office by President Harrison in 1889. He also served as Governor of the State until 1893 when he returned to Watertown to practice law. The Mellette home is a rambling house with block towers and encircling porch. It is on the summit of Mellette Hill and offers a fine view of the country west and south of the city. There have been unsuccessful attempts to have the State purchase this property but it is still in private hands. The transmitter of the local radio station is here.

2. SWIFT & CO. PLANT, along the Great Northern tracks on River St., is one of the largest meat packing plants in the State. Cattle, hogs and sheep are processed here and shipped East. The plant has added to the city's commerce, besides employing a large number of workers.

3. An AVIARY of pheasants, ducks, geese and many other species of bird life is on 3rd Avenue N.W. bet. 3rd and 4th Sts. Many varieties of pheasant including the beautiful golden pheasant are here. The first ring-necked pheasants planted in South Dakota were distributed from this point. The birds were purchased from a breeder in New York and shipped to Watertown.

4. CODINGTON COUNTY COURTHOUSE, 1st St. bet. Maple and Bdway., was constructed in 1928 of white Indiana limestone, and was one of the first courthouses in the State of modern

architectural design. It is adorned with tapering columns, topped with Ionic volutes. Two murals representing "Wisdom and Mercy" and "Justice and Power," were painted by Vincent Aderentti of New York City. Indirect lighting sets off the decorated dome. County offices are on the first and second floors; the third floor is the State headquarters of the American Legion. Architects of the building were Perkins, McWayne and Freed.

TOUR 1—6.6 m.

R. from Kemp Ave. on Kampeska Blvd.

5. The MUNICIPAL AIRPORT, at 1 m. on Kampeska Road, was completed in 1937 and has three large buildings of native stone. It is an outstanding port in a region where air transportation is comparatively new. It is a mail and passenger station on the Omaha to Minneapolis, and Minneapolis to Cheyenne routes. The hangar, work shop and administration building are grouped together; the stone was taken from the shores of Lake Kampeska by WPA workers in building the airport.

6. The OLD STATE CAPITOL, Kampeska Road and Lakeshore Drive, was never used as a government building and now it houses a night club. In 1889 when South Dakota was admitted to the Union, Watertown business men built the Capitol as an inducement to locate the seat of government there. The optimistic men raised $60,000 for the building and campaign expenses, and then, to their discomfiture Pierre was selected.

R. from Kampeska Road on Shore Line Drive.

7. CITY PARK comprises 140 acres along Lake Kampeska (Ind.: *Shining-shell-like*). Bathhouses, concessions, picnic grounds, band shell, baseball park and playground equipment are under municipal supervision. In the northern part of the park is a marker designating the first site of Kampeska City.

8. The STATE PIKE HATCHERY, Shore Line Drive at outlet, (*open daily; free*) raises and transplants 15,000,000 wall-eyed pike annually in lakes of the State. The pike are seined from Lake Kampeska and stripped of their spawn which are then hatched and shipped.

9. MEMORIAL PARK, N. end of lake, is a memorial to the U. S. S. South Dakota which was used in the World War. The bell of the battleship is in the park. Bathhouses, picnic grounds and fishing equipment are available.

10. STONY POINT is a resort with bathing, boating, fishing, skating and other recreational facilities. Three hundred yards from shore is MAIDEN'S ISLAND. A legend is told of a hunter and his daughter, Minnecotah, who made friends with the Sioux tribe. The young warriors of the tribe vied with each other to win the affection of the pretty maiden. She decided that whoever of them could hurl a stone farthest into the lake would be the recipient of her love. The man of her choice had journeyed to the west and was not expected to return for several months. The warriers hurled rocks and boulders, exerting every fibre of their muscles to out-throw their competitors, not realizing the wily diplomacy of Minne-cotah in this contest. No one could judge the exact distance be-cause of the waves. After days and nights of rock throwing the braves realized the trickery used on them. So many rocks and boulders had been thrown that a stone island had been formed a few hundred yards out from shore. The maiden was forcibly placed on the island without food or shelter, the Indians believing that her choice of one of them would be forced by suffering and exposure.

A great white pelican at night brought Minnecotah fish for food and saved her from starvation and after many days her lover re-turned to learn of her predicament. Quietly paddling his canoe through the stillness of night, he took her from the stone island and escaped to the west. Upon finding the maiden gone the following morning, the braves decided that the white pelican had been sent by the sun god to transport her to other regions.

THE BLACK HILLS

Railways: Central portion of the Black Hills served by the Chicago, Burlington & Quincy, running from Edgemont to Deadwood; eastern edge of Hills served by Chicago & North Western, running from Nebraska Line to Belle Fourche; cross lines joining these run between Deadwood and Whitewood (North Western), Mystic and Rapid City (Crouch Line), and Minnekahta and Buffalo Gap (Burlington to Hot Springs, North Western to Buffalo Gap).

Highways: E. and W.—US 14, northern Hills; US 16, central Hills; US 18, southern Hills. N. and S.—US 85 and US 85A, central Hills; US 14, US 16, and State 79, eastern Hills.

Bus Lines: Black Hills Transportation Co., connecting all major towns, also operates fleet of sightseeing observation motor coaches.

Airports: Black Hills Airport (serving Lead, Deadwood, and Spearfish, US 85 and US 14, 5½ m. S. of Spearfish); also Belle Fourche, Rapid City, and Hot Springs. No commercial airline in area.

Hotels (State-owned and operated): State Game Lodge, Sylvan Lake Hotel, Blue Bell Lodge, all in Custer State Park.

Camp Grounds: Scattered about at many points throughout Custer State Park, Black Hills National Forest and Harney National Forest.

Recreational Areas: Custer State Park, Black Hills National Forest, and Harney National Forest.

Precautions: (1) Against fire — do not smoke while traveling through the forests; clear ground and dig hole before building fire; put out fire with water before breaking camp; do not build fire near brush nor against log. (2) Policing camp—do not wash dirty dishes or clothes in streams; burn all dry trash; bury garbage and tin cans before leaving.

The Black Hills region is geographically, geologically, socially, and economically a unit, differing from the rest of the State in each of these regards. Its most common title is the "richest hundred square miles in the world," this chiefly in reference to its

PAUL BUNYAN BURYING THE BLUE OX
TO FORM THE BLACK HILLS

many valuable mineral deposits, the principal one of which is gold. But the region is more than that. It is one of the chief recreational areas of the Middle West, and its vacational facilities are being enjoyed by an ever-increasing throng of visitors. The attractions of the various Hills cities are well known—the Homestake gold mines at Lead, Deadwood with its graves of famous frontier characters, and Rapid City with its Museum and Dinosaur Park. But outside the cities there is still much to be seen, the giant sculptures of nationally known Mt. Rushmore, the unique granite spires of the Needles, and the almost ethereal beauty of Sylvan Lake. Still this does not exhaust the possibilities of the Hills region.

With regard to the physical origin of the Black Hills, there is a wide diversity, not to say conflict, of ideas. According to the Paul Bunyan school of thought, it all came about through that mighty logger's Big Blue Ox, Babe, who was 42 ax handles and a plug of tobacco broad between the eyes. It seems that the Big Blue Ox ate a red hot stove—a stove with a griddle so big that Paul Bunyan had negro boys with hams strapped to their feet slide around on it and grease it. At any rate as soon as the ox had committed this gustatory indiscretion, he left for parts adjacent, contiguous, outlying and still more distant. It was while traveling the more distant parts, far out on the plains, that the ox finally fell down and died of exhaustion or heartburn or whatever oxen do die of when they eat red hot stoves. Paul Bunyan, meanwhile, had been in swift pursuit of his pet ox, but he arrived too late to do him any good. He could only weep floods of tears that flowed in all directions and then ran together to form the Big Missouri River. Then he set about burying the ox. It was out of the question to dig a grave big enough to hold him, so Paul began to heap earth and rocks upon him until he had covered all of the mighty bulk, making an immense mound at the place where the ox had died. But in time the rains came and washed gullies in it, and the wind and the birds carried seeds there and the mound became scored with gulches and canyons and covered with trees and grass. And so this great mound of earth and rocks which was heaped up to cover Paul Bunyan's ox became the Black Hills that we know today.

However there are certain quibbling and hair-splitting scientists who reject this reasonable theory altogether. According to them, these so-called "Hills" are in reality an old mountain chain. In very ancient times, even considering the age of the earth, a great dome or batholith like an overturned wash basin, was slowly thrust from the depths of the earth by some tremendous convulsion of nature. (*See NATURAL SETTING.*) The granite core, which formed the center of the mass, thrust aside as it rose all the sedimentary layers which had been deposited at the bottoms of successive oceans. Before the Alps and the Rocky Mountains were formed, and while the site of the present Himalayas was still a stagnant marsh, the Black Hills were already old. Thousands upon thousands of feet of sedimentary deposits have been washed off their summits leaving spires and crags of upthrust granite exposed. And while these ancient Hills do not have the snow capped peaks of the younger Alps nor the rugged grandeur to be seen in Glacier Park, nevertheless they have a charm and beauty all their own. The roads of the Hills lie through an almost primeval forest of pine, with rushing streams rather than mountain torrents, with unexpected parks and meadows, with glimpses of shy deer and industrious beaver. Or less frequented trails may be followed, trails that apparently lead into the wilderness, only to end at some abandoned mine. And beside them one may fish for trout in unspoiled streams, or spend whole days in solitude and contemplation of "Nature in her various forms."

Almost the whole of the Black Hills area is contained within the boundaries of the Black Hills National Forest and the Harney National Forest. The former comprises the northern Hills and the latter the southern. Originally one, they were later divided for administrative purposes. Between and within these two forests are smaller independent areas, such as Custer State Park (*see below*), Wind Cave National Park (*see Tour 14*), Jewel Cave National Monument (*see Tour 5*), and Fossil Cycad National Monument, (*see Tour 7*).

The Black Hills and Harney National Forests, of slightly over half a million acres each, are for the most part in the same state in which nature left them. Their rolling hills and ridges are covered with ponderosa pine, which comprises 98 percent of their total timberage. For the remainder there are the silver trunks of birch, quaking aspen, and cottonwood, the slim gray shafts of ironwood, and thickets of plum, buffalo-berry and other bushes. Through the open forest glide the timid deer, venturing out into the parks and glades to graze at twilight. In the deepest fastness of the Hills may be heard the bugling of the seldom-seen elk, and the broad slap of the beaver's tail sounds like a pistol shot on many a mountain stream. Gamy and wary trout lurk in the shadows of the deepest pools, their number swelled from year to year by recruits from State and National hatcheries. The woodchuck ambles awkwardly across the road and the stupid porcupine stolidly strips the bark from the trees. The coyote skulks around, robbing a bird's nest or tearing at an ancient carcass with equal relish and gusto. Among the trees flit innumerable birds, while high over all soars the stately eagle, making his nest on inaccessible granite crags.

But while wildlife pursues its untrammeled course, the comforts of civilization are not lacking. At appropriate spots near the stream or scenic wonder, the Forest Service has provided camp sites, with conveniences that eliminate camping hardships. Here and there are artificial lakes, with bathing, boating, and still-water fishing adding their attractions. Footpaths lead intriguingly through the forest and horseback trails extend for miles through territory impossible of access by any other means. Throughout this region the visitor may be as primitive or civilized as he pleases. It is his to choose.

One of the most interesting phases of conservation work on the part of the Forest Service is represented by the lookout stations on various mountain peaks. There are five within the forest area. Of these the most accessible and most visited is that on Harney Peak (*see Tour 14A*). More than ten thousand people a year make this trip. The view amply repays the effort. The fire guard who is on constant duty will tell you that the question invariably asked him by visitors is "Don't you get lonesome up here all by yourself?" "And," he adds "I probably speak to more people a day than any of them."

Custer State Park, one of the largest State parks in the United States, contains more features of unusual interest than any similar area in the Black Hills. To name a few of them, there is the State Game Lodge that became the Summer White House in 1927, when occupied by the late President and Mrs. Coolidge (*see Tour 5*); Mt. Rushmore, on whose granite face Gutzon Borglum is carving the likenesses of four of the greatest Presidents (*see Tour 5B*); beautiful Sylvan Lake and Harney Peak, with its tree-shaded trail connecting the two (*see Tour 14A*); Legion Lake with its attractive lodge and surroundings (*see Tour 5*); Mt. Coolidge, with its thrilling approach and wonderful view (*see Tour 5D*); and the incomparable Needles, those granite spires and minarets, like so many fingers pointing skyward above the trees (*see Tour 14A*). Besides these outstanding features there are miles upon miles of winding road, of shady bridle paths, and of attractive footways. There are hotels, cabin camps, and camp grounds. There is the scenic Iron Mountain Road (see Toùr 5), where through three successive tunnels one may see framed the distant carving on Mt. Rushmore, more impressive as seen through these rocky telescopes than even close at hand.

There are accommodations within the park for 1,000 people daily, and the nearby towns are able to take care of any overflow. Within certain areas anyone may select a building site and lease it from the State at a nominal rental of $10 a year. Many of the canyons are dotted with cabins erected under this plan.

TOURS

Whether travel is by motor, train, or airplane, horseback or afoot, the tours that follow penetrate every region and community of the State, covering in all more than five thousand miles.

The main tours, connecting at the borders with like tours in surrounding states, crisscross South Dakota from north to south and from east to west, following in general the main Federal highways. These tours numbered from one to eight, such as Tour 2 (The Yellowstone Trail), run from east to west, while those that run north and south are numbered from nine to fourteen. Fifteen is a mountain railway tour. Tours bearing a number followed by a letter, such as Tour 5B (the road that passes Mt. Rushmore), indicate alternate routes, perhaps not as direct but often more interesting than the main tours. Side trips from the main highway are indicated by smaller type, indented. The introduction to each tour is a description of the region through which that tour passes.

These tours may be followed in reverse order by subtracting the mileages given and by changing "right" to "left" and vice versa.

With the aid of the Key Tour Map on the following page, showing where the various routes cross one another, circular or regional tours may be planned.

The tours in this book are designed for South Dakotans as well as for visitors. Few people living in the Black Hills have visited the Lake Region; and it is said that more people from Illinois registered at the Rushmore Memorial in 1937 than from South Dakota.

If in spite of the map and directions you suddenly find yourself lost, build a fire, throw in the book, and make smoke signals. There may be an Indian over the next ridge.

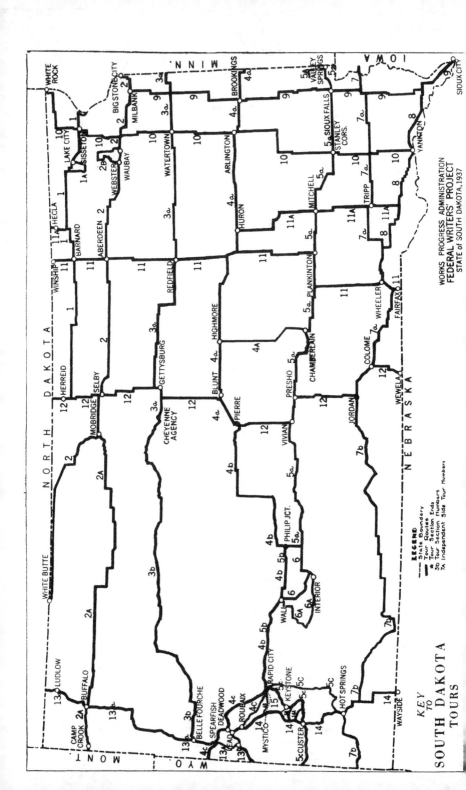

KEY TO
SOUTH DAKOTA
TOURS

WORKS PROGRESS ADMINISTRATION
FEDERAL WRITERS' PROJECT
STATE of SOUTH DAKOTA, 1937

LEGEND
State Boundary
Tour Routes
Tour Section Ends
Tour Section Numbers
Independent Side Tour Numbers

TOUR 1

(Browns Valley, Minn.) — Sisseton — Britton — Eureka — Junction
with US 83. State 10.

Minnesota Line to Junction with US 83, 176.6 m.

No railroads parallel the highway, but several branch lines are
crossed.

The roadbed is graveled throughout.

Hotel and tourist accommodations available at above towns, and at
numerous lake resorts on or near the highway between Sisseton and
Britton.

State 10 crosses northern South Dakota's lake region in the Coteau des Prairies and levels off through the James River Valley. In
the northeast corner of the State is the Sisseton Indian Reservation,
triangular in shape and bisected by State 10. This section is also
dotted with lakes, spring-fed and tree-fringed. It is developing into
a resort area slowly and with little fanfare; few people from other
parts of the State have ever been there. Although the highway
passes through an Indian Reservation, few Indian homes are seen,
for it has been open for white settlement since 1892. Here the Indians and whites live and work side by side, observing no tribal or
racial boundaries. Off the main highway, groups of Indian families
are clustered along lake shores; large numbers loiter in the streets
of Sisseton, agency headquarters.

Swedes, Norwegians, Poles, and Germans settled the eastern
area through which State 10 passes, and farther west are communities of Finns, Russians, and Germans. In the Indian country, intermarriage between the whites and Indians has brought about
many unusual names and degrees of color. There are dark-skinned,
black-haired persons with Swedish, Norwegian, Polish, British, and
German names, and blue-eyed, clear-skinned youths with Indian
names.

State 10 crosses the South Dakota-Minnesota boundary, 0.5 m.
W. of Browns Valley, Minn., between Big Stone Lake on the
south and Lake Traverse on the north. When it rains on this road,
the water falling on the south side is said to drain into the Gulf of
Mexico, and that on the north into Hudson Bay. Lake Traverse,
headwaters of the Red River, is famous in the history of the Northwest; from Big Stone Lake flows the Minnesota River, which later
joins the Mississippi.

At 3 m. the SISSETON INDIAN RESERVATION extends westward. (*The boundary is not marked, and the reservation is open. The agency headquarters is at Sisseton.*)

The Sissetons and the Wahpetons (*dwellers among the leaves*), bands of the Sioux Nation, found this region of cool crystal lakes, wooded ravines, edible berries, buffalo, and fish an earthly paradise when they migrated westward (*see INDIANS*). Good hunters and fishermen, these peaceful people never strayed far. They welcomed the visits of Jean Duluth, Father De Smet, Francis Rondell, and Stephen Return Riggs, trading with Duluth and Rondell, and listening to the religious teachings of De Smet and Riggs.

Following the Minnesota Massacre at New Ulm, during the Civil War period, the Sissetons were advanced upon by troops from Fort Snelling, Minn. The tribal council made a law that all whites in their lake country would have to dress like Indians to keep from being massacred. Fleeing Indians, pursued by soldiers, came into the Sisseton country bringing their captives with them; the Sissetons were instrumental in having the captives released to the soldiers, and in return the military advance was discontinued. Another troop, however, came into the Indian country, burning gardens and tents. Attempts were made towards peace, but continued misunderstandings arose, followed by actual warfare. Old Indians enjoy relating how, while fleeing, they turned about so that the cannon would be brought into use. To their extreme amusement they dodged the baseball-sized cannonballs directed toward them. In 1863 the Sissetons, who had been driven W. across the Missouri River and into Canada, returned to their lake country. Camped at Enemy Swim Lake (*see Tour 2B*), the soldiers surrounded them. There a treaty was made which, in Indian language, was to the effect: "There will be no more wars; we will be brothers."

With the help of the Indians, Fort Sisseton was established in 1864 (*see Tour 1A*), and in 1876 a treaty was made establishing the Sisseton Indian Reservation. The Indians settled around the lakes—Enemy Swim, Pickerel, Blue Dog, Red Iron, Piyas, Two Mile, Four Mile, Six Mile, and Nine Mile—in family groups. In 1892 the Federal Government purchased the reservation from the Indians, opening it to homesteaders. The Indians were allotted 160 acres for each individual; there is no unallotted land there at present. As families have grown, there has been no new land for the children, so that today one plot and one house serves an old man and his wife, together with their married children and families.

There are 2,740 Indians on the reservation roll, only 775 of which are full-blooded. A small annual increase in the Indian population is reported by the superintendent of the agency. The close proximity to the whites during the past 45 years has resulted not only in intermarriage, but adoption of white men's customs. The Sioux language is used at pow-wows, church, and meetings, but English is understood by nearly everyone. There is no tribal property; instead, 70,630 acres of Indian-owned land is rented, and 5,781 acres cultivated by Indian farmers. Native handicraft is no longer engaged in to any degree. Wild fruits are still gathered and processed by old methods; corn is dried on cheese cloth; and chokecherries and wild plums are ground with meat. There is still some fishing, particularly in winter through the ice. "Store clothes" are worn exclusively, and few old-time garments survive. At summer pow-wows, the washtub has taken the place of the hide tom-tom, and lipstick the place of war paint. There are 306 permanent homes used by Indians and less than a dozen log cabins. A few tents are seen in summer as temporary dwellings. There are about 200 Indian children in public schools on the reservation, 200 in Federal boarding schools, and 100 in church boarding schools. The churches—mostly Episcopal, Catholic, and Presbyterian—furnish the social life. Wagons and old cars start toward church on Saturday, loaded with Indians, staying all night with friends or relatives who live near the edifice.

At 3.6 m. is a series of MOUNDS (R) whose origin is controversial—whether built by Mound Builders, Ree Indians, or Sioux (*see INDIANS*). The mounds have been excavated and the artifacts have not been preserved. It is generally agreed, however, by archaeologists that they were burial grounds of that race known as the Mound Builders.

SISSETON, 14 m. (1,202 alt., 1,840 pop.), is the agency for the Sisseton Indian Reservation and the trading center for a large diversified farming area. The word Sisseton means in Sioux language, *dead fish*, or less literally, *fishing village*. As the town is the administrative center of the reservation, Indians are seen at any time on the streets. There are a few older women who wear blankets or shawls, but for the most part their color differentiates the Indians from the whites. The AGENCY is at the top of the hill, one block E. of Main St. A COLLECTION OF INDIAN RELICS is on display at the high school, one block E. of lower Main St. Construction of a large, modern hospital for Indians was started in 1936.

Sisseton has been the home of some interesting Indians, one of whom was Asa Sweetcorn, a football player with Jim Thorpe at Carlisle Institute. The giant Sweetcorn, who is supposed to have worn a size 21 collar, was arrested 40 times for intoxication and assault and battery during his varied career. One of his feats to raise money was to bet he could ram his head through wooden doors. On one occasion six splintered port holes in the side of a barn were said to have been made by him following as many runs and dives into the wall. Another time Asa encountered his match in an impromptu wrestling engagement, and his opponent bit off his ear. Earless Asa carried the auditory appendage in his pocket four days before visiting a doctor. The heading in a local paper read: "Chews Sweetcorn Ear in Winter."

The seat of Roberts Co. is at Sisseton.

At Sisseton is the junction with US 81 (*see Tour 10*).

At 21 *m.* is the eastern edge of the COTEAU DES PRAIRIES (*hills of the prairies*). This range of hills rises abruptly above the level prairie, and the road winds through the hills with sharp curves and steep grades; going E. a car can coast 7 m. into Sisseton from the last hill.

At 22.2 *m.* is LONG HOLLOW, a deep wooded ravine which has been a gathering place for Indians since the Sioux first occupied the region. Late each summer members of the Sisseton band still gather there for pow-wows. A church has been built 2 m. N., and can be reached by walking up the draw. There is good pasture in the bottom-land and shelter from icy winds; tall trees cast cool shadows during the summer. When enemies came, the Sissetons often followed the long ravine S. into a deeper and more secluded gulch, known as BAD HOLLOW.

At 25.4 *m.* is the junction with a graded road.

> Left on this unnumbered road to the first of a chain of lakes, known as BUFFALO LAKES, 1 *m.*, with the main lake at 5 *m.* On their sand beaches and thickly-wooded banks picnic places can be found. The lakes received their name from a variety of fish that abound there—buffalo fish, frying-pan-shaped and small-boned. This is also a popular duck and goose hunting region.

At 27.8 *m.* is RED IRON LAKE, divided by State 10 into two bodies of water. Privately operated resorts along the highway offer fishing, boating, swimming, and picnic facilities. Bluegills, perch, and pickerel are caught in the lake.

At 28.4 m. is CLEAR LAKE, which borders the highway. A
public sand beach near the road is used by bathers. A resort with
fishing supplies and bathing accommodations is in the wooded area
(L). At 28.9 m. is the headquarters of a State Game Warden where
hunting and fishing licenses can be secured (*see GENERAL IN-
FORMATION*).

At 31.1 m. is a junction with a dirt road.

> Right on this road is LONG LAKE, 0.6 m., one of several lakes
> in the State by that name. Somewhere on its shores there is,
> according to Indian legend, a cached flour sack containing gold
> coins. Indians relate a story told by Gray Foot, a Santee, who
> on his deathbed gathered his sons together and told them of
> the gold he had buried at Long Lake. A band of Santees, he said,
> raided the agency at Martin, Minn., during the Minnesota Massa-
> cre, killing some of the soldiers stationed there. The payroll had
> recently arrived and gold coins were heaped on the table. Each
> Indian took a share. Gray Foot had filled part of a flour sack
> and tied it on his horse. When the War Department sent out
> notice that anyone found with gold in his possession would be
> considered guilty of murder by that evidence, Gray Foot buried
> his loot, he said, between two straight willows near the shore
> at the E. end. But the treasure has never been found.

LAKE CITY, 33.3 m. (192 pop.), is a country village named
for the surrounding lakes, particularly Cottonwood Lake on the
N. edge of town.

> 1. Left from Lake City, on a graveled road, are EDEN and FORT
>   SISSETON (see Tour 1A).
> 2. Right from Lake City, on a graded road, are FLAT LAKE,
>   8 m., and several marshes suitable for duck hunting.

Lake City is at the western boundary of the Sisseton Indian
Reservation (*see above*).

At 34.8 m. is SIX MILE LAKE.

At 35.4 m. is SQUAW HILL (R), which was named about 100
years ago by the Sioux. A large group of Sioux women was picking berries. The men of the tribe had gone southward, trailing a
buffalo herd. One young woman, with a papoose on her back,
noticed a movement among the bushes. Peering closely she spied
a Chippewa man. Without showing alarm, she quietly dropped a
word of the impending danger to the others, who were talking
loudly; seeing nothing, they accused the young woman of having
a vision. Slipping stealthily among the brush, the young squaw
worked her way to the lake and hid. The piercing war cry of the

Chippewa was followed by screams and crying. When all was quiet the woman returned to the hill, only to find the bodies of the Sioux women and babies mutilated and strewn about the hill. When the Indian men returned from their hunting trip they found the bodies and, amid great lamentation, buried them on the hill's summit.

At 36.2 *m.* is the SISSETON GAME PRESERVE, a sanctuary for wild waterfowl.

At 37.4 *m.* is NINE MILE LAKE (R), last of the "mile chain," named by soldiers from Fort Sisseton.

State 10 winds through the western portion of the Coteau des Prairies (*see above*); beyond are flat plains, dotted with red and white farm buildings, green meadows, yellow fields, purple plowed patches, and a distant clump of town buildings at Britton.

At 48.2 *m.* is the junction with State 25.

> Right on this road is the junction with a graded road at 6 *m.* R. here to another junction with a graded road; R. here to SWIFT'S PEAK, 16 *m.* (2,240 alt.), the highest point in the eastern half of the State. From the top is a view of a dozen towns in North and South Dakota. The lights of Aberdeen, more than 50 *m.* away, are visible at night. North from this point is WINDY MOUND, 22 *m.*, from which the Indians watched for buffalo on the plains. The North Dakota boundary is immediately to the N.

BRITTON, 57.1 *m.* (1,354 alt., 1,473 pop.), reflects the prosperity of a rich farm region where the soil is said to be as productive as any in the Northwest. The raising of purebred beef cattle is an important local industry. The town was named in honor of Col. Isaac Britton, its founder and the prime mover in the building of the Dakota and Great Southern R.R., which before completion became part of the C. M. St. P. & P. R.R. Britton has a municipal hospital. Because of its location in a hunting and fishing region, its stores feature outdoor supplies. It is the seat of Marshall Co.

At 60.2 *m.* are the RICE RACING STABLES, where horses are raised and trained for harness races at fairs and celebrations in the Northwest.

HOUGHTON, 77.3 *m.* (200 pop.), is a rural village where the farmers bring their produce to trade for staples.

At Houghton is the junction with State 37.

> Right on this road is HECLA, 6 *m.*, HOME OF THE SCHENSE QUADRUPLETS. Jay, Jimmie, Jean, and Joan were born in an Aberdeen hospital on Jan. 13, 1931, to Mr. and Mrs. Fred Schense. They received Nation-wide publicity until the arrival of

the Dionne quintuplets. Schense, a tenant farmer, encountered considerable difficulty in providing for his increased family. When the quadruplets were little more than a year old he took them on an exhibition tour of county and State fairs through the Northwest. The venture yielded hardly sufficient remuneration to pay expenses, and they returned to Aberdeen destitute. Their mother died when the children were two years old, and a year later their father married the housekeeper. Besides the quadruplets the family included three older children and a new baby sister. Schense operates a 160-acre farm near Hecla now The height and weight of the four youngsters vary, and no two of them are the same size. They closely resemble one another as to features, complexion, and hair.

At 79.5 m. the highway crosses the James River.

At 83.8 m. is the junction with a graveled road.

Left on this unnumbered road is SAND LAKE and the U. S. BIO-LOGICAL SURVEY STATION, 0.4 m., where a steel tower rises high in the air. The station supervises 2,400 acres of the Sand Lake Game Refuge. Boys in a CCC camp developed the refuge for waterfowl.

COLUMBIA, 8 m. (1,304 alt., 307 pop.), prior to 1900, was expected to be one of the largest cities in the State, but a series of events caused it to become a small, inconspicuous town. The town was started in June, 1879, by Bryon Smith of Minneapolis, who led a party of settlers to the confluence of the James and Elm Rivers. The next year Brown Co. was organized, and Columbia became the county seat. A large lake was formed by damming the river at the western edge of the new town, and steamboats began to ply its waters, carrying grain and produce northward. The C. M. St. P. & P. R.R. chose to build its road through the thriving young town, but the city demanded a drawbridge over the lake. Then things began to happen. The railroad withdrew and built through Aberdeen; the dike and the lake disappeared; Aberdeen won the county seat, and the citizens of Columbia moved to the newer town. The first county courthouse is now used as a school building.

BARNARD, 95.4 m. (60 pop.), is at the junction with US 281 (see Tour 11).

At 97.1 m. is a junction with a dirt road.

Right on this road is the COLIN CAMPBELL TRADING POST SITE, 1.6 m., marked by a monument. This stockaded post was established in 1822 by Colin Campbell for the Hudson's Bay Co., and was occupied six years. The Indians residing near the stockade were a band of Yanktonnais Sioux, of which Chappa (Red Thunder) was chief. His son Waanata was born there and became a prominent figure through his exploits in the War of 1812. Waanata distinguished himself at the battle of Fort Stephenson near Sandusky, Ohio; at the close of the battle it was found that nine bullets had hit him. He fought with the British Army, was cited for bravery, given a captain's commission, taken to England, and presented to the King. Waanata's last years were spent in North Dakota where he and his band exercised a protectorate over a band of Arikaras. In return for protection against the Sioux, Waanata demanded tribute from the Arikaras, which enabled him to live in comfort and comparative luxury. He was buried near Fort Yates, N. Dak.

At 100 *m.* is the junction with a dirt road.

Left on this road is WILLOW LAKE, 1.6 *m.*, an artificial lake built to furnish Aberdeen with its water supply. The dam, built with relief labor, backs up Willow Creek.

LEOLA, 118.4 *m.* (1,587 alt., 812 pop.), was named for Leola Haynes, daughter of a pioneer family. The town was started in 1885 when a group of Russian-German immigrants and people from other midwestern States settled on the "flats" S. of Leola. A prairie fire in 1889 burned all but 12 of the 100 buildings, leaving the school, McPherson Co. courthouse, and other buildings of brick or stone. It was not until 1906 that Leola obtained railroad facilities for shipping the large amounts of grain and hogs raised in that area; but in 1936 the railroad inaugurated a truck line to supplant the trains. Duck hunting brings sportsmen to Leola each fall; there are a number of hills and marshes N. of the town.

Between Leola and Eureka is a part of the Russian-German community that settled in McPherson and Campbell Cos., prior to 1900. The vanguard of the immigrants arrived in 1884 from the southern part of the State; in 1889, trainloads of them arrived, having come direct from their homes in Russia, taking practically all land available for homestead entry in the whole Eureka section. While generally termed Russians, these people are descendants of Germans who had emigrated to Russia in the time of Catherine the Great. The older people use their native tongue at home and in the stores, but the young people have adopted the English language and American ways. A trace of the influence of Old World architecture is still seen among the farm houses (*see ARCHITECTURE*). The original buildings were long and narrow, designed to conserve wall space and for convenience; one end of the building housed the family, the center was used to store grain, and the third section for the livestock. The entrance door to the house was divided, so that the top part might be swung open, leaving the bottom half closed to keep children in and animals out. Most of the immigrants have had a degree of prosperity, and now the long narrow buildings are used to house the family or livestock exclusively, and other buildings have been erected nearby. There is a South Russian influence still noticeable in the use of vivid, contrasting colors in painting houses. In the country and town purple houses are trimmed in green, pink houses have blue borders, yellow houses are decorated with orchid, and no lack of originality is discernible.

EUREKA, 153.7 m. (1,884 alt., 1,430 pop.), is an example of a small city founded and still peopled by European immigrants who have provided themselves with most of the conveniences and comforts of modern American towns. The soil was productive for these newcomers, and during the 1890's Eureka maintained that it was the largest primary wheat market in the world, 36 elevators being required to care for the flood of grain produced by the immigrant farmers. The town has a large number of retired farmers who, after acquiring a competence, have left their farms to sons and daughters. They brought with them the traditional German love for beer; before prohibition it required 18 saloons properly to satisfy the thirst of the Eureka community. With the legalizing of liquor sales in 1935, Eureka promptly voted to operate a municipal liquor store. German dishes can be had in the restaurants, but are not featured. Services in German are held in the Lutheran and Catholic churches.

At 176.6 m. is the junction with US 83 (see Tour 12), 3 m. N. of Mound City.

TOUR 1A

Lake City—Eden—Fort Sisseton. Unnumbered road.

Lake City to Fort Sisseton, 16.3 m.

Roadbed is graveled.

Minneapolis, St. Paul and Sault St. Marie R.R. parallels this route between Lake City and Eden.

Branching S. from State 10 (See Tour 1) at Lake City, the unnumbered road passes through a part of the lake region in which the lakes have not been developed commercially. Camping and picnic places are numerous, but none are improved or set aside for that purpose. The Fort Sisseton area is in a game reserve, and no hunting is allowed.

At 0.8 m. the road skirts ROY LAKE, where there is good fishing.

At 4.9 *m.* TWIN STINK LAKES are passed, one lake on each side of the road. They received their name and dubious renown from the alkali odor caused by receding stagnant water.

EDEN, 7.7 *m.* (1,355 alt., 168 pop.), developed from a community nearby to which the name, Eden Park, was given by a group of Polish Catholic immigrants who were impressed by the beauty of the surrounding lakes. That was in 1909, and six years later the town was started at its present location when the Soo R.R. built a branch line through the region. There are a large Catholic church and school in Eden, and also a number of Polish Jews.

Left from Eden the road passes unnamed sloughs and crosses a series of hills.

At 13.1 *m.* the road turns R. Along this road in the 1860's ox teams grunted and carts creaked as they hauled rocks to build the new fort, long before white settlers had penetrated the region. Indian scouts on fast ponies rode the trail with dispatches; and a few years later a telegraph line connected the fort with Webster. Fancy buggies bearing the society folks of homestead days rolled down the road on their way to fort balls, and military expeditions passed over it in the early 1880's.

At 16.3 *m.* is the entrance to FORT SISSETON. (*Parking space at entrance; cars not allowed in quadrangle.*)

On the E. side of the quadrangle are the barracks and commissary; to the N. are the hospital, blockhouse, and stables; to the W. are the Commanding Officer's headquarters and officers' quarters; and to the S. the Quartermaster's office, saddle shop, guardhouse, chapel, and blockhouse (*see CHART*).

Historic Fort Sisseton, manned at different periods in its history by Indians, whites, and Negroes, and having recently served as a playground for wealthy duck hunters, is being restored to its old-time dignity with the aid of the Works Progress Administration, the National Park Service, and Marshall Co., which have combined to roll back the calendar to the days when the fort was the social and military center of young Dakota Territory. Electric lights are being replaced by candles, faucets by buckets, and the garages are to be filled with hay.

The fort was established, following the Minnesota Massacre in 1864, by Major John Clowney, commander of troops recruited in Wisconsin. Acting upon orders from General John Pope that the post be set up "not east of the James River," Major Clowney led

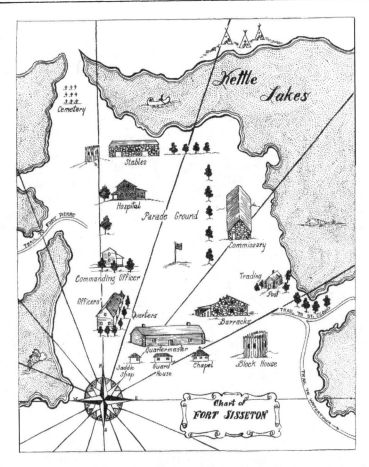

his soldiers into Dakota Territory, which at that time was inhabited only by Indians and a few traders of French origin. The Sisseton-Wahpeton tribes of the Sioux Nation had surrendered peaceably the year before at Enemy Swim Lake (*see Tours 1 and 2B*), and when the soldiers entered their domain the Indians guided them to the advantageous fort site. It was, contrary to order, 40 m. E. of the James River.

Situated on the elevated tablelands known as the Coteau des Prairies, the fort was partly surrounded by the Kettle Lakes where lived 1,200 Sioux Indians. It was named Fort Wadsworth originally in honor of General James S. Wadsworth of New York, who died in the Battle of the Wilderness. During the time that Colonel

W. D. Boyce, Chicago millionaire newspaper publisher, leased the fort a few years ago, Congressman James W. Wadsworth, a grandson of the man for whom the post was named, was a frequent visitor. In 1876 the fort took the name of the tribe living in that region, the name which it still bears.

Building a fort in an undeveloped country was no easy task. Supplies had to be brought 244 miles from St. Paul. Stones for the barracks, commissary, officers' quarters, and stables were dragged by oxen from as far as Wahpeton, N. Dak., although many native stones were used. In 1868 brick was brought in wagons drawn by oxen from St. Cloud, Minn., for the permanent buildings, including the hospital. Large oak trees were cut and sawed by a portable sawmill for the storehouse, which was 150 ft. long and built entirely of logs. The two towering blockhouses were also made of logs. The stone buildings, 240 ft. long and 36 ft. in width, caved in from lack of care, hard usage, and the effects of vandalism after the troops were withdrawn in 1888.

In the early 1880's Fort Sisseton was the social center of the eastern half of Dakota Territory. For a civilian in Watertown, Fargo, Webster, or Browns Valley to receive an invitation for dinner at the fort was considered a high honor. A silver service was used exclusively in the officers' quarters, with an orchestra playing for the dinners and balls. During vacations when the young men and women returned from Eastern schools, brilliant social functions were in order and delicacies were brought by pony express from St. Paul for the occasions.

The soldiers stationed at the fort, ready to quell Indian uprisings and protect the whites, were of Irish, German, and Scotch descent. Physical hardships were common during the hard winters, and many are the stories of heroism.

Old Indians like to recall the days when their fathers were scouts at the post. One man in particular is legend. He was Samuel J. Brown, the half-breed son of the first white trader in the region. In April 1866, word was received at Fort Sisseton that the Indians were crossing the James River near Jamestown to make raids on the settlers. Brown, who was chief of scouts, was sent to Ruilliard's trading post, about 10 m. NE. of Aberdeen and 55 m. from the fort, to warn them. A large tribe was living on the Elm River near Ruilliard's post, and Brown was to persuade them not to join in the fighting. Brown left Fort Sisseton near sundown and rode hard, arriving during the night. He was told that Indian carriers, who were much swifter than the Government mailmen serving the fort, had brought word that President Johnson had signed a treaty to stop the soldiers from fighting the Indians. Brown knew that he had to get back to the fort before the troops left in the morning for Jamestown to meet the Indians; he decided, therefore, that he must retrace his steps before another Indian war should commence, with the soldiers at fault. So he traded horses with Ruilliard and started back for the fort. Soon after he left, a terrific blizzard began. He angled E. more than N. because of the stiff, cutting wind and found himself among the Waubay Lakes at daybreak. Having gone too far S., he turned due N. and spurred his plucky pony into the raging blizzard. Brown reached the fort in time to halt the troops, after riding steadily since he had left the evening before. When he was taken from his pony he was unable to move his limbs, stiffened by the cold weather and the wearisome 135-mile ride. And he remained paralyzed until the end of his life!

After the Civil War two companies of hand-picked Negroes were stationed at Fort Sisseton. Despite the fact that every man was over six feet tall and an athlete, they did not relish their situation. First, they were afraid of the Indians; next, they were ridiculously out of place when wintry winds swept tons of snow across the prairie; then too, and worst of all, they were given the job of digging up the bodies of the soldiers who had been buried there, for removal to another fort! Many of the dead were deserters who had been shot and dragged back behind horses for burial. One of the stories related by old-timers about the Negroes and their grave-digging activities is as follows: one big, husky Negro was standing on a rough box in a grave, loosening the dirt around the sides so that the box could be pulled out. A board gave way and the Negro's foot sank into the body of a dead soldier! A superhuman leap vaulted him out of the grave to the solid ground, where he emulated the feats of Jesse Owens and Ralph Metcalfe for speed. He never returned to the fort, and his whereabouts have never been entered upon the records.

Between 1910 and 1927 the fort was in the hands of private interests. Hunting parties from Minneapolis and St. Paul found the neighboring passes perfect for hunting ducks and geese.

In 1920 Col. W. C. Boyce, Chicago newspaperman, leased the fort and hospital to be used as a dwelling house. Colonel Boyce began his newspaper career at Britton (*see Tour 1*). At the time of his death in 1928 he owned newspapers in Chicago and Indianapolis. One room in the renovated hospital was the poker room, where games continued day and night every fall during the hunting season. Many of the visitors hired hunters to do their shooting in order that they might have ducks to ship home. Jerry Wilson, professional Sisseton trapshooter, was hired at $25 a day to hunt for several of the visitors. Colonel Boyce, known as the man who started the Boy Scout movement in the United States, astonished Webster citizens once when, after arriving by train from the West Coast, he had his Rolls-Royce sent out from Chicago in an express car. Motor boats, a putting green on the parade grounds, and the poker table furnished entertainment for most of the guests.

In 1935 a Federal transient camp was set up at Fort Sisseton as an Emergency Relief Administration activity, and work on the restoration of the fort was started. An error in the reconstruction was soon discovered when a hip-roof was placed on a building which originally had a straight, pointed roof. The National Park Service, Works Progress Administration, and Marshall Co. co-operated in continuing the project, and the restoration is being accurately followed. A ditch has been dug around the fort to the same depth it was originally, and the dirt used, as was formerly done by the soldiers, to build a mound wall on the inside. It will require several years to complete the project.

TOUR 2

(Benson, Minn.)—Milbank—Webster—Aberdeen—Mobridge—Lemmon—(Hettinger, N. Dak.). US 12.

Minnesota Line to North Dakota Line, 328.5 m.

The C. M. St. P. & P. R.R. parallels the highway throughout.

Between the Minnesota Line and Aberdeen the roadbed is mostly bituminous surfaced; the rest gravel, with short stretches of tarvia.

Hotel and tourist accommodations excellent in larger towns, with lakeside camping places in Lake Region.

US 12, known as the Yellowstone Trail, crosses northern South Dakota through the lake region, the James River valley, the Missouri River ranges, and the Buttes and Badlands section, each different from the others. The north-eastern part of the State is dotted with lakes, spring-fed and tree-surrounded, abounding in game fish and wild fowl. Unfortunately, when the railroad and highway were built an attempt was made to avoid as many lakes as possible, and only a few can be seen from US 12. With the coming of the homesteaders and the building of the railroad in the early 1880's, small towns sprang up almost overnight. The fertile land of the broad James River valley was settled quickly, and farms through that region are large and modern. In spring the valley is checkerboarded with green fields of grass and black plowed lands, with occasional clusters of trees, all of which have been planted by the farmers. In the fall the golden fields wave like the sea, with tall corn rows forming the shore. Here is a prairie country, vast and apparently endless, telling a story of ceaseless labor to make things grow. Farther west, in the Missouri River breaks, the land is less suitable for grain crops and better for livestock purposes. Attempts to farm on a large scale have met with little success and cattle now roam the stone-studded hills. Beyond the Missouri River are the Badlands, fantastic in shape and spotted with ranches. Raising of cattle, sheep, and horses forms the basic industry, with a little farming to obtain feed.

US 12 crosses the Minnesota Line 40 m. W. of Benson, Minn. (*see Minn. Tour 10*), and touches the southern end of BIG STONE LAKE, which stretches northward for 36 m. On a windy day whitecaps roll high, the lake turning into a frothy, greenish-gray, roaring sweep of water. The lake was named for the outcroppings of granite rocks nearby, and is on the boundary between Minnesota and South Dakota. It is stocked with game fish, particularly pickerel, pike, bluegills, sturgeon, perch, crappies, and sheepshead, a variety peculiar to this lake.

US 12 passes over a 100-ft. dike between the States, known as the WHETSTONE DIVERSION PROJECT. A cooperative arrangement was made between the Minnesota and South Dakota governments, acting with the Works Progress Administration, to divert water from Whetstone River (L) into Big Stone Lake (R), which during the drought years was sadly depleted. For 50 years attempts had been made to divert the Whetstone River into the lake, which has as an outlet the Minnesota River. Work was started in October 1934, and in March 1937 water from the river began pouring into the lake. Residents of Big Stone City, S. Dak., and Ortonville, Minn., left their work to watch the lake level rise, and one onlooker—a pioneer—exclaimed, "By gad! It's flowing uphill after all."

At the eastern edge of Big Stone City is a CORN CANNERY, 0.5 *m.*, that operates each fall when the corn from the surrounding fields has been picked. A corn king is crowned each year—the man who can eat the most corn on the cob.

BIG STONE CITY, 0.8 *m.* (979 alt., 675 pop.), overlooks the lake from which it takes its name, and, in addition to being a summer resort center, has a brick factory, corn cannery, and granite quarry; yet the normal population is small. During summer and fall, however, it becomes considerably larger. The town was first known as Inkpa City, named for the renegade Indian, Inkpaduta, who held captive there several women, taken in the Spirit Lake massacre.

1. Right from the center of Big Stone City, on an improved road, is CHAUTAUQUA PARK, 1 *m.*, a popular summer resort with cottages, boating facilities, swimming, and fishing. Sheltered by trees, the resort is a center for week-end picnics and camping parties. At 9 *m.* is LINDEN BEACH, in a setting of tall linden or basswood trees. A trading-post, established in 1865 by Moses Moreau and Soloman Robar, once occupied the site but now a hotel and cabins with modern facilities have taken its place. HARTFORD BEACH, 11 *m.*, with its large, old-fashioned hotel with two tiers of open porches around the building, roller skating rink, bathhouse, and shell boats, is an interesting resort. All kinds of freak boats are found there. A feature is the midnight swimming during the summer months, which visitors enjoy, the air and swimming water at that time being about the same temperature. Immediately W. of the resort are the Hartford Mounds, in which skeletons and artifacts of the Mound Builders have been found (see INDIANS).

2. On the shores of Big Stone Lake at Big Stone City, or at any of the resorts (see above), boats can be rented by the hour or day. Flat-bottomed and clinker rowboats and various types of outboard motorboats are available, together with fishing supplies, poles or rods, lines, bait, and other equipment. Because of the length of Big Stone Lake (36 *m.*), waves roll high with a heavy wind and it is advisable to stay near the shore. Trolling, casting, and still-fishing are all possible in Big Stone Lake, where sturgeon, northern pike, pickerel, wall-eyed pike, catfish, crappies, bass, bluegills, sunfish, perch, and bullheads abound. On the W. side of the lake are Chautauqua Park, Linden Beach, and Hartford Beach resorts.

At the western edge of Big Stone City, 1.2 *m.*, is a brick factory utilizing native clay.

At 1.9 *m.* the Whetstone River is crossed, and US 12 begins to wind over a range of low, rambling hills, where frequent, clean-looking farm buildings are set in groves of trees.

At 7.9 m. is a junction with a graveled road.

Left on this road is the DAKOTA GRANITE QUARRY, 0.5 m., with its huge piles of stone, like a strange fortress. A few years ago a young man named Stringle obtained control of a quarry in which there was a quantity of mahogany granite. He built a cutting and polishing plant, and today carloads of gravestones are shipped to all parts of the United States. The various kinds of granite quarried here are Hunter, royal purple, and mahogany.

MILBANK, 14 m. (1,148 alt., 2,549 pop.), was named for Jeremiah Milbank, a director of the Milwaukee R.R., which was extended through the city in 1880. The railroad established a division headquarters here, which attracted many families of Irish and Dutch origin to work in the shops and on the line. A windmill, once used to grind grain from the surrounding country, has been moved to the center of the city, L. of US 12.

Milbank became the seat of Grant Co. after a heated three-town contest. In 1880 Big Stone City won the first election for county seat; but the next year Milbank had outgrown Big Stone City, so the latter induced Wilmot, a town nearby, to enter the contest. Milbank won by 25 votes, but Big Stone City officials charged fraudulent voting and retained the records; Milbank at the same time established itself as the county seat, and residents filed their papers in both towns, to be on the safe side. The case was taken to court and Milbank was recognized as the official seat. Big Stone City officials, however, refused to give up their records until they had been reimbursed for campaign funds.

Milbank granite, quarried within the city limits, is well known and widely used. The town has been long noted in the State for its high school athletic teams and for the All-conference and All-American football players it contributes to Midwestern universities. One of the best known was Jack Manders, star player of the University of Minnesota and later of the Chicago Bears (professional).

At Milbank is the junction with US 77 (*see Tour 9*).

MARVIN, 31.6 m. (1,657 alt., 136 pop.), was originally known as Grade Siding, owing to its situation on the railroad; but in 1882 a post office was to be established and a more dignified name was needed. There was a Marvin safe in the railroad office and a local punster suggested that Marvin was a "good, safe name."

Between Marvin and Summit, US 12 winds into the Coteau des Prairies, *hills of the prairies,* so-named by early French explorers.

The hills have gullies and draws lined with oak, ash, and elm trees. From the crests of the hills are splendid views of Big Stone Lake, Lake Traverse, and far into Minnesota, a jumble of purple, yellow, and green.

SUMMIT, 39.9 m. (2,000 alt., 503 pop.), is the highest point along the railroad in the Coteau range, about 1,000 ft. above Big Stone Lake. Because the town had an altitude greater than any other between the Mississippi and Missouri Rivers, it was named Summit. Each year a celebration is held to observe the anniversary of the opening of the Sisseton Indian Reservation (*see IN-DIANS*). Although the reservation was opened April 15, 1892, the celebration occurs the latter part of June.

At 44.1 m. is a junction (L) with US 81 (*see Tour 10*), which unites with US 12 to 46.1 m., where US 81 branches R.

ORTLEY, 49.2 m. (168 pop.), is gradually moving toward the highway to take advantage of the tourist traffic. Originally named Anderson for the first resident in 1906, it was later given the name of a prominent local Indian. An Indian celebration is held here each June.

At 53.1 m. is BITTER LAKE (L), a shallow body frequented by mudhens during the summer, but having an unpleasant odor.

Although actually a part of the original Sisseton Indian Reservation, the lands in this rural area were ceded and sold to homesteaders, particularly Scandinavians, many years ago, so that few Indians live along the highway here. Most of them returned to their former haunts, the lake shores.

WAUBAY, 57.3 m. (1,813 alt., 976 pop.), is the English corruption of the Indian word "wamay" (*where wild fowl build their nests*), first given to the chain of lakes NW. of Waubay. The town is popular with the Indians, many families making their homes in Waubay, one of the few towns in which Sioux Indians actually reside. On the streets are Indian women in shawls and blankets, old men in moccasins, but with regular "store clothes" or, commonly, overalls. The younger Indians have been so influenced by their white environment, chiefly through intermarriage, that they are difficult to distinguish. Being comparatively an old town, having been founded in 1880, Waubay has many frame buildings, holds square dances with old-time music as often as modern dances, and nearly every male resident is a good fisherman. Blue Dog Lake is to the N., with fishing and bathing facilities.

Waubay is at the junction with an unnumbered graveled road (*see Tour 2B*).

At 60 *m.* is RUSH LAKE, so called because of its tall rushes and boggy marshes. Muskrat houses—mounds of mud, sticks, and rushes—are in the water; ducks also nest and swim about the lake during the spring and summer. Often in spring great white pelicans are seen far out on the water. Hunting clubs from Chicago, Milwaukee, and Sioux City have lodges here for fall duck and goose hunting.

An Indian legend of Rush Lake relates how ducks and other waterfowl received their beautiful colors. A young warrior who had from childhood been very fond of gay, bright colors, walked far from camp, lured by the beautiful colors of Indian summer. Now and then he would stop and take from his pouch clay and oil which he mixed to make shades and tints to his liking. As the shadows began to lengthen, he suddenly realized that it would soon be time for the night fire, so he made his way to Rush Lake where he built a small lodge of rushes. As he sat looking at the setting sun, he heard the talk of waterfowl not far away. Then he saw before him, diving and playing, ducks, mallard, teal, gray geese, and loons. They were his friends and were always glad to see him, so he put his hands to his mouth and called to them. They were startled at first but they soon recognized him, and paddled to shore as fast as they could. The Indian invited them to his lodge, where they took turns telling of what they had done that day. When he told that he had been studying and mixing colors, the mallard became interested and said, "You are our friend; would you be so kind as to paint us with some of your beautiful colors?"

"I will," said the warrior. "Choose your colors."

The mallard said that he wanted a green head, a white stripe around his neck, a brown breast, and yellow legs. When he was painted, the mallard said, "Now I do not want my mate to have the same colors as I do." So she was painted mostly brown.

The teal had his family and himself painted as he desired. By this time the paints were almost gone, so there were no bright colors left for the goose and the loon.

At 62.3 *m.* is a junction with an unnumbered road (*see Tour 2B*).

WEBSTER, 68.4 *m.* (1,842 alt., 2,033 pop.), is the seat of Day Co., and styles itself the "gateway to the Lake Region." Platted in 1880 and named for the first settler, J. B. Webster, the town attracted young businessmen to the new farm frontier. With a Norwegian farming community growing up around the town, a Scotchman, two Englishmen, a German, and a few others who came from eastern States, started business enterprises, namely, a livery, real estate office, jewelry store, grain elevator, bank, general store, newspaper, and saloon. The livery stable and saloon are gone, but around the others a prosperous, civic-minded town has developed until now it has a paved main street and two newspapers, one of which, *The Journal*, is widely known in journalistic circles for its rhyming headlines.

Right from the highway is a MUNICIPAL TOURIST PARK, with good accommodations.

HOLMQUIST, 73.1 *m.* (85 pop.), has three large white houses, pretentious in the 1890's, and identical in appearance. It is a safe wager that every third person in the community is named Holmquist, Olson, Peterson, Johnson, Helvig, Sundstrom, or Jensen.

BRISTOL, 78.2 *m.* (1,775 alt., 624 pop.), has the largest creamery in the region, the farms around having large dairy herds. The town was named for Bristol, England, in 1881, when it became the terminal of the Milwaukee R.R., but it was not until 1921 that it was actually incorporated. The village was the western terminal of the railroad for a year.

Between Bristol and Andover the range of hills dwindles to level prairie, and large wheat fields spread out in all directions. Occasionally early in the morning coyotes are seen on the hills near the road, and in the spring large flocks of geese feed in the cornfields along the highway.

ANDOVER, 90.4 *m.* (1,475 alt., 324 pop.), was first known as Station 88 by railroad graders, but when the town was platted in 1881 it took its present name from Andover, Mass. This market town for a rich farming region has a large, old-fashioned hotel, the Waldorf.

GROTON, 101.3 *m.* (1,304 alt., 1,036 pop.), is a grain and implement market for a large portion of the James River valley. Groton was the birthplace of Earle Sande, a few years ago the premier jockey in American horse racing. As a youth he first rode ponies, and then farm horses, bareback, and eventually because of his experience and small stature, became a professional jockey.

In the winter of 1936-37, after drought had ravaged the crops, townsmen and farmers found a remunerative business in shooting jackrabbits, the fur from which is used in the manufacture of coats and hats. At Groton the Boy Scouts staged gunless rabbit round-ups, using clubs instead.

Between Groton and Aberdeen US 12 passes through the James River valley, one of the richest farming areas in the Middle West, the soil of which is a rich black loam, a deposit of the glacial period. Around each farm is a grove of trees, reminiscent of homestead days when a claim could be had for planting 20 acres in trees.

At 109.6 m. US 12 crosses the James River, in the spring, a clear, fast-flowing river, in the summer a sluggish stream, and in the fall often completely dry or consisting of a series of pools. Dikes can be seen along the banks, to keep the river from flooding the bottom-land in high water. During the drought period the river was dry most of the time. Pheasant hunting is especially good along the river, and the bright-colored ring-neck pheasants are to be seen any day, any season, somewhere along the highway. The river contains bullheads and a few pickerel (*see SPORTS AND RECREATION*).

At 119.7 m. is the ABERDEEN MUNICIPAL AIRPORT, stopping place for transport and mail planes (*see TRANSPORTATION*).

ABERDEEN, 121.8 m. (1,300 alt., 16,725 pop.), (*See ABERDEEN*).

> Northern State Teachers' College, Wylie and Melgaard Parks, German-Russian community.

Here is a junction with US 281 (*see Tour 11*).

At 122.4 m. are the Milwaukee R.R. STOCKYARDS, in which trainloads of cattle, sheep, and hogs from the ranch country of western North and South Dakota and Montana are unloaded for rest, water, and feed on their way to packing centers farther east. There are 150 pens for cattle, each holding a carload, and 109 pens for sheep. From 200 to 2,000 carloads of stock pass through the yards each month during the fall shipping season. The yards are interesting by night as well as by day, when trains unload under bright lights.

At 126.9 m. is a junction with a graveled road.

> Right on this road is RICHMOND LAKE 2 m., which was formed by a dam built with the aid of the Works Progress Administration, flooding an area of 1,000 acres to make one of the largest man-made lakes in the State.

At 135.4 m. US 12 crosses the neck of MINA LAKE, formed by damming Dry Run Creek. Construction of the dam was started by private subscriptions from Aberdeen and Ipswich residents who wanted a recreational site. It was completed with the help of the State Game and Fish Department and Federal relief agencies. The lake is stocked with game fish, and is a State game reserve. Another arm of the horseshoe-shaped lake is crossed at 136 m. over a rock spillway.

IPSWICH, 149.3 m. (1,530 alt., 943 pop.), was named by Charles H. Prior, superintendent of the Milwaukee R.R., for the English city of that name. It is the seat of Edmunds Co., and has a new modern-style courthouse. A PUBLIC LIBRARY, presented to the city by the heirs of Marcus P. Beebe, pioneer resident, is built of native stone from the prairies. There is also a church constructed of the same kind of material. The town is rendered more attractive by the large ZINNIA GARDENS along Main St.

The promotion of the Yellowstone Trail (US 12) from "Plymouth Rock to Puget Sound" was begun at Ipswich by Joseph W. Parmley, and the organization, now known as the U. S. No. 12 Association, still maintains its national headquarters here. A World War MEMORIAL ARCH spans the highway, bearing the name of the Yellowstone Trail and its founder.

South of Ipswich, in Powell township, a colony of Welsh people settled and made their characteristic national contribution to the music of the region, three of them having been members of the Royal Welsh Glee Club which sang before the King and Queen of England.

Between Ipswich and Mobridge the glacially-formed hills rise like a rumpled blanket. Near the Missouri River there is more grassland, and grazing cattle are seen.

ROSCOE, 164 m. (1,826 alt., 540 pop.), is a trade center for a farming community, not unlike the small towns of the movies, with pool halls, tall red grain elevators, general stores, square houses, and large frame churches.

BOWDLE, 179.2 m. (1,995 alt., 773 pop.), came into being with the advent of the railroad, which was gradually pushing toward the Missouri River. The town was named for a banker who represented the railroad's interests in that region. Bowdle in the 1880's was an important sheep and wool shipping point, but with the coming of German farmers, diversified farming has become more important. Most of the businessmen in Bowdle are of German extraction, and the language is used on the streets. Churches form an integral part of social life, both in town and the rural communities. There are both Catholic and Lutheran churches.

JAVA, 194.4 m. (2,045 alt., 514 pop.), was once noted throughout the State for its girls' basketball teams, which for several seasons defeated all opponents. Cattle and horses are raised extensively in the surrounding region, forming the basis of the town's business. Pioneer residents are unable to recall how the town received its name, but it is generally believed that railroad engineers named it facetiously for coffee.

At 200 m. is the junction with a graded road.

> Right on this road is HIDDENWOOD LAKE, 3 m., a recreational center for this region; there is a good beach, and picnic grounds.

SELBY, 202.3 m. (1,877 alt., 613 pop.), was founded in 1899 when the town of Bangor, then county seat 5 m. S., was moved to the railroad line. Selby became the seat of Walworth Co. and the trade center of a large area in which cattle and horse raising is carried on extensively as well as farming. Selby sends a large percentage of its high school graduates to college, and many of the residents are college graduates. Although Selby is several miles from the Missouri River, nearly every spring one resident builds a houseboat, pulls it to the river, floats down to New Orleans for the winter, sells his boat and returns to build another.

At Selby is the junction with US 83 (*see Tour 12*).

At 219.3 m. the crest of the Missouri River breaks is reached, with a view of the river and bottom-land stretching N. and S., fringed with cedar, willow, and cottonwood trees. Here farming and livestock-raising are carried on together, and proposals for large irrigation projects are made annually. The most successful crops have been alfalfa and other forage plants. Thick timber, matted with dense underbrush along the river, gives testimony of what is possible where moisture is sufficient in this area, often classed as semi-arid.

MOBRIDGE, 221.6 m. (1,657 alt., 3,464 pop.), was formerly the site of Arikara and Sioux Indian villages, but it was not until 1906 that the present city was founded. At that time the Milwaukee R.R. built a bridge across the Missouri River, and when a telegrapher used the contraction "Mo. Bridge" in his reports a name originated that has remained with the town. Several build-

ings were moved from Old Evarts, a town which had been started
8 m. S., now deserted. As the division headquarters for the Pacific
extension of the railroad, the town grew rapidly. A large railroad yard still remains, but the offices have been moved. On the
grounds of the railroad station are two large stones called the
CONQUERORS' STONES. It is said that defeated Indian chiefs were
forced to kneel on the stones, placing their hands in the hand-
shaped grooves in token of submission to their captors. An excellent
collection of Indian relics taken from Arikara village sites near
Mobridge (*see below*) is displayed on Main St., by O. L. Lawein.
Unlike towns along US 12 to the E., in Mobridge are seen ranchers with ten-gallon hats and cowboy boots, and Indians in overalls or shawls.

At the western edge of the city is the NORTHWESTERN LUTHERAN
ACADEMY, a sectarian school.

At 222.9 m. is a junction with a graveled road.

> Right on this road is RIVERSIDE PARK and the FOOL SOLD-
> IERS BAND MONUMENT, 2 m., erected in honor of the "Fool
> Band" of Indians who rescued a party of white prisoners. Dur-
> ing the War of the Outbreak (see HISTORY), a band of Santee
> Indians attacked Shetek Lake, Minn., and took captive two wo-
> men and seven children. The white captives were taken to the
> Missouri River, at its junction with Grand River. Word of their
> whereabouts came to Fort Pierre. A party of eleven young Indian
> men, known as the Fool Soldier Band because they had taken an
> oath to help the whites, set out with Martin Charger, reputedly
> a grandson of Capt. Merriwether Lewis, the explorer, as their
> leader. The other Indian men were Kills Game and Comes Back,
> Four Bear, Mad Bear, Pretty Bear, Sitting Bear, Swift Bird, One
> Rib, Strikes Fire, Red Dog, and Charging Dog. They found the
> Santee camp of White Lodge, leader of the hostile band, and
> bargained for the captives, offering horses, food, and weapons.
> Finally a trade was effected and on Nov. 20, 1862, the captives
> were released to the Fool Soldiers. Having traded all but two
> guns and one horse, the rescuers made a basket for the children
> to ride in and placed one of the women, who had been shot in
> the foot, on the horse. Martin Charger gave his moccasins to the
> other woman who had no shoes.

> At 3 m., is an ARIKARA VILLAGE SITE, the outlines of which
> can be seen, as a different shade of grass fills the circle where
> the mud huts once stood. Each hut was from 20 to 30 ft. in
> diameter. Mounds are still visible beside each circle; these were
> refuse piles, and fragments of pottery are still found in these
> heaps. Several of the mounds were excavated by the Smithsonian
> Institution and the artifacts are on display in Washington, D. C.

At 224 m. is a junction with a graded, winding road.

Left on this road is LINCOLN PARK, 0.4 m., which has a public swimming pool, dance pavilion, tourist cabins, picnic places, and shade trees.

At 224.5 m., is the Missouri River bridge built by the State in 1924. North of the bridge is the railroad bridge, which rests on piers sunk 90 ft. into the river bed.

From the highway bridge, up the river, ASHLEY ISLAND is visible (R). It was named for Gen. William H. Ashley, a partner in the Rocky Mountain Fur Co., who in the spring of 1823 conducted a party of 100 men and a cargo of merchandise up the Missouri River, on flat boats, to his trading post on the Yellowstone River in Montana. Arriving at the Arikara Indian villages opposite the island on May 30, he traded trinkets for horses. Some of the Ashley party planned to continue the trip overland the next day, but at dawn the Indians made a surprise attack, killing 12 men and wounding 11. The land party returned to the boats and, taking the dead and wounded, drifted down the river. The boats halted where the highway bridge now stands, and the journals record how Jedediah Smith made a "powerful prayer" for the wounded. It was the first recorded act of public worship in South Dakota. General Ashley sent a message with news of the massacre to Col. Henry Leavenworth at Fort Akinson, Kan., who immediately dispatched an expedition to punish the Rees. On the way the soldiers met a party of trappers under Major Pilcher, and the remainder of the Ashley party, augmented by several hundred Sioux, set out in search of the enemy. Major Pilcher and the Sioux went ahead to hold the Rees until the arrival of the artillery. Hostilities began, but the Rees, camped on the E. side of the river, refused open battle. A six-pound howitzer, which had been brought and mounted on a nearby hill, began a bombardment of the Arikara village. The very first shot beheaded the chief. By noon the Rees sent a plea for peace, agreeing to return the goods stolen from the Ashley expedition. They returned a few buffalo robes, and further negotiations were postponed. In the morning it was discovered the Rees had escaped during the night with their belongings.

At the western end of the bridge the time meridian is crossed; W. of the bridge is mountain time, E. is central. (*Going W. turn watches back one hour; going E. turn them ahead one hour.*)

At *225.2 m.* on top of a high hill, at the junction with State 8 (*see Tour 2A*), is the SACACAWEA MONUMENT to the most famous of all Western Indian women. Sacacawea was a Shoshoni Indian girl who was captured by the Mandans at the age of 12, and later sold to a French trapper, Charbonneau, who married her. Charbonneau was hired by Lewis and Clark in 1805 to guide their expedition through the Rocky Mountains (*see HISTORY*). He took along with him his wife and infant son. Sacacawea, known as the Bird Woman, served as scout for most of the journey, and was also the nurse. On the return of the expedition in 1806 Sacacawea and her husband stayed with the Mandans for a while, but later, at the urgent invitation of Capt. Clark, visited him at St. Louis. He persuaded them to leave their son with him to be educated. Shortly after the return, according to two contemporary journals, a wife of Charbonneau died of fever, supposedly at Fort Manuel, on the Missouri River S. of the State line, and was buried there. There is some question, however, whether the wife referred to was Sacacawea. Charbonneau had more than one wife, and records of the Wind River Reservation in Wyoming offer evidence that a woman known as Sacacawea died there after having lived to a considerable age. Fort Manuel was destroyed during the war of 1812, and the site eroded into the Missouri River, so neither the fort nor the grave can be located accurately today.

The STANDING ROCK INDIAN RESERVATION, *231.3 m.* covers the eastern half of Corson Co. in South Dakota, and extends into North Dakota, with the Agency at Fort Yates, N. Dak. (*No permission necessary to pass through open reservation; office of agent at Fort Yates, N. D.; Federal offense to transport intoxicating liquors into or through reservation.*)

There are 3,828 Sioux Indians on the reservation roll, 2,565 of which are listed as full-bloods by the agency superintendent. The native bands within the Sioux Tribe (*see INDIANS*) on this reservation are: Hunkpapas, Yanktonai, Teton, Minneconjou, Itazibeo, Oohenupa, Sihasapa, Ogalala, Sicungu, and Isanyati. The Indian population is increasing. All persons under 40 years of age can speak English, but many speak the native tongue at home. The native language is used by 90 percent of the people over 40, and by half the children of pre-school age. It is used very little by school children.

Rodeos are held at irregular intervals during the summer months.

From US 12 Indian farms are seen, but a better view of the life on the reservation is obtained on the winding, dirt side roads. There are 222 frame houses occupied by Indians on the reservation, but none have modern facilities; 426 families use log houses today. Nearly every family has a tent in addition to its regular home. "Store clothes" are worn by 80 percent of the tribe, while old time garments such as moccasins, shawls, and petticoats made of flannel, with many gathers for fullness, are still worn by older women. Skins are still dressed by removing the hair with wood ashes, soaking the hide in water, and greasing it; after this it is worked by hand until it is soft and pliable. Other surviving customs include the general "give away" when a death occurs in the family. Clothing, household articles, and furnishings are given away, and the survivors of the family are obliged to replace things as best they can. The social life on this reservation consists of much visiting and dancing. When families go visiting, they take their tents and camp on the premises of those they are visiting. Usually they bring their own bedding and, if they have it, their food. Old time dances such as square dances and waltzes are popular, as well as the kahomani and other Indian steps. The Sioux enjoy the fairs and rodeos in the summer, taking their tents to the celebration where they camp until everything is over. The traditional tribal music prevails, but there is no set time or place where it can be heard. Funeral songs, rain songs, war songs, songs for the rejected lover and for those who are downhearted are heard wherever a group gathers in the evening. Native cults are not active on the Standing Rock Reservation, and 99 percent of the Indians are affiliated with some Christian sect. The Catholic, Episcopal, and Congregational denominations are strongest in point of numbers.

A tribal council of 14 members has some administrative powers; and a tribal judiciary of two judges, appointed by the Government, holds court over crimes of minor nature. The inhabitants of the reservation participate in county and State administration, with usually two or three holding elective county offices. The tribal wealth is approximately $11,000, but the per capita wealth averages only about $20, not including land. All property is now individually owned, but there are 95,000 acres of unallotted land. About 320,000 acres of Indian-owned land are rented. There are 21 Indian-owned stock ranches. During the past few years, the drought period, the farms have not been self-supporting. Several Indians have built up various types of individual businesses, including two newspapers, a creamery, a shoe repair shop, and two dance orchestras. There are cooperative livestock associations. Native handicraft forms a means of partial support, but it is not practised extensively.

At 235 m. is ST. ELIZABETH'S SCHOOL (R), an Episcopal boarding school for Indians. In front of the white buildings, situated on a high hill, is a monument erected to the early Christian leaders, and especially to the native minister, Rev. Philip Deloria.

WAKPALA (Ind., *stream*), 236.6 m. (1,633 alt., 200 pop.), is a settlement of whites and Indians. The one-street village, of dull frame buildings and a bright new community hall, has board sidewalks. A modern, brick schoolhouse contrasts with log cabins and tents in the wooded outskirts of the village.

At 253.3 m. is a junction with a dirt road.

> Left on this road is ELK BUTTE, 5 m. (L), one of the old sacred hills of the Sioux People. At 6 m. is LITTLE EAGLE, an Indian village of cabins and tents. It was here that probably the last Sun Dance ever to be held by the Sioux was staged in 1936 in quest of rain. Chief White Bull, nephew of Sitting Bull, led the three-day dance. At Little Eagle is a monument to Indian soldiers who died in the World War.

At 255 m. is the junction with a graded, dirt road.

> Left on this road is SITTING BULL PARK, 11 m., where the Sioux chief was killed during the Messiah War. (Indian guide available during summer.)
>
> It was during the early dawn of the crisp, frosty morning of Dec. 15, 1890, that Sitting Bull, last chief of the Hunkpapa Sioux, fell riddled with bullets at the hands of his own people, the Indian police, sent to arrest him. Here Sitting Bull last exhorted the wavering fragments of his once powerful band. Today the site of the medicine man's home is a public park, unimproved in order to preserve the actual setting. The sites of the cabins, the spots where each man fell, the common grave of the seven followers who died with Sitting Bull, and various relics of the famous "struggle in the dark" are preserved in this park.
>
> The old chief spent most of his life in South Dakota, but his body was taken to Ft. Yates, N. Dak., the agency, for burial. There in a solitary grave, in a corner of the old army post cemetery, Sitting Bill sleeps; bodies of white men, once buried near him, have been removed.
>
> Probably no figure in all Sioux history has caused more controversy, more uneasiness, was more colorful, more disliked, and more respected. When Sitting Bull was killed and his followers

were dispersed on that cold, hazy morning, the dim lamp of hope that had flickered so long in Sioux breasts, suddenly flared crazily, resulting finally in the Battle of Wounded Knee and the pitiful crushing of the dying spirit of the Indians. The ghost dance had been the last straw at which the Indians, in their final stand against civilization, had grasped. Believing that the white men, "Wasicun" (pronounced waseeehun), would suffer for their greed and selfishness, the Sioux imagined a Messiah would soon come and punish their enemies. The Wasicun had crucified their saviour, and retribution, they were sure, would overtake them.

Many books have been written about this chief, part of whose influence rested on his fame as a medicine man. Some disparage him; others praise him. Those who knew him declare he was canny, treacherous, deceitful, and cowardly. He never was a brave warrior in battle. At the Little Bighorn battle he was busy making medicine in his tipi, while braver leaders were in the thick of the red tide, directing the extermination of Custer's detachment or engaged in driving Reno across the river. But, at any rate, he always exerted a powerful influence, and caused no end of worry to white authorities, especially Maj. James McLaughlin, for many years agent on the Standing Rock Reservation where Sitting Bull lived. When McLaughlin learned that Sitting Bull was preparing to leave the reservation, he deemed it wise to place him under arrest. Detailed for the uncertain and risky task were 43 Indian policemen, under the command of Lieutenant Bullhead, a cool and reliable man, and an avowed enemy of Sitting Bull, as well as of his chief bodyguard, Catch-the-Bear.

The police approached Sitting Bull's camp quietly, at daybreak Dec. 15. The medicine man was sleeping when the police burst into his cabin, struck a light, and read to him the order of arrest. He consented to go with them and sent one of his wives to saddle his favorite mount, a trick circus horse he had brought back with him from Buffalo Bill's Wild West show, with which he had traveled at one time.

While the police were hurrying him into his clothes, word was spread about the camp of the arrival of the police, and quickly the medicine man's followers began to assemble about the cabin. The police, seeing the impending danger, hastened to get Sitting Bull out of the cabin and whisked away before bloodshed should occur, and half-dressed, he was dragged outside. Once out of the cabin and in view of all his loyal tribesmen, he hesitated; and while jibes from his young son, Crowfoot, from one of his wives, and others in the group, stung him deeply, he made up his mind that he would not be taken without a struggle. Lieutenant Bullhead and Sergt. Shave Head held Sitting Bull, each by an arm, Sergt. Red Tomahawk was guarding the rear, while the rest of the police (Metal Breasts, the Sioux called them) were trying to clear a path through the barricade of menacing red bodies, which hemmed them against the cabin.

When Catch-the-Bear, rifle in hand, appeared among the warriors, shouting threats at Lieutenant Bullhead, his personal enemy, Sitting Bull cried out, "I am not going! I am not going!" Catch-the-Bear threw up his rifle and fired. Bullhead fell, a bullet in his leg. But as he fell he turned and sent a slug into the body of Sitting Bull, who was shot from behind at the same time by Red Tomahawk. Shave Head was struck simultaneously with a bullet, and the three—Sitting Bull, Bullhead, and Shave Head—all went down in a heap. Then began a terrible hand-to-hand struggle between about 43 policemen and about 150 of Sitting Bull's warriors. It was no common fight; with Indian against Indian, Hunkpapa against Hunkpapa, the result was frenzy, brutality—Indians clubbing, stabbing, choking each other. Some of the police were Yanktonnais and Black Feet; the rest were Hunkpapas, Sitting Bull's own people.

Soon after the firing started most of the police dodged behind the cabin where they had the advantage, while the enemy took refuge behind trees that fringed the stream nearby. They held each other at bay until the arrival of the troops.

An event that almost struck panic to the more superstitious of the Indian police was the behavior of the gray circus horse, which Sitting Bull had ordered saddled and brought to his door. During all the fighting he sat calmly down in the midst of the melee and lifted one hoof as he had been trained to do. Then he performed other tricks he had learned with Buffalo Bill's Wild West show. This spectacle frightened some of the police, who feared that the spirit of the dead Sitting Bull had been reincarnated in the horse and had returned to punish them for their deed. Despite the fact that the air was alive with bullets, the old horse came through without a wound.

The seven warriors who had fallen with Sitting Bull on December 15 lay unburied for two weeks after the battle. Relatives were afraid to return because they thought the soldiers were still there. It was then that the Rev. T. L. Riggs, son of Stephen R. Riggs, pioneer missionary of South Dakota, volunteered to go with them and assist in the burial. They were placed in a common grave near the scene of the fight. Dr. Riggs is still living at Oahe, and through this act, which at the time he thought inconsequential, he endeared himself to the hearts of Sitting Bull's people.

McLAUGHLIN, 257 m. (2,002 alt., 633 pop.), is a young town in a comparatively new country, and while its trade is largely with Indians, it reflects the effect of prosperous years in this ranching and farming community. The town was named for Col. James McLaughlin, Indian Inspector of the Bureau of Indian Affairs.

McINTOSH, 283 m. (2,276 alt., 654 pop.), is the oldest town in Corson Co., having been incorporated in 1910; it is also the county

seat. The town was named after the McIntosh brothers who were
the subcontractors in charge of building the railroad grades through
the Standing Rock Reservation.

Between McIntosh and Lemmon the rolling country breaks into
occasional sharp buttes and grassless mud flats. Less than 30 years
ago the prairie was covered with shacks, hastily put together by
homesteaders who came, only to leave as soon as the land became
theirs. The few who remain, living along the little streams, have
gradually acquired herds of cattle. This country was once the paradise of cattlemen; it still is, but in a different sense. The cattleman must rent his land today; yesterday it belonged to anyone or
no one. Here, where there are few towns and the roads are impassable in wet seasons, the temptation to go to town is less; families are large and live to themselves. Men and women are wind-
burned the year around, and children are virtually raised in the
saddle.

MORRISTOWN, 299.8 m. (2,240 alt., 235 pop.), named for the
C-7 ranch proprietor, Nels Morris, supplies the surrounding ranchers with such supplies as they do not get from mail order houses.

THUNDER HAWK, 308.1 m. (100 pop.), has a general store
where on Saturdays commodities, politics, and gossip are exchang-
ed over the cracker and pickle barrels.

LEMMON, 318.4 m. (2,567 alt., 1,785 pop.), was named for
"Ed" Lemmon, pioneer and cattleman who for years was foreman
of the large L7 cattle outfit. The town is the trade center for a
large territory in both North and South Dakota, which produces
grain, cattle, horses, and sheep. Thus, it is one of the few towns
in the United States where cattlemen, sheepmen and farmers—each
uncomplimentary to the other—meet on a common ground—the
store, poolhall, bar, dancehall, or courtroom. Situated on the North
Dakota Line, part of the town is actually in the adjoining State.
It has enjoyed rapid growth during recent years, due to the fact
that it is the only town of appreciable size within a wide area and
commands a very large trade territory. Attempts at farming in the
immediate vicinity have resulted in much distress during recent
drought years, although the soil is exceptionally fertile.

Although Lemmon is the outstanding town in Perkins Co., it was
forced to concede the county seat to Bison, an inland hamlet,
about 40 m. SW.

The PETRIFIED WOOD PARK, on Us 12, contains several buildings, and numerous curios, built entirely of petrified wood obtained toward the southern part of the county. Petrified wood and agate rings are also sold in Lemmon, many different designs being obtainable.

On a convenient knoll at the northwest edge of town is the city's STANDPIPE, and nearby is the town's new SWIMMING POOL, completed under the Works Progress Administration program.

A fire that burned several tanks of petroleum products in 1935 created billows of smoke that drifted S. a hundred miles. Ranchers on the Cheyenne River told of seeing the smoke high in the air.

Left from Lemmon, on State 73, is a MASS BUFFALO BURIAL, 18.1 m. The site is difficult to reach, requiring several turns and the fording of a river; at 12 m. is a junction with a dirt road; R. on this road; at 15 m. L. on a winding road, past a country schoolhouse and through the woods, to Grand River. The river can be forded in most seasons. Left along the river at 18.1 m. is a cutbank, where a wedge-shaped mass of bones is exposed, 12 ft. under the surface of the earth. There are thousands of bones, and they are not fossilized. Several theories have been advanced for their presence. One is that a herd of buffalo may have been mired down in a morass; another is that the buffalo were driven over a cutbank by a severe storm and piled up at the bottom. There is evidence to refute every theory advanced thus far, and the presence of the bones has puzzled paleontologists who came to study the phenomenon.

WHITE BUTTE, 328.5 m. (85 pop.), the last town in South Dakota on US 12, is a typical Western movie village, its few houses evidently built without much idea of the town's coherence. Since it is a railroad town with a favorable location as a stock shipping point, it is a familiar sight to see cows or sheep dodging behind houses as the herds are driven to the stockyards for their long journey to market.

At White Butte US 12 crosses the North Dakota Line, 16 m. SE. of Hettinger, N. Dak. (*see N. Dak. Tour 9.*)

TOUR 2A

Junction with US 12—Trail City—Timber Lake—Isabel—Bison—
Buffalo—Camp Crook—(Miles City, Mont.). State 8.

Junction with US 12—Montana Line, 201 m.

Between junction with US 12 and Isabel this route parallels a
branch of the C. M. St.P. & P. R.R.

Hotel and tourist accommodations at Timber Lake, Isabel, Bison,
and Buffalo.

Gravel and dirt roadbed throughout, in good condition.

West of the junction with US 12 the road goes through a more
or less level country for 125 miles, but from that point on it is
more picturesque. It passes through the Reva Gap of the Slim
Buttes, and thence westward is never out of sight of pine-clad hills
—whether the Slim Buttes, the Cave Hills, or the East and West
Short Pines. For a number of miles west of the Slim Buttes the
road parallels Grand River, although not always in sight of it.

State 8 branches W. from US 12 (*see Tour 2*) 3 *m.* W. of Mobridge.

TRAIL CITY, 12 *m.* (2,143 alt., 300 pop.), is at the junction
of two branches of the C. M. St.P. & P. R.R., running to Isabel and
Faith (*see Tour 3*), respectively.

TIMBER LAKE, 32 *m.* (2,161 alt., 560 pop.), was built on the
edge of Timber Lake, which, paradoxically, has virtually no timber. In recent years the lake, crossed by a bridge, has been almost
dry. The town is the seat of Dewey Co.

FIRESTEEL, 41 *m.* (2,340 alt., 148 pop.), became well-known
for the State-operated coal mile there until its sale in 1936. Acres
of ground around the town were excavated for lignite coal, veins
of which are close to the surface. The State operated the leased
mine at a severe loss, but during the "depression" years coal was
given to needy, relief families. Coal beds are so common in the
area from this point W. that coal is sold for $1.00 to $1.50 a ton
at the mine.

ISABEL, 49 *m.* (2,402 alt., 420 pop.), is the terminus of one
branch of the C.M.St.P. & P. R.R. and serves a large territory
to the W.

COAL SPRINGS, 85 *m.* (15 pop.), is a general store and post
office, and was originally a quarter of a mile N. of its present site.

At 94 m. is the junction with State 73.

Right on this graveled road 15 m.; L. on old scenic round-up trail to the SITE OF OLD SIEM, 18 m., a discontinued post office dating back to range days. Left of Old Siem, across Grand River by ford and up a steep hill by footpath, is the HUGH GLASS MONUMENT, 19 m. Hugh Glass, in the summer of 1823, was a hunter and guide for a trading party under Gen. William A. Ashley, en route from the Missouri River, following the route of the earlier Astorians. Glass was scouting ahead of the main party near the forks of the Grand, when he came upon a grizzly and her cubs. He had no time to retreat, and a terrific battle ensued between him and the bear. When his companions found him, the bear was dead and Glass was unconscious, badly clawed about the face and mauled. Ashley left two men to stay and take care of him. They watched the unconscious man for four days and then, concluding that he would not live, they took his gun and ammunition, his knife, and even his matches, and left him. When they overtook the Ashley party, they reported that Glass had died and that they had buried him.

Glass recovered consciousness some time after they

HUGH GLASS
AND THE BEAR

had left. He knew, by the campfires, that someone had been left to aid him, and he was enraged that they should have left him defenseless and deserted. When he tried to move, he found that his leg was broken. For several days he lived on what bear meat he could tear off with his teeth. Then the meat commenced to spoil and from that time he lived solely on roots and berries. He decided that if he were to save his life, he would have to crawl to the nearest white settlement, Ft. Kiowa on the Missouri River, over a hundred miles away. It took him weeks to accomplish this incredible feat, setting a record for grit and endurance.

His wrath at the men who had betrayed him had grown to be a consuming fire, and, as soon as he was able to travel, he started in pursuit of them. He joined a keelboat party bound for the mouth of the Yellowstone; but when they reached Mandan, the ice closed in and the party had to remain there for the winter. But Hugh Glass' anger would not let him wait. He started overland alone and he found the Ashley party at the mouth of the Big Horn. He strode into the cabin and demanded to be shown the men who had deserted him. One of them cowered against the wall. Glass covered him with his gun and, walking over to him, kicked him lightly. "Get up!" he said, "and wag your tail. I wouldn't kill a pup." He inquired after the other man, a youth whom he had befriended, and found that he had gone to Ft. Atkinson with dispatches. After a few weeks' rest Glass set out to find him; but when he reached the fort, he found that the man had gone up river again. He finally overtook him and in the end forgave; "and that fact," Neihardt says, "raises his story to the level of sublimity."

John G. Neihardt, poet laureate of Nebraska, immortalized this feat in "The Song of Hugh Glass." On the hill 0.5 m. S. of the forks of the Grand, is the monument with the following inscription:

1823-1923

This altar to courage was erected by the Neihardt club August 1, 1923, in memory of HUGH GLASS who, wounded and deserted here, began his crawl to Ft. Kiowa in the fall of 1823.

MEADOW, 96 m. (60 pop.), is a small prairie town with garage, filling stations, and a few stores.

BISON, 108 m. (2,500 alt., 275 pop.), was named for the large shaggy animals that roamed the plains in countless thousands when the first white man came. It is a typical prairie town with one main street, from which the false front wooden stores of early days are not entirely lacking. The residence portion is more attractive; each house is surrounded by a large yard, and a beginning of tree planting has been made. Although towns like Bison are negligible in comparison with Eastern towns, they are economically much more important with relation to the region which they serve. Bison and Buffalo, its neighboring county seat to the W., each with a population of less than 300, are both on mail order house maps of the Northwest. Surrounding Bison are cattle ranches and large grain farms. This town is the seat of Perkins Co.

At 115 *m.* is the junction with a graded road.

> Right on this road at 7 *m.* is a sign, "Petrified Tree"; L. here 3 *m.* to a PETRIFIED TREE, claimed to be the largest in the world. Competent observers have declared that there is no record of a larger mass of petrified wood all in one place. The tree, buried in a hill, was discovered only recently. Seventy-five feet of it have been uncovered and there is still more in the hill. At the base the diameter is 2 ft. There are several large knots where limbs once grew and rings indicating the growth of the tree are plainly visible. Scientists say that this gigantic tree is a member of the Sequoia family.

REVA, 146 *m.* (12 pop.), is a store and post office just E. of the Slim Buttes. At 146.5 *m.* is the junction with a graded road.

> Left on this road is the post office, GILL, at the ROCK RANCH, 12 *m.* This ranch is remarkable for the beauty of its buildings and their setting. As the name implies, they are all of stone, and two stone arches give entrance to the parklike grounds. The stonework is interspersed with pieces of petrified wood and fossil specimens. Within the house there are many fossil remains gathered in the surrounding hills. Here are fossil bones of the three-toed horse, the oreodon, and the cephalopod. There are also fossilized turtles and snails, and the imprints on rock of ferns and leaves that grew in early geologic ages.

> At 16 *m.*, (R) up Deer Draw 0.5 *m.*, is a picnic ground. Here is a spring of good water and all camping facilities.

> At 16.5 *m.* there is a gap in the Buttes known as CEDAR PASS. This is second only to Reva Gap in beauty. The view from the top of the pass over the prairies is remarkable, with Castle Rock and Square Top in the distance, and on the horizon the faint blue outlines of the Black Hills. To see sunlight and shadow chasing each other over fifty miles of prairie is a sight long to be remembered.

At 148.5 *m.* (L) is SLIM BUTTES BATTLEFIELD MONUMENT, a simple shaft, eight ft. high, commemorating the Battle of Slim Buttes, which took place in the immediate vicinity. This was one of the three major conflicts between soldiers and Indians in the history of the State, the other two being the Battle of Wounded Knee and Colonel Leavenworth's campaign against the Rees.

The Battle of Slim Buttes was fought on Sept. 9, 1876. General Crook's troops were hastening S. to protect the settlers in the Black Hills, when an advance guard under Maj. Anson Mills encountered a small force of Indians in Reva Gap of the Slim Buttes. Major Mills held the Indians off until the arrival of reinforcements under General Crook. The Indians, meanwhile, had been reinforced by members of Crazy Horse's band. The two forces fought one entire day, at the end of which three white men and a dozen or more Indians had been killed, and a few Indians were taken captive. The battle was more or less of a stalemate, but the Indians withdrew during the night. The next morning General Crook burned what was left of the Indian villages and buried his own dead, causing his whole column to trample over their graves as he broke camp, to conceal their location from the Indians. Of the white men killed, one was a well-known scout, William White, a friend and follower of Buffalo Bill, whom he admired intensely. So noticeable was White's constant companionship with Buffalo Bill that General Sherman gave him the nickname "Buffalo Chips," because, he said, where you saw one you always saw the other.

At 150.5 m. the route enters the SLIM BUTTES, a long range of pine-topped hills, with limestone cliffs facing the W., and broken ridges and wooded valleys sloping to the E. For 20 m. this ridge stretches N. and S., and at the southern end it bends slightly SE. for another 15 m. towards an isolated peak known as Sheep Mountain. Through this entire stretch of 35 m., the range is never more than six miles wide, and more frequently two or three. It is this characteristic that has given it the name, Slim Buttes. The white limestone cliff to the W. is broken in three places: at Reva Gap near the N. end, at the JB Pass 10 m. S. of Reva Gap, and at the elbow where beautiful Cedar Pass permits passage (*see above*). These are the only points in the range where any kind of vehicle can cross.

The Slim Buttes have a history more replete with incident than any other part of this region. The first white men to see them were the members of the Astorian party under Wilson Price Hunt, who, in 1811, followed Grand River from its junction with the Missouri in order to avoid the long northward curve of the larger stream. The traders marveled at the buttes and mentioned them in their journals. Next to see them were the members of the Ashley party, who followed the trail of the Astorians in August 1823. This was the party of which Hugh Glass was guide, when he performed his almost incredible feat (*see above*). The next to note the Slim Buttes was a detachment of soldiers under Maj. Anson Mills who encountered a force of Indians in the Reva Gap and fought the Battle of Slim Buttes (*see above*).

At the north end of the Buttes is a sharp, detached rock rising to a peak, known as the Saddle Horn. There also are two great cliffs, 200 ft. high, facing each other across a deep draw. Farther S. along the western edge is a lofty knoll, rising above the skyline of the rim. This is called Government Knob, because on its summit is a marker of the Coast and Geodetic Survey, a brass-capped pipe thrust into the earth. This is the highest point in the county. From this and almost any other point along the Western rim, there is a really superb view. To the W. are the hills known as the East and West Short Pines, and beyond them the long blue line of the Long Pine Hills in Montana. To the NW. are the rounded shoulders of the Cave Hills. To the N. are jagged peaks that rise along the North Dakota border, and to the S. Castle Rock, Square Top and the faint blue outlines of the Black Hills, a hundred miles away.

South of the mile-wide Reva Gap the unbroken ridge extends for ten m. to the JB Gap, a lofty pass with scarcely a break in the line, but with an auto road descending its W. side with tortuous windings and terrific grades. This pass was named for the famous JB HORSE RANCH nearby (*open to visitors*), which has existed from the earliest days of white settlement.

A few miles S. the buttes make their bend to the SE., and at this point is a break, beautiful Cedar Canyon (*see above*), down which the road winds on its way S. From Cedar Pass the Buttes extend 15 m. farther and then cease as abruptly as they began, with Sheep Mountain standing beyond, a lonely sentinel.

In general, the western edge of the buttes is abrupt and commanding, with limestone cliffs the entire distance; the eastern side is broken up into long sloping valleys, with jutting points between. Springs are found throughout the buttes, the grass is long and thick, the draws are wooded, and it is an ideal place in which to winter stock. It is a part of the Custer National Forest, and neighboring stockmen acquire the right from the Government to run stock on the Reserve, paying by the head.

The buttes are also rich in fossils. Bones of the three-toed horse, the oreodon, the cephalopod and the sabre-toothed tiger, turtle shells of unusual size, fossil tracks of animals, and other interesting specimens have been picked up. In Reva Gap Indian relics have been found, such as bones, arrows, and an abandoned tipi that gives its name to Tipi Canyon.

In the buttes are numerous outcroppings of lignite coal, and in Reva Gap there is a coal mine that has been worked for many years. It has been estimated that there are a quarter of a billion tons of lignite coal in Harding Co. alone, and that the whole Slim Buttes region is underlaid with it.

At 151.5 m. the crest of REVA GAP (3,100 alt.), of the Slim Buttes is reached. This is the beauty spot of Harding Co. South of the road strange formations of rock and clay rise perpendicularly in many different forms. One of the largest of them has been named Battleship Rock because of its resemblance to the prow of an enormous ship. Many other narrow formations stand out here and there, or in line. They resemble nothing so much as individual pieces of stage scenery waiting to be pushed into position. At the highest point of the pass (L) is a perpendicular column of rock and earth rising two or three hundred feet, with grass and trees on its summit. This has become known as Flag Rock. It is climbed, but with difficulty. Just W. of Flag Rock a dirt road turns off (L) and follows the crest of the divide for half a mile. Along this trail are many camp sites with permanent ovens and other conveniences. Water can be obtained from nearby ranches.

West of the crest of Reva Gap the road winds down a horseshoe curve to lower ground.

At 159 m. is the junction with a dirt road.

Left on this road; at 2 m. L. through gate; at 2.5 m. is the STATE ANTELOPE PRESERVE (visitors welcome).

This is the only place in the world where antelope in large numbers are reared in captivity, so that this interesting and deer-like creature may be preserved for future generations. A 6-ft. fence of heavy-mesh wire topped by two strands of barbed wire surrounds the preserve; the heavy posts stand only a rod apart, a tubular steel post set in cement alternating with a pitch pine post, making a durable fence around this tract of over 14 sections.

Much of the land now enclosed was part of an old cattle ranch that dates back to the early 1890's, and the original ranch buildings are now the home of the Park Superintendent. It is the intent of the State Game and Fish Commission, under whose auspices the park exists, to preserve the buildings in the same form as they were when the ranch was taken over, for there are comparatively few examples left of the ranch architecture of the early days. The main dwelling is a typical log ranch house, roomy, low-ceilinged, and homelike. This ranch is ideally situated on the banks of Squaw Creek, a spring-fed stream that flows the length of the park and, with its twists and turnings, supplies sufficient water to all parts of it.

In a comparatively small enclosure, near the ranch building, are the baby antelopes that are being reared by hand. Every year from a dozen to 20 young antelopes are picked up in the large pasture to be brought up as "bottle babies." A baby antelope three days old, or younger, can be picked up off the ground. Instinct tells the young antelope to trust to its power of concealment at this stage it flattens itself to the earth, with its long neck outstretched and only its eyes betraying signs of life.

Antelopes are difficult to rear, being high-strung, delicate creatures. They must be fed often and a little at a time. They cannot take pure cow's milk at first, but must have it diluted with water. The proportion of milk is gradually increased until at about five weeks they are taking it undiluted.

The object of rearing a certain number by hand each year is twofold. They are kept in a smaller enclosure near the buildings, as an exhibit for visitors; also it is planned that the place with its increasing herd of antelopes (about 450) shall become a supply station for foundation herds of State and National Parks. The commission will not supply antelopes for municipal parks, because it has been repeatedly proven that these prairie animals will not live in close confinement; and the commission feels that to place them under conditions in which they cannot survive is to impose a needless cruelty.

As many as 175 antelopes in one band have been seen on the prairie just outside the fence. But they are much more likely to be seen in groups of six or a dozen, both inside the fence and out.

The antelope is a graceful, tawny creature, somewhat smaller than a deer, with a white rump that under excitement or fear flares out in all directions to twice its size and makes that antelope "flag" of glistening white which is seen for miles. It is their danger signal to one another, the sign that it is time to employ their great weapon of defense, their marvelous speed. They are said to be the speediest animal in the world. The coyotes are obliged to relay on them in order to catch them. They are protected by law, and are increasing outside the park as well as inside. Their flesh is dark and tender, even more so than venison.

A feature of the antelope preserve is a large dam that holds back some of the waters of Squaw Creek. In a lakeless country this dam has been very popular as a swimming place, with people coming for 20 m. Two bathhouses are conveniently placed near the dam face. The dam has also been stocked with fish and should afford good sport in time to come. The fish are of two kinds, bullheads and black bass. The former are intended for fishing by children and those who simply desire to get fish, while the black bass are for those who look on fishing as a sport and wish to pit their skill against a game fish.

From the junction with the road to the Antelope Preserve, State 8 runs for about 3 m. through the sheep ranch of A. H. Dean, for whom the author of *Sheep*, Archer B. Gilfillan, herded for 16 years. It was here that he obtained material for his book, which he wrote after he had herded sheep ten years. A graduate of an Eastern university, he drifted into herding through force of circumstances and continued the occupation because he liked it. The author described the country he knew best, and those travelers who may have read the book can judge of its truthfulness. The book, moderately successful, sold two editions and is at present being reprinted. The buildings of the Dean ranch are plainly visible a mile (R) from the road at 160.5 *m.*

At 171 *m.* is the junction with US 85 (*see Tour 13*). Between this point and Buffalo US 85 and State 8 are one route.

BUFFALO, 173 *m.* (2,800 alt., 250 pop.) (*see Tour 13*).

Here is a junction with US 85 (*see Tour 13*).

Within a radius of 50 m. of this point there are more sheep than in any similar area in the United States. Sheep wagons are seen on the top of many a hill, and bands of sheep graze along the roadside. A visit to one of these wagons will be of interest perhaps to anyone who has never seen one. But first locate the herder. He may object to strangers invading his home without permission. He will be somewhere close by with his sheep, and will gladly show how he, the last of the nomads, lives. But do not expect to find him different from anyone else who tends animals or works on a ranch. He wears no distinctive garb and talks no special "lingo."

The sheep wagon is reminiscent of the pioneer covered wagon, except that it is much shorter and the canvas is pulled taut, eliminating that ribbed appearance. Mounting a set of steps, or walking up the wagon tongue, to the doorway, the visitor sees before him a marvel of compact and convenient living quarters for one person. At the right, close to the door, is a small camp stove and above is a set of shelves for dishes and utensils. Along either side are benches, formed by extending the wagon bed over the wheels;

SHEEP HERDER

in the center of each of these benches is a trapdoor that opens into a "grub box," extending down into the space between the front and back wheels. Here the herder keeps his bread, cereal, meat, and light groceries. The two benches terminate in a bed across the end of the wagon—a board bunk, which may or may not have a set of springs, but has a mattress and bedding such as is found in any bunkhouse. Under the bed is a recess which sometimes has a drop door in front. Here the herder keeps his potatoes and bulky articles; and here his dog sleeps at night—and retires to it in the daytime when the herder inadvertently steps on his foot. Over the bed is a small window, hinged at the top and manipulated by a rope attached to the bottom, so that the herder can open and hold it at any angle desired by simply tying the rope. This window, being at the opposite end of the wagon from the door, insures perfect ventilation and also permits the herder to look out over his sleeping flock at night without getting out of bed. For this reason the wagon is always placed with its door facing away from the bedground. The door is cut in two, crosswise in the middle, the upper and lower halves swinging independently on their own hinges, making it easier to keep the wagon at any temperature desired without a direct draft on the stove. There is no table in sight until the herder either swings it up from the front of the bed and props it with its one leg, or, more likely, pulls it out flat from beneath the bed, the exposed part being held firm by the part that remains beneath the bed.

Such is the herder's happy home, a model of compactness and convenience. His personal belongings are kept on a shelf above his bed. There is plenty of room in the wagon for one person, but two would crowd it. Perhaps that is the reason why there are so few married herders, or at least herders whose wives live with them in the wagon. There is distinctly no room for temperament, and the sheep wagon will probably continue to be in the future as it has been in the past, the refuge of the married man and the hiding-place of the bachelor.

On the tops of many hills in this part of the country are small monuments made of piled stone, often two or more on one hill. These monuments, locally called "stone Johnnies," are as characteristic of sheep country as the sheep themselves. They are the work of herders. Many explanations have been given for them. One, obviously unfair to the herder, is that when he feels himself mentally slipping, he piles up rocks in order to occupy his mind. Another theory is that by the shape or size of the monument he can assure himself of his location in case of fog or darkness. The fact that there are not half a dozen foggy days a year in this region would seem to argue against this theory. Perhaps the most reasonable explanation is that the monuments are the result of the conjunction of an idle hour and a convenient scattering of stones, which usually are found on hilltops. Herders spend much of their time on hilltops, since it is easier to watch the sheep from an elevation.

The country W. of the buttes is somewhat different from that to the E. It is rougher and the soil is lighter. There are few small farms, but large ranches. Often for miles there is not a house. But the landscape is more picturesque and varied. To the E. are the white, pine-topped cliffs of the Slim Buttes; to the W. are two shorter ranges of the same formation and appearance, the East and West Short Pine Hills. To the N. are the rounded outlines of the Cave Hills, from which the limestone cap has been worn away.

Petrified wood is also plentiful throughout this region; it is found in almost every creek bed and in Grand River, where it should be looked for on the riffles. There are isolated small patches of badlands where an occasional fossil specimen is picked up, although the best have been taken. In the mud buttes leaf impressions are found by those who know how to look for them.

At 191 *m.* is the region known as the JUMP-OFF. At this point is a junction with a prairie trail.

> Left on this road, following the rim of the Jump-Off, which is really a fault in the earth's surface extending N. and S. for many miles, the country is much like the Badlands on a smaller scale. It is rough and broken, with many bare hills. Grotesque formations, washouts, and cut banks make it a very difficult country for travel. Along the rim on the western edge is a good view of this region, but only on foot or horseback can the remarkable formations be explored. As in the Slim Buttes, there have been found a considerable number of fossils, including dinosaur bones. Some of these are on exhibition at the Harding post office, and a number of them are in the School of Mines Museum in Rapid City (see RAPID CITY).

> It was in the heart of the Jump-Off that Tipperary, South Dakota's most famous bucking horse, lived his entire life on the ranch of his owner, Charlie Wilson. He retired an undefeated champion and lived to be more than 20 years old. In spite of good care, he was caught in a severe winter storm and his remains were not found for many weeks.

At 194 *m.* is the junction with a dirt road.

> Left on this road is the old town of HARDING, 12 *m.* (25 pop.), in a most picturesque setting between the East and West Short Pine Hills. It consists of only a few stores, dwellings and post office, but in the early days it served a large territory and had a very good trade. There is a display of fossils at the postoffice (see above).

The SHORT PINE HILLS are so named to distinguish them from the Long Pine Hills of Montana, just across the line. The "Short" refers to the length of the hills and not to the pines. The hills are in two groups, the East and West Short Pines, respectively. They are limestone-capped ridges of the same general character as the Slim Buttes, and are a part of the Custer National Forest. These hills are covered with ponderosa pine, which upon designation by the forest ranger may be cut into lumber by the ranchers. The hills are easily accessible, and afford many delightful camp sites.

CAMP CROOK, 198 m. (186 pop.), was named after Gen. George Crook, the Indian fighter of the middle '70's in this region. Like Harding, Camp Crook is an old pioneer town. Like Buffalo, it serves a very large ranching territory. Its trees make it more attractive than the average prairie town. There is bathing and fishing in the Little Missouri, on whose banks the town is built.

~ It was in this region that the last of the great northern herd of buffalo were killed. When the terrific slaughter of these animals by the hide hunters took place, they split into two great bands. The northern herd was slaughtered along the Little Missouri River.

At 201 m., State 8 crosses the Montana State Line, 129 m. SE. of Miles City, Mont.

TOUR 2B

Waubay—Enemy Swim Lake—Pickerel Lake—Waubay Lakes—Junction with US 12.

Unnumbered road.

Waubay—Junction with US 12. 36 m.

Graveled roadbed.

Resort, hotel, and cabin accommodations at Enemy Swim and Pickerel Lakes.

This circular route passes through the lake region north of Waubay and Webster, where chains of small lakes weave through the hills. Fishing, swimming, motorboating, aquaplaning, camping, picnicking, waterfowl hunting, ice skating, ice boating, and skiing are popular sports, and lodges, resorts, and cottages have been built to promote these activities. This section has been visited little by people from other parts of South Dakota, largely because of its location; however, groups of people from Chicago, Milwaukee, and Akron spend weeks here each year. The route through this region is in the Sisseton Indian Reservation (see INDIANS and Tour 1).

The Sisseton and Wahpeton bands of the Sioux Nation found the lake country to their liking, withstood attacks from the Chippewas, and moved no farther until they were driven out by U. S. soldiers in 1862. They returned the next year and settled permanently around the lakes. The early settlement of the lake country is the story of white immigration and intermarriage with Indians. For instance, there was Albert Barse and E. P. Owens, a printer. After the Civil War, with jobs scarce, the two men sought employment from Horace Greeley, whose, "Go West, Young Man" campaign was starting. The editor hired them to write stories of the Northwest, and the pair started on their adventure. Settling first at Graceville, Minn., they married twin cousins of One Road, a noted chief, in order to secure the confidence of the tribe. Barse used to relate how the women were afraid to stay with them because of their white color and unusual language, so One Road had to move in too. Later Barse moved to the Waubay Lakes (*see below*), and Owens homesteaded at Minnewasta. They never returned to New York; their descendants are still prominent in the lake region. An influx of ·Norwegian and Swedish homesteaders, followed by groups of Poles, came in the 1880's. The effect of hybridization through the marriages of whites and Indians is noticeable; most of the Indian families have mixed blood, and have taken the names of the white members.

From the junction with US 12 at WAUBAY (*see Tour 2*), this route runs N. to BLUE DOG LAKE, 0.4 *m.*, which was named for one of the Sisseton chiefs whose descendants still live near Waubay and the lake. Bullheads, carp, and eels are most abundant in the lake, which has a mud bottom.

At this point is a junction with a graded road.

Left on this road is a DANCE PAVILION, 0.8 *m.*, where boats are for rent. There are numerous picnic spots along the lake beside this road.

At 0.9 *m.* the road crosses a SLOUGH full of rushes and cattails. Varieties of ducks are often seen here during the nesting season, and mudhens, protected black waterfowl, are usually abundant.

At 1.7 *m.* is BLUE DOG CREEK, where in the early summer large yellow water lilies bloom, one of the few places in the State where lilies grow wild. Beside this creek were old Chief Blue Dog's log house and three log cabins, one for each of his wives..

At 2 m. is the junction with a dirt road.

Left on this road is an old resort where boats can be rented and fishing equipment secured.

The road passes through a rolling, farming country; a small house, unpainted barn, several dogs, small garden, and two or three horses usually comprise an Indian home, while the more pretentious homesteads are those of white farmers. The Polish farms can be distinguished from the Indian homes by a two-story house and the color of the numerous children in the yard.

At 7.5 m. is a junction with a dirt road.

Right on this road is reputedly the BURIAL MOUND OF CHIEF BLUE DOG, 0.7 m., which has been opened by vandals who removed relics; at 1.4 m. is GUDERIAN BEACH, a small resort in a grove of linden and elm trees. At 1.7 m. is a canal to raise the level of CAMPBELL SLOUGH (R), a bass-spawning and waterfowl refuge.

From the highway ENEMY SWIM LAKE can be seen (R). The lake is the setting for a famous Indian legend which has several variations, but it is generally agreed that its name was derived from a battle between the Sioux and Chippewas. According to the old legend, handed down for generations, a band of Sisseton Sioux was camped in the woods of the peninsula which extends from the southeastern shore and almost reaches a long, high island. A powwow was in progress one evening and the squaws had been sent out for more firewood while the others sang and danced around the fire. Meanwhile a band of hostile Chippewas from the Mississippi country, who were on a hunting trip, saw the reflection of the fire in the sky and followed the light to the lake shore. Leaving their horses in the woods on the eastern side of the lake, the Chippewas planned a surprise attack on the village after the dance was over and all were asleep. Sioux guards being stationed on the mainland, the Chippewas quickly made rafts and landed on the island, which provided an approach from which no attack was expected. As the tom-toms beat loudly, the Chippewas quietly crossed the waistdeep neck to the peninsula and hid in the bushes waiting for the village to retire. But one of the squaws, picking up sticks, heard her dog growling; when she went to find it she saw a stranger in war paint crouching nearby. She screamed. There was no escape from the excited, war-whooping Sioux. The Chippewas splashed back to the island and, as the Sioux followed, they swam for the shore and their waiting horses. "Toka nuapi!" (*the enemy swim*), cried the Sisseton chief. Some of the Sioux rode their horses around the bay and as the swimming enemies reached the shore they were trampled to death.

At 8 m. is the junction with a graveled road, where there is the small brown house of an Indian family, in which pow-wows are often held during the early fall on Saturday nights. Here the young Indian people gather for the rabbit dance, and legion dance, two favorites in which couples circle the room side by side while singing. A few white people, friends of the Indians, are often present and join in the dance. Unbuttered bread and coffee are served during the dancing, which lasts until a late hour and is followed in the morning by church.

Right on this road at 0.6 m. is the entrance to CAMP CHEKPA, regional Boy Scout Camp. Chekpa means "twin" in Sioux, and Chief Chekpa was noted in local history as a peaceful leader. The beach, known as SANDY BEACH, is excellent for swimming (open to the public). At 0.8 m. is a pond and private refuge for mallard ducks (R); L. is a bay full of stumps which in normal years is a fine bass-fishing region. The BIOLOGICAL STATION of Northern State Teachers College (see ABERDEEN), 1.2 m., holds summer classes in biology, zoology, and botany; women students live in cabins and men in tents.

At 1.3 m. is CAMP DAKOTAH, an attractive summer resort operated by Jack Rommell, hunter and sportsman. (Hotel, dining room, cabins, boats.) The camp is situated on a peninsula that extends into Enemy Swim Lake. In the hotel lobby are Indian relics and fishing and hunting trophies. The fireplace is made of Indian hammerheads, tomahawks, mortars, pestles, and other implements picked up in the vicinity. There are three types of fishing in Enemy Swim Lake—casting for black and silver bass; trolling for northern pike, pickerel and wall-eyed pike; and still fishing for bluegills and perch.

Visitors seeking Indian relics can often find flint arrowheads along the beaches or high ground nearby. Diamond willows, stripped to make ornamental canes, are found near the lake shore, the most suitable being those from 6 to 10 ft. high. Buffalo beans and sweet-flag, the root of which is used by the Indians as an antidote for colds, grow on the hills beside the lake.

At 8.8 m. is an INDIAN CHURCH (Episcopal) and CEMETERY. In 1863 when the Sissetons, who had fled W. across the Missouri into Canada, returned to their lake country and camped at Enemy Swim Lake, U. S. soldiers surrounded them (see Tour 1). Here a treaty was made, and on this ground where they agreed to "be brothers" with the whites, the church that was built still stands

(R); but there is a new, glistening white edifice nearby. To the L. is the rectory, a house and barn, for the minister and his family. In front of the church is the cemetery in which a variety of gravestones mark the burial places. On many of the markers is a daguerreotype set in stone, showing an old Indian dressed in the clothing of white men. Some of the graves are covered with brightly colored glass and others have flags to show their participation in wars. Several markers are for white men who have lived with the Indians, including Albert Barse (*see above*).

Between Enemy Swim and Pickerel Lakes the road cuts through a series of hills and draws.

At 11 *m.* is the junction with a graveled road.

Right on this road is PICKEREL LAKE, 1.3 *m.*, a slender, fish-shaped, tree-bordered lake about three miles long. Spring-fed and deep, its waters are cold even in summer, but swimming, aquaplaning, rowing, canoeing, motorboating, and sailing are popular and regular sports. Northern pike, pickerel, wall-eyed pike, black bass, silver bass, crappies, bluegills, perch, and steelhead trout are caught here. At the foot of the hill is SOUTH END, 1.5 *m.*, a village of summer cottages grouped around the shoreline for over a mile. A hotel and dining room are in the center. (The beach is public and boats, swimming suits, and fishing equipment are available at the hotel.)

1. Right from South End on a winding dirt road is a STATE FISH HATCHERY, 0.5 *m.*, where pike, pickerel, and lake trout are hatched for lakes in the region. The low white hatchery building is beside a stream which flows from a natural spring farther up the ravine. Behind the row of cottages along the lake are Indian homes.

2. Left from South End, on a dirt road between rows of cottages, is the PEABODY GARDEN, 0.6 *m.*, where an irrigated garden affords a botanical exhibit.

3. Behind the South End hotel is a path to a MOUND 1.1 *m.*, which overlooks both Enemy Swim Lake and Pickerel Lake. From this vantage point one can see the chain of Waubay Lakes (SW) and Webster, 25 m. away. The hill is sacred to the Indians, as it was here that the medicine men and holy men went to fast and have visions. Wailing for days, and without food, the men would fall into swoons and usually experienced hallucinations. These they would interpret to their tribe, and future plans would be made accordingly. Among the stories handed down from father to son is the prophecy of Tasonkesapa 200 years ago. He was asked to have an understanding with the Great Spirit about the coming of the white men, of whom they had met several. His reply was: "The Great Spirit answered, 'The buffalo and wild things will disappear'."

At 12.3 *m.* is a junction with a dirt road.

> Right on this road is RAMONA BEACH, 1.2 *m.*, a private resort owned by Aberdeen people.

At 13.2 *m.* is a junction with a dirt road.

> Right on this road is Maloney's, 0.9 *m.*, a resort (open).

At 14.2 *m.* is the northern end of Pickerel Lake and a junction with a graveled road.

> Right on this road is the ABERDEEN Y. M. C. A. CAMP, 0.6 *m.*, a summer camp for boys and young men. Across the narrow neck of water is ADAMS BEACH, a public resort.

This route turns L. at the junction with the graveled road and for a few miles crosses rolling prairie land. At 19 *m.* is a junction with a graded road where the route turns L. to GRENVILLE, 22 *m.* (1,815 alt., 282 pop.), which was incorporated in 1918 as a town, but had been a village since 1885 when a group of Poles established a Catholic church there. The church has been rebuilt and an academy has been established for the Polish farm children.

East of Grenville the route passes between two bodies of water, known as Waubay Lakes. In the lake to the R. is an island which is frequented by white pelicans every spring during mating season.

At 27 *m.* is the HILDEBRANDT RANCH on an oak-covered hill, behind which is the site of the old BARSE TRADING POST.

At 27.4 *m.* is the junction with a sandy road.

> Left on this road is the U. S. BIOLOGICAL STATION, 1 *m.*, where a refuge for waterfowl in this area is being established, this being usually a hunting region; L. is an observation tower.

At 29 *m.* is a junction with another graveled road and this route turns R. to another of the WAUBAY LAKES, 30.7 *m.*

At 32.5 *m.* is a junction with a dirt road.

> Right on this road is HEDTKE PASS, 0.8 *m.*, a natural shooting pass—a strip of land between two large, marshy lakes. The pass is owned by the State Game and Fish Commission and only restricted duck and goose shooting is allowed. On the western edge of the pass is a wooded area in which are clusters of bittersweet, a red berry with open orange peel, often used for decoration.

At 33.2 *m.* is another WAUBAY LAKE, in the middle of which is CORMORANT ISLAND, so called because of the number of long-necked black waterfowl that build nests there each spring, so close together that there is no room to walk. This lake is used in winter for ice boating because of its size, but it is not used for either swimming or fishing.

At 35 *m.* is LAKE MINNEWASTE (Ind., *good water*). This lovely lake is shaped like an hourglass. Although there are no public bathhouses, swimming is popular in summer and ice skating in winter.

At 36 *m.* is the junction with US 12 (*see Tour 2*), 5 *m.* W. of Waubay.

TOUR 3

(Dawson, Minn.) — Watertown — Redfield — Gettysburg—Faith — Newell — Belle Fourche. US 212.

Minnesota Line to Junction with US 85 at Belle Fourche, 429.8 m.

Between Watertown and Gettysburg US 212 is paralleled by the C. & N. W. R.R.; between Le Plant and Faith, by the C. M. St. P. & P.; and between Newell and Belle Fourche, by the C. &. N. W.

Hotels and tourist camps at larger towns.

Roadbed hard-surfaced 68 miles in vicinity of Watertown; remainder graveled with short stretches of dirt grade.

US 212 passes through the State's lake region and level prairies and thence across the rugged, broken cattle country west of the Missouri River, which merges into a region marked by steep-walled buttes, jutting upward at intervals like numerous large haystacks. Continuing through the irrigated section, where water has miraculously transformed the drab prairie into a veritable oasis, the route halts in the shadows of the Black Hills.

Between Faith and Newell there are towns in name only, for none of them can boast of much more than a store and post office. There are no hotel or tourist accommodations in this distance, although gasoline and oil can be purchased along the highway. Despite the fact that much of US 212 traverses a sparsely settled, open country, the route is quite picturesque, hills and buttes providing constantly changing scenery.

Section a. Minnesota Line-Cheyenne River Reservation, 214.3 m.

US 212 crosses the South Dakota line 15 m. W. of Dawson, Minn. (*see Minn. Tour 11*).

At 11.5 *m.* (L) is LAKE ALICE, one of the numerous bodies of water in a section of the State noted for its many lakes.

At 13.6 m. is the junction with US 77 which crosses the State's richest farming area (*see Tour 9*).

KRANZBURG, 25.8 m. (155 pop.), consisting of a few scattered buildings, including a night club, garage, and gas stations, is the only town directly on the highway between the Minnesota Line and Watertown.

WATERTOWN, 35.8 m. (1,734 alt., 10,246 pop.) (*see WATERTOWN*).

> Summer resort center at Lake Kampeska, first State Capitol, Mellette Home, Aviary, State Pike Hatchery.

Here is the junction with US 81 (*see Tour 10*).

At 49.5 m. is the junction with a graveled road.

> Right on this road is MEDICINE LAKE, 12 m., called in the Sioux Indian language "Min-ne-pe-juta." This small body of medicinal water covers approximately 400 acres and is fed by subterranean springs. A chemical analysis reveals that this lake contains chemicals similar to those found at French Lick, Ind.

> Skin eruptions and irritations are relieved by these waters. The Indians who named the lake made use of its medicinal properties. Water from it is bottled and sold throughout the country. A short time ago a movement to establish a sanitarium was started, but as the lake is rurally located, funds were lacking for the completion of the project. A fine sand beach encircles the entire lake, and two resorts, one on the east and another on the west shore, provide bath-houses, lunches, and picnic grounds.

HENRY, 54.4 m. (1,812 alt., 358 pop.), might be termed the eastern edge of South Dakota's most thickly stocked pheasant country, and into this section every year pour hundreds of sportsmen, not only from other parts of the State, but from adjacent and often distant States. These popular birds are also found in other parts of eastern South Dakota, but natural haunts, good feeding grounds, and shelter make this section outstanding.

Henry is one of the many towns that, during early railroad days, were given the names of railroad officials, their wives, daughters, or even sweethearts, other towns included in this list being Florence, Wallace, Lily, Bradley, Raymond, and Butler. Henry has a well-equipped tourist park.

CLARK, 67.5 m. (1,779 alt., 1,290 pop.), seat of Clark Co., was founded in 1882 and has always been the center of a prosperous farming region. Its courthouse, completed in 1935, is one of the outstanding structures of its kind in northeastern South Dakota.

The interior decorations are of Carthage marble topped by ala-
baster.

DOLAND, 86.2 m. (1,355 alt., 538 pop.), has a population composed of many nationalities, intermingled to such a degree that
they can only be called Americans. The town has a large trade
territory and is situated in a productive farming region.

FRANKFORT, 97.2 m. (1,296 alt., 346 pop.), like Henry is
noted for the abundance of pheasants in the surrounding country.
The town was named for the German city in honor of an early
settler, Frank I. Fisher, who shot the last buffalo in Spink Co. The
animal's head was mounted and is now displayed in the courthouse
at Redfield.

At 100 m. is the junction with a graveled road.

> Right on this road is FISHER'S GROVE, 0.2 m., a public park on
> the James River with picnic and recreational facilities. This park
> was developed in 1936-37 in a heavy stand of timber. In the river
> is Motley Island.

REDFIELD, 108.4 m. (1,295 alt., 2,573 pop.), is the largest
town on US 212 between Watertown and the Black Hills. Four
hotels and a tourist park afford ample accommodations. In Redfield
is the new EASTERN STAR HOME OF SOUTH DAKOTA, designed to take
care of old and indigent members of the order. It is housed in the
buildings formerly occupied by Redfield College, now non-existent.
The town also is the home of PLEASANT VIEW ACADEMY, a denominational school.

Redfield has the distinction of having had to take up arms in a
struggle over the site of the county seat, a fight which began in
1880 and was not permanently settled until 1886.

By the election of 1880, Redfield, then Stennett Junction, was
selected as the seat of Spink Co., but for some reason the county
records were not moved from Old Ashton. In the next election,
1884, there were more votes cast than there were people in the
county. The towns contesting for the county seat sent delegations
to attest to the voting in every polling place and it was believed
that the totals were correct, but when the ballots were counted apparently dead men had voted, as well as all the railroad construction crews and others.

Following this fraudulent election there was much discussion as
to where the county seat should really be, and a delegation from
Redfield, sworn to secrecy, stole the county books and records,
after picking the vault.

Feeling ran high, and before long word had been passed throughout the northeast part of the county and in the early morning about 300 "Minute Men" gathered at Old Ashton, armed with various weapons.

On the morning of Dec. 7, 1884, an army of about 1,500 men from the northern section arrived at Redfield and made camp near where the Milwaukee depot now stands. Mayor Hunt of Redfield attempted to parley with the "Army of the North", but they sent the Redfield mayor a message that 2 hours would be allowed to get the women and children out of town, as at that time they would invade the town, take the records, and destroy the place if necessary.

Acting upon the suggestion of an attorney, that, inasmuch as Redfield had won the election of 1880, an injunction be applied for to prevent the removal of the records, a Chicago & North Western engine was chartered for a trip to Watertown. From there the party went across country to Milbank to obtain the injunction. In the meantime marksmen were posted at convenient points as unrest became apparent in the ranks of the "Ashton Army." The arrival of the train bearing the injunction, which was promptly served, was perhaps the only thing that averted bloodshed.

Later, sixteen leading citizens of Redfield were named in warants issued by Justice Bowman of Ashton. All gave bonds except one, who demanded immediate trial; the case was transferred to Athol and heard by Justice Oakland. Attorneys from Watertown, Huron, and Aberdeen appeared for the prosecution and the entire Redfield bar presented the defense. The defendant was dismissed with a word from the judge, "Not proven; but don't do it again."

Although Redfield continues to be the county seat, there are many old-timers who still hold strong opinions on this subject.

At Redfield is the junction with US 281 (*see Tour 11*).

> Right from the center of town on a graded road that crosses Turtle Creek, is the STATE SCHOOL AND HOME FOR THE FEEBLE MINDED, 1 *m.* In connection with the school is an excellent herd of nearly 200 Holstein-Fresian cows, cared for by the institution. This herd has won national fame and received many awards. The spacious barns and other buildings of the school are visible for many miles.

At 111.9 *m.* is the junction with a graded road.

> Left on this road are the SINK HOLES, 0.6 *m.*, large openings in the ground, partially filled with water. They were created when

blasting for a spring several years ago. They are about 1,000 ft. from the point where the blasting occurred and their presence is attributed to an underground stream that probably washed out loose gravel beneath, the blast then causing the cave-in.

ROCKHAM, 125.5 m. (1,394 alt., 258 pop.), is a grain and produce market for the large and thrifty German community that surrounds it.

FAULKTON, 149.1 m. (1,595 alt., 713 pop.), seat of Faulk Co., also draws business from a large territory, as it is a considerable distance from any town of appreciable size. It was named for Andrew J. Faulk, an early governor of Dakota Territory.

Like many early towns, Faulkton also engaged in a county seat fight. The other contestant was LaFoon, now a ghost city, 5 m. east of Faulkton. LaFoon won the first election, but Faulkton became the permanent seat with the advent of the railroad in 1886. That sounded the death knell for the town of LaFoon, and its residents moved to Faulkton.

At 149.7 m. is the junction with a graded road.

Left on this road to LAKE FAULKTON, 1 m., a large artificial lake which provides water sports for Faulkton and vicinity. It was built under a Government work program.

SENECA, 170.3 m. (1,911 alt., 295 pop.), is a short distance (R) from the road.

It was named for Seneca Falls, N. Y., by Eastern homesteaders. In 1936 a fire leveled many buildings here.

LEBANON, 182.5 m. (1,956 alt., 345 pop.), for many years was the thriving center of a prosperous farming area, but trucks and automobiles robbed it of much of its earlier business. The town has an excellent swimming pool and park.

At 189 m. is the junction with US 83 (see Tour 12); US 83 and US 212 are united for 10 m.

GETTYSBURG, 194.1 m. (2,082 alt., 1,414 pop.), was named for the Pennsylvania battlefield by a group of Civil War veterans who first settled here. Founded in 1881, the town has kept its main street neat and attractive by considerable paving and the preservation of many old trees. Today several large cottonwoods protrude through the sidewalks and tower above the adjacent buildings.

The town presents a colorful sight, with visitors from farm, ranch and reservation. The Indians live at the Cheyenne Agency, headquarters for the officials of the Cheyenne River Reservation (*see below*). Gettysburg has a wide trade area and normally is the busy center of a prosperous farming section.

At 199.4 *m.*, is the junction with US 83 (*see Tour 12*).

At 211.3 *m.* is the junction with a winding graveled road that follows the Missouri River and is flanked by trees on either side.

> Left on this road is FOREST CITY, 3 *m.* (65 pop.). The town was originally located farther up the river and was one of the stopping places for numerous fur traders and military expeditions. In the 1890's a railroad was built from Gettysburg, but abandoned soon after 1900. Before the bridge was built above the present town, a ferryboat plied between Forest City and Cheyenne Agency, but with the completion of the bridge all business was diverted from the town. Today, with only a handful of scattered inhabitants, the village is gradually joining the long list of ghost towns. It was the first seat of Potter Co., but following a county seat fight it lost to Gettysburg.

At 211.6 *m.* a dim but passable road leads R. through a gate over a small hill.

> Right on this road to MEDICINE ROCK, 0.4 *m.*, long held sacred by the Indians, and a subject of controversy among scientists. On it are the imprints of three human feet, a hand, and many animal tracks. Although the footprints are of enormous size, they are perfect in outline. This fact caused Indians to tie bags of medicinal herbs on poles above the rock with the belief that the herbs would absorb additional powers. They also laid gifts upon the rock, offerings to the "Great Spirit." The presence of the rock was known before 1825, for on that date Gen. Henry Atkinson and Col. Benjamin O'Fallon, having heard of it, visited the site while on a trip up the Missouri River, and reported the fact to Washington.
>
> For a long time it was generally believed that the imprints were made by some man of prodigious size who walked across the rock before the clay had hardened into stone. Some believed it was the work of an artist-jokester, who desired to give future generations something for speculation. However, scientists are now of the opinion that the prints were made by some sagacious medicine man who wanted further to impress his followers.

At 212.2 *m.* is WHITLOCK CROSSING, a small hamlet founded when the bridge was built, and at 216.6 *m.* is the Missouri River, which for years was a natural barrier to western migration. The western bank of the river is the eastern edge of the Cheyenne River Indian Reservation, 214.3 *m.*

Section b. Cheyenne River Reservation-Belle Fourche, 215.5 m.

The CHEYENNE RIVER RESERVATION (*open to visitors*) is one of the nine Indian reservations in the State. A Federal law imposes severe penalties on persons convicted of selling or giving intoxicants to Indians. Possession of liquor and its transportation across a reservation are also prohibited. Order is preserved through a system of Indian police who have authority to arrest any law violators.

The reservation covers all of Armstrong and parts of Dewey and Ziebach Counties. Indian life, however, is not confined to these specific boundaries, there being many families in the adjacent territory. Here the "vanished American" is no longer vanishing; in the last 10 years there has been an annual increase of about 10 persons per 1,000 population.

There is now a total of 3,418 Indians on this reservation, of which only 1,378 are full bloods. Included in the group are numerous native bands designated by the names; Miniconjou, Sans Arc, Two Kettle, Blackfeet, Uncapapa, Upper and Lower Yanktonai, Oglala, and Sisseton. Nearly all the older Indians speak only the Sioux language, but with improved educational facilities on the reservation, only 2 percent of those between the ages of 20 and 40 use their tribal language exclusively.

These Sioux, with few exceptions, have never been entirely self-supporting. At times the Government has made payments to them, but these have been from the sale of inherited lands or interest on tribal funds. Very little money accruing to them is given in a lump sum, but rather is divided into periodic payments. Various funds, which in most cases have their sources in treaties, include the Trust Fund, Three Percent Fund, and Sioux Benefit Funds. Their total wealth consists of $455,334 in tribal funds and $1,429,085 in tribal lands.

Farming is another source of income, although few of the Sioux have made much progress in this respect. Furthermore the reservation is not situated in the best agricultural section of the State. Some forage crops are raised along the Cheyenne River, but this treacherous stream has a habit of suddenly changing its course during flood periods, thus making the permanence of homes erected on its sandy bottoms decidedly uncertain.

Despite the fact that education and attempts to foster better living conditions have made noticeable inroads on old tribal customs, many of the Indians, especially the old ones, live in a manner similar to that of 40 or 50 years ago. Regardless of the fact that little credence is given to tales of the dog as a source of food, the custom still exists. Take away the dog and the Indian would be robbed of a major food source. Dog meat is never eaten except in soup, canine steaks being practically unknown.

After a wedding the parents of the bride and groom generally give a feast. Feasts are also given after funerals, often on the same day. This is an old custom, and unless the Indian observes it he rapidly loses the esteem of his fellows. Sometimes the more fortunate members of the tribe are persuaded to give a feast and invite their destitute friends. At these festivities the meal begins with meat. In addition there are bread, or biscuits, and perhaps a vegetable. Sometimes "wasna," a concoction of chokecherries, meat, and grease pounded together and dried, is served. Often there is "tipsla," or Indian turnips, dried in the fall and served in a kind of soup. If a guest cannot eat all that is served him, he wraps up the more solid food and takes it home to be consumed later.

Changes in habits of eating have come slowly on the reservation. Only in recent years has there been a tendency to buy canned milk, cereal, and fruit. The Sioux still use large amounts of lard, potatoes, onions, tomatoes, and baking powder; the last item has always been a consistent seller among post traders, for the Sioux like biscuits. Habits of dress have changed more rapidly than other customs, virtually all the Sioux dressing as do their white brothers.

Superstitions have not disappeared, even among those with comparatively good educations. When a family camps for the night, a cloth is usually hoisted on a pole above the tent in the belief that it will keep rattlesnakes away. Shaking a blanket out the door will frighten away any ghosts or supernatural visitors, according to local belief.

A few years ago many Indians with various ailments journeyed to the Pine Ridge Reservation where lived a woman who claimed to have fallen into a trance, mistaken by her friends for death, and upon awakening discovered at her side a jar of salve. Her sleep left her withered and emaciated, but in her vision she was told to administer this salve to her people, who would be cured of their infirmities.

One legend that received wide belief told of a squaw and a she-wolf who lived together in a cave for several months, each talking to the other in some language that both understood. Every day the wolf brought food to the woman, until a party of her tribesmen happened along. She was informed by the wolf that her people were near, whereupon the woman went off with them. The cave is on Cherry Creek and bones found there tell a mute tale of the food that was brought the squaw by the wolf—so the Indians say.

Between 200 and 300 of the Indians have comfortable homes and a similar number own cabins and log houses; however, the average family spends much of its time roaming about the reservation, their home consisting of a tent, a few cooking utensils, and some bedding. Although nearly all have permanent homes, many of them prefer living in a tent much of the time.

Under the present system, a tribal council comprises the chief governing body among the Sioux. It consists of 15 members, and carries on negotiations with the Federal, State, and local governments; it presents and prosecutes claims and demands of the tribe; and it administers tribal lands, funds, and property within the control of the tribe.

Cattle and other property have been issued on the Cheyenne River Reservation, with the expectation that the Indians would be encouraged to start in business for themselves. Many have been in a measure successful, and figures show 376 Indian-owned ranches. Accustomed to a roaming life and looking upon cattle mainly as providing food for the moment, the Sioux, generally speaking, have not built up many herds.

CHEYENNE AGENCY, 1.7 m. (121 pop.), is the headquarters of the Cheyenne River Reservation. Living here are Government officials, traders, missionaries, school teachers, and Indians. Government officials at the agency will answer questions of visitors concerning all parts of the reservation.

Approximately 250 children attend the boarding school; and an up-to-date hospital, well-staffed, takes care of patients from all over the reservation.

In the western part of town is an INDIAN VILLAGE of log cabins and tents, typical of Indian life. School buildings are modern, and a large gymnasium aids pupils in competing with other towns in athletics. West of the school the Indians have erected a monument to their dead chiefs. There is a growing tendency among the Indians to mark spots of historical interest and to honor heroes of past generations.

LA PLANT, 22.7 *m.* (61 pop.), has long been known as a prairie trading post for Indians, cowboys, and ranchers. The village, strung haphazardly along a hillside, is representative of the towns of the transition era between the open-range and homestead periods.

Over this part of the country, before the advent of the homesteader, roamed great herds of cattle—released by large outfits who staked their chances of success on the favorable weather. Sometimes they lost; often they won. Occasionally the cattleman's fortune was wiped out in a few days. Such was the case in the memorable Thanksgiving blizzard of 1896 which raged three days, when thousands of head of livestock blindly drifted into draws and wash-outs, were covered with snow, and perished. Spring round-ups revealed that most of the cattle outfits had suffered more than a 50 percent loss.

For many miles US 212 winds and dips over the rolling prairie, with only occasional houses to lend assurance of the fact that human life is near, even if infrequent. There is no attraction in this region for anyone who sees it only on the surface. But to the Westerner or to anyone else with imagination it brings to mind loping herds of buffalo relentlessly pursued by bands of Indians, ponderous freight wagons, drawn by swaying teams of oxen; great herds of cattle; the decline of the big outfits and the rise of the nester; and the tide of homesteaders and their subsequent drift back East. All this is typical of the evolutionary process of western South Dakota. In some sections where climate and soil conditions permitted, the farmer came to stay; but generally speaking, this range country will remain for some time to come the realm of the stockman.

RIDGEVIEW, 33.7 *m.* (72 pop.), was so named because of its position on the divide between the Cheyenne and Moreau Rivers. The swift-flowing Cheyenne is the largest feeder of the Missouri in western South Dakota. Its hundreds of tributary creeks and draws reach out on either side, like the legs of a centipede, to cut sharp creases in its basin. The Moreau, a smaller stream, often dries up entirely in the course of an extremely dry season, but during rainy periods, or during the melting of heavy snows, it becomes a roaring and impetuous torrent.

At 42.9 *m.* (L) is MOSSMAN, merely a shipping point for the many cattle that the railroad carries annually from this vast ranching country. The place itself is significant only because it was named in honor of Capt. Burton C. Mossman, chief owner of the Diamond A, South Dakota's largest cattle ranch. Captain Mossman for more than 50 years has led a colorful life on the range in various capacities, including that of a cowboy, range foreman, range superintendent, general manager, and owner of cattle outfits, besides serving as first captain of the Arizona Rangers. Thrust among the reckless, dangerous characters of the Southwest, his bravery and acceptance of responsibility have been the source of many border stories.

The Diamond A Ranch was started in 1903 in the days of open range, but in 1909 a tide of homesteaders forced the leasing and buying of much land. As a result Captain Mossman leased thousands of acres and at one time controlled most of Armstrong Co., the only county in the United States without a postoffice. Drought years have necessitated the selling of a part of the cattle, but the ranch still retains many of the customs of the old free-range days. Cowboys, round-ups, branding time, and line camps exist today as they did a half-century ago. The Diamond A in reality comprises several ranches, headquarters being established at various points where feed and water are most easily available. Although drought years and restrictions on the leasing of Indian land have reduced the extent of the holdings, the ranch is still the largest in the State. Before the homestead tide, about 50,000 cattle wore the Diamond A brand.

EAGLE BUTTE, 59.5 m. (2,415 alt., 310 pop.), was named for a nearby butte on which Indians hunted eagles for feathers to make war bonnets. According to legend, deep pits were dug, covered with light branches, and a rabbit laid on them for bait. The trapper concealed himself in the pit and caught the eagle by the foot as it swooped down to get the rabbit. The town was started when the railroad was extended through the locality in 1910, and today is supported by a mixed population of farmers, ranchers, and Indians.

LANTRY, 71.6 m. (40 pop.), was also founded in 1910 when the railroad entered the region, but did not enjoy the growth of the neighboring towns. Near here is a large dam used by the railroad as a water supply.

DUPREE, 81.1 m. (2,356 alt., 364 pop.), for 25 years after its founding retained its board sidewalks, typical of early cow towns. It was named for Fred Dupree, an early French trapper. Although founded largely through the influx of homesteaders, it has lost little of its Western color. Cowboys, Indians, and ranchers still give it most of its business.

Following its founding, the real estate business enjoyed a flourishing period, the first land office being in a tent on Main St. Pointing out the sites of surveyed quarter-sections to prospective homesteaders was a lucrative business in those days. The business was called "locating," and the newcomer, for a fee ranging from $25 to as much as he could be induced to pay, was taken out into the country where the corners of his prospective claim were pointed out to him. In those days the automobile had not yet displaced the horse as a means of conveyance; consequently nearly all of the "locating" was done by using a horse and buggy for transportation. Often a handkerchief was tied around a buggy spoke and the revolutions counted as a help in measuring the approximate distance to the next corner.

Every period has its attendant stories. One, told of homestead days, referred to the improvements required by law before the filee was given a patent to his land. One homesteader of lethargic tendencies, who was required to have broken a certain number of acres on his land, was asked how many he had plowed. He replied: "Around twenty." Investigation showed that he had not lied, for he had broken a single furrow around 20 acres.

During normal years Dupree is a busy marketing center for livestock, flax, and small grain. When the prairie was first broken, large yields of flax brought small fortunes to the early farmers. It was not an uncommon occurrence to have one crop of flax pay for the land.

Left from Dupree on an unnumbered graded dirt road is CHERRY CREEK, 35 m. (100 pop.), sub-agency of the Cheyenne River Reservation. During average times it is composed of a few Government buildings, two post traders' stores, and heterogeneous group of scattered Indian homes—log huts with dirt roofs, tents, temporary homes of hundreds of Indians from all parts of the reservation. Cherry Creek was the home of Chief Hump, famous Sioux leader, and was a point of tension during the Messiah War of 1890. It was to Cherry Creek that Sitting Bull's followers fled after the old medicine man was killed on Grand River and it was a few miles above the town that Big Foot and his band were first overhauled by soldiers prior to the Battle of Wounded Knee.

The village received prominence in South Dakota literature through the descriptive and colorful essay by former Governor

Charles N. Herreid during one of his visits to Cherry Creek. The essay, called "The White Squaw," relates the tragic episode of a white woman in an Indian environment, besides presenting a vivid picture of the reservation town. It is reprinted in part by permission of O. W. Coursey's "Dakota Literature."

". . . It was ration-day at the agency. About 1,500 Indians belonged to this station and at this time, Indian fashion, most of them were camped in their tents and tipis—some on the plains and some on the heavily timbered bottom-lands — altogether forming an improvised, semi-barbarous, picturesque village.

"On the banks of the Cherry Creek and the Cheyenne immense quantities of red buffalo berries burdened the bushes—forming a most appropriate and artistic setting in the luxurious foliage, tinged with nature's announcement of the passing season. It was an ideal camping ground, an ideal fall day. It was Indian summer, Indian feast day, Indian village, Indian country. Smoky eyes, smoky complexions harmonized perfectly with smoky skies. Man and nature were attuned. The atmosphere was languid, peaceful, dreamy, melancholy. To me, with my intense love for the wilderness and sympathy for the Red Man, it was a day of intense interest and enjoyment.

"The agent informed me that among the squaws was an old 'white' woman, who had lived among the Indians since infancy. This aroused my curiosity. I asked permission to see her and talk to her and a messenger was sent to find her. After some time the messenger returned saying he had found her, but that she refused to appear at the office of the Agent. The Chief of the Indian police, named Straighthead—a magnificent Indian— was sent out, with orders to bring her to the office. While waiting for developments I pictured to myself the helpless baby girl, snatched by savages from her tomahawked parents. I saw the restless pioneers leaving civilization; the emigrant train, traversing and trespassing upon the broad domain of the aborigines. I saw the wild attack of the red men, made ferocious by the resistless rush of the venturesome white men. I saw the red and white both dominated by the same powerful motives—the comfort and happiness of his family and himself.

"Presently the policeman ushered into the room a decrepit and most wretched-looking woman, apparently at least seventy years old. She shuffled into a corner, crouching upon the floor, trembling with fear. She knew that she was a white woman, that her folks had been killed in a skirmish on the plains; that she had been with the Indians since she was about one year old. She could not speak a word of English and, excepting her blue eyes and features, looked like the most degraded and miserable savage. The poor old woman did not show the least desire to know anything about her own people, nor to come in contact with white people or civilization.

"Near the agency building was a slaughter house, where beef cattle were being slaughtered and the meat parceled out to the Indians as part of their regular rations. It seemed to be the special prerogative of the squaws to secure the meat supplies and with their children they hung around this very repulsive establishment. Nearby later during the meeting, I saw a number of the more voracious eagerly devouring like choice tid-bits, the cast-off, raw intestines and offal, and among them was the gray-haired, ragged, wretched white squaw. As I viewed the distressing scene I shuddered at the horrible tragedy of a wasted human life. Under different circumstances this woman, now feasting on refuse with savage satisfaction, might have graced the banquet room of the White House."

FAITH, 103.9 *m.* (2,600 alt., 564 pop.), is at the end of a branch of the C. M. St. P. & P. R.R. It is another of the towns founded during the homesteading wave of 1910. It was named, according to a story, because an early resident expressed his belief that it required *faith* to live on the rolling, semi-arid prairie. The town has a trade territory reaching in four directions, extending into the expansive hinterlands of the cattle and sheep country to the N., W. and S. and the farming region to the E. It is typically a town with Western flavor, dominated by ranchers and cowboys and colored by a mixture of Indians who come from the nearby reservation to trade. A large earthen dam S. of the town provides a lake that is used mainly for stock-watering purposes.

The country between Faith and Newell is devoid of railroads, the region being a vast open-range domain of the cattle and sheepmen. There are no towns or even hamlets, but merely post offices and stores with gas pumps outside.

EDSON, 113.8 *m.* (20 pop.) FOX RIDGE, 129.3 *m.* (7 pop.), MAURINE, 134.3 *m.* (12 pop.), are merely hold-overs from homestead days, unable to muster much population because of lack of railroad facilities. Once busy little centers of the homesteader's trade, they now serve small groups of ranchers in their vicinity.

CEDAR CANYON, 137.5 *m.* (10 pop.), so named because of a nearby canyon with a thick growth of cedar trees, is the point where US 212 first crosses the OLD BISMARCK TRAIL, angling from the NE. This old historic trail, which formerly wound across 275 m. of broken, treeless country, uninhabited except for Indians, was the road over which an assorted throng of gold-seekers, adventurers, and get-rich-quick men of many types, lured by prospects of sudden wealth in the Black Hills, traveled in early days. The name of Ben Ash is closely associated with the Bismarck Trail, for it was he who first marked the route. In 1876, during the gold rush, it happened that Bismarck, N. Dak., was one of the railroad points nearest Deadwood.

Starting at Bismarck, there was first the Missouri River to be crossed, then the Cannon Ball, Grand, Moreau, and Belle Fourche Rivers, besides numerous creeks. The stagecoach furnished the transportation used by most of the people making the trip, and for those days the service was first class. There were stage stations at convenient points where drivers and horses were changed. The bullwhackers were the most picturesque characters who traveled the trail. With a wagon and trail wagon drawn by four or five yoke of oxen, and with several outfits traveling together for protection, these caravans traveled 10 or 15 m. per day. Unlike the stage drivers, the bullwhackers made their own camp. If the weather was fair, they usually made the trip without mishap, but if it was rainy the long stretches of gumbo made traveling impossible. Although fields, fences, and roads have partly obliterated the old trail, the deep ruts made half a century ago are still visible in many places.

MUD BUTTE, 147.3 *m.* (3 pop.), was named for a butte that, with its absence of any vegetation, resembles a prodigious handful of dark mud slapped rudely upon the grassy prairie which surrounds it.

SULPHUR, 157.3 *m.* (3 pop.), is also on the old Bismarck Trail. The town was so called because it is near Sulphur Creek, a stream which has no apparent relation to its name. Sulphur is one of the homestead towns that for several years thrived on the trade of newcomers. Like most other mushroom towns it boasted several commercial enterprises, including a newspaper. In those days persons who filed on Government land were required to advertise their readiness to make final proof. They were then required to swear that they had lived up to the stipulations of the law. The usual charge for several weeks of advertising was $5, and there were often several hundred advertisements inserted during the homestead boom. As a result newspapers sprang up, flourished for a few years, and then vanished. Various names were given these newspapers; some were simple, some cleverly associated with a peculiar name of a town, others with the idea of permanency. The editor of the Sulphur paper incorporated a pun in its title and called it *The Sulphur Match.*

NEWELL, 191.8 m. (2,820 alt., 580 pop.), although in a dry section of the State, has streets lined with luxuriant trees, and shrubbery, and is surrounded by farms where green vegetation stands out in striking contrast with the dun prairies beyond. All this is because Newell is in the heart of the Government Reclamation Project, which brings water from the Belle Fourche Dam to irrigate the level areas lying along the Belle Fourche valley. Sugar beet production is the chief industry, while in wide, shallow valleys alfalfa is grown for forage and seed. Bear Butte, 25 m. to the S., is plainly visible from Newell. At Newell is the junction with State 79.

> Right on State 79 is a sub-station of the STATE EXPERIMENT FARM. 1.5 m. (L), operated in connection with the principal experiment station at Brookings. It was established here because being in an irrigated region, numerous experiments can be carried on relative to irrigation problems. The station is also the headquarters of the U. S. Bureau of Reclamation and Belle Fourche Irrigation Project. A farm picnic is held here every year in July.

NISLAND, 199.5 m. (2,855 alt., 234 pop.), is another town in the irrigated section of South Dakota. In recent years the growing of cucumbers, made possible through fertile soil and abundant water, has been stimulated by a large pickle-salting station at Nisland. The town is also the scene of the annual Butte Co. Fair.

At 207.8 m. is the BELLE FOURCHE DAM (R) — locally called Orman Dam — largest earthen dam in the State, and one of the largest in the world. It is built on shale or heavy compact clay, locally known as gumbo, and is 6,200 ft. long, 115 feet high, and 19 ft. wide on top. The reservoir, approximately 10 m. long, with an average width of more than 2 m., supplies water to more than 75,000 acres in the Belle Fourche valley. The dam is on Owl Creek, but water is supplied by a diversion dam in the Belle Fourche River, which turns flood waters into the reservoir.

Construction was begun in 1905; in 1908 the first unit was opened for settlement, and water was applied to 12,000 acres. Extension of the work continued until 1917, when water became available for about 82,000 acres.

The Inlet Canal, constructed for the purpose of conducting the flood waters of the Belle Fourche River to the storage reservoir on Owl Creek, is 6½ m. long and has a capacity of 1,600 ft. per second of water.

The irrigation season extends from May to September, inclusive, although spring rains are generally sufficient to germinate crops, and often makes irrigation unnecessary before June.

BELLE FOURCHE, 215.5 m. (3,013 alt., 2,314 pop.), (*see Tour 13*) is the junction with US 85 (*see Tour 13*).

TOUR 4

(Lake Benton, Minn.)—Brookings—Huron—Pierre—Rapid City—Sturgis—Spearfish—(Beulah, Wyo.), US 14.

Minnesota Line to Wyoming Line, 478.1 m.

Except in a few places the Chicago & North Western R.R. parallels the route between the Minnesota line and Sturgis. Between Sturgis and the Wyoming line there is no parallel railroad.

All-weather roads.

Good hotel and tourist accommodations in larger towns and cities.

Crossing a level, almost unforested plain for about 225 miles, with only a few tree-fringed lakes and occasional hills to break the monotonous expanses of prairie, US 14 drops abruptly into the Missouri River valley and winds over rolling country to the Black Hills. Appearing first dimly distant, the Black Hills rise sharply from the prairie land surrounding them. Within their pine-covered portals is a rugged, picturesque mountain region including many points of scenic and historic interest.

This highway traverses the State, east and west, and affords a composite picture of the eastern farming area, western grazing region, and mountain country. Yucca, cactus, buffalo berries, occasional prairie dog villages, magpies, eagles, and perhaps a coyote are seen west of the Missouri River.

Section a. Minnesota Line—Pierre, 222.1 m. US 14

US 14 crosses the Minnesota Line 8 m. W. of Lake Benton, Minn. (*see Minn. Tour 12*), and enters one of the best farming regions in South Dakota.

ELKTON, 2 m. (1,751 alt., 807 pop.), is at the junction of the C. & N. W. and the C. R. I. & P. R.R. Along the railroad track is a park with a band shell, walks, and elm trees; similar parks have been established in nearly every town along the line in eastern South Dakota, as a compliment to the railroads that brought the towns into being.

Free coinage of aluminum was tried in Elkton three years before the Presidential campaign of 1896, when William Jennings Bryan stumped the country for free coinage of silver. Suffering from a lack of anything to use as a medium of exchange, mainly because of hard times, Elkton businessmen concocted a plan to employ aluminum money in lieu of a more precious metal. Accordingly, they hired a St. Paul firm to "make money" for them. Thin strips of aluminum were cut to imitate the respective denominations of coins and the name of a firm was printed on one side.

The plan worked remarkably well for a time. When purchases were made with legal coin the substitute would be given out in exchange. Mr. Jones would take his change from the grocer and buy meat with it. The butcher would spend it in other stores or buy a calf or a hog from a farmer. But retribution was not far distant. A United States inspector dropped in one day and notified the businessmen that they must cease the practice. Furthermore, he told them that they were subject to a fine of $100 in real money for every aluminum coin dispensed. From Elkton the inspector went to St. Paul where he closed the money-making plant. Satisfied that the Elkton men had no fraudulent intent, he gave them time to call in the illegal coins. Eventually all the bogus money was redeemed, and Elkton returned to the gold standard.

AURORA, 14.2 m. (1,630 alt., 234 pop.), platted in 1880 at the time of the extension of the railroad into this part of the State, has tall red grain elevators, white houses, and a few towering cottonwood trees, which break the level expanse of rich farm land.

BROOKINGS, 20.3 m. (1,636 alt., 4,723 pop.), named for Judge W. W. Brookings, was platted in 1879. For a short time its name had been Ada. Depending to a large extent upon student trade for its support, Brookings might be considered a typical college town. A prosperous farming area surrounding it is also stimulative to business, and many retired farmers live here. With neat, well-kept lawns and many shaded homes, Brookings possesses much quiet beauty.

The many departments of the SOUTH DAKOTA COLLEGE OF AGRICULTURE AND MECHANIC ARTS include numerous industrial courses and practically every branch of science connected with agriculture, ranging from agronomy to veterinary courses. (See EDUCATION.) There are also courses in chemistry, engineering, journalism, pharmacy, and other subjects. One of the institution's greatest services is to farmers, through one main experiment station at Brookings and substations at Highmore, Cottonwood, Vivian, and Eureka. Both four-year and short-term winter courses can be taken.

The college campus comprises attractive lawns and 18 well-equipped buildings, including two dormitories for women and a spacious armory that serves a multiple purpose. Celebrating its 50th anniversary in 1934, the college during the half-century has graduated about 23,000 students, while about 100 graduates are professors and instructors in leading colleges and universities in the United States.

Each fall the college holds its Hobo Day, a time-honored event. For this event men students make preparations weeks before by foregoing the task of shaving. The result is that when Hobo Day arrives, many amusing and grizzly types of beards of assorted colors are offered by the wearers in competing for the prize that goes to the nearest perfect facsimile of the typical "Knight of the road." The day is featured by a football game with a traditional rival.

THE COUGHLIN CAMPANILE AND CHIMES, rising 165 ft. and dwarfing all other buildings in the city, was given to the college by Charles L. Coughlin, an electrical engineering graduate, on the occasion of the 20th anniversary of his graduation. He was a South Dakota farm boy from near Carthage, and is now a prominent Milwaukee manufacturer.

The total cost of the tower was approximately $75,000. It measures 30 ft. square at the base, not including the approaches, and 47 ft. square with the approaches. It is built of white Indiana limestone, red brick, and concrete, to harmonize with the beautiful LINCOLN MEMORIAL LIBRARY and the COOLIDGE SYLVAN THEATRE nearby. There are 180 steps leading to the balcony, the highest point that can be reached by visitors. The balcony floor is 112 ft. above the ground, or almost exactly two-thirds the height of the tower.

A glass-covered hatchway in the ceiling of the balcony room permits a view of six of the eighteen tubular chimes, and also of Old Faithful, a bell cast for State College in 1885, and one of the 8,-000,000 candlepower beacon lights. There are 18 tubular bells in the belfry, which are struck with electrically operated hammers fitted with rawhide tips to give a mellow tone. Electrically operated dampers silence a vibrating chime the instant another is struck, thus preventing discords. While the entire program control and playing mechanism appears complicated, it is very reliable. It operates automatically and requires practically no attention, all changes being made by the clock and program device.

An 8,000,000 candlepower aeronautical beacon, revolving at the rate of six revolutions per minute, is in a glass ball eight ft. in diameter at the top of the tower. Another beacon of the same power, but not revolving, throws its beam towards the BROOKINGS AIRPORT to the W. These beacons are charted on the United States airway maps and must be kept in contant operation from sunset to sunrise. They are turned on and off automatically by special clock-operated switches. Eight 350-watt white floodlights illuminate the stone top of the tower at night, and 12 lights of the same kind are used to throw the college colors, yellow and blue, on various parts of the tower. These lights are likewise thrown on and off by clock switches.

It is planned to use the walls inside the tower for the display of materials and facts about the history and development of State College.

At Brookings is the junction with US 77 (*see Tour 9*).

VOLGA, 29.4 m. (1,636 alt., 557 pop.), was named for the Volga River in Russia, though the people of the community are not of Russian descent, but Scandinavian.

A story is still current in Volga about a salesman from Chicago who, in 1880, came to Volga for the first time. Learning of a trading post at the inland town of Oakwood, he hired a livery team and drove there. It was apparent that he expected to find the country wild and woolly, and during the evening some of the local men concluded that it would be too bad if he returned disappointed. He was taken to Charlie Porter's drug store, where a group of men were apparently gambling for high stakes under the influence of liquor. Suddenly a violent quarrel started and Porter rushed behind the counter, returning with a huge cheese knife. Another man came reeling out of the back room, swinging a double-barreled shotgun. Three men rushed at him, when both barrels were discharged into the ceiling. This was too much for the salesman, who bolted out of the door for the livery barn, forgot about collecting his money, and never returned.

At 39.7 m. is the junction with US 81 (*see Tour 10*).

ARLINGTON, 41.8 *m.* (1,846 alt., 557 pop.), originally called Nordland because of the large number of Scandinavians who first settled here, has an artificial lake and a native rock island. Although a small, two-street town, people get confused in directions, as the streets are diagonal to the compass.

Here is the junction with US 81 (*see Tour 10*).

HETLAND, 47 *m.* (207 pop.), is also the center of an extensive Scandinavian community, named for a settler by that name who came from Hetland, Norway.

The life of the homesteaders who settled in this prairie country in the 1880's was hard but often romantic. In the spring of 1880 Hod Phelps brought his family from Minnesota and filed on a homestead near here. As money was none too plentiful, he made a temporary home in a dugout in a steep bank that faced the east. He spent the summer breaking the prairie with his walking plow and horse, making a stable for his cow, digging a well, and putting up hay. During the same summer a young woman, May Wheeler, came from Baraboo, Wis., and filed on a homestead near the Phelps land, as she had known the family previously; however she returned to Wisconsin to earn more money before building. In the meantime, Mrs. Phelps' unmarried brother, Willis Atwater, came from the East and filed on a nearby homestead. In October a blizzard began on the morning of the 15th, followed by several storms until by mid-January travel and communication were cut off. On the last train to break through the snow blockade, Miss Wheeler arrived at Nordland (now Arlington). After buying lumber and equipment, she found she could not start building while the storms continued, and so she moved in with the Phelps. The storms increased in fury and frequency during the rest of January and February, and it was not long until there were 12 ft. of snow on the level. Each new storm buried the dugout completely, making it dark as night the day around. The kerosene supply was soon exhausted, and the only source of light was a saucer of grease with a rag in it. Wheat was ground in a coffee mill, and they burned hay and straw hauled by manpower on a home-made sled.

Through the long, cold winter a romance between Atwater and Miss Wheeler developed. The first thaw came on April 17, and the weather turned suddenly warm. Water flooded the land and ran in torrents through the ravines. Those who had vowed to leave during the winter now began making plans for their homes on the prairie. Among them were Atwater and his bride, who eventually built up a large and prosperous farm.

LAKE PRESTON, 56 *m.* (1,722 alt., 1,009 pop.), received its name from the lake nearby, which was discovered and named in 1839 by Gen. John C. Fremont, noted pathfinder, who surveyed the levels of the water on his journey through the Northwest. He named the lake for Senator Preston of North Carolina.

This area is an excellent farming region during normal years, its prosperity attested by large barns and farmhouses.

DE SMET, 66.2 *m.* (1,726 alt., 988 pop.), first settled in 1879, was named in honor of Father Peter J. De Smet, early apostle to the Indians of South Dakota (*see HISTORY*). Lying in the heart of a dairying section, it has been called the Cream City. Many of the merchants and professional men in De Smet are sons of pioneers, and modern buildings show the town's development.

1. **Right from De Smet on State 25, a graveled road, to the BIRTHPLACE OF ROSE WILDER LANE (1887-), the writer, 2.5 *m.*** Only a few gnarled boxelder trees mark the place that was her home, although the remains of the sod shanty in which she was born are marked by two slight elevations near the trees. Laura Ingles Wilder, author of children's stories and mother of Rose Wilder Lane, came here as a bride. Rose Wilder Lane has said that the pattern of her whole life was formed in that pioneer setting. At the age of six she became so intensely interested in writing that she developed writer's cramp and was taken out of school. For a time it was feared she would lose the use of her arm. Leaving the country in a covered wagon at the age of seven, she remembered, however, the prairies and the town, which have been used as the settings of her books. The Earnestine Series of stories which were published in the "Saturday Evening Post" had descriptions of De Smet and subtle characterizations of its early inhabitants. In "Let The Hurricane Roar" the description of the blizzard and cold is that of the Dakota prairie. In a recent book, "Old Home Town," De Smet can easily be recognized.

2. **Left from De Smet on State 25 to a junction with a graveled road, 8 *m.*;** L. on this road is LAKE THOMPSON, 10.7 *m.* (R), which covers an area of 20 sq. m. LAKE HENRY (L) is a smaller body of water. It was at Lake Thompson in 1857 that a party of Santee Sioux overtook Inkpaduta, after he had committed numerous depredations. A fierce battle ensued. Inkpaduta, chief objective of the long chase by the Santees, escaped, but two of his sons were killed. South Dakota and Minnesota history records the "high spots" in the life of Inkpaduta, infamous son of Wamdesapa, whose cruel traits he inherited. Recently, human bones, thought to be those of Indians, were unearthed in the vicinity.

At 74 *m.* is a junction with a graded road.

Left on this road, 2 *m.* (R), is the BIRTHPLACE OF HARVEY DUNN, the artist. Only two mounds of dirt remain to mark the site of the sod house in which he was born in 1882. At the age of 14, Harvey Dunn was doing a man's work on the farm. In school the teacher made a practice of hiding the chalk, as Harvey emptied the chalk box every day. His strong fingers sketched everything, from delicate flowers to powerful locomotives. Harvey wished to study at the Art Institute in Chicago, but he was without funds. A De Smet landowner, Charles Dawley, offered to pay $2 an acre to summer-fallow 200 acres of land, and a deal was made. Working from sunup to sundown, Dunn saved his money and left for Chicago to attend school in 1902. Finishing his course in Chicago, he went to New York. When the World War began, Dunn was sent to France by the War Department to portray scenes of American activities as historical records. Many of his war pictures were on covers of the "American Legion Monthly" from 1928 to 1936. He has illustrated many magazine stories and articles. Among his best known paintings are: "Artillery in Action," "A Corner In Hell," "The Raiding Party," "In the Wire," "The Raid," "The Vigil," "The Homesite," "The Rail-splitter," "Kamerad," "Armistice." and "Camouflage." The original painting of "The Sniper," cover design of the American Legion Monthly in 1928, is hung in the De Smet American Legion Post clubhouse.

IROQUOIS, 80.3 *m.* (1,401 alt., 531 pop.), was named for the Iroquois Indian tribe. Nearby are an artificial lake and game preserve.

CAVOUR, 89.4 *m.* (1,311 alt., 196 pop.), received its name from Count Cavour, Italian statesman and builder of railroads in Italy.

HURON, 99.6 *m.* (1,285 alt., 11,733 pop.) (*see HURON*).

Home of the State Fair, Huron College; meat-packing and farm-trading center.

Here is the junction with State 37 (*see Tour 11A*).

In the vicinity of Huron the dust storms of 1933 and 1934 were particularly devastating, taking off the top soil and piling it in the ditches along the road. Between Huron and Wolsey piles of dust are seen, but the U. S. Soil Conservation Division has made furrows to prevent further shifting of the soil. Also, the shelterbelt program includes planting of trees in this area to prevent severe dust storms in the future.

At 111.4 *m.* is the junction with US 281 (*see Tour 11*) with which US 14 is united through the town of Wolsey.

WOLSEY, 114.5 m. (1,353 alt., 445 pop.), was named for Cardinal Thomas Wolsey of 16th century note. It was in Wolsey, according to a story related there, that the late Richard Sears, of Sears, Roebuck & Co., received the impetus that caused him to embark upon the mail order business. In 1882 he was the first railroad station agent at Wolsey. Having several small C. O. D. shipments of varied articles that remained unclaimed, he notified the consignors. A jewelry company suggested that he try to dispose of the articles on commission. This he did, and was so successful that he was soon doing a small mail order business. After two years he left Wolsey, found a partner, and organized one of the world's largest mail order houses.

North of Wolsey US 14 branches L.; US 281 R.

WESSINGTON, 129.5 m. (1,419 alt., 564 pop.), which received its name from the range of nearby hills, is often confused with Wessington Springs, located about 30 m. S. On its main street are often seen huge transportation trucks parked beside the teams and wagons that bring produce from the back country.

ST. LAWRENCE, 145.3 m. (1,580 alt., 356 pop.), is the center of a rather extensive dairying region, and at different times has led all other towns along this branch of the Chicago & North Western R. R. in shipment of cream.

MILLER, 147.3 m. (1,587 alt., 1,468 pop.), was named for its first settler, Henry Miller. The town has a large new SWIMMING POOL (*open to visitors*; *moderate charge*). On the second floor of the Hand Co. courthouse here is a free exhibit of Sioux and Arikara Indian relics.

At 152 m. is the junction with an unimproved road.

Left on this road to CAMP DAKOTA, 6 m., a deep-wooded gulch in the Ree Hills, where Boy Scouts gather annually for an outing and instruction. The camp has abundant shade, good spring water, a swimming pool, mess hall, and many rustic bridges; tables, chairs, and benches were constructed by the scouts during encampment. Several hiking trips can be taken either up and down the ravine, or among the hills nearby.

The REE HILLS to the S. were named for the Arikara Indians, commonly known as the Rees. Wooded ravines and lookouts from which miles of country can be seen, were used in pioneer times as a hide-out by horse and cattle rustlers, according to tradition. Cattle and horses stolen as far south as Nebraska were brought into the Ree Hills and hidden; later they were taken in small bunches to various markets—Pierre, Bismarck, Aber-

deen. When traffic on the trail to Fort Pierre became heavy, the
hills were abandoned by the rustlers and were then used by bull-
whackers as a place to rest and view the trail ahead.

At 157.5 *m.* is a junction with a graded road.

Left is REE HEIGHTS, 0.8 *m.* (1,731 alt., 307 pop.), from
which picnic trips to the Ree Hills can be taken.

HIGHMORE, 169.3 *m.* (1,890 alt., 1,002 pop.), seat of Hyde
Co., received its name through a foreign railroad worker's imper-
fect command of English. The foreigner, attempting to inform his
fellow workers that the land rises gradually to the W. of Ree
Heights, announced repeatedly, "high more," and as a consequence
named a growing community. A STATE EXPERIMENT FARM (*open*)
on the highway (L) is used especially for testing leguminous crops.

Here is the junction with State 47 (*see Tour 4A*).

HOLABIRD, 177.1 *m.* (63 pop.), consists of a garage and oil
stations along the highway.

HARROLD, 184.1 *m.* (1,801 alt., 260 pop.), was founded with
the coming of the railroad in 1881, and might be termed a "mushroom village," as it grew to approximately its present population
in about one month in 1883.

BLUNT, 201 *m.* (1,621 alt., 477 pop.), for more than 20 years
was the center of a wide trade territory, and at one time had a
population of more than 2,000. But with the building of a new
railroad line to the N. in the early 1900's, the town's prosperity
waned steadily.

At 203.5 *m.* is the junction with a dirt road.

Left on this road is MEDICINE KNOLL, 3.1 *m.*, a long narrow
mound, rising 400 ft. above the valley. According to an Indian
legend, a young Sioux chief went to the knoll to fast, sing, and
pray before battle. On the third day, seeing the enemy creep-
ing toward him, he sang louder, thus bringing to his aid his
fellow tribesmen who defeated the Arikaras. A gigantic stone
serpent, placed here by the Sioux, commemorates the event.

At 203.7 *m.* is the junction with US 83 (*see Tour 12*); US 14
and US 83 are united between this point and Fort Pierre.

At 218.5 *m.* is the junction with a dirt road.

Left on this road is LAKE ARIKARA, 1 *m.*, an artificial body of
water formed by damming a dry creek. The lake was named for
the Indian tribe that once inhabited the region. When full it
covers 11 acres and serves as a fishing and boating spot, as well
as a game preserve. The spillway of the lake was originally ex-

cavated as a railroad cut for a line between Blunt and Pierre, over which no trains ever passed.

At *220.8 m.* is the junction with a graveled road.

Right on this road, 1.6 *m.*, on the summit of Snake Butte (L) is the CENTER MONUMENT, erected in 1923 to mark the geographical center of South Dakota and approximate center of North America. On the monument is inscribed; "Erected by Charles L. Hyde and Doane Robinson, 1923." The monument when first erected, was at the base of Snake Butte, near a four-road terminal. In the interests of traffic safety, it was moved here and a fence was erected to protect it from souvenir hunters, intent on chiseling pieces from its surface.

The long winding ridge on which the monument stands is called SNAKE BUTTE, the scene of another Indian legend of a brave young Ree who ran into an ambush of his arch enemies, the Sioux. Though mortally wounded and reeling with pain, he ran a lurching, swaying course until he dropped. In admiration of his bravery the Sioux placed a rock on every drop of blood that dripped as he ran. At the center they placed their own symbol, the turtle. The result is a winding line of rocks, nearly a half mile in length. A fence has been placed around the figure of the turtle.

At 8.6 *m.* is the "Gray Goose" corner; L., at 13.6 *m.*, is the junction with another road; R. on this road at 14.6 *m.* the route follows an unimproved dirt road, winding over hills, through woods, and across river bottoms, to the SITE OF FORT SULLY, 23 *m.*, built in 1866 as a consolidation of the old and new forts of the same name. During the Messiah War of 1890 it was used as a central point for outfitting military expeditions. Mayor Fiorella H. La Guardia of New York lived here as a youth, while his father served as post bandmaster. Foundations of the old buildings are still almost intact and the several cisterns used there are in a good state of repair. (Note: Visitors are warned to watch for uncovered cisterns.) The buildings of the fort occupied the rim of a flat and extended along the slopes. On the hill is a monument recently erected to mark the historic site. The fort was abandoned in the early 1890's.

South of the site of the fort, 1.2 *m.* (R), are traces of an old Arikara Indian village, depressions and mounds. Pieces of pottery and occasionally arrowheads can be found.

US 14 winds over the Missouri River range of buttes and down to Pierre, *222.1 m.*

Section b. Pierre—Rapid City, 189.5 m.

PIERRE, (1,440 alt., 4,013 pop.) (*see PIERRE*).

State Capitol, Memorial Hall, Riverside Park.

At 2.4 *m.*, after crossing the Missouri River, is a junction with a graded dirt road.

> Right on this road, at 0.4 *m.*, is a junction with the old canyon road (L), where the famous DEADWOOD TRAIL climbed the hill out of Fort Pierre in the days before the railroad came.
>
> Winding serpent-like across approximately 200 m. of prairie, the Deadwood Trail in gold-rush days served as the main artery of travel and transportation from Pierre to the feverish mining camps of the Black Hills. Over this trail passed the huge, slow freight wagons, the stagecoaches with their relays of fast horses, and the colorful, motley throng of adventurers, gold-seekers, cowboys, gamblers, and outlaws.
>
> It was on this trail near Grindstone, in 1876, that four luckless freighters mysteriously met their death and were buried in a wagon box near the scene of the tragedy. The creek near where the murders were committed has ever since been called Deadman's Creek. The mystery, incidentally, was never solved. Still another episode, recalled by old-timers of Haakon Co. today, was the gruesome multiple murders by a rancher named Kunneche, living NE. of Ottumwa, who made a practice of killing his hired men instead of paying them long-accumulated wages. He is said to have killed at least five men, hacking their bodies to pieces.
>
> The first successful automobile trip was made over the trail in 1905 by Governor Peter Norbeck, later U. S. Senator. Today only remnants of the old trail remain; a few deep ruts off the traveled highway show where wagon wheels once passed.
>
> Continuing N. past the gulch of the old Deadwood Trail, the dirt road reaches the SITE OF OLD FORT PIERRE, 2.4 *m.* Relics of the early days, when fur traders, trappers, and soldiers made the vicinity their headquarters, can still be found. Several other so-called forts, actually only trading posts, were once established in this vicinity. They were designated on the map as Ft. Tecumseh, Ft. Galpin and Military Fort. Although the original fort was established near the site of the present town of Fort Pierre, it was moved to this point two years later. Construction of a reproduction of the old fort was begun by CCC boys in 1937.
>
> Beyond the site of old Fort Pierre (L) is the HOME OF JAMES "SCOTTY" PHILIP, 3 *m.*, formerly called the "buffalo king," because when the shaggy range lords were virtually exterminated, he purchased a small herd and built it up in a mammoth pasture near his home. At the time of Philip's death in 1911 there were nearly 1,000 buffaloes in the herd. In the yard around his home is his grave.

Continuing N. along the road a few hundred yards (R) is the SITE OF AN OLD ARIKARA VILLAGE, designated by a large red gate.

FORT PIERRE, 3 *m.* (1,437 alt., 777 pop.), at the confluence of the Missouri and Bad Rivers, has a history crammed with events of first importance in the annals of South Dakota. Perhaps no other point in the State boasts as many "firsts" as this quiet little town, which still retains a touch of the days when it was the boisterous center of a far-reaching cow country. Fort Pierre represents the eastern edge of the range country and is approximately on the dividing line between the agricultural east and prairie west of the State.

Because of the buried Verendrye Plate (*see VERENDRYE HILL below*), Fort Pierre claims to be on the site of the first spot visited by white men on South Dakota soil. The establishment of a fort, near the site of the present town, by Joseph La Framboise in 1817, marked the beginning of the oldest continuous settlement in the State. In 1840 the Rev. Stephen R. Riggs, a missionary from Minnesota, preached the first sermon delivered in the Dakotas. In 1855 the Government bought Fort Pierre and General Harney moved 1,200 troops to that point. In 1865 the Indian War of the Outbreak was settled by a treaty at Fort Pierre.

With the building of the railroad to Pierre in 1880, Fort Pierre became the starting point for freight outfits on their long overland trek to the Black Hills. It was also here that the river steamers unloaded their cargoes for the Black Hills haul.

With the rise of Pierre, the importance of the older town declined. Today it is a rambling, sleepy village, filled with memories of voyageurs and trappers.

Across Bad River, at the first street, a road leads (L) to LEWIS AND CLARK PARK, one of the chief points of interest in the town.

At Fort Pierre is the junction with US 83, (*see Tour 12*).

At 3.3 *m.*, a few rods up the hill W. of Fort Pierre, a marker indicates a road (L).

Left on this road is the VERENDRYE HILL AND MONUMENT. It was on this gumbo knoll, overlooking the Missouri and Bad Rivers, that the Verendrye brothers—Louis and Francois—in 1743 buried a lead plate and claimed a vast territory for France. This is the first record of white men on Dakota soil.

In 1742 the Verendrye brothers set out from Canada to seek a route to the western sea. After reaching what is now central

Montana, they turned back, arriving at the Missouri River near Ft. Pierre on March 15, 1743. They remained here with a band of the Little Cherry Indians until April 2. While camped here, they buried a lead and zinc plate bearing the date March 30, 1743. Here, at the joining of Waksicha, or Bad River, and the Missouri, later centered the activities of the river trade which were of commercial and historical importance.

The burial spot of the plate was marked by a rough pyramid of stones. The Frenchmen told the Indians the stones were a memorial, for they did not want them to know of the plate. The late William Frost said that a pile of stones, probably part of the pyramid, was on this hill when he came to Fort Pierre in 1877. Other early residents have spoken of hauling stones from there to use in building.

The years passed, bringing changes in the growth and development of the little town of Ft. Pierre. The new school building was erected nearby and the school children made this hill their playground. One Sunday, February 17, 1913, as a crowd of boys and girls were walking about, one of the girls, Hattie Foster, noticed something protruding from the earth and pulled it from the ground. The children could see it was a flat piece of metal but so covered with dirt that all they could read of the writing was the date. Not knowing its value, they made laughing comments and speculations as to what it might be, and were about to throw the plate away, when one of the boys, George O'Reilly, took possession of it. He showed it to his father, William O'-Reilly, who had a collection of pioneer articles, and he got in touch with members of the Historical Society. Historians had been searching for the location of the buried plate, mentioned in the Verendrye journals, and the finding of this one caused much excitement and speculation. Deciphering of the carving disclosed on one side the following inscription in Latin:

> "In the 26th year of the reign of Louis XV the
> most illustrious Lord, the Lord Marquis. of
> Beauhurnois being viceroy, 1741, Peter de La
> Verendrye placed this."

and on the reverse side, in French:

> "Placed by the Chevalier de La Verendrye
> Lo (Louis) Jost (Joseph Verendrye)
> Louis La Londette
> A Miotte
> The 30th March 1743."

The plate, 8½ inches long, 6½ inches wide, and ⅛ of an inch thick, was purchased by the Historical Society for $700, and is now in the Historical Museum of the Memorial Building in Pierre. The scene of this historic discovery was left unmarked for 20 years. On September 1, 1933, a monument was dedicated by the South Dakota Historical Society and the Fort Pierre Commercial

Club on the opening day of the Stanley County Fall Festival. The French Government took official notice of the event and sent Rene Weiller, consul in Chicago, to represent that country. After a historic pageant, which wound through the town to the summit of the hill, the monument was formally dedicated with speeches by Gutzon Borglum, the sculptor, George Philip, nephew of "Scotty" Philip, and Lawrence Fox, State Historian. Among the honored guests was John Stanage of Yankton, born at Ft. Pierre in 1857, the first white boy in old Dakota Territory.

A few rods to the NE. of the Verendrye Monument is the concrete and stone map of South Dakota constructed of stones from each county, gathered by the Young Citizens League. It was dedicated on the last day of the Y.C.L. Convention in May 1935.

At 10.3 m. is the junction with a graded dirt road.

Right on this road to the STANDING BUTTE "OIL WELL," 22 m., which is merely one more venture added to the long list of blasted hopes of wealth from "liquid gold." The road to the well is a combination prairie road and river view drive. After traveling 10 m. on the main road in a northerly direction, a sign, "To Orton," indicates the route straight ahead. Soon the road dives down a steep descent and rises as abruptly on the other side. At 15.5 m. the road veers to the L. until it reaches a butte —Standing Butte—whence it angles L. 2.2 m. to a well-improved horse ranch. Here is the well.

The well was promoted before the World War and drilling continued until a shaft was sunk several hundred feet. The well never produced anything but warm artesian water, which now flows free and unharnessed to join the Cheyenne River.

At 13 m. US 14 crosses WILLOW CREEK, which in freighting days, between Fort Pierre and the Black Hills, was an almost impassable hazard in wet weather, the heavy gumbo soil of its valley clinging to wagon wheels and paralyzing travel.

HAYES, 38 m. (40 pop.), in the era of the big cattlemen, was a typical cowboy center with most of the characteristics of the "wild and woolly" days—saloon, dance hall, general store, hitching posts. The site of the original town was one-half mile S. of the present hamlet, and a tall, unpainted building was at one time used as a dance hall.

At 40.5 m. is the Methodist Episcopal LITTLE BROWN CHURCH ON THE HILL (R). Just as the town of Nashua, Iowa, became famous through its *Little Brown Church in the Vale,* immortalized in the hymn of Dr. William S. Pitts, this little prairie church is known in a lesser degree throughout most of western

South Dakota. As the Church in the Vale earned wide attention for its many weddings each year, the Hayes Church is receiving similar note in its community, many couples having taken their marriage vows here since the present structure was erected in 1923. Beginning in 1908 with a handful of homesteaders as a nucleus, the church has weathered the years of depopulation caused by continued droughts, when settlers, discouraged, left their holdings to return East.

At 63.3 *m.*, just before descending into the Bad River Valley at Midland, is the junction with a dirt road.

> Left on this road is CAPA, 10 *m.* (85 pop.), of interest because of its hot mineral baths. The source of the water for baths is a deep artesian well. The water is piped to a pool in the Capa Hotel, where treatments are given for all kinds of rheumatism and muscular pains.

MIDLAND, 64.2 *m.* (1,878 alt., 296 pop.), was given its name because it was supposed to be midway between the Missouri River and the south fork of the Cheyenne River. It was one of the towns engaged in a riotous county seat contest in 1914, when rambling Stanley Co. was divided (*see PHILIP below*). At the NW. edge of town is LAKE CHO-KA-YA, an artificial body of water where swimming and fishing are available.

At 90.5 *m.* is SUNSHINE LAKE (L), built under a Federal program to provide a water supply, a road grade, and swimming and fishing facilities for the community.

PHILIP, 93.5 *m.* (2,159 alt., 887 pop.), was named for James "Scotty" Philip, the "buffalo king" (*see above*). The town was started with the extension of the railroad to the Black Hills in 1907. With many new business houses and a large new auditorium, Philip is the center of a vast farming and ranching section, its trade territory extending N. as far as 50 m.

Always a thriving little town, it staged a lively campaign in 1914 in an effort to become the seat of the newly created Haakon Co. Almost overnight five towns in the county—Philip, Nowlin, Powell, Midland, and Lucerne, the last merely an inland post office in the center of the county—joined the race. The result was an easy victory for Philip.

At the County Fair Grounds on the western edge of town a graded dirt road makes a slight turn and then runs directly W.

On this road is the SILENT GUIDE MONUMENT, 8 *m.*, a recent improvement on an original rude stone monument, built in early days by a sheepman to mark the location of a waterhole that never failed. It figured in many disputes between the sheep and cattle ranchers and was torn down and rebuilt several times during the range feuds between the two traditional enemies. It was customary for cowboys to express their contempt for sheepherders by roping the monument and toppling it over whenever they happened along. At last one sheepherder, imbued with more courage than the rest, mounted the monument with a rifle and threatened to shoot any cowboy who attempted to molest him.

The monument, on a high hill near the road (L), is visible for miles. It was rebuilt in 1924 through public subscription.

US 14 turns L. at Philip, crosses Bad River and winds over a series of hills.

At 98.5 *m.* is the junction with US 16 (*see Tour 5*); US 14 and US 16 are united for 91 m., between the junction and Rapid City, 189.5 *m.* (*See Tour 5, Section b.*)

Section c. Rapid City to Wyoming Line, 66.5 m.

RAPID CITY, (3,196 alt., 11,346 pop.). (*See RAPID CITY.*)

State School of Mines and Museum, Dinosaur Park, Alex Johnson Hotel, Municipal Park and Canyon Lake, and Hangman's Hill.

Here is a junction with US 16 (*see Tour 5*); with State 79. (*see Tour 5C*); and the Rim Rock Trail (*see Tour 4B*).

At 1.3 *m.* is the junction with a graded road.

Right on this road is the SOUTH DAKOTA STATE CEMENT PLANT, 0.8 *m.*, one of several enterprises undertaken by the State during the period 1915-25. It has been financially successful. Located where materials used in the manufacture of the product are easily accessible, the plant, since it began operations in 1925, has virtually monopolized the cement business in South Dakota, $2,000,000 in profits having been turned into the State Treasury. Operating on a non-political basis and controlled by a five-man commission, the plant has been run on tested business principles, which have built up a volume that one year showed an output of 643,000 barrels. It employs 110 persons, and has an annual payroll of $175,000.

One commissioner is appointed each year by the governor for a term of four years ending July 1, thereby necessitating a new appointment every year. From the first the board has been formed of men of different political parties. For the 11 years that this plant has been in operation, the management has been unhampered.

The product is sold only through dealers, who have to pay taxes to the State, except when highway paving is being done for the State and sales are made direct to contractors. All profits are returned to the State through the plant.

The total gross sales amounted to more than $16,000,000 and the credit losses were less than $4,000 from 1925 to 1937. In all of that tonnage of cement there never has been a rejection, although every contractor who buys in large quantities has a laboratory, and tests are continuously going on while a building is being constructed. The purity of the cement sent out from this plant is well guaranteed, for chemists make tests every hour of both raw and finished products while the plant is operating. This project at first was regarded with suspicion by some of the privately owned plants, but there now exists a most friendly feeling among the manufacturers of cement. More than 98 percent of all cement used in the State has been made in the Rapid City plant.

Cement is made from lime rock, shale, and gypsum. The limestone is quarried just back of the plant from a layer of rock 45 ft. thick. The shale is from the State's own bed five m. E. of town. Gypsum is purchased from the U. S. Gypsum Co. of Piedmont, S. Dak.

Lime and shale are ground together in proportions of 80 and 20 percent. After the mixture is "burned" and prepared as "clinkers," a small percentage of gypsum is added to govern the time it takes cement to set.

The plant owns two engines, one of which is a narrow-gauge that is used in the quarry; 12 railroad cars haul the shale.

At 1.9 *m.* (L) is the new NATIONAL GUARD HEADQUARTERS, formerly part of the Indian School property, the 84-acre plot was set aside as a permanent camp for the State's National Guard. Construction began June 25, 1934, and the rough work was carried on by relief organizations.

The camp is complete in every respect, with an administration and warehouse building built with the aid of the Works Progress Administration, tent floors, storage house for target material, sliding targets with a tunnel leading to the storage house, a firing range equipped with a telephone, Kennedy Stadium capable of seating 3,000 spectators, and a lake fed with running water. The guard assembles for training each year in June. In addition to all this, the Government has beautified the grounds by picturesque landscaping.

From Rapid City US 14 goes in a northerly direction along the eastern edge of the Black Hills.

At *2.4 m.* is the junction with a graveled road, a scenic drive connecting with US 85A (*see Tour 4C*).

The highway passes through rolling country of interesting soil formation. On one side of the road is red clay, and on the other is yellow, each making a sharp contrast with the grass and evergreens. This area is alternately wooded and barren, with occasional small ranch houses.

BLACKHAWK, *7.6 m.* (60 pop.), is a small town on Blackhawk Creek, with souvenir shops, gas stations, and a schoolhouse.

At *9.3 m.* is a marker at the point where US 14 crosses the trail General Custer made as he was returning to Ft. Abraham Lincoln in North Dakota in 1874.

At *12.5 m.* (R), near the highway, is a reproduction of the SIDNEY STOCKADE, an important stage station on the old Sidney-Deadwood and Pierre-Deadwood stage lines during gold rush days. It was the first station N. of Rapid City.

At *12.6 m.* is a junction with a graded road, built on the roadbed of a narrow-gauge railroad used formerly by the Homestake Mining Co. to carry timber out of the Hills.

> Left on this road to STAGE BARN CAVERNS, *2.2 m.* (open; adm. fee; trip requires an hour). There are five openings, and the underground caves extend about one-half mile. The cave is situated in a limestone formation 500 ft. thick, and the walls show markings which indicate that the water remained at different levels for long periods of time. The rooms vary in height from a few feet to 20 ft. The walls are covered with calcite crystals and the cave has both stalactites and stalagmites. The cave is considered "alive," as its features are still in the process of formation. Various colors are present, and iron in solution gives many of the stalactites a reddish tinge.

At *13.8 m.* is a junction with a graded road.

> Right on this road is the TIMBER OF AGES, *1.2 m.* (adm. charge), comprising a collection of petrified wood. The 60-acre tract has huge stumps and long logs which show the structure of trees in petrification, such as the limbs, roots, bark, growth rings, knotholes, indents of rot, mineral coloring, agate, crystals, and cycads. Small pieces are plentiful. This group of petrified trees is in the Minnewasta layer of the Dakota Sandstone, and, according to scientists who have examined the area, it is considered approximately 100 million years old.

PIEDMONT, *14.5 m.* (150 pop.), furnishes supplies to ranches of the region and caters to tourists who stop there.

US 14 follows Elk River valley and crosses Elk Creek at 17.1 *m.*

BLACK HILLS ROCK MUSEUM, 17.3 *m.* (L), is a private collection of rocks, crystals, and petrified wood, some specimens of which are for sale.

At 17.4 *m.* is the junction with a graveled road.

> Left on this road is the route to CRYSTAL CAVE, 5.5 *m.* (longer route, $1.00, shorter route, $0.55; children under 12 free; under 17, half-price. Free crystal souvenir to every visitor. Trips every half hour, ·day or night, year around.)
>
> The cave has been compared in appearance to a huge sponge, with all its windings, galleries, rooms and turnings. Unlike the dead color of a sponge, each. of these passages is lined with glittering crystals, above, below, and on the sides. Every projecting rock is covered and every recess lined with gleaming calcite crystals. In the wealth of crystals there is no monotony. In one room the formations are pointed and glittering; in another rounded and dull. Impurities have given some of them a deep yellowish tinge, and in one room they resemble a quantity of prodigious baked beans. Sometimes boxwork, deeply encrusted with crystals, is visible on the ceiling. The cave has 50 m. of explored rooms and 22 m. of paths.
>
> In the lower room of the explored part—some of the cave is still inaccessible—there are pools of clear, cool water with stalactite and stalagmite formations, sometimes with a combination of the two. There are places where the crystals have been of necessity broken in making passages, the exposed rock resembling choice cuts of beef with streaks of fat running through. Occasionally a crack in the crystal walls will be marked by a thin red line where water seeping through has deposited iron and left it to oxidize.

At 17.6 *m.* is the junction with a graveled road.

> Left on this road is WONDERLAND CAVE, 5.4 *m.* (adm. $0.50 and tax; children under 17, $0.25; under 12, free). Competent guides conduct regular trips through the cave, an hour and 15 minutes being required to make the trip.
>
> Though not as large as some in the region, it has many strange and fantastic formations such as "The Sheep," "The Frozen River." "The Madonna and Her Child," "The Icicle Fence," and many other weird and beautiful forms, built through countless ages by the steady drip of mineral-laden water. The cave, discovered in 1931, is now equipped with a complete electric lighting system. Stalactites hanging from the roof join with stalagmites reaching up from the floor.

DEAD MAN CREEK, 28.5 *m.,* is crossed just S. of Sturgis. On its banks (R) is a monument of varicolored stones to the memory of Charles Nolin, a pony mail carrier, who was killed and scalped by the Indians at this point. The monument is in the form of a shaft and is surrounded by an ornamental fence with posts constructed of like material. Behind the monument are five black walnut trees growing from the slips obtained from five historic American battlefields including Gettysburg, Valley Forge, and Antietam.

STURGIS, 28.6 m. (3,432 alt., 2,591 pop.), was named for Maj. S. D. Sturgis who was in command of the military post in 1878 when the site was laid out. It is in the extreme southwestern portion of Meade Co., and it is said that many residents of the county, particularly in the northeastern portion, have never visited their county seat. Meade Co. is the largest in the State, its area exceeding the combined areas of Rhode Island and Delaware.

The town was nicknamed "Scooptown," or "Scoop," from the fact that Sturgis was originally populated by the usual type of camp following. There was a saying among the soldiers that when you visited in town you were apt to get "scooped" or "cleaned out."

The early population of Sturgis was made up largely of bull-whackers and bull trains, due to the large amount of supplies required by the military post and citizens. With the building of toll roads into Deadwood from the N. in 1877-78, all heavy freighting was routed to circle the Hills along the eastern flank, this being a much easier route to follow. All travel from the S. came this way, and the route from Pierre was forked at the Cheyenne River to head in directly for Sturgis with all freight intended for Deadwood and the northern Hills. This made of Sturgis quite a metropolis in a very short time, so that its one main street was literally teeming with life all day long and most of the night. Sturgis today is an important center of a large territory, with a growing population, as shown by the more than 50 percent increase in the last 10 years.

1. Right from the center of Sturgis on State 24, a paved road, is FORT MEADE, 2 m. It was established in 1878 and named in honor of Gen. George B. Meade, leader of the Union forces at the Battle of Gettysburg. Entering the grounds from the W., the first building used by officers in 1878 stands alone on the hillside to the R. Residence buildings are along the road from the entrance as far as the fort hospital. Here the road forks and forms an oval parade ground. To the R. are the officers' residences, to the L. the fort headquarters and post office; N. of the barracks is another street on which are warehouses, several stables for the horses, and the new riding hall. The parade ground, bandstand, and ball diamond are between the two streets. Polo and baseball games are the major sports of the soldiers. There is a landing field for planes N. of headquarters. The fort reservation consists of 13,127 acres.

The Fourth Regiment of Cavalry now occupies the fort. The
Seventh Cavalry at one time was stationed at Fort Meade. When
Gen. George A. Custer led this regiment in the battle of the
Little Big Horn, the Indians killed every living being except one
horse, "Commanche," and he was found two days later, riddled
with bullets, standing in a small stream of water. He was taken
first to Fort Lincoln and later moved with the regiment to Fort
Meade where he lived for 10 years. When the regiment was
transferred to Fort Riley, Kan., he was moved also. When he
died at an advanced age he was accorded military honors.

2. Right from the center of Sturgis on State 79 is an improved
road to BEAR BUTTE, 5 m. (4,422 alt.). Rising like a huge
mound of dirt dumped there by human hands, the Butte was
named "Mato Paha" (Ind. bear hill) because to them it resembled a huge bear, as seen from the NE. Standing detached
from the Black Hills proper, like a last outpost, this mass of
earth rises 1,200 ft. above the prairie surrounding it. The N. and W.
sides are so abrupt that they are inaccessible, even to experienced
hikers; but the eastern slope is more gradual, and from this
direction the summit can be reached.

Legends of the Butte tell how different tribes held possession of
this sacred mound, which was the goal of an annual pilgrimage
of worship as well as their watch and signal tower. Traces on
top show that fires have been kept burning for days at a time.
Records were kept by different tribes by placing rocks in the
forks of trees and thereby showing which tribe was in possession.
The Mandans are said to have made annual pilgrimages to Bear
Butte as long as they were permitted to do so. The Cheyennes
took the territory from the Mandans ,and later the Sioux absorbed the Cheyennes who held possession when the white man
claimed it by treaty. The Mandans held an annual religious festival called "Mee-nee-ro-da-ha-sha" (sinking down or settling
waters).

Nu-mahk-muck-a-nan, they believed, was the only man saved
from a flood. He landed his canoe on a "high mountain in the
West." Every year the Mandans believed they must make some
sacrifice to the water, and this sacrifice must be of sharp-edged
tools, as the canoe was made by similar instruments. They also
believed they must visit the mountains or else another flood
would come and no one would be saved. The time for pilgrimage
was when the willow leaf was in full growth. According to tradition, a turtle dove was sent out from the canoe and it returned
with a willow twig on which the leaves were in full growth.
Therefore the dove was regarded as a medicine bird and the Indians considered its destruction a crime.

Close to Bear Butte to the W. is the LARGEST ARTESIAN
WELL in the State. It was sunk in 1921 by a company of specu-
lators who were seeking oil. A 10-inch hole was drilled and the
flow was two million gal. per day. The waste was so great that

authorities soon after reduced the capacity by putting a six-inch pipe on top. Later a hole was drilled in the side of this pipe and the top plugged to prevent further waste.

At 29.7 m. is a junction with State 24.

Right on this road, the eastern edge of the Black Hills is skirted as far as Whitewood. At 3.8 m. is an unusual view of Bear Butte (R), and at 7.3 m. State 24 crosses WHITEWOOD CREEK. The water in this creek is a dull black, caused by the mill tailings from the Homestake Mine at Lead (see DEADWOOD). WHITE-WOOD, 8.3 m. (3,625 alt., 421 pop.), is a picturesque village, so named because of the extensive growth of aspen and birch trees in the vicinity. It became a town with the advent of the C. & N. W. R.R., while Crook City, just over the hill, joined the many ghost towns of the Hills, The reason was that early residents had pinned their hopes on the building of the railroad through Crook City. WHITEWOOD HILL, 8.5 m., is a steep climb, from which is a striking view of the valleys leading out of the northern Hills. At 12.3 m. State 24 rejoins US 14.

Between Sturgis and Deadwood, US 14 rises 1,000 ft. through BOULDER CANYON with its high limestone cliffs and heavy pine timber, a scenic drive.

At 41.4 m. is a junction with US 85 (*see Tour 13*); US 14 and US 85 are united to Spearfish.

At 42.4 m., at the summit of the hill above Deadwood, is PINE CREST CAMP, the municipal tourist camp of Deadwood. There are many cabins in a picturesque setting on a pine-covered slope. There are laundry facilities, a camp store, and playground equipment.

Left from this point is the CABIN OF DEADWOOD DICK, 0.3 m., where Deadwood Dick of dime novel fame lived until his recent death. (Open to visitors; free.) Up the mountain side from the cabin, is a footpath to the summit of Sunrise Mountain, where, blasted out of solid rock, is the GRAVE OF DEADWOOD DICK. It is close to the junction of the old Bismarck Trail with the Pony Express trail between Pierre and Deadwood, and overlooks the town which is so closely associated with the romance of his name. From this point can be seen not only Deadwood and Lead, but also Terry Peak, Custer Peak, and Mt. Roosevelt, with Bear Butte in the distance.

Deadwood has always had a penchant for Deadwood Dicks. The original was Richard Clark, who is said to have driven the first stage into Deadwood. It was he who was the apocryphal hero of a thousand hair-raising, blood-and-thunder Wild West tales written in New York City and not intended to be believed by anyone. But they spread the fame of Deadwood and its mythical

hero to the four corners of the country. Whether the occupant of
the present "grave of Deadwood Dick" is the original of that
name is beside the point.

At 43.3 *m.*, the crest of the hill, is the PREACHER SMITH
MONUMENT. The Rev. Henry Weston Smith, a Methodist
minister and itinerant preacher, was the first to exercise his profession in the Hills. On the 20th of August, 1876, he set out from
Deadwood for Crook City, in spite of the fact that he had been
warned that to do so was dangerous. Shortly after, word was
brought to Crook City that he had been found, killed by Indians,
five m. from Deadwood at a place called "The Rest." A party of
men set out from Crook City and carried his body to Deadwood.
On Aug. 20, 1914, exactly 38 years after he had been murdered,
the Society of Black Hills Pioneers unveiled a monument to his
memory on the spot where he met his fate. On each anniversary
of his death, his last sermon is read at a memorial service.

From the Preacher Smith Monument the road runs for miles
down a narrow winding gulch, and clings to the hillside above the
creek, with thickly wooded hills on either side. Since most of the
timber is pine, it is difficult to say whether the scenery is more attractive in summer or in winter when the pines show green against
the snow. This is the far-famed DEADWOOD HILL, one of the
memorable drives in the Black Hills.

At 47.6 *m.* is the St. Onge Corner, where the road branches E.
to the old French settlement of St. Onge. This whole region, a rich
upland valley, is called Centennial Prairie, because it was settled in
1876, the year of the Philadelphia Centennial.

At 50 *m.* is the BLACK HILLS AIRPORT, dedicated in the
summer of 1936 and serving the towns of Deadwood, Lead, and
Spearfish. The airport is one of the best-equipped in the Northwest. There are three main buildings constructed of native limestone quarried nearby. The main hangar has accommodation for
thirty planes. There is a repair shop of almost the same size for
the servicing of planes; also an administration building, with accommodations for pilots and passengers, a coffee shop, radio room,
and lobby. Between the hangar and the repair shop is a large concrete apron, and the runways are oiled. The field itself is a level,
square quarter section. It is unusual to find so large a tract of
level ground within the borders of the Hills. The field is surrounded by the usual marked posts of aviation. The airport was
built as a Works Progress Administration project.

SPEARFISH, 54.5 *m.* (3,637 alt., 1,738 pop.), took its name from a rather apocryphal incident of the early days. One old-timer was supposed to have remarked to another as he stood on the banks of a stream, "This would be a good place to spear fish," and forthwith the creek and future town were named.

The nickname of Spearfish is "The Queen City," because the hills surround it like a diadem. To the E., overlooking the town, is the lofty peak of Lookout; to the W. is Crow Peak; and to the S. Spearfish Mountain.

Spearfish lies on both sides of Spearfish Creek, at the mouth of Spearfish Canyon. It is not an industrial town but an important tourist center, the tourist business ranking high in the town's activities. There are five tourist camps in town, including the municipal park. One of these, the Central Cabin Camp near the depot, has an interesting collection of petrified wood and fossil specimens.

The municipal tourist park is in two sections. One of these is a cabin camp just opposite the U. S. Fish Hatchery. The other, without cabins, serves as a city park as well as a place where tourists may pitch their tents or park their trailers. It is one of the most attractive parks in the Hills. Bordering Spearfish Creek and faced by a rock cliff on the other side, it is shaded by great trees. Red squirrels and robins glean the scraps that the visitors leave. Campers may catch trout within a few yards of their tents.

There is also a community building with a good collection of native and other curios. A store supplies the needs of the campers, and gas for cooking, as well as laundry facilities are available. There is a large dance pavilion in which dances for the townspeople are held weekly.

Just S. of the city park is the U. S. FISH HATCHERY (*open to visitors*), established in 1899 for the purpose of hatching fish with which to stock the streams and lakes of the Black Hills region. This hatchery is now engaged in the propagation of brook, rainbow, Loch-Leven, and black-spotted trout. A brood stock of rainbow and brook trout is maintained at the hatchery in open ponds. This stock supplies part of the eggs from which the small fish are hatched to be used in stocking streams. Additional eggs of these species are sometimes shipped to this hatchery from other States.

The Spearfish hatchery raises approximately 2½ million fish each year, varying in size from two to five inches. These fish are supplied to any person free of charge for stocking public waters. There is one commercial hatchery in Spearfish which sells trout to hotels and restaurants.

The Black Hills region is the only part of South Dakota where trout are found in great numbers, although they are found to some extent in the waters of the Pine Ridge and Rosebud Indian Reservation. The reason for this is that only clear cold water is suitable for this species.

This hatchery conducts extensive feeding experiments relative to the merits of numerous artificial fish foods. During the fiscal year 1935, the station fed approximately 38,000 lbs. of fish food, consisting of beef and sheep livers, beef lungs and spleens, and ground salmon eggs. During the present year the station has received 10,000 lbs. of ground seal meat from Alaska. This meat is cooked, dried, ground, and put up in burlap bags.

The Spearfish station is a very attractive spot, the grounds being surrounded by large rim rocks and containing many trees and beautiful lawns. A large number of pools containing fish of various sizes are an attraction to visitors. The hatchery building contains the hatching troughs, a small aquarium, and a display case showing the different stages of egg development. Employees are glad to answer questions regarding the operations.

Spearfish has a golf course, a modern high school, a volunteer fire department, a hotel, and a moving picture theatre.

At Spearfish is a junction with US 85 (*see Tour 13*).

West of Spearfish US 14 passes the campus of the BLACK HILLS TEACHERS' COLLEGE, one of the four normal schools of the State. The school, founded in 1883, has had a steady growth until a few years ago when it was reduced, in an economy wave, to a two-year course. It also has a large summer school. The buildings are placed in a row, facing a well-kept park. The northernmost is the dormitory and refectory, then comes the administration and recitation building, next the gymnasium, and finally the training school, which is a grade school taught in connection with the normal school.

Northwest from Spearfish US 14 angles through scenic country, the foothills of the Black Hills, crossing wooded ridges and fertile valleys, with the Hills to the L. and the open country stretching N. to the R.

At 63 *m*. there is a fine view of the Wyoming hills.

At 64.8 *m.* is the GAME PRESERVE of the Black Hills' Rod and Gun Club.

At 66.5 *m.* US 14 crosses the Wyoming Line 2 m. E. of Beulah, Wyo. (*see Wyoming Tour 10*).

TOUR 4A

Highmore—Crow Creek Reservation—Fort Thompson—Lower Brule Reservation—Chamberlain. State 47.

Highmore to Chamberlain, 55.2 m.

No R.R. paralleling this route; no bus line.

Usual accommodations at Highmore and Chamberlain.

Graveled roadbed.

State 47 branches south from US 14 at Highmore, o *m.* (*see Tour 4*). Few houses are seen along the highway between High-more and Fort Thompson. For the entire distance of 30 m. between the two towns the road is straight as a plumb line, and the topography, except when State 47 plunges down into the Missouri River valley, is level or gently rolling.

The CROW CREEK RESERVATION (*open to public*) is entered at 17.2 *m.,* and the region is featured by upland stretches covered with buffalo grass, where great herds of shaggy buffaloes grazed in the days of Indian hunters. During the hard winter of 1934, farmers in the country N. of this section drove their wagons over these flats and gathered loads of dried cow dung for fuel, just as in the early days homesteaders picked up "buffalo chips" to burn. At the western edge of the reservation, in the pocket formed by the Big Bend of the Missouri River, are sheep and cattle ranches and small farms owned by both white and Indian settlers.

At 19.3 *m.* is the junction with a dirt road.

Right on this road is STEPHAN MISSION, 0.7 *m.,* where pupils from Crow Creek and other reservations, principally the Sisseton, are enrolled in the Immaculate Conception School. There are usually about 250 pupils attending the boarding school, which extends through the 10th grade. The large chapel is the central church for the adult Catholic people of the surrounding country. The gymnasium is used as a center of community recreation. Community sewing and work in Indian handicrafts are sponsored by this mission.

FORT THOMPSON, 30.2 *m.* (180 pop.), is administrative headquarters for the Indians on the Crow Creek Reservation. As late as 1880 Crow Creek, as the post office was known, was an important stopping point on the stage route which began at Yankton and extended along the river, through Pierre, to northern posts. Traders' stores in Fort Thompson are typical of reservation posts —visiting and loafing places, as well as trading centers. Buildings are arranged in the form of a square, the office being in the center. The square is a hold-over from the days when a stockade surrounded the group of buildings.

The fair grounds and exhibit hall are on the right of the entrance to the agency. All is quiet and deserted around this spot except on Fridays, when the Indians gather for business meetings of the tribe, or to engage in old Indian dances. In early September a fair is held here.

The reservation roll at the last census showed 943 Indians. As on other reservations, an Indian council governs many of the affairs of the tribe, the group holding regular meetings in the council room at the office building. The 10th and 25th of each month are ration days. At 8 a. m. on these days a food ration of flour, baking powder, coffee, sugar, pork, tomatoes, and prunes is given out at the commissary building to about 70 old and indigent Indians.

An excellent water supply plant was built in 1934 and pumps send purified water into the institutions and homes of the employes. The Indian population in general live in cabins, tents, and open-air shelters. Unsanitary conditions prevail, the water being hauled in open barrels to their homes.

A large proportion of the children of school age attend five schools on the reservation, the largest one of which is on the western edge.

A large collection of examples of old Indian art and craft work, decorated clothing and rude implements, is housed in the EPISCOPAL MISSION HOUSE (*open to public*). Modern pieces of beadwork and carving, products of a group of 20 Indians who use the name Crow Creek Crafts, are for sale.

Just W. of Fort Thompson SOLDIER CREEK marks the limits of the agency. On a bank of this creek, near the bridge, eight people were drowned in September 1933, when their house was carried away in a disastrous flood that rushed down the valley following a cloudburst.

Several small log and frame cabins in this vicinity are excellent examples of the type of houses that most Indians throughout the reservation occupy today. Sometimes a shade, or shelter, is built for summer use in front of these cabins. Shades are built of forked poles set in the ground, with more poles laid horizontally and thickly covered with leafy willows to form the roof. This well-ventilated room, sometimes called a "squaw cooler," is used as a special center for the family and visitors, its open-air sides enclosing a combined kitchen, dining-room, living room, bedroom and workshop. A village of white tents is generally seen in the vicinity of Fort Thompson. Round shades of bent willows, covered with fresh leaves, are set up in front of the tents to take advantage of the breeze and for additional sleeping quarters. Tuberculosis is prevalent here, as on other reservations.

At 32.2 *m.* is a junction with an unimproved dirt road.

Right on this road is a FERRY, 6.2 *m.*, reminiscent of the early days, which makes regular trips across the river to the LOWER BRULE RESERVATION, 6.9 *m.* The jurisdiction of this reservation has recently been combined with that of Crow Creek, only a sub-agency being maintained here now.

LOWER BRULE, 7.5 *m.* (50 pop.), is the headquarters for the little reservation on which barely 600 Indians reside. The small population was the chief reason for combining it with the Crow Creek reservation. Teton Sioux of the Sicangu tribe live on this reserve. "Brule" was derived by French traders from their translation of Sicangu (burned thighs). An old map of 1829 marks this area as occupied by "Tetons of the Burntwood." These Indians are closely related to those of the Rosebud Reservation. Until 1890 the reservation extended S. to White River. When the reservation boundaries were changed, part of the Indians moved W. to Rosebud.

At Lower Brule is the lower end of the famous BIG BEND, a 45 m. loop, noted in the journals of every river explorer. At the time of the War of 1812, Manual Lisa was made agent for all the Indians on the upper Missouri River. He established a strong trading post in the vicinity of Big Bend. When fur traders ascended the river, parties often left their boats at the turn and walked the 4 m. across the neck of the loop. The account of Elias J. Marsh (1859) tells how such a party had to wait overnight for their boat to navigate the distance around the bend to rejoin them.

From Lower Brule the dirt road winds a sinuous course along the rough, jumbled breaks of the Missouri River to IRON NATION, 12.3 *m.*, a store and post office situated near the river. Along the road, spread fanwise from Iron Nation, are the scattered homes of Indians comprising this community. A white church—Messiah Chapel, Episcopal—stands on a hill near the road. Below the hill a large spring has been walled in and a

pump placed over it. Lower Brule Reservation is marked by
scenes that vary little from those of a hundred years ago, the
few Indian houses, rude outbuildings, and occasional barbwire
fences, comprising the only advance upon the primitive.

The post office was named for Chief Iron Nation, leader of the
Brules when this tribe began to adopt civilized ways. Over this
area Iron Nation and his band roamed during the last days of
the red man's untrammeled wanderings. Medicine Creek in this
vicinity was the headquarters for the bands, as they sallied into
the prairie country to hunt buffalo. Numerous dams, constructed
under a Government works program during recent years, with
many wells placed at advantageous points on the several reservations, have helped solve the water problem that periodically becomes acute. The average Sioux Indian is not particular about
the source of his water supply, sanitation playing an insignifi-
cant role in his choice.

From Fort Thompson, State 47 spirals down the valley of the
Missouri River, winding near the shores, dipping into hollows, and
lifting over ridges. Remains of Indian life are still seen at various
places near the road. Arrowhead seekers have found many relics
of early days scattered along the valley. Trenches, used by the Ree
or Arikara Indians more than a century ago for defense, are found
in different places, and when State 47 was constructed it cut
through a forgotten Indian burial ground.

At 40.1 m is CROW CREEK, for which the reservation is
named. Several miles of the valley can be seen from the highway
along the hilltops, and many Indian homes are visible, the stream
being a favorite camping ground of the Sioux. At the mouth of
Crow Creek tribes once met for councils. The place is called the
"Sioux Pass of the Three Rivers" in Lewis and Clark journals,
because two other creeks, Elm and Campbell, empty into the Missouri River near here.

At 40.2 m. is a junction with a dirt road.

Left on this road is the CROW CREEK DAM, 1.3 m., a huge
earthen structure built across Crow Creek to impound a lake
10 m. long. It will be the second largest earthen dam built under the CCC program in the United States. A crew averaging
about 250 boys, has been working on the dam, which will provide
a recreational center for a wide territory. The dam has to be a
veritable fortress, for it will be called upon sooner or later to
stop the torrential waters that will surge down the valley, inun-
dating the lowlands and becoming a churning, roaring river after
a heavy rain.

CHAMBERLAIN, 55.2 m. (1,363 alt., 1,506 pop.) (see Tour 5),
is at the junction with US 16. (see Tour 5).

TOUR 4B

Rapid City—Junction with US 85A (Pactola). An unnumbered road known as the Rim Rock Trail, 18.5 m.

The Rapid City, Black Hills & Western R.R. ("Crouch Line") roughly parallels this trail.

Usual accommodations at Rapid City.

Roadbed graveled.

This road, known as the Rim Rock Trail, is primarily a scenic route, but it also affords a short cut between Rapid City and US 85A, 2 m. N. of Pactola. The views, after the road has climbed the hill above the valley of Rapid Creek, are exceptional. Typical Black Hills scenery, pines, parks, and mountain streams, are in evidence for the rest of the route.

This route branches S. from US 14 (*see Tour 4*), just E. of Baken Park in RAPID CITY, 0 *m.*

At 0.2 *m.* the road crosses the bridge over Rapid Creek. This creek is one of the best trout streams in the Hills.

At 0.8 *m.* is the SOUTH DAKOTA NATIONAL GUARD CAMP (*see Tour 4*).

At 1.1 *m.* (R.) is a Federal Indian Hospital which, when completed, will care for Indians from surrounding States, especially those suffering from tuberculosis. The old buildings were formerly used as an Indian school and later as a transient camp.

At 2.6 *m.* is CANYON LAKE, formed by damming the waters of Rapid Creek. Here are a city-operated beach and bath house (*admission free*), rowboats, and picnic grounds. A "fish fry," constructed of native rock and logs, has a cooking range 22 ft. in length. The land covered by the 45-acre lake was donated by Dr. R. J. Jackson of Rapid City on the condition that no motor boats ever be permitted on its waters.

At 3.2 *m.* (L) is a STATE FISH HATCHERY (*adm. free*). Here several different kinds of trout are raised to "fingerling size" and then planted in the creeks. This service to fishermen has succeeded in keeping a normal supply of trout in the streams. The pools in the hatchery have been repaired and in some cases entirely remade to improve the rearing ponds. Full-grown rainbow and Loch-Leven trout are in the N. pond.

At 4.5 *m.* is a junction with a graded road.

> Right on this road is NAMELESS CAVE, 2 *m.*, which compares favorably with other caves in the Black Hills from a scenic point of view, since many rooms contain beautiful crystalline formations. Here are stalactites and stalagmites—"The Frozen River," "Palisades." "The Devil's Kitchen," "Fairies Hallway," and many other unusual formations. Well-formed crystals and frostwork of crystal aggregates coat the rock surfaces in great profusion and delicacy. The cave is 75 ft. below the surface of the ground and is easily reached by a stairway.
>
> Since the cave was discovered recently, it has been explored only 1.5 *m.* There are many passages which have not been penetrated but they are being developed as rapidly as possible. The cave is lighted by both indirect and flood lights.
>
> The limestone formation in which the cave is found is said to be 290 million years old and contains fossils such as corals, gastropods, and brachiopods.

At 4.9 *m.* the road forks, the trail (L) going to Dark Canyon (*see Tour 15*). Right here on Rim Rock Road.

At 6.7 *m.* the road emerges upon the RIM ROCK, overlooking the valley below. Many beautiful views are obtainable along this stretch of road. Below lies the trail just traveled, and the creek which cuts its way along the bottom of the gorge.

At 7.4 *m.* the road enters the Black Hills National Forest and winds through the pines.

At 10.2 *m.* (L) is the junction with a graded road.

> Left on this road is TRIANGLE I RANCH, 0.2 *m.* At 1 *m.* is Hisega R.R. station (RCBH&W) and TRIANGLE I LODGE (see Tour 15), formerly Pierre Lodge, a summer camp among the trees, where cabins and swimming pool are available. The fishing is good. Many persons suffering from hay fever and asthma spend the summers here and find relief for the duration of their stay. At the Triangle I Ranch nearby, established in 1882, saddle horses and guide service are available for those who wish to explore the surrounding hills. Winter sports are featured, and the lodge is available for hunters during the deer hunting season.

At 10.6 *m.* is a road leading L. to the power-house of the Dakota Power Co. At this point the water is returned to Rapid Creek after being used for the generation of electric power.

At 12.3 *m.* (L), in the creek, is a wheel used to bail out water for use on an irrigation project consisting of a small plot.

At 12.8 *m.* the highway approaches the FLUME (L), which carries the water from Pactola to Big Bend, to furnish power to operate the hydroelectric plant.

At Pactola a low dam backs up the water of Rapid Creek and turns it into the upper and open part of the flume. This part is 12,773 ft. in length, and is made of heavy planking in the form of an open trough. For most of its length it is supported on high trestles as the country through which it passes is very rough. About 0.5 m. below Pactola (*see Tour 14*) it is siphoned under the tracks of the Crouch Line, and less than half a mile beyond passes over the track on a trestle more than 30 ft. high.

The flume follows, roughly, the course of Rapid Creek and the railroad right-of-way, but in many places it is far from both. It runs as an open ditch on the top of a tableland for 3,933 ft.; a pipe-line, about 5 ft. in diameter, extends 11,257 ft., and a tunnel, through solid rock, 612 ft. The penstock which conveys the water to the turbines is 724 ft. long. The flume, pipe-line, and ditch, are 5.5 m. in length, and have a drop of more than 300 ft. from Pactola to Big Bend, developing 2,000 horsepower.

The flume was first built in 1894 by the Pactola Placerville Mining Co., to convey water to placer mines between Pactola and Placerville, 2.5 m. below. It was then only an open flume and ditch. The mines did not produce as much gold as expected and the flume and ditch were taken over by the Dakota Power Co. in 1906, and they extended it to Big Bend.

The water drops 83 ft., generating electric power which is sent to Rapid City over steel towers and a 2,400 volt transmission line. Due to difficulty caused by freezing in winter, the plant and flume are shut down from about December 1 to March 15 each year.

At 13.2 *m.* (L) is a burned-over area which is beginning to be reforested.

At 13.3 *m.* (R) is JOHNSON SIDING, on the Crouch Line (*see Tour 15*).

At 17.3 *m.* (R) are ledges of slate rising above the surrounding forest growth.

At 17.9 *m.* (R) is a CCC dam, and at 0.5 *m.* beyond (L) is another CCC dam.

At 18.5 *m.* is the junction with US 85A (*see Tour 14*), 2 m. N. of Pactola.

TOUR 4C

Junction US 14 (Rapid City—Nemo—Roubaix—Junction with US 85A (Pluma).
Junction US 14—Junction US 85A, 39.1 m.
Unnumbered, graveled and dirt road; not paralleled by railroad.

Winding westward through one of the most scenic parts of the Black Hills, this route provides many points of interest. In order fully to appreciate the trip it is advisable to take plenty of time in driving the distance, stopping at the numerous points of attraction along the road. For one accustomed to riding, much of the route can be covered on horseback.

This road branches W. from US 14 (*see Tour 4*), 2.4 m. W. of RAPID CITY, 0 m. at junction indicated by a sign.

At 1.7 m. the road enters the cool, shady mouth of SOUTH CANYON, a deep gorge with tree-covered slopes flanking the road on either side. Occasionally sheer walls of solid limestone interrupt the green forest covering.

At 2 m. is a ranch house, where saddle horses are for hire by the hour or day. From the ranch several hiking and bridle trails can be taken.

Farther up the canyon, 4.3 m., at the foot of a bluff (R), is a large cave extending back into the mountain. Ponderosa pine, oak, elm, aspen, boxelder, and spruce cover the hillsides and extend to the edge of the creek along most of the drive. Birch is seen frequently, but most of the white-barked trees are aspen.

At 6 m. the road passes over the divide between South Canyon and Box Elder Creek, the canyon walls merging gradually into picturesque valleys and farm land. At 9.7 m. the road crosses the boundary of the BLACK HILLS NATIONAL FOREST (*see BLACK HILLS RECREATIONAL AREA*). There are numerous beaver dams along the creeks, where anglers may match their skill with the shrewdness of the elusive trout.

At 9.8 m. the highway strikes the TRAIL OF GENERAL CUSTER'S EXPEDITION on its return in 1874 from French Creek, near the present town of Custer, to Fort Abraham Lincoln, near Bismarck, N. Dak. General Sheridan secured permission from Washington in the spring of that year to send an expedition into the Black Hills for the purpose of exploration and scientific survey of the territory, to determie its mineral and geological possibilities. By the first of July Custer set out with about 1,000 soldiers, a supply train, and 300 beeves which were to be killed as needed.

Their route skirted the Montana-Dakota boundary to Mt. Inyan Kara, thence SE. to French Creek. Three exploration parties went out from the permanent camp, one down French Creek from which Charley Reynolds took dispatches to Fort Laramie. The return trip took the same course to Castle Creek, thence past Nemo and along Box Elder Creek to the point where it joins BOGUS JIM CREEK, 10 m. On this site Custer camped and while there, a story says, the expedition buried arms, ammunition, and some whiskey. However, no discovery of the reported cache ever verified the truth of the story.

The story of Bogus Jim dates back to early Black Hills days. When the region was the favorite haunt of gold prospectors, a certain Francis Calabogus located a mining claim and established a camp on the creek. From the contraction of Calabogus comes the name, Bogus Jim. Many claims were filed along the creek and farther back in the hills. Lead and silver ore were found in large quantities, and one or more copper veins were uncovered. But the prospectors wanted gold. There was little market for the other metals. Facilities for smelting were poor, transportation difficult, and most of the miners lacked the capital to develop their claims; consequently, there was little development of mineral resources in this part of the Hills.

Green Mountain, (5,101 alt.), highest peak in this region, commands a beautiful view of the surrounding forest and country. Rocky Point is another nearby attraction; it can be reached by a little hard climbing and affords a good view.

At 11.6 m. the highway passes CUSTER'S GAP through which the expedition passed on the journey to Fort Abraham Lincoln. During the ascent of the gulch several wagons were overturned. Today there is still a wagon road up the gulch. The route follows Box Elder Creek through deeply-wooded canyons. At 13.1 m. (L) there is a dark streak, largely iron ore; and at 14.7 m. is a formation which resembles a castle wall with high battlements.

At 16 m. is a ranch house where rooms are rented to tourists.

At 16.4 m. is STEAMBOAT ROCK (R), so named because of its resemblance to the hull of a boat stranded upon a huge reef; with considerable effort and about a day's time one can reach the top, from which there is a broad view of the surrounding country. To the W. is Bogus Jim valley; to the NW., Custer Peak (6,794 alt.); to the N., the town of Nemo; while to the E. are rolling prairies and the distant Badlands.

The U. S. Forest Service has developed a picnic ground, 16.5 *m.*, at the foot of the mountain. Along the cliff (R.) the formation of the rocky ledge resembles ancient castles. At 17 *m.* is a small store and filling station.

NEMO, 19.5 *m.* (4,616 alt., 240 pop.), is a quiet little village where the Homestake Mining Co., maintains a logging-camp and sawmill. There is also a ranger station here. Forest quietness, broken only by the occasional hum of a motor or the whistle of a sawmill, prevails. There is a LOG CHURCH (R) and across the street from the church is an old TOWN HALL. Just inside of the door of a shack along the board sidewalk is an old-fashioned fire hydrant and hose.

Beyond Nemo the country is more rugged, the steep slopes of the mountains having been swept by forest fires several times.

At 21.5 *m.*, on each side of the road, are two abandoned mines, reminiscent of an earlier day.

At 23.1 *m.* is a concrete-encased spring. The water is clear and cool and of the usual pure quality found in most Black Hills springs. Two m. farther there is a dam and a dry lake bed.

At 31.2 *m.* the road enters a forest of young trees with a distant glimpse of Custer Peak. The wooded area is often broken by out-croopings of schist and milk white quartz. This type of quartz contains gold in free-milling form.

The ANACONDA GOLD MINE is passed at the little Hamlet of ROUBAIX, 34.2 *m.* (5,392 alt., 45 pop.). The mine was discovered in the early 1880's and was first named the Uncle Sam Mining Co. The vein which the prospectors discovered contained what is known as free-milling gold. Simple stamping and washing was all that was necessary to recover the metal. This vein played out, and the property was later worked by the Clover Leaf Mining Co. until 1905, when the water broke through into the seventh level, about 700 ft. down. If the shaft leading to the pump had not broken, the mine could have been pumped out. The Anaconda Mining Co. acquired the property in 1934 and began operations to drain the mine. For months the draining of the mine went on until by September 1935 the mine was emptied of all water, including the seventh level. Since September 1935 the company has been busy cleaning up and locating ore drifts preparatory to actual production. The present equipment will take care of about five times the water which enters the mine per minute. The mine has a Diesel power-plant and also a steam outfit.

There are no stamps in operation at present; but there is a daily production of from 80 to 500 tons. The property covers 2,200 acres, and the mine and mill employ (1937) about 100 men.

At 39.1 *m.* is the junction with US 85A, 5 m. S. of Pluma (*see Tour 14*).

TOUR 5

(Luverne, Minn.)—Sioux Falls—Chamberlain—Rapid City—Custer —(Newcastle, Wyo.). US 16.

Minnesota Line to Wyoming Line, 486.6 m.

All-weather roads entire distance, hard-surfaced for the most part.

Except for a few deviations the C. M. St. P. & P. R.R. roughly parallels the route between Sioux Falls and Rapid City.

Good hotel and cabin camp accommodations are available at the larger towns.

Camp sites open to travelers at all towns.

Passing through one of the best farming sections of South Dakota at the start, US 16 crosses the State westward through a gradually changing country. Tree-sequestered farm homes with many improvements slowly give way to farms with less pretentious buildings. Dairy herds and cornfields become less numerous, pasture land replaces improved fields. After the road descends into the Missouri River valley, the scene changes rapidly, and the road lifts again in long, easy spirals into the open West-river country, the "wide open spaces," marked by widely separated farms and grazing herds of cattle. The change becomes more pronounced as the route continues west. Winding snake-like over rolling prairie, touching the scenic Badlands, skirting ridges, sinking into hollows, the road finally abandons its sinuous course and heads straight for the Black Hills. At a distance of about 25 m. these unusual mountains are dimly visible, jutting from the horizon line like smoke-shrouded thunder clouds. The Black Hills region is vastly different from the prairie stretches to the east.

Section a. Minnesota Line—Junction with US 14, 310.4 m.

U. S. 16 crosses the Minnesota Line 14 m. W. of Luverne, Minn. (*see Minn. Tour 13*), and passes through rolling country, with occasional groves along the highway. The oak trees are almost the last of that variety to be seen on the route, as farther west there are only a few, scattered along the Missouri River.

VALLEY SPRINGS, 1 m. (1,395 alt., 411 pop.), was settled in 1873 and had the first railroad station in Minnehaha Co. It received its name because of the number of springs along Beaver Creek.

At 3.1 m. is the junction with County H (*see Tour 5A*).

At 4 m. is the BEAVER VALLEY CHURCH, the center of a Swedish community noted for its *smorgasbord*—a spectacular array of appetizers generally served as an evening meal at the community meetings held at the church. An enormous table is spread and loaded with Scandinavian specialties—herring, sardines, anchovies, cold ham, and several other cold meats, liver loaf, vegetable salads of every description, headcheese, and three or four other kinds of cheese, including getost, a chocolate-covered cheese made of goat's milk. A large dish of boiled lobsters is generally on the table, and with this course a generous supply of the Swedish national bread, flatbrod, is served. Some special fish is commonly used for the second course, perhaps herring in cream, or meat balls of a special Swedish type, with tea and marmalade, rye bread and Swedish rusks. For dessert frozen whipped cream is served with a bowl of strawberries when seasonable. Perhaps the most pleasant features of a Swedish *smorgasbord* are the coffee and the many varieties of sweet rolls and rings and fancy cookies that have helped make a reputation for Swedish cooking.

At 8 m. is the junction with a graveled road.

Right on this road is BRANDON, 1.5 m. (192 pop.), a little village in the center of a community where "earmarks" of the old-time husking bee have been partially retained in a new and exciting sport—the corn husking contest. A national contest is scheduled at Brandon in 1938. Whereas the husking bee was a social gathering for the small farmers whose "heap" of corn was counted by scores instead of thousands of bushels, the husking contest is primarily a competitive game, the number of bushels husked being important only in determining the winner. The husking bee in homestead days was a major social event, for that was long before automobiles, movies, or night clubs. Neighbors helped one another and, while husking was only incidental to the social end of the gathering, every man kept at his task, lured by the prospects of finding a coveted red ear which entitled him to kiss the lady of his choice.

But the husking contest is a game of skill, speed, and endurance. The growth of the sport in South Dakota is evinced by the fact that 14 counties entered the State contest in 1935. An outgrowth of an idea of Henry Wallace, Secretary of Agriculture, who believed something should be done to develop a sport from the subjects farmers talk about, the husking contest was slowly evolved to settle the perennial arguments of braggarts as to who was the best husker in the community. Despite the progress of husking machinery, many young farmers today are pointing their efforts toward competition in the annual meet.

Strict rules have been devised to make these contests genuine proofs of skill and endurance. These rules must be obeyed to the letter. With two rows assigned to each man, the contestants line up at one end of the field. The equipment of each consists of a team and wagon, selected by lot among the entrants. The wagon has a high bang-board on one side to deflect the corn into the wagon-box. Behind each man is a gleaner, a sort of umpire who picks up the nubbins left to determine the thoroughness of the contestant. The husker is required to take loose corn lying either in the two rows, or between them. If he does not take it, the gleaner will pick up what he missed and this will be counted against him. Coaching is prohibited, but hundreds of spectators follow the huskers.

The contest lasts 80 minutes and is started by two shots, a minute apart. The first shot is a warning to get ready; the second a signal to begin husking. With the second shot the excitement begins, simultaneously the huskers swing into action. The golden ears beat a rapid tattoo against the bang-boards, and blend with the cheers of the spectators who throng the field behind the wagons, each trying to stimulate his favorite contestant to greater speed. A single shot stops the contest, and the winner is determined by subtracting deductions for gleanings and husks from the total weight of corn brought in from the field.

Taking root first in the southeastern part of the State, the husking contest idea is slowly spreading to other sections. In 1934 Richard Anderson of Brandon won the South Dakota championship and was runner-up in the national contest.

The mounds left by the Mound Builders, known locally as the BRANDON MOUNDS, 8.2 m. (R), are on a hill between the Split Rock and Big Sioux Rivers. There were originally 38 easily distinguishable mounds. Relic-seekers have opened several of them; but the only scientific investigation was made in October 1921, under the auspices of the Smithsonian Institute. William E. Meyer, who supervised it, died before his findings could be published, and the Smithsonian has artifacts but no record of the investigation. Most of the available knowledge concerning the Brandon Mounds is based on the word and unpublished manuscripts of Dr. W. H. Over, curator of the University of South Dakota Museum in Vermillion. Dr. Over was present when the excavation was made and carefully kept notes concerning all of the skeletons and artifacts which were uncovered.

It is thought that the Mound Builders migrated from the East. They are said to have been less inclined toward a nomadic life than the Sioux Indians, but eventually they crossed the width of Minnesota and settled near where the Split Rock River flows into the Big Sioux River. Modern Indians are of the opinion that the village could not have been very far from the mounds; and white settlers in the vicinity have found many arrowheads on the site, and some rubbish-piles still exist.

The most unusual bit of information concerning the Brandon Mounds, disclosed by the investigation of 1921, was that the Sioux Indians reopened the mounds for their burials. At the depth of 7 or 8 ft. there were found the older remains and artifacts; and at the depth of 5 ft. the bones were in a better state of preservation, and some of the relics are made of metal.

The upper, shallow burials, are credited to the Sioux Indians, and the deep, lower burials are considered to have been those made by the Mound Builders.

SIOUX FALLS, 15.6 m. (1,422 alt., 33,644 pop.) (*see SIOUX FALLS*).

> State's industrial center and largest city. State Penitentiary, Morrell Packing Plant, Manchester Biscuit Company, Pettigrew Museum, Terrace Park, Sherman Indian Mounds, Coliseum.

Here is a junction with US 77 (*see Tour 9*).

At 26.1 m. is the junction with a graveled road.

> Left on this road is WALL LAKE, 1.5 m., one of the most popular resorts in Minnehaha Co. The lake covers about 240 acres and is included in a 960-acre game preserve. Stocked annually with fish, the lake gives up thousands of several different varieties each summer. Here are cottages for rent, two dance pavilions, a skating rink, bathhouse, refreshment stands, and boats for hire. A sandy beach and playground add to the many recreational facilities.

PUMPKIN CENTER, 33.6 m. (4 pop.), unlike the mythical town of the Uncle Josh stories, has actually existed for many years at the crossroads of US 16 and State 19.

At 48.6 *m.* is the junction with US 81 (*see Tour 10*).

BRIDGEWATER, 54.6 m. (1,420 alt., 808 pop.), was originally called Nation, for Carrie Nation, the prohibition-crusader who carried on a bottle-smashing campaign. According to stories, the present name was given because railroad workers were required to carry their drinking water across a bridge during the time the Milwaukee R.R. was being constructed. The town has received Nation-wide publicity through its Colony Band, a group of musicians who dress in the garb of Mennonites while giving their programs at national American Legion conventions.

Bridgewater was another of the many towns in the State that engaged in a determined county seat fight. The town had won the honor in 1880, but it was claimed that their victory was the result of unfair practices. Accordingly, a group of Salem citizens drove to Bridgewater after dark and waited until it was safe to proceed with their business. The county clerk, in sympathy with the Salemites, left a window unlatched to expedite the coup d'etat. The records were procured and the men returned to Salem where they set up an improvised courthouse. When the Bridgewater citizens learned of the loss, they went to Salem, heavily armed, expecting to retrieve the records; but at the latter town everyone feigned ignorance of the entire affair and the Bridgewater men returned home, defeated. Salem was later named the permanent county seat.

EMERY, 65.5 *m.* (485 pop.), since early days has been known for its musical societies, both in the schools and in the town.

It was through Emery that the old Sioux Falls-Black Hills Trail passed in the days of oxen and prairie schooners. The county was surveyed in 1876 and opened for settlement. Soon Easterners were pouring in, some remaining to take up claims, others continuing westward to the Black Hills, where the lure of gold had already precipitated a turbulent rush of fortune seekers.

ALEXANDRIA, 74.7 *m.* (1,352 alt., 812 pop.), seat of Hanson Co., is on the northern edge of a large German farm area. The many pretentious farm houses and substantial buildings in the community indicate years of thrift and thoroughness. It is still related in Alexandria that, in 1884, when a tornado swept through the town, a woman who took her children into the cellar came up after the storm, lifted the trapdoor, and found the house gone.

Left on a graveled road is LAKE HANSON, 1.9 *m.*, an artificial lake built by the Works Progress Administration, and fed by

Pierre Creek and springs, insuring an abundance of water during dry periods. Cottages have been built and it is being developed as a summer resort.

At 8o.3 *m.* is a junction with a graded road.

Left on this road is the ROCKPORT MENNONITE COLONY, 8.3 *m.*, the home of a stern religious sect of Swiss-German people who had lived in Russia before settling here. They retain the curious dress, customs and beliefs of their ancestors, living in secluded rural colonies where their industry and thrift enable them to become prosperous farmers. In 1895 several groups of these people emigrated to this country from Russia to escape persecution and settled in colonies along the James river between Mitchell and Yankton.

The sect originated in Switzerland in 1530 when Menno Simons, a leader of the Anabaptists, founded a new branch which became known as Mennonites in his honor. Because of religious persecution they later emigrated to Austria and Germany. Near the close of the 18th century the Czarina of Russia offered them land and freedom from military service, so in 1774, followers of Jacob Hutter, one of their religious leaders, emigrated into Russia and the members became known as Hutterites. After several decades the Russian ruler repudiated her agreement and again they moved, this time coming to the United States.

Men in the colony never shave after they marry and thus are easily distinguished from the single members. Men and boys wear gray-black jackets and trousers, black felt hats in summer and fur caps in winter. Women and girls wear long, full, black calico dresses, and have shawls tied over their heads. Small children are cared for in a day nursery; the older ones receive religious training as well as grade school education. Large chalkstone buildings house several families, with one room usually assigned for each. Household duties are divided among the women, and farm work among the men. An overseer or elder, who also serves as spiritual leader, is elected to supervise the work and commercial life. A treasurer handles all the money and makes all the purchases for the community. If one marries outside the colony, he forfeits his claim to a share of the wealth. One may join by turning over all his property to the colony and accepting its customs. Those who leave the colony are unable to recover their property or shares. Besides not believing in war, the Hutterites disapprove of the use of firearms, tobacco, and moving picture shows. They are efficient farmers. steady workers, and live with little thought for their modern neighbors. Man is king in the colony; at meals the men are served first and the women do not eat with them.

Imbued with deep religious convictions, the Hutterites devote Sundays mainly to spiritual teachings. In everyday life these people live up to their ideals. Physical punishment is unknown.

If a member commits a minor offense, he may put himself in the good graces of the community by asking forgiveness from all members.

Proud of the fact that not once during the depression or drought did they seek help, the Hutterites continue to farm the fertile valley of the James River. It is especially noteworthy that these people of strange dress and customs are unusually polite and willingly explain the plan of their community. They permit pictures to be taken of their buildings and fields, but never of themselves.

MITCHELL, 89.5 m. (1,301 alt., 12,834 pop.) (*see MIT-CHELL*).

Corn Palace, Lake Mitchell, Custer Battlefield Highway Building, Indian Village site.

Here is a junction with State 37 (*see Tour 11A*).

MOUNT VERNON, 102.5 m. (1,413 alt., 460 pop.), in 1889 was entirely destroyed by a prairie fire, fanned by a 60 m. gale that swept the town. The result was that original buildings were replaced by newer types of architecture. Much of the surrounding area is underlaid with Dakota sandstone, an excellent building material. In order to obtain a satisfactory well it is necessary to reach this sandstone, which sometimes is more than 700 ft. below the surface.

At 113.9 m., just E. of the Plankinton city limits, is a junction with a graded road.

Right on this road is the SOUTH DAKOTA TRAINING SCHOOL, 0.8 m., where incorrigible and delinquent children under the age of 18 are committed by law until they are 21, unless discharged by the Board of Charities and Corrections. The school opened in 1887 with one delinquent. The land, comprising about 800 acres, is farmed by boys of the institution. Girls are segregated and have their own buildings, playgrounds, and teachers. They are taught housework and sewing, and are required to show improvement in their work before they are eligible for release. Boys learn carpentry, cement work, and mechanics, besides their detailed housework. The institution boasts a good band, and through encouragement of athletics develops consistently good teams. Noted for its purebred Holstein dairy herd, the farm also raises fine poultry and hogs.

PLANKINTON, 114.9 m. (1,528 alt., 715 pop.), is the seat of Aurora Co. Although Mitchell is generally believed to have had the first corn palace, the honor in reality belongs to Plankinton, for in 1891 a grain festival was held here. The bold statement, "Dakota Feeds the World," was printed on the outside of the building, a plain wooden structure, its exterior covered with grains and grasses. A story of the event at the time related how people came from a wide area on foot and horseback, in buckboard and wagons, to see the grain palace, which was abandoned after 1892.

At Plankinton is the junction with US 281 (*see Tour 11*); US 16 and US 281 are united for 19 m.

WHITE LAKE, 126.9 m. (1,646 alt., 506 pop.), is the site of the successful landing of the balloon, *Explorer II*, on Armistice Day, 1935 (*see Section c. below*).

At 134 m. is the junction with US 281 (*see Tour 11*).

KIMBALL, 139.8 m. (1,789 alt., 1,150 pop.), founded in 1880, was first called Andover, which was later changed to Kimball in honor of a railroad commissioner.

At 151.8 m. is the junction with a graveled road.

Left on this road 0.1 m., then L. 0.1 m., and finally R. 1.6 m., is the NELSON ROADHOUSE, now called the Custer Farm, on the old trail from Yankton N. along the Missouri River. In early days a supply line started from this point, connecting with forts stationed in several places up the river. The house was constructed with timbers two ft. apart, which were then filled in with home-made mud bricks, also used to build the chimney. The outside walls were boarded over and the inner brick covered with plaster. The roof was thatched with long grass cut in nearby lowlands. The house was later shingled and sided. It was here that Gen. George A. Custer and his troops stopped on their way to the Black Hills in 1875. The Nelson Roadhouse enjoyed a lucrative business during the gold rush days of the late 1870's.

PUKWANA (Ind., *peace-pipe smoke*), 154.8 m. (1,546 alt., 238 pop.), was well known for many years as the headquarters and shipping point for a device designed to save gasoline consumption in automobiles. With a large office force and trade territory which extended even to foreign countries, Pukwana became nationally known as the smallest town in the United States with a first-class post office. The business still operates on a small scale.

CHAMBERLAIN, 164.8 m. (1,363 alt., 1,506 pop.), like several other early towns on the Missouri River, was for many years a ferrying point for passengers and freight. Its picturesque location on the eastern slope of the river valley, its numerous park and recreational facilities, and its recently paved streets combine to make it one of the most attractive towns along the route. The fact that it is situated on the Missouri River, which is the approximate dividing line between the East-river farming region and West-river ranching country, gives the town an added touch of color, there being an intermingling of the characteristics of the two sections. On the extreme western edge of town is the CHAMBERLAIN SANITARIUM, operated by the Seventh Day Adventist Church but open to all patients. It specializes in the treatment of rheumatism and associated diseases.

Land W. of the Missouri River was opened for settlement in 1890, and the sole means of crossing the river was by a ferry that was operated only at certain hours of the day. In 1893 a pontoon bridge was strung across the river at Chamberlain. This floating structure was so built that the deck of the bridge rested on flatboats tied side by side. When river steamers approached, one end of the pontoon was released from its anchorage on the bank and allowed to float free. Although unsafe, especially in high water or freezing weather, the pontoon served as the connecting link between the markets at Chamberlain and the open range westward. In 1905 the C. M. St. P. & P. R.R. built a bridge across the treacherous river, which continually threatens to change its course. In winter the only way in which teams and cars could cross the river was on the ice. In 1920 Charles Bolling and his wife of Oacoma were drowned, leaving nine helpless children, and a drive was started to secure a highway bridge. In 1923 the State Legislature passed a bill to build five bridges over the Missouri, one of which was constructed at Chamberlain.

At Chamberlain is the junction with State 47 (*see Tour 4A*).

AMERICAN ISLAND, 165.3 *m.*, is a popular recreational center for a wide area. While not an island today, it has retained its name from an earlier day when a portion of the Missouri River flowed on either side. Immediately after crossing the bridge is MUNICIPAL PARK (L), in which are facilities for many kinds of amusement and recreation. A modern swimming pool, dance pavilion, picnicking and camping grounds, are in the dense timber fringing the river bank. In connection with the park are a golf course and rodeo grounds.

The history of the island dates back more than 125 years. In 1809 a trading post, called Fort Aux Cedras, was built here. Fort Recovery replaced it is 1822, following the burning of the former. The latter fort was afterwards abandoned.

In 1925 a reenactment of the Custer massacre was staged on

American Island to feature the completion of the bridge. About 5,000 Indians took part, and just as they were the first to cross the river before the white men came, they were also the first to cross the new bridge. Dressed in full Sioux regalia, they presented an impressive spectacle as they marched with moccasined tread, bells tinkling at every step, gaudy war bonnets flashing a half-dozen colors in the sun, the older Indians doubtless recalling the days when there was no bridge, no town, and no vestige of the white man. Indians came to the celebration in automobiles, on ponies, and in wagons loaded with camp equipment, in a seemingly endless line. An Indian camp was pitched on American Island, the tipis as nearly as possible like the original type before the advent of the canvas tent. Also aiding in the sham battles were 250 soldiers from Fort Meade (*see Tour 4*). The performance was staged on the hills across from the island where seats were provided for 15,000 people in a natural amphitheater; approximately 35,000 witnessed the performance.

OACOMA (Ind., *place between*), 168.8 m. (1,338 alt., 175 pop.), was so named because it lies between the Missouri River and the bluffs beyond. Manganese was discovered in the hills NE. of the town, but the deposits have not been utilized to any extent, though some attempts have been made in this direction. Loss of the county seat to Kennebec, together with the completion of a highway bridge, which diverted much former trade to Chamberlain, caused a rapid decline in population. Today many empty buildings give the impression of a ghost town in the making.

RELIANCE, 186.6 m. (1,780 alt., 247 pop.). A large artificial lake, which backs water nearly a mile, has given the town a much needed addition to its water supply as well as improved recreational facilities.

This section of the country was stimulated to a sudden growth in population in 1907 when the railroad was built, tying together the eastern and western parts of the State. Homesteaders took up the available land, and soon many thriving communities had developed. Some of the new residents were able to withstand the unusually dry years of 1911-12-13; others, unable to make a living, returned to the East. The deserted houses—generally small shacks—were soon appropriated by neighbors, sometimes for a financial consideration, sometimes for nothing. Today many homes comprise a group of shacks joined together to form a composite house—not the most graceful type of architecture.

KENNEBEC, 201.3 m. (1,687 alt., 385 pop.), seat of Lyman Co., boasts a new courthouse as a result of its victory in an exciting county seat race, with Presho and Oacoma as opponents. A large dam, built under the Federal Emergency Relief Administration, is NE. of the town. It is in a new game preserve.

At 210.7 m. is a junction with a graveled road.

> Right on this road is a new, unnamed lake, 2 m., where the CCC boys constructed a large dam designed to afford an ample water supply for practical and recreational use. The camp was one of the first to be built in the State under the CCC program, and has a complete set of buildings and equipment.

PRESHO, 211.3 m. (1,764 alt., 517 pop.), was the "bedding down" place for extensive round-ups in the days of the large cattle outfits. Ample water and feed were usually found on Medicine Creek nearby. Twenty years ago it was considered one of the largest hay-baling and shipping points in the United States. At one time its mushroom population neared the 3,000 mark. According to a story, eight minutes after the first town lot was offered for sale in 1905, a bank, composed of two barrels and a plank, opened for business. At first the bank operated day and night in serving the frantic rush of homesteaders, and the cashier was compelled to carry a six-shooter and all the currency with him when he went to lunch.

At Presho is the junction with US 83 (see Tour 12); US 16 and US 83 are united for 14 m.

VIVIAN, 223.4 m. (200 pop.), is one of the many typical prairie towns on this route. Straggling along a slope of Medicine Creek, Vivian retains its board sidewalks and the roofed porches of 30 years ago.

> Right from Vivian on a graded road is a STATE EXPERIMENT FARM, 1 m., where experiments with crops of a fairly wide area are carried on. Corn, oats, alfalfa, and Odessa barley are the chief crops, and a special kind of dent corn—Vivian 13—is produced. Recent drought years have seriously hampered the farm's experiments.

At 225.3 m. is a junction with US 83 (see Tour 12).

DRAPER, 237.3 m. (2,230 alt., 176 pop.), perched on a hill, is visible for many miles in all directions. The name honors a railroad conductor.

MURDO, 247.4 m. (2,217 alt., 625 pop.), the largest town on the long, undulating stretch of prairie along US 16 between Chamberlain and Rapid City, was named for a pioneer cattleman, Murdo McKenzie. Handicapped by a scarcity of water during dry years, the situation has been remedied through the construction by the Works Progress Administration of a large dam just S. of town.

OKATON, 257.2 m. (70 pop.), and STAMFORD, 267.2 m. (30 pop.), are two small prairie hamlets that were founded when the railroad was extended to the Black Hills in 1906.

There have been periods when this area has produced large wheat crops, and farming has been attempted since homestead days. However, it probably will always remain principally a stock country, scanty rainfall combining with other natural conditions to render farming a doubtful venture.

BELVIDERE, 279.4 m. (2,308 alt., 193 pop.), invites the traveler to stop and enjoy bathing, boating, or fishing in Lake Belvidere, near the town and US 16 (R). South of Belvidere is the 30,000-acre cattle ranch of Tom Berry, South Dakota's "Cowboy Governor," 1933-37.

KADOKA (Ind. *hole in the wall*), 293.4 m. (2,467 alt., 412 pop.), was so named because the town is near the rim of the Badlands' wall.

Kadoka has been called the "jumping off place," not in the usual sense, but because W. of the town is an abrupt entrance to the scenic Badlands. The town is attractively built, clean looking, and has three excellent tourist camps. It is the principal outfitting point for the Badlands.

At Kadoka is the junction with State 73.

> Left on this highway is KODAK POINT, 14 m., a vantage point from which the Badlands is viewed and photographed in three directions. After driving 12 m. the road follows the rim of a precipice, and in the distance the formations of the Badlands, with their many shapes and colors, stand out like strange spectral ruins of a vast medieval city.

At 301.4 m. is the junction with State 40 (*see Tour 6*). US 16 turns sharply (R) and unites with US 14 at 310.4 m., the two routes continuing W. as one highway to Rapid City.

Section b. Junction with US 14—Rapid City, 91 m.

At 14.2 m. is a STATE EXPERIMENT FARM (L) (*open to visitors; guides available*), where various experiments with leguminous and drought-resisting crops are given considerable attention. Other soil crops and livestock are also raised.

COTTONWOOD, 15.3 *m.* (2,414 alt., 150 pop.), first called Ingham, was given its present name because of the groves of cottonwoods growing nearby. This has always been a favorite area for grouse and sage hens, rigid hunting laws having restored their numbers in recent years.

QUINN, 28.2 *m.* (2,607 alt., 144 pop.), once was the trading point for a group of Jewish farmers and ranchers who settled nearby. Ruts of the old Deadwood Trail and an early telephone line are still visible 10 m. N. of the town, which was named for Michael Quinn, one of the early-day freighters. Mrs. Charles Waldron, a Fort Pierre woman, is finishing a book, begun by her late husband, dealing with early freighters on the Deadwood Trail, and a brief biography of Quinn is included.

WALL, 34.2 *m.* (2,713 alt., 325 pop.), received its name because of its situation near the edge of the Badlands. Its founding in July 1907 was marked by a lively celebration, an event which has become an annual affair. Called the "Gateway to the Badlands National Park," the town is the trading center of a farming and stock-raising country.

South of Wall, in 1905, thousands of cattle and horses drifted over the wall of the Badlands and perished during the tragic May blizzard that left in its wake utter ruin for nearly every stockman in the western part of the State. The storm, starting as rain, gradually turned to snow which fell steadily and thickly. Riding in on a strong north wind, the blizzard howled across the open stretches with unleashed fury. What had been balmy May weather soon changed to the bitterest storm a severe winter could offer. Striking at a time when livestock had just shed winter coats, the blizzard forced the bewildered animals to drift with the wind until they floundered helplessly into snow-filled draws to die. Barbwire fences of homesteaders added to the toll, for large numbers of stock drifted against them and piled up. South Dakota is a country of extremes, evinced by the fact that a mild warm day, may, in a few hours, be changed into one of biting cold, and vice versa. People who have lived in the State long will recall how they have often retired at night with the thermometer hovering near zero, to be awakened in the morning by water dripping from the roof, the sudden change being due to a chinook wind from the Rocky Mountain area.

Here is a junction with the unnumbered Badlands Monument highway (*see Tour 6*).

West of Wall US 16 winds down into the valley of the Cheyenne River. Before the days of highway improvement, the breaks of this river were always a knotty problem to freighters, especially during wet weather.

At 46.4 m. is one of the forks of the Cheyenne River, the two branches of which envelop the Black Hills area and carry away the water from the numerous creeks that dash down from the mountains. Noted for its swift current, the river often becomes a swirling, roaring torrent, carrying with it trees, brush, and silt gathered from its many dry tributaries, each transformed into a rushing river following a heavy rain. The Cheyenne River is also noted for its treachery. During normal periods it can be forded by team or on horseback, but it may rise two feet or more in an hour. Many instances have been known where a stranger to the wiles of the stream would attempt to cross, only to have his rig swept away by the swift waters, fortunate if he escaped with his life.

WASTA (Ind., *good*), 49.4 m. (2,320 alt., 181 pop.), was named by Doane Robinson, first State Historian. Nestling at the foot of massive gumbo bluffs, it is the trading center for a vast cattle country to the N. In the early 1880's this region was a vast range territory with large cattle outfits, their herds often numbering tens of thousands. Ranches were generally near some stream, and the cattle were turned loose to roam at will until round-up time called for a check-up. No ranches of comparable size remain today.

Many youths with a desire for Western life obtain work on a modern ranch with the expectation of "cowboying," but to their dismay usually discover that the work in the main consists of endless drudgery—haying, chores, fencing, cleaning sheds, and other manual tasks similar to those on a farm. The boss is the one who usually does the "cowboying." There are two reasons for this. In the first place he likes to keep in daily touch with his stock, and in the second place it is the easiest work on the ranch. Fences, smaller herds, and the shrinkage of open range, have all combined to take the glamour from the once colorful role of the cow "waddy."

NEW UNDERWOOD, 70.2 m. (275 pop.), is situated on Box Elder Creek, one of the numerous streams that drain the Black Hills. Tumbling down from the mountains, the creeks gradually slow their pace as they stretch out across the plains before joining the Cheyenne River. The mouths of these little streams often provide good fishing.

BOX ELDER, 80 *m.* (30 pop.), is a small railroad town, principally important as a shipping point.

RAPID CITY, 91 *m.* (3,196 alt., 11,346 pop.) (*see RAPID CITY*).

> State School of Mines and Museum, Dinosaur Park, Halley Park and Indian Museum, Alex Johnson Hotel, Municipal Lake and Camp.

Here is a junction with US 14 (*see Tour 4*) ; Rim Rock Trail (*see Tour 4B*) ; and State 79 (*see Tour 5C*).

Section c. Rapid City—Wyoming Line, 85.2 m.

LOOKOUT TOWER, 3.2 *m.* is on Rockerville Hill; from the tower, by means of a telescope (*fee nominal*), is a clear view of the Rushmore Memorial figures and Harney Peak (R), and the Badlands and Cheyenne River breaks (L).

At 6.4 *m.* is a graded road to HIDDEN CITY (*see Tour 5C*).

Brilliant brick-colored outcroppings (Opeche) begin at 8.5 *m.*, with three exposed cut banks along the highway showing the nature of the soil.

At 10.3 *m.* is a junction with a graded road.

> Left on this road are the SITTING BULL CAVERNS, 1 *m.*, first known by the Sioux Indians as Two Bear Holes, from the fact that two large bears made their homes in the entrances. The location was popular, and old Indians recall that Sitting Bull's band used to camp there. The caves were not extensively explored until 1934, and in 1935 they were opened to the public.

At 11.2 *m.* is SPRING CREEK. It was in connection with this stream, in gold rush days, that the tale of *When a Mule-Skinner Kisses a Mule* originated. There was a gold stampede in Rockerville, which was becoming a town almost overnight. The Indians had held up a mule train on the Sidney road between Rapid City and Spring Creek, and the next day a merchant approached one Johnny Hunt and asked him to haul a load of goods from Rapid City to Rockerville immediately. As Johnny and his mules would have to go over the road on which the Indian hold-up occurred, he asked the merchant if he thought the trip advisable. "Oh yes," said the merchant, "I'll go over with you, but you will have to come back alone."

After a lot of thinking on Johnny's part and a great amount of coaxing from the merchant, Johnny finally agreed to make the trip, but first went home for his 50-70 needle-gun. After he had delivered the goods, some miners told him of a new trail whereby he could save five miles. Although the new trail was treacherous, he was still worried about Indians and decided to try it. Everything went well until he came to Spring Creek Canyon. Here he found himself and the mules looking over a precipice of about 300 ft., inclined at a 45-degree angle. Not wishing to retrace his steps for 15 miles, and anxious to get back to Rapid City, he resolved to make the descent.

After chaining an old tree top to the rear end of the wagon to act as a brake, locking both rear wheels, and adding a little persuasion intermingled with much profanity, Johnny coaxed the mules to take off. They gathered momentum as they slid down, the wagon zigzagging and careening, the mules skidding along on their haunches. Johnny's mind had been centered on Indian raids so earnestly that he had forgotten to secure the wagon box to the chassis, and about halfway down the precipice it slid roughly onto the mules' backs. Johnny managed to hang on somehow until they reached the bottom, where he was catapulted over the dashboard ahead of his mules. Searching thoroughly for broken bones and finding none, he scrambled to his feet and walked over and jubilantly kissed the nose of one of his dour-faced mules. This was too much for the mule, which immediately broke away and bolted down the trail. About two hours afterwards he was found with his nose in the waters of a creek.

At 12.2 m. is the junction with an unimproved dirt road.

> Right on this road, through a gate, is the rim of the Stratosphere Bowl, 1 m. (see below). From this vantage point the entire bowl can be seen, including the floor, 425 ft. below.

At 13 m. is the junction with a dirt road.

> Right on this road is the floor of the STRATOSPHERE BOWL, 1.3 m. (3,500 alt.). (Steep descent, drive in second gear, and sound horn at turns.) The bowl was used for the National Geographic Society-U. S. Army Air Corps record-breaking flights into the stratosphere. On Armistice Day, 1935, the balloon, "Explorer II," rose to a height of 13 m. from the rock-walled basin. The bowl was chosen because it is sheltered from surface winds in an area where cloudless days are frequent, and to the E., the direction in which the balloon was expected to travel, are hundreds of miles of level plains, assuring a good landing. Here for weeks scientists, balloonists, and Army troops toiled day and night in preparation for the flight. Finally, on November 10, the long-awaited high pressure area drifted in from the W., indicating the weather would be ideal for a flight the next day. All

guests were barred from the bowl; truck loads of soldiers arrived from Fort Meade to hold the balloon in leash while the helium gas flowed into it. At night a huge battery of floodlights, placed in a circle around the floor of the basin, were turned on, lighting the bowl so brightly that it was possible to read a newspaper at any time during the night. Mooring ropes were attached to each of the points in the scalloped edge of a girdle encircling the balloon near the top, and these ropes were payed out by the soldiers as the balloon filled with gas. Soon after inflation began, some gas formed a pocket in the fabric underneath and caused a 17 ft. tear, resulting in more than an hour's delay while it was being mended. As the first streak of dawn was seen above the cliffs, the important task of fastening the gondola to the balloon was completed. The gondola, rolled out on a rubber-tired "dolly," was suspended below the bag with bridles of parachute webbing. The 40 bags of lead dust, the emergency parachute and heavy scientific equipment, which was later released and floated to earth by parachute as the balloon came down, could be seen hanging from the gondola's sides, as the craft was maneuvered to take advantage of favorable air currents. Inside were Capt. Albert W. Stevens, scientist, and Capt. Orvil A. Anderson, pilot, making last preparations.

At 7:01 a. m. word was given to cast off, and the giant balloon, clearing the rim of the bowl by only 50 ft., floated upward. Because of northwest winds blowing at the time, it was necessary to take off over the very highest cliffs. To lighten the load for a quick ascent, 700 pounds of ballast were removed before the start. When the balloon was 100 ft. above the trees, a downward trend of air forced it earthward, but Capt. Anderson, who was standing on top of the gondola, quickly dumped 750 pounds of ballast. Immediately the immense bag rose rapidly, ascending to the height of 13.71 m. above sea level—exceeding all previous attempts to rise into the stratosphere.

After the balloon reached an altitude of 15,000 ft., Capt. Anderson slowed the rate of ascent so that Capt. Stevens could have an opportunity to rig the instruments which trailed underneath the gondola. The ports were then sealed and the pilot continued the ascent, maintaining as nearly as possible a speed of 400 ft. a minute. As they neared the ceiling and the balloon became fully expanded the rate of climb was reduced to 200 ft. a minute. The balloonists maintained their position at the ceiling for 1½ hours, making observations and collecting scinetific data. In mid-afternoon, during the descent, a radio hook-up was arranged whereby the two men in the metal gondola talked to the commander of the China Clipper flying over the Pacific Ocean and also to a newspaper editor in London.

After remaining aloft for more than eight hours, and reaching an altitude of 72,395 ft., the two sky explorers managed a perfect landing in an open field near White Lake, S. Dak. (see above, section a), 240 m. E. of the natural amphitheatre from which the craft took off.

Explorer II, the world's largest balloon, was made of 2 2/3 acres of cloth, had a capacity of 3,700 cu. ft. of gas, and weighed 15,-000 pounds including the gondola, instruments and crew. Its height at the take-off was 316 ft.

The successful flight of 1935 was the third attempt and the second ascension, sponsored by the National Geographic Society and the United States Army Air Corps, to be made from the Stratosphere Bowl. The first flight took off at dawn, July 28, 1934. The balloon had attained a height of slightly over 60,000 ft., when the bag commenced to rip and the descent was begun. The flight ended that afternoon when the huge bag and the gondola crashed in a field near Holdredge, Neb. The balloonists saved their lives by using their parachutes. The second attempt to penetrate the upper air was disastrously halted when, an hour before the scheduled time for the take-off, the balloon ripped at the top, collapsed to the floor of the bowl, and its charge of helium escaped.

The LOG CABIN in the bowl was built in 1881 by Col. J. H. Wright; the large fireplace is made of rock and mud. The field is now used as a potato field.

ROCKERVILLE, 13.3 m. (4,371 alt.), has been almost completely abandoned. except for campgrounds. Along the highway are the Silver Mt. Camp and Memorial Tourist Camp.

At 18.1 m. is the largest SHINGLE MILL in the Black Hills.

An old gold mine is (L) on the limestone bluff at 21.1 m.

KEYSTONE, 22.1 m. (4,342 alt., 250 pop.). is one of the pioneer towns of the Hills. The older part follows the creek (L), with unpainted houses on one side and store buildings on the other. The newer part follows US 16 and caters to travelers with its markets and camps.

A FELDSPAR MILL (L) is at the fork of two roads, its large building covered with a coat of white dust. The plant has been operating day and night since repeal to furnish feldspar to be used in making glass, and also false teeth, bathtubs, linoleum, and other articles. Breaking naturally into cubes, the rock is ground with Belgian granite until it is pulverized. Some of the rock is reduced to a powder four times as fine as flour. The spar is mined from the mountain behind the mill, and other minerals are also extracted, particularly lithium, used in making soft drinks, and mica, used in the manufacture of isinglass.

The RUSHMORE POTTERY MARKET is L. of the highway, mid-town.

Native clay, hand-turned on a wheel, is made into vases, bowls, pitchers, and novelties. Two sculptors working on the Mt. Rushmore Memorial discovered the clay and began experimenting with pottery. A glaze has been perfected to add to the beauty of the product. The kiln is situated a mile behind the market.

At 22.7 *m.* US 16 enters the HARNEY PEAK GAME SANCTUARY. A large crag of jesset is near the road (R) at 22.9 *m.*

At 23.1 *m.* US 16 enters the eastern end of CUSTER STATE PARK, one of the largest State parks in the United States, comprising 128,000 acres. Created in 1913, with the exception of modern hotels and improved highways, this park remains in a wilderness-like state and is a wildlife sanctuary where over 600 buffaloes, 2500 elk, and 2000 deer roam freely.

At 23.8 *m.* is the junction with the RUSHMORE MEMORIAL HIGHWAY (*see Tour 5B*). From here US 16 traverses the Iron Mountain Highway.

At 24 *m.* are the GRIZZLY PARK campgrounds, in rugged seclusion.

From the PIGTAIL BRIDGE, 24.3 *m.,* is an excellent view (R) of Washington's face carved on Mt. Rushmore in the distance. At 25.2 *m.* is another Pigtail Bridge, claimed to be the longest spiral bridge in America. The bridge is built so that each succeeding upward curve passes over the last one until the road reaches a sufficient height to take to the hillside in its upward climb.

A TUNNEL, 26.4 *m.,* is cut through solid granite for 176 ft. The whole tunnel is focused on the Rushmore figures, the sides of the tunnel forming a frame, and the whole making a most effective telescope; but the view is backward through the tunnel.

At the end of the tunnel the road forks into two one-way drives through a grove of quaking asp and birch.

At 26.7 *m.* another bridge approaches a tunnel, which again is focused on Mt. Rushmore, but this time the view is straight ahead. The road winds upward with sharp curves and pitches, and divides again into one-way roads.

At 27.6 *m.* is the summit of IRON MOUNTAIN (5,500 alt.), from which a view of surrounding mountains is available. To the W. is Harney Peak, NW. is Mt. Rushmore, and E., through the trees, are the yellow Badlands; below, the road drops away in ribbon-like curves and loops. Iron Mountain is estimated to have 55 percent iron content. Such a deposit is known as "Iron Hat."

At 28.6 m. is another tunnel, with a rear view focused on Mt. Rushmore, and for the next few miles ironwood trees replace the pine, until a treeless plain is reached.

At 32.4 m. is the junction with a dirt road.

> Left on this road is the SPOKANE MINE, 1 m., one of the mines reopened during the gold boom.

Continuing down the mountain side, US 16 recrosses Iron Creek several times until the foot of the mountain is reached.

GRACE COOLIDGE CREEK, 40.1 m., was named for the wife of former President Calvin Coolidge, who spent the summer of 1927 in the Black Hills. It was previously called Squaw Creek.

At 42.2 m. (R) is the CUSTER STATE PARK ZOO (open to public). A variety of native animals, including bear, deer, elk, bobcats, mountain sheep, wolves, porcupines, foxes, coyotes, and badgers, are kept on exhibit.

At 42.3 m. is a junction with a graded dirt road.

> Left on this road which immediately enters the BUFFALO PASTURE a Buffalo Round-up is held every year in mid-July. As a part of the round-up activities, the bulls for the annual exchange with out-of-State parks are taken from the Custer State Park herd.
>
> The park herd, which numbers 600, roams free over the pastures. Usually buffalo remain in a herd, but sometimes the quiet, shaggy creatures are seen singly or in small groups beside the road. They pay little attention to passers-by, but as they possess agility and speed contradictory to their clumsy appearance it is advisable not to leave the car when they are near.

STATE GAME LODGE, 43.1 m. (4,225 alt.), is a State-owned hostelry built of native stone and pine. It gained national notice as "The Summer White House" of President and Mrs. Calvin Coolidge in 1927. The ground floor, with the exception of the dining room, contains a museum of Indian relics and geologic specimens.

At 43.5 m. is the CUSTER STATE PARK MUSEUM (open to public), a low rambling rustic building constructed of native stone and lumber, built in 1934-5-6. The main exhibit room, is entered through a massive and attractive portico fronting the highway to the S., and will be used for the geological exhibit. To the E. is a wing having two additional exhibit rooms that will be used for the historical and forestry displays, respectively. In another wing are the office and the laboratory for preparing exhibits. At the R. of the entrance is the library and reading room, and around the north side and east end of the east wing is a large flagstone terrace 18 ft. wide.

At 48.9 *m.* is the junction with the Needles Highway (*see Tour 14A*). Between the arms of the Y is the forester's residence.

LEGION LAKE, 49.5 *m.*, was formed by damming a creek and flooding the canyon. This lake, known for its striking beauty, has a huge, rounded rock at the south end. It has been stocked with lake trout and blue gills.

At this point is the junction with a graveled road.

> Left on this road is the AMERICAN LEGION CAMP, 0.3 *m.*, a hotel and cabin camp operated by the South Dakota American Legion. In addition to the public hotel, there are 21 cabins, bathhouses, a diving tower, slide, boats, and a recreational playground.

> East of the hotel, on a one-way road, is THE BADGER HOLE, 0.3 *m.*, home of Badger Clark, South Dakota poet laureate, and author of "Sun and Saddle Leather," "Sky Lines and Wood Smoke," "When Hot Springs Was a Pup," and "Spike." Much of his poetry has the "southern Hills" as a setting.

BALANCED ROCK, 49.6 *m.* (R).

At 50.3 *m.* is a junction with State 87.

> Left on State 87, at 1.6 *m.*, is a junction with a dirt road; R. on this road is MOUNT COOLIDGE, 2 *m.* (6,400 alt.). This peak, formerly Sheep Mountain, in the summer of 1927 was renamed in honor of President Coolidge, as a memorial of his visit to the State. The road leading to the summit is considered the most thrilling in the Hills. Its final stretch is along a "hogback," with steep slopes dropping away on either side and no guardrail. On the summit is a log tower with an inside stairway. From the tower's top can be seen all the higher peaks of the Hills, even those in the northern section, and parts of three States—South Dakota, Nebraska, and Wyoming.

> At 4.7 *m.* is BLUE BELL LODGE, a summer resort with a log hotel and several cabins. It is owned and operated by the State.

At 51.9 *m.* US 16 enters HARNEY NATIONAL FOREST (*see BLACK HILLS RECREATIONAL AREA*).

At 52.4 *m.* US 16 reaches the east edge of STOCKADE LAKE (5,189 alt.), a long, narrow, 135-acre artificial lake, formed by damming French Creek. At the east end are a beach, diving tower, and boat dock (*open to public*). The road winds along the shore, over the dam and spillway. Left of the dam, close to the creek, is CAMP DORAN, 53.2 *m.,* which houses the company of CCC youths who built the dam. A pear-shaped peninsula reaches into the lake (R). A campground and picnic area, 53.7 *m.,* overlook the lake.

ANNIE D. TALLENT MONUMENT, 54.4 *m.,* is a memorial to the first white woman in the Black Hills. Born in York, N. Y., and educated in the East, she came to the Black Hills with the Gordon Expedition in 1874. When all the trespassers were taken to Fort Laramie, Wyo., in 1875, she was transported on a government mule. She returned with another expedition a year later. She wrote a book, *Black Hills,* or *Last Hunting Grounds of the Dakotas,* in which she described the early days of the Black Hills. When she died in 1901, a special train was furnished by the Society of Black Hills Pioneers to carry her body to Elgin, Ill.

At 54.5 *m.* US 16 passes the western edge of Stockade Lake opposite the old Gordon Stockade site; at this point is the junction with a dirt road.

Right on this road is a reproduction of the GORDON STOCKADE, 0.2 *m.,* originally built on the banks of historic French Creek in gold rush days.

Reports from the Custer expedition that penetrated the Black Hills in the summer of 1874 stated positively to the Government that there was "gold in them thar hills." The news created considerable excitement, especially at Sioux City, Iowa. Charles Collins became active in organizing an expedition to the new El Dorado. By October a small band of 26 men and a woman and her boy, together with six covered wagons, each drawn by four oxen, and provisions enough for six months, were assembled for the trip.

The van started Oct. 6, with the pretense of having O'Neill, Neb., as their goal. After a few days it was deemed best to elect one of their number as leader and pilot. Their choice was John Gordon and his ability proved the wisdom of their selection. A few weeks after the train passed O'Neill one of their number, Moses Aaron, became seriously ill, died Nov. 27, and was buried that evening on a knoll near where the town of Wall now stands.

The expedition reached General Custer's old camping grounds on French Creek, about 2.5 m. E. of Custer, Dec. 23, 1874, after a trip of 78 days, marked by sufferings and privations. The weather turned extremely cold but, fortunately for the pioneers, fuel was handy. The large pine logs, filled with pitch, burned freely.

For protection against hostile Indians the band decided to build what later became known as the Gordon Stockade. US 16 now passes the place, and a signboard, about 200 yards distant, marks the spot where gold was first discovered July 27, 1874, by Horatio N. Ross and Wm. McKay, who were prospectors with Custer.

The stockade was, as the reproduction shows, an enclosure 80 ft. square, built of logs 12 to 14 in. in diameter, set 3 ft. in the ground, making a fence about 12 ft. high. The structure was placed on level ground beside French Creek, 400 ft. from either timber or rocks. Cracks were filled from the inside by smaller timbers. Bastions were built at the corners so that occupants could protect themselves by shooting along the outside of the fence in every direction. The double gate was made of 10-inch hewn logs and opened inside. A well 7 ft. deep was sunk 2 rods from the gate.

Six log cabins were erected inside, and companions were chosen according to compatibility. Some of the cabins had puncheon floors and the rest only the ground. Each cabin had a good fireplace built of rock and mud. The roofs were made by splitting 12-inch logs into halves and hollowing them out like a trough. Cracks in the roofs were filled with grass and mud. No nails were used.

After the stockade and cabins were finished, they began the search for gold, occasionally taking a day off to get a deer, elk, or mountain sheep, to keep up the supply of meat. By the end of January 1875 the miners had panned out $40 in gold, enough to prove the metal was there.

To keep their word with Collins, who organized the party, Gordon and Eaf Witcher started Feb. 3, 1875, for Sioux City with their gold for proof, and also to bring back reinforcements and provisions before the Indians should begin to come into the Hills in the spring.

In March the colonists were so sure they were making a permanent settlement that they laid out a town and named it Harney. It proved to be only another dream, for on April 3, 1875, two army officers accompanied by Rodger Williams and Red Dan McDonald appeared in camp to inform the band that they were under arrest and must prepare to move immediately to Fort Laramie. Confusion was rife at once, for they were to take only what was absolutely necessary. Many of the men hid their tools, so sure were they that they would be back. Of the 28 oxen they had turned out, only 15 would be rounded up. Camp was broken April 7, and the band started for Cheyenne.

Upon their arrival at Fort Laramie they were paroled, and were surprised to learn that their friend, Collins, had sent money for their transportation back to Sioux City. A few of the men went back, and when they arrived they were met at the depot by the mayor and thousands of citizens.

John Gordon was not daunted. Openly backed by thousands of citizens, he organized another expedition of 300 members and crossed the Missouri River three days before a special message from Washington reached Sioux City, forbidding anyone to leave for the Black Hills. When the wagon train reached the Indian reservation, Government troops overtook it, burned all the wagons and supplies that were not needed by the trespassers for their return trip, and placed Gordon under arrest at Fort Randall. Even this treatment did not stop the movement. Adventurers still sifted through until a treaty was signed and the restrictions raised.

Through the Commercial Club of Custer, the stockade was rebuilt in 1924. A huge mass of pegmatite, covering several acres at the base, rises behind the stockade to a height of about 500 ft. It is called Calamity Rock, and is named for Calamity Jane, whose widespread activities are alleged to have extended even to this rocky peak.

At 54.6 *m.* FRENCH CREEK is crossed. It was from this creek that the first gold in the Black Hills was panned, starting the gold rush of '76. Gold is still being panned in the creek, but with suction pumps and mercurized pans.

At 54.8 *m.* is a native-stone marker where Gen. George A. Custer's soldiers camped in 1874. Beside it is the grave of John Pommer, a private of the U. S. Cavalry.

The FIRST GOLD CLAIM, 55 *m.*, was registered by soldiers and posted on this site.

At 56.7 *m.* is SENTINEL HILL PARK, a tourist camp with a large picnic shelter. A 9-hole golf course (*public*) adjoins the camp.

At 57.4 *m.* is a junction with US 85A (*see Tour 14*); US 16 and US 85A are the same route for 1 m.

CUSTER, 57.9 *m.* (5,301 alt., 1,398 pop.), seat of Custer Co., is the oldest town in the Hills. It is on French Creek near the place where gold was first discovered July 27, 1874, by Horatio N. Ross, a prospector with General Custer's expedition into the Hills.

The town was staked out in 1875 and named Stonewall in honor of the Confederate general, "Stonewall' Jackson. The group of miners first on the site, like the Gordon party that previously settled on French Creek and erected the Gordon Stockade, was ordered out because no treaty had as yet been signed with the Indians. In this case, however, the authorities permitted seven men to remain as custodians of the property of all. Many of those who left never returned. After the withdrawal of the Federal troops, leaving the country open to settlement, the town was named Custer at a miners' meeting and lots were divided among the miners present.

Immigrants began to come in great numbers, and by April 1876 the population had increased to 5,000. After the discovery of the rich placer mines at Deadwood, in the short space of three weeks the 5,000 population had dwindled to less than 100 residents. But Custer had been publicized throughout the East, and its natural advantages of location in the hills, abundance of water for placer mining in the French Creek valley and neighboring gulches, and the discovery of large quantities of mica, all tended to render the city important once more in the eyes of settlers.

The first post office in Custer, and in the entire Black Hills region, was a spacious cave in the rock just a mile W. of town, on the N. side of the road. Here, in the earliest days of placer mining, everyone who came in from the "outside" deposited the mail he brought. And there the miners would come, each one sorting out his own mail and leaving the rest. The next post office, in the rear of a general store in Custer, consisted of an apple box into which all mail was thrown and from which each person took what belonged to him. This was satisfactory to all until the arrival of a U. S. postal inspector. Horrified at this unorthodox handling of the mail, the inspector in no uncertain terms told the storekeeper just what he could and could not do. As he left the building, the irate merchant overtook him on the porch and thrust the apple box into his arms. "Here's your darned post office!" he said, "Take it with you."

Between the years 1881 and 1890 the town began to build for permanency, several brick structures being erected. In 1890 with the arrival of the railroad, Custer was at last connected with the world outside its little valley. Today, because of its proximity to such points as the Needles, Harney Peak, Sylvan Lake, and other scenic spots, the town has become a mecca for tourists. A historical pageant (*see below*), held on the anniversary of the discovery of gold in French Creek, attracts increasing thousands of people yearly. Situated in a favorable hunting region, the town is a gathering place for deer hunters during the fall open season. There is still some placer mining being done in Custer, while local and nearby lumber mills bring in a considerable amount of trade. A feldspar mill at the edge of town ships several carloads of ore weekly. In addition, quartz, gold, mica, beryl, tantalite, amblygonite, soda spar, tourmaline, and gypsum are shipped in commercial quantities. With its wide streets, laid out "so that four yoke of oxen could be turned around without driving around the block," Custer has retained many of its original rugged characteristics, and is still a typical frontier town.

The GOLD DISCOVERY DAYS PAGEANT GROUNDS, on a grassy tree-bordered slope at the SE. edge of town, are the scene of part of a two-day celebration held each year, July 27-28, to commemorate the discovery of gold on French Creek in 1874 (*see HISTORY*). The pageant, held on the actual date of the discovery (July 27) presents, first, an allegorical representation of creation, with costumed groups of children symbolizing flowers, young girls representing the stately pines, and with small boys, dressed as gnomes, planting gold in the earth. The following scenes show the Custer expedition, the arrival and removal of the Gordon Party, the gold rush, the Metz massacre, the hanging of Fly Speck Billy, Indian battles, and an attack on a stagecoach. All the white actors in the drama are residents of Custer, while a large number of Indians from Pine Ridge Reservation play historic roles. The production is in charge of the Women's Civic Club of Custer, and the author of the script is a life-long resident of the city. Besides the pageant, there are rodeos and Indian dances in an arena NE. of town, and a street carnival.

SCOTT'S ROSE QUARTZ CO. STORE is housed in a large concrete building near US 16 at the east end of town. The cement doorstep to the salesroom is inlaid with small pieces of rose quartz, laid in parallel lines spaced about a foot apart. In the salesroom are displayed different kinds of mosaic work and stones, all on sale. The articles are made in the workshop in the rear of the salesroom. Outside is a rock garden, its borders and paths outlined with large slabs of petrified wood.

The LOG CABIN MUSEUM, on Main St., opposite the courthouse, is the oldest standing building in the Black Hills. It was built by General Crook's soldiers under Captain Pallock of the Fifth Cavalry in 1875. It stands in Way City Park, which was named for Harry E. Way, pioneer resident and antiquarian, who donated the park and museum, originally his private collection, to the city. The building, constructed of hewn logs, is 16 ft. wide and 20 ft long. Loopholes in the walls are bullet-scarred at the outer ends. Since it was first built a fireplace and floor have been added, and the roof has been shingled. It contains a collection of stuffed animals and birds—hawks, a mounted lion, bobcats, and eagles—and also a large collection of mineral specimens and historical relics dealing with the history of Custer and the Black Hills.

The ROSS MONUMENT, just a short distance W. of the Log Cabin Museum in the park, was erected in 1921 by the Association of Black Hills Pioneers in honor of Horatio N. Ross, who first discovered gold on French Creek. The monument is composed of rocks set in cement, the rocks being contributed by pioneers and friends of Ross. One crystal was taken from the post office room in Wind Cave 40 years ago. Among other rocks are diamond drill ores, rose quartz, tourmaline, purple and yellow lapidolite, petrified moss, calcite crystals, mica, and gold and copper ore.

Large pieces of petrified wood make up the entire front of the ARTCRAFTERS' STUDIO, W. Main St., built in early English design; it contains a huge fireplace, which has a base of petrified wood and is surmounted by large slabs of varicolored but harmonizing native 1ocks. The Artcrafters use various native stones and minerals in making articles such as lamps, vases, and garden seats.

1. Right from Custer, on the Deerfield road, is a junction with a dirt road (L), 6.9 *m.* This road leads to the summit of BEAR MOUNTAIN, 11.4 *m.* with an elevation of 7,172 ft., Bear Mountain competes with Harney Peak in altitude; however, only a handful of people visit this densely forested summit, where from a lookout tower is a generous view of rugged peaks, the Needles, limestone ridges in the southern Hills, and an especially clear view of Custer Park in the northern Hills.

2. Right from Custer, on the Limestone road, 1 *m.* (L), in the Custer cemetery, is the GRAVE OF HORATIO N. ROSS, who first discovered gold in the Black Hills, and who died a pauper.

At 9.1 *m.* the Limestone road begins an ascent toward a plateau of approximately 6,000 ft., and the Limestone Cliffs appear. In the rugged recesses of the region is some of the best hunting in the Black Hills. The first shot in the more accessible parts of the Hills is the signal for the deer and the elk to stampede to the seclusion of the limestone buttes where snow is deep, and where sound and odors are carried for long distances. The BULL SPRINGS HUNTING CAMP at 13.7 *m.* is a privately owned but public lodge for deer hunters. At 17.8 *m.* (L) is SIGNAL HILL (6,500 alt.). Here a ranger scans the Limestone country for forest fires and watches deer come to the salt licks in the evening. At 25 *m.* the road passes into GILLETTE CANYON, and a road branches (R) at this point toward ICE CAVE, 26 *m.* Ice Cave is unusual not only for its 75 ft. limestone archway, but because it is one of the few un-commercialized and seldom-visited caves in the Hills. The cave leads back 90 ft. in the rock, and is very cool even in the heat of the summer.

At 58.4 *m.* is a junction with US 85A (*see Tour 14*).

At 58.8 *m.* is an OPEN PIT GOLD MINE, in which a dragline and bucket are used to sift what gold is left in French Creek. The operations have been successful. This is placer mining by machinery.

At 62.8 *m.* is FOUR MILE RANCH, a resting place on the old Cheyenne Trail; here is a junction with a graded dirt road which follows the old trail down the valley.

Left on this road is HEUMPHREUS' TWELVE MILE RANCH, 8 *m.*, one of the oldest ranches in the southern Hills, so named because it is 12 m. from Custer on the Custer-Cheyenne Trail. It was a favorite stopping place in the early days and its hospitality has always been proverbial. In these latter days when the swift auto has replaced the slow freight wagon, the old traditions are upheld by the presence of numerous rustic cabins clinging to the hillside underneath the pines. At the foot of the hill sprawls the comfortable old ranch house, with the barns and corrals that identify it for the cattle ranch that it is. There are three collections at the ranch that are well worth seeing—books, mineral specimens, and art objects. The library, one of the largest in this section, is especially rich in books on the botany and geology of the region. The mineral collection is unusually valuable and complete. There are over 1,000 speciments of minerals and fossils gathered in the Black Hills and vicinity, all named and identified. The art collection contains 70 drawings in color of the native wild flowers of the region, together with numerous wood carvings of exquisite artistry done in native juniper wood, and drawings and oil paintings of Indian, pioneer, and Western life.

Camp sites in the forest along the road are numerous. At 68.7 *m.* are two excellent campgrounds. Along the cuts the soil is streaked vertically with shades of yellow, red, and purple.

At 71.7 *m.* is a side road.

Right on this road is JEWEL CAVE, 1.5 *m.* (5,500 alt.), a national monument. The cave was first discovered by two brothers, Albert and Frank Michaud, while prospecting, and remained in their possession until 1928 when the Custer Cammercial Club and the Newcastle, Wyo., Lions Club took it over for development and exploration. In July 1934 it was made a national monument by the Federal Government.

The cave derives its name from its crystal formations. There are two routes in the cave, one having been explored 2 m. and the other 1 m.

At 72.1 *m.* US 16 crosses HELL'S CANYON (5,092 alt.), so named by frontiersmen because it was "hell to cross."

At 74.2 *m.* begins a mile stretch where trees have been uprooted by a tornado. Stumps are all that remain to mark the scene of the catastrophe; the timber was logged and the debris burned.

The heavy timber is being gradually replaced by smaller trees, and the top of the tableland is covered with sagebrush.

At 85.2 m. US 16 crosses the Wyoming Line, 8.2 m. SE. of Newcastle, Wyo. (see Wyo. Tour 8).

TOUR 5A

Junction with US 16—Garretson—Sherman. County H, State 11.
Junction with US 16—Sherman, 14.8 m.
Roadbed graveled.

County H branches N. from US 16, 2 m. W. of Valley Springs (see Tour 5), and leads to a region of scenic charm and bizarre beauty, one of the most attractive spots of eastern South Dakota. Its strangeness, its chaos, and the sharp break from the level or moderately rolling prairies surrounding it, make the region a spectacular little world of its own.

GARRETSON, 9.8 m. (1,492 alt., 677 pop.), was incorporated in 1891; Palisades, 3 m. W., vanished when a railroad junction was formed at the site of Garretson, and joined the long list of ghost towns of South Dakota. An old mill anchor is the only physical reminder of the once prosperous village. Garretson, known principally as the center of a region of fantastic beauty, is a stopping place for visitors.

An outstanding annual summer event in Garretson, as well as in several other towns in the region, is the ROLEY POLEY TOURNAMENT, a favorite sport of the scattered Belgians in the neighboring communities. The game is similar to horseshoe pitching, but instead of horseshoes round wood disks of varying weights are used. The players pick out whatever disks they can handle best and the object of the game is to see how close to the peg one can roll the disc. The task appears easy until tried. When tournaments are held, a two-or-three-day holiday is declared and the town generally joins in the celebration. Hearty Belgian greetings are shouted across the streets and playing ground. It is a time of gaiety and an invitation is extended to everyone in the town. There are usually many different teams. The tournament is arranged so that it will last the entire day, and even darkness does not stop the play, the contests often continuing far into the night on a lighted field.

One block E. of Main St. is an improved dirt road.

1. Right on this road to the tree-hidden canyon called DEVIL'S
GULCH, 0.4 *m.*, often referred to as "Spirit Canyon." Its fascination lies in its weird beauty, solemn and almost oppressive. A
jagged wound, burnished by nature's hand, across the gently
rolling plain, Devil's Gulch is a sanctuary of charm and inspiration. The chasm is featured by bold walls of pink and purple
rock, cleft by crevices, some so deep that they are thought to be
bottomless; mysterious green water reflects the cedars clinging
to the stone and the fronds of ferns that thrive in the moist, cool
air.

Surrounding this gulch is a park, maintained by the town's
authorities. However, aside from providing tables and seats for
the convenience of picnickers and building the footbridges, nothing has been done to disturb the beauties of nature. The winding paths follow a natural way among the rocks and from the
peak of the last one a glimpse of the red rock can be caught
through the branches of many varieties of trees and shrubs that
thrive there.

The footbridge, protected with iron guard rails, affords a splendid
point from which to view the perpendicular cliffs of quartzite.
Striking is the coloring of the rock in sun and shadow, red in
the light and purple in the shade. Bushes and ferns grow wherever a little earth has become lodged in the narrow ledges, but
the cedars cling to the bare rocks in a fantastic manner. These
beautiful trees grow luxuriantly on the very top of the cliffs
where nothing but bare, weather-beaten stone can be seen, and
the wonder is that they grow nowhere else in the vicinity except
on similar formations at the Palisades (see below), and at the
Dells (see Tour 9).

Just under the bridge is the BOTTOMLESS PIT. The water is dark
and oily and seems to have no current, but there is a powerful
undertow that forces the plumb line against some projection of
the walls, so that no one has been able to measure the depth
below 600 ft. under water level.

Crossing the bridge, the path leads along the edge of the canyon.
Many platforms of smooth, bare rocks afford points of observation to those who can stand on the very brink of the chasm
without becoming dizzy. The black shadows on the water at the
foot of the cliff opposite create an illusion that the great wall
overhangs a deep cave, and if one gazes fixedly for a moment at
that dark reflection, the cliff seems to approach silently and
menacingly, as if it had become the prow of a giant ship.

At the head of the gulch is the famed DEVIL'S STAIRWAY. Only
those with strong muscles, steady heads, and sound hearts are
advised to attempt the descent. There are several long jumps and
huge steps; but those who are brave will be well rewarded. From
the bottom, the view is almost bewildering. The contrast of blue
sky and dark green waters and the red, pink, and purple cliffs

overhanging threateningly would delight an artist. Seen from below, the cedars and ferns seem to cling to the rock by some inexplicable magic. The strange moaning of the wind adds to the feeling of being in the abode of some unearthly being. At night, or when a storm rages and thunder echoes and reechoes within the walls, one can easily imagine that the devil of the Indian legend is about to emerge from some dark crevice to gather in another soul. The climb upward is easier than the descent. The visitor, slowly retracing his steps along the canyon, discovers new rocks and new platforms, each with new and startling effects.

2. Right from Garretson on a dirt road winding SW. are the PALISADES, 2 m., an interesting and unusual outcropping of red quartzite (adm. 10c). Split Rock River adds the magic of dark, silent waters to the bizarre, entrancing picture made by the great pillars of granite-like stone—red, gray, and purple—that tower high above the many trees, like ruins of a gigantic palace. The nature of the formation creates this striking illusion, for the quartzite is marked into regular blocks by lines and surface fissures, so evenly distributed from top to bottom that it resembles skilled masonry work. Cedars—dark blue, almost black against the sky—cling to the bare rock.

Westward from the bridge that spans the river at the entrance of the park, a path, shaded by oaks and elms, winds around masses of tumbled blocks of rock that have fallen from the cliffs to the R., over projections of jutting stone worn smooth by the elements, and along the water's edge of the King and Queen Rocks, their cedar-crowned heads more than 100 ft. above the mirror-like water. The view from these perilous points of vantage is so thrilling that the exertion necessary to reach their summits is amply rewarded. For those who are not in mountain-climbing trim, an easier path to the R. is available for ascending the cliff. However, the beauty of the many colored, cedar-topped walls on the other side can be enjoyed from the water's edge, where the coolness of the air that blows from the river and the shade refresh those who do not care for climbing in the hot sun.

BALANCE ROCK, on the opposite side of the river, is a formation that seems to defy the laws of gravity, for it stands on a narrow base at the top of a cliff and looms larger above, apparently lopsided. The mass of alternating red and gray stone, seems to hang precariously—on the verge of crashing to the depths below; yet the rock has evidently been there for ages, a bold sentinel against the sky, defying wind storms, lightning, and raging blizzards.

Other attractions in the park include the DEVIL'S KITCHEN, an enclosure walled in by red rock where queerly-shaped stones, jutting through the floor, might be imagined as some banished devil's store and kitchen furniture.

CHIMNEY ROCK is sometimes missed because part of its bulk is hidden by tall trees; the color of the stone is a deep vivid red.

On both sides of the stream are paths that are full of surprises, leading to unexpected crevices and queerly-shaped rocks. Cool places for picnics are available, with tables provided. Excellent fishing can be enjoyed during the season, the cold waters yielding channel catfish, speckled trout, black bass, rock bass, and pickerel.

North of Garretson the route follows State 11; at 11.4 m. is the junction with a dirt road, in good condition. A sign (R) bears the legend: "Jesse James' Cave."

Right on this road to a farmhouse, 3 m., where inquiries must be made for the route to JESSE JAMES' CAVE, 0.4 m., (adm. 10c each if not more than 2 in party; 25c for group of 3 or more).

This reputed hide-out of Jesse James has no sunken lake, underground river, or sparkling stalactites, but it is the only cave in this part of the country, and from the entrance is a magnificent view to the N.

Twenty-five years ago a farm hand, who was working for the farmer owning the land on which is the cave, found the name, Jesse James, carved in the wall of the strange hole in the rocky cliff of the Split Rock River. Early settlers knew of the place, and there was a sort of legend about the notorious desperado having hidden there after the robbery of the bank at Northfield, Minn.

No one unacquainted with the area could find the beginning of the rough and slightly dangerous stairway made of coarse blocks of stone in the cliff. Extreme care must be taken while descending this steep incline, as the rocks are slippery and no rail or guard of any sort is provided.

The only way to the cave from the foot of the natural stairs is through a narrow tunnel, a little more than 3 ft. in diameter and perhaps 12 ft. in length. One must crawl through, but the walls are smooth quartzite and the floor solid. There is no danger. It must be understood that the cave is not at the bottom of the cliff, where the clear water of Split Rock River flows noiselessly, but halfway down, about 30 ft. from the base.

The little tunnel gives access to a sort of ledge, a level platform of red granite about 10 ft. square, from which is a beautiful view of the valley. The scenery is fascinating with color effects of red, purple, and gray cliffs, blue sky and mirror-like water. Directly across the river, green meadows extend to the broken cliffs, which resemble ruins of a gigantic wall. Cedars clinging to the bare rocks, and groups of thickly foliaged trees growing where the cliffs have collapsed, add to the beauty of the picture.

The cave itself is quickly explored, A flashlight is necessary, because of many jutting rocks and projecting ledges. Legend has it that Jesse James used to creep in the shadows and hide on one of the high shelves when enemies came near. After crawling through some narrow places, and passing through chambers with very rough walls, for a distance of about 50 ft., the end of the cave is reached.

At 14.8 *m.* is Sherman (1,495 alt., 205 pop.).

TOUR 5B

Junction with US 16 (Keystone)—Mount Rushmore—Junction with US 85A (Hill City). Rushmore Memorial Highway (unnumbered).

Junction with US 16—Junction with US 85A, 13.7 m.

Hard-surfaced road to Memorial; sharp curves require careful driving.

The scenic Memorial Highway climbs westward from US 16 (*see Tour 5, Section c*), 1 m. S. of Keystone, and at several vantage points the carved figures on Mount Rushmore can be seen in the distance. For full benefit of light and shadow upon the memorial, it is advisable to make the drive in the late afternoon during the summer months, and early in the morning during the fall and winter.

Viewed from the highway between the junction and Mount Rushmore, the chiseled stone faces of George Washington, Thomas Jefferson, Abraham Lincoln, and Theodore Roosevelt stand out in silvery profile, towering above surrounding mountain peaks.

At 0.3 *m.* is a spring (R); springs are numerous along the route and many of them are piped to the road so that the traveler can lean from his car for a drink.

At 0.9 *m.* is another spring and camping area.

At 1.8 *m.* is DOANE MOUNTAIN and a parking space for the MOUNT RUSHMORE STUDIO (5,500 alt.). Doane Mountain was named for Doane Robinson, for a quarter-century South Dakota's State Historian, who conceived the idea for the Mount Rushmore Memorial in 1924. The large, stained-log studio houses the plastic models of the sculptored figures and the office of Gutzon Borglum, sculptor of the memorial. The studio models are in proportion to those on the mountainside. On the top of each is a compass and plumb bob, which are used in measuring the distance and degrees of the model profile points; similar instruments and measurements, but on a larger scale, are made on the mountain to guide the sculptors. Pictures and souvenirs are sold in the studio, and on the porch is a telescope through which can be seen the memorial and the men at work.

THE MOUNT RUSHMORE MEMORIAL (6,040 alt.), across the sharp valley, is said to be the largest sculpture undertaken since the time of the ancient Egyptains; the gigantic figures in granite are carved to the proportion of men 465 ft. tall. George Washington's carved face is 60 ft. from hair line to chin, and one can stand in Jefferson's eye. When the memorial is completed, the busts of Washington, Jefferson, Lincoln, and Theodore Roosevelt will command the view for miles, a stately, cloud-draped monument to four Presidents of the United States—to perpetuate the founding, the expansion, the preservation, and the unification of the United States. The head of Washington—wig, high forehead, large nose, and resolute jaw—emerges prominently from the most forward cliff, and presents a striking profile from either side. Lapels of his coat are visible and, when completed, his coat will show to the waistline. The face of Jefferson is set back into the precipice, the features, however, showing plainly. The head of Lincoln, which was unveiled Sept. 17, 1937, as a part of a program, nationally broadcast, inaugurating Constitution Year, is in the protruding rock farthest to the R. The Roosevelt figure is set deep into the mountain. When completed, the Washington and Lincoln figures will stand out from each side, with Jefferson and Roosevelt lower and farther back.

Following the gold rush period of the late 1870's, Charles E. Rushmore, an attorney from New York, visited the Black Hills in the interests of his mining clients. While touring the Hills, by horse and buggy, the attorney inquired the name of the granite-crested mountain. One of the party jokingly answered: "Why that is Mount Rushmore." And it still bears that name.

In 1924 a plan to carve a colossal national memorial on one of the rocky peaks of the Harney range was originated, and Gutzon Borglum became interested in the proposal. Three years later the South Dakota Legislature authorized the creation of the Mount Rushmore Memorial Association, which raised the funds by subscription to begin work. President Calvin Coolidge dedicated Mount Rushmore, August 10, 1927, during his vacation in the Black Hills, and blasting began. The funds were depleted in 1928, at which time Congress released $50,000 of the appropriation outright, and work was resumed. The Federal Government in 1935 took over the project, placing it under the Department of Interior.

During the interim, the face of Washington was chiseled, and the features of Jefferson, to Washington's right, became prominent.

However, when a fissure in the rock was discovered by Borglum the face of Jefferson was blasted out. It is being carved on the other side of the Washington profile, now, and deeper into the mountain.

The magnitude of the figures to be carved in the mountainside necessitates engineering as well as sculptural skill. After the surface rock has been blasted, large drills operated by compressed air cut out the features. Holes are bored into the rock to the desired depth and the pieces between broken out. Another air drill, with a chisel point, takes off the rough surfaces. Polishing will be the last job.

The workers are let down in small seats by gear-rigged cables over the edge of the mountain, using their feet to push them away from the rock. Scaffolds to hold several men are also built on the figures. The regular staff consists of 36 men, about 19 of whom operate the carving drills. There is a blacksmith to sharpen the drills, engineers to operate the three large compressors, a powder man to blast the rough work, and hoisting men to lower the carvers on the mountain face.

The stone is a greyish-white granite with black flecks in it. Outlines are drawn on the rock in red to show where the rock is to be cut away, and the faces are chiseled out from top to bottom.

At the studio is a footpath.

Right on this path to a CABLE HOUSE 40 ft., which operates the car used to transport tools and some of the workers. The tools are sharpened several times during the day to pierce the tough granite of the mountain. Down the steps and along the path is a RESTAURANT (open to the public) and the OFFICE OF THE SUPERINTENDENT, 150 ft. From here a walking trip to the top of Mount Rushmore can be made (permission only from Borglum or Superintendent; guide furnished) up a flight of 400 wooden steps, through a crevice in the rock. Along the steps trees appear to grow out of the granite, and squirrels are seen. At the summit is another studio (private), the tool house, and hoisting apparatus room. Behind the cliff is a third studio, slightly higher and facing Harney Peak. A MUSEUM, carved out of a rift in the rock, is planned when the memorial is completed.

From Doane Mountain, Rushmore Memorial Highway twists below the figures.

At 2.1 m. a person can stand directly under the nose of Washington, 500 ft. above, and sense the magnitude of the project.

NEEDLES EYE, 3.1 m., is a granite formation with a great slit, which is shaped to suggest the eye of a needle.

At 3.2 *m.* (R) is the LEANING ROCK, another granite formation, appearing to lean dangerously toward the road.

At 3.5 *m.* (L) there is a beautiful view of the northern hills.

At 4.6 *m.* (R) is a huge GRANITE FORMATION. These particular formations seem to rear up out of the earth, a surprising contrast with the forest lands surrounding them.

At 4.7 *m.* (R) is a large camp area containing an open fireplace; here is the junction with a graded road.

> Right on this road is HORSE THIEF LAKE, 0.3 *m.*, a small body of water so named because it was in this area that Lame Johnny, infamous robber of the Hills region during the early 1880's stored his loot. And it is said that the lake covers gold and jewelry whose value is a small fortune. Here also is an abandoned CCC camp.

At 5.7 *m.* (L) is a PUBLIC PICNIC GROUNDS and spring.

At 6.9 *m.* (R) is the beginning of a one-way road. On this road there is not enough room for two cars to pass. Birch and aspen trees line the avenue and in some spots grow into the road.

At 7.1 *m.* is the end of the one-way road.

At 9 *m.* is a rock formation which looks almost as if piled by hand.

At 9.6 *m.* (L) is a shale formation.

At 10.1 *m.* is a side road.

> Right on this road is PALMER GULCH LODGE, 1 *m.* (4,900 alt.). This dude ranch caters to vacationists wishing to fish, hike, golf, and ride horseback. The cabins are furnished. (Rates: $25 to $40 per week.) A caretaker is in charge the year round.

At 11 *m.* (L) is an excellent view of Harney Peak.

At 11.7 *m.* begins a one-way road which crosses an area of thick timber, spruce and aspen predominating.

At 12.3 *m.* is an area of dead trees skirting the road, the trees having died from an attack of beetles.

At 13.1 *m.* (L) is the GRIZZLY BEAR HORSEBACK TRAIL. Here also is the approximate center of a burned area 1 m. long.

At 13.7 *m.* is the junction of Rushmore Memorial Highway with US 85A (*see Tour 14*), 3 m. S. of Hill City.

TOUR 5C

Rapid City—Hermosa—Fairburn—Buffalo Gap—Junction with US
85A (Hot Springs). State 79.
Rapid City—Junction with US 85A, 61.1 m.
The Chicago & North Western R.R. parallels this route throughout.
Usual accommodations at Rapid City.
Roadbed is graveled and well maintained.

Between Rapid City and Buffalo Gap State 79 skirts the western
edge of the Black Hills, gradually drawing farther from them as
it goes south. This country, without definite character, is neither
a farming region nor a good stock country, although these are
the main uses to which it is put. It is almost uninhabited, the towns
being very small and far apart, and few houses are visible between
towns. At Buffalo Gap the road turns directly west and enters the
Hills, joining US 85A five miles north of Hot Springs. Along this
stretch of road there are rolling ridges, usually wooded, and frequent open spaces called "parks." From Rapid City to Buffalo Gap
the road is fairly level, but from the gap to the junction wtih US
85A there is a steady climb.

RAPID CITY, o m., (3,196 alt., 11,346 pop.) (*see RAPID
CITY*).

At 1.1 m. (L) is a paved curving drive leading to the School of
Mines (*see RAPID CITY*).

At 1.8 m. (R) is a tourist camp.

At 6.4 m. (L.) is the HIDDEN CITY (*admission 50c*) consist-
of a long wall below ground, excavated for a distance of a quarter
of a mile and roofed over to protect it from the weather. This wall
is thought by some to have been the work of a prehistoric race, the
sole surviving remnant of a "hidden city." But others, among them
the faculty of the School of Mines, believe it to be a natural
though very unusual formation, a series of sandstone dikes. The
subject is still controversial.

At 7.5 m. the road enters a region of bluffs and bare, broken, and
eroded hills.

At 10.4 m. the road crosses Spring Creek.

At 11.4 m. (L) is an odd-appearing butte, resembling a volcanic
cone.

HERMOSA (*beautiful*), 18.8 *m*. (3,278 alt., 108 pop.), was founded by the Pioneer Town Site Co. in 1886. The principal point of interest is the little white CONGREGATIONAL CHURCH (R) at the northern edge of town. Here President and Mrs. Coolidge attended service each Sunday during the summer of 1927, when the Summer White House was at the nearby State Game Lodge (*see Tour 5*). A student pastor had charge of the church that summer but President Coolidge was faithful in his attendance. At his request, no mention or reference was made to his presence at any time. The only formality observed was that after the service the congregation remained seated until the President had left the church. At the end of the summer the President and Mrs. Coolidge entertained the student pastor at dinner.

At 19.5 *m*. is a junction with a dirt road leading (R) along Battle Creek, to RUSHMORE CAVE, far back in the Hills. The cave is similar to other crystalline caves in the Hills.

At 19.6 *m*. the road crosses BATTLE CREEK. This creek originates high in the Hills, descending from the NW, and has long had a part in the history of the Hills. At one time it was one of the best trout streams in this region, and, though still considered good, cyanide from the mines near Keystone and Hill City has killed quite a number of the fish.

At 21.1 *m*. (R) is a splendid view of Mt. Rushmore if the atmospheric conditions are right (*see Tour 5B*).

At 24.9 *m*. there is a glimpse of Harney Peak and Mt. Coolidge (*see Tours 5 and 14A*).

FAIRBURN, 32 *m*. (3,430 alt., 95 pop.), was platted in 1886 by the Pioneer Town Site Co. Its name is a combination of the adjective "fair" with "burn," the Scotch name for a brook or creek. In this instance it has reference to an unnamed creek in the town.

At 43.2 *m*., after passing over a flat, monotonous stretch of country, there is a view of the Badlands in the distance.

At 46 *m*. State 79 crosses LAME JOHNNY CREEK, which was the scene of the execution of the bandit, Lame Johnny. Like most mountainous or forest regions, the Black Hills became the hiding place for many fugitives from the law, and the rendezvous of various gangs who preyed upon travelers, miners, prospectors, and settlers. Lame Johnny, who walked with a limp, was one of the most ambitious thieves of the Hills' country. A college man,

HEIGHTS AND DEPTHS OF
THE BLACK HILLS

Illustrations

BEFORE the Rushmore Memorial was started and the U. S. Army-National Geographic Society Stratosphere flight held, it was the general conception east of Akron that the Black Hills were just "out West some place."

Since then, thousands of persons have visited Mt. Rushmore to see the figures of four Presidents being carved in the mountainside, and in the pages that follow are three views of the Memorial. There is also a photograph of Explorer II, world's largest balloon, emerging from Strato Bowl near Rapid City on its way to a record-breaking ascent of 13 miles.

South Dakotans are particularly proud of Sylvan Lake and the new State-owned Sylvan Lake Hotel in Custer State Park. The hotel, opened late in 1937, is considered one of the finest park lodges in the Nation.

Also included among the pictures are two caves, for the Black Hills have many underground passages, some still unexplored.

he wandered into Texas from the East and engaged in the profitable trade of stealing horses from the Indians. After a time he
moved into the Black Hills and took up the well-ordered life of
the average pioneer, serving as deputy sheriff of Custer Co. and
then for a time worked in the Homestake Mining Co. office, where
an acquaintance recognized him as a horse thief from Texas. Soon
there was a rumor that he was back at his old trade of running
off Indian horses as well as those belonging to white men. In the
fall of 1878 he and his gang engaged in the holdup of a coach
on Gilme and Sanlabury stage line on Lame Johnny Creek in Custer Co.; shortly after the robbery Lame Johnny was arrested on a
charge of horse stealing previous to this time. Later it developed
that he was wanted for the stagecoach robbery and was put on a
coach at Red Cloud to be brought into Deadwood for trial. A short
distance from Buffalo Gap when the coach reached the small creek
that now bears his name, Lame Johnny was taken from the coach
and hanged to the limb of an elm tree, at the place where he and
his gang had robbed the coach.

At 48.6 *m.* (R) is the gap in the hills, appropriately called Buffalo Gap, because it was here that the first settlers saw great droves
of buffalo making their slow, ponderous way.

BUFFALO GAP, 51.2 *m.* (3,257 alt., 150 pop.), named from
the nearby gap in the hills, is a station on the Chicago and North
Western R. R.; it was founded in 1885. The country around is
associated with the bandit, Lame Johnny, who often hid in the
nearby hills. It is the center of a ranching region and has never
quite lost the glamour of cowboy days.

At 55.4 *m.* the road crosses Beaver Creek and, for about a mile,
twists in and out between high hills, crossing and recrossing small
draws and gulches.

At 61.1 *m.* is the junction with US 85A (*see Tour 14*), 5 m. N.
of Hot Springs (*see Tour 7*).

TOUR 6

Junction with US 16—Badlands National Monument—Wall. State 40 and Badlands Monument Highway (unnumbered).

Junction with US 16—Wall, 49 m.

Cabin accommodations at Cedar Pass and the Pinnacles.

Graveled roadbed.

State 40 branches W. from US 16 (*see Tour 5*), 8 m. W. of Kadoka; this section of State 40 and the unnumbered Badlands Monument Highway will probably become a part of US 16 in the near future, as the monument is developed.

In the Big Badlands of South Dakota the BADLANDS NATIONAL MONUMENT (*adm. free*) has been established by the Federal Government and placed under the supervision of the National Park Service. It comprises 50,000 acres in a strip 40 m. long and 20 m. wide.

In developing this region, it is the aim of the Government to preserve its pristine freshness, and to restore the animal life that formerly abounded there. While they cannot bring back the dinosaur and the triceratops, the oreodon and tyrannosaurus rex, they plan to have the Rocky Mountain sheep once more look down from the jagged pinnacles, as they have done within the memory of man, while the Rocky Mountain goats sit staring to windward for hours from some inaccessible mountain shelf. On the plains at the base of the white-walled formations, wary antelope and deer will once more roam, and the lumbering buffalo will file through the passes and browse in the draws. Only the slinking coyote will be banned, the robber of birds' nests and the killer of defenseless young animals. So the region will return to a primitive state, almost as it was perhaps when the little three-toed horse roamed the plains "unrestrained by the nearest rider, fifty million years away."

"Mako (*land*) sica (*bad*)" was the expression used by the Indians to describe the strip of barren land, ghostly peaks, lofty pinnacles, spires, and terraces that make up the White River Badlands of southwestern South Dakota.

"Mauvaise terres" (*bad lands*), said the early French explorers of this region when confronted with the problem of travel through this fantastically weird country, with its countless formations of marvelous size and structure, its varied shapes and colors.

"A part of Hell with the fires burned out" was the way Gen. George A. Custer described them.

Half a mile away is a skyline with a broken and serrated edge as sharply etched against the sky as if just struck off by the sculptor's chisel. The broken edges of this skyline assume every conceivable shape and form, with here a minaret and there a castle, here a pyramid and there a tower, and here a projection that started out to be a peak and became a glistening candelabrum; this fantastic skyline stretches in either direction as far as the eye can see, with infinite variation.

Likewise, there is no sameness in the mighty wall below. At one point the clay has been whipped by wind or water into a series of fluted columns supporting a giant table. At another, a sheer wall rises to a peak in a gigantic pyramid of dazzling whiteness. Here and there are subtle bands of color, harmonizing with one another, and yet distinct; while at intervals is a band of red. And sometimes upon the benches there is a touch of green where grass or shrub is striving for a foothold, or where the stunted cedars raise their wizened heads against the white wall behind them.

The region is particularly fantastic by moonlight, with no clearcut edges, but ghostly shapes and shadowy walls; it is a city dead, untenanted; a thousand monuments, their faces blank, their feet in shadow. And over all there rests a deep silence, except when some late car roars through a pass, leaving a stillness deeper than before.

Frank Lloyd Wright, the noted architect, had this to say of the Badlands, on a recent visit:

"As we rode, or seemed to be floating upon a splendid winding road that seemed to understand it all and just where to go, we rose and fell between its delicate parallels of rose and cream and sublime shapes, chalk white, fretted against a blue sky with high floating clouds—the sky itself seemed only there to cleanse and light the vast harmonious building scheme. Here, for once, comes complete release from materiality. Communion with what man often calls 'God' is inevitable in this place."

Millions of years ago this part of the earth was probably covered by a great marsh. Amidst the terrific, steaming heat, huge, lumbering animals and reptiles lived and fought and died, to be covered with sediment deposited through many centuries. New species of animals appeared upon the scene—a three-toed horse, a small camel, a saber-tooth tiger.

As time rolled on the many animals and reptiles of those dim ages died, leaving almost no visible trace of their existence. Then the forces of erosion began to operate. As centuries passed, slowly and steadily the numerous growing streams carved their way into the soft, yielding soil, molding the present Badlands formation and uncovering in places the prehistoric skeletons that are rich sources of information to the modern scientist. After a heavy rain, fossilized bones are often found lying exposed on the ground. The Badlands are a treasure storehouse of ancient animal life, and specimens and skeletons from this region have found their way into museums all over the world. One of the largest collections of Badlands fossils is at the South Dakota State School of Mines at Rapid City (*see RAPID CITY*).

West of the junction with US 16 part of the Badlands Wall, which rises to the L. in high, jagged peaks is visible for several miles. At 13 *m.* the road turns L. and the wall looms ahead; the formations are larger and more numerous, and the route passes near the peaks and pinnacles. These cathedral-like spires are composed of the harder types of strata that have withstood the wear of erosion; the different layers are of many colors—gray, tan, buff, green, cream, and orange.

Approaching the crest, the road winds between towering peaks and freak formations until, from the top of CEDAR PASS, at 17 *m.*, the valley below and the interior of the Badlands present a panorama bewildering in its immensity. Directly ahead (R) is VAMPIRE PEAK, so old in legend that even the oldest residents of the section do not know why it was so named. It is a tall, majestic peak, circular at its base and growing slimmer until capped by twin spikes. Nearer at hand are a few scattered clumps of cedar trees growing upon the peaks or springing from the fissures, all that remains of the heavy growth of trees that once gave the pass its name.

At 18 *m.* is CEDAR PASS TAVERN AND CABIN CAMP, lying at the base of the formation on the level, grassy floor of the valley. A collection of Badlands rocks and fossils is on display in the dining room; examination is permitted, and some specimens are for sale.

At Cedar Pass Camp saddle horses are available for those who would like a closer view of the Badlands without the exertion of walking through them. But for those who are able to do rough walking, there are rich returns in a hike through and over some of the formations. A start can be made from Cedar Pass Camp by car or horse.

Right from Cedar Pass Tavern on State 40 to Cedar Pass at 1 *m.* Right on dim trail at 1.5 *m.* This trail leads over low mesas through shallow draws, up to the base of the formations at 2 *m.* From here there is a footpath. Fossil remains are exposed from time to time as the formation weathers away, and they fall or are washed to the bottom of it. When several bits of bone are found close together, it is often possible to trace them to their source directly above where they lie. Whole bones are rare, but fossil teeth are not uncommon, either embedded in part of the jaw or singly.

Along this stretch of wall are various low places called "windows," which look out over that desolate region aptly termed DANTE'S INFERNO. Through these windows are seen a series of striking views, each different from the rest. The infinite variety of scene is one of the most striking characteristics of the Badlands, and even the same place looks quite different when viewed at dawn or at twilight, in the glare of the noonday sun or by moonlight.

A climb to the top of the formation at any point is difficult but well rewarded. Here are rows of barren ridges, with sheer sides and thin walls, a welter of chaos and desolation. In either direction is seen mile after mile of Badlands wall, with occasional jagged peaks and serrated skyline.

At 18.2 *m.* is the junction with the unnumbered Badlands Monument Highway R. which this route follows; State 40 continues W. (*see Tour 6A*).

For 20 m. the road winds through the heart of the Badlands, one of the most scenic stretches of road in the State. Now it skirts the base of the formation, now it winds up narrow canyons with towering peaks of white clay on either side, and now it climbs the almost vertical wall by a steady grade, and then follows the snake-like contour of the formation's brink for miles, with all the panorama of the Badlands spread out below, with the breaks of White River visible to the S., and to the N. and W. the level plains stretching to the distant Black Hills. Far to the W., Sheep Mountain stands like a lone sentinel, marking the end of the Badlands.

At 28 *m.* (R) is BIG FOOT PASS. It was through this natural opening that the wily Indian chief, Big Foot, led his band of 400 warriors, eluding the United States soldiers who had thought every possible pass was guarded. John J. Pershing, then a captain, was one of the soldiers attempting to stop Big Foot. After penetrating the Badlands, Big Foot and his warriors met a disastrous end at the Battle of Wounded Knee (*see Tour 7*) when he and almost all of his band were annihilated in the last conflict between the whites and the Indians, the culmination of the Messiah War.

After a steep, circling climb up Big Foot Pass the road follows the freakish wall until Dillon Pass leads down into another, perhaps a more wonderful, region, the PINNACLES, where are seen likenesses of huge ancient cathedrals, turrets, spires, and altars. After a few winding miles among the foothills of the Pinnacles, the road passes through the upper tunnel to the Great Wall.

At 40 m. is the PINNACLE POINT TOURIST CAMP, overlooking the great formations of the Badlands; here the gorgeous coloring at sunrise, once seen, is never forgotten. At the edge of the wall the view commands a bewildering maze of valleys, ravines, and jutting peaks, like the ruins of an ancient city. There are furnished cabins, a dining room, and other conveniences.

At 40.1 m. is the junction with an unnumbered road (*see Tour 6A*).

From Pinnacle Point the road runs northward, and at 49 m. forms a junction with US 16 at WALL (*see Tour 5*).

TOUR 6A

Junction with Badlands Monument Highway—Interior—Scenic—Pinnacles. State 40 and unnumbered road.
Junction with Badlands Monument Highway—Pinnacles, 61.8 m.
Chicago, Milwaukee, St. Paul and Pacific R. R. parallels this route.
Limited accomodations.
Roadbed graded; good in dry weather only.

State 40 twists westward from its junction with the unnumbered Badlands Monument Highway, 18.2 m. W. of the junction with US 16 (*see Tour 6*), passing between the Badlands Wall and White River, and a new (unnumbered) road winds northward from Scenic along the outer side of the wall. This region lies in lonely isolation, with only an occasional ranch, whose cattle are the sole moving objects on the landscape. This unnumbered road is off the beaten paths of travel and skirts the entire western end of the Badlands region.

INTERIOR, 1.8 m. (2,381 alt., 155 pop.), is so named because of its position within the Badlands wall. It is an old town for this region, having been founded in 1891. Although it is in a ranching country, its principal source of income is derived from catering to the wants of tourists, who flock to the Badlands in increasing numbers.

At 3.8 *m.* is a junction with a dirt road.

Left on this road at 2 *m.* is WHITE RIVER, named for the white clay that washes off the hills and colors its waters in flood time a milky white. Here is a fork, L. up the hill winding through the breaks, past log and sod shanties, to the HEADLEE RANCH, 18.2 *m.*, a country store and post office. At 21.2 *m.* in a draw is a windmill, the landmark for a prairie trail (R) which winds 1.4 *m.* to RATTLESNAKE or DEVIL BUTTES. It is advisable to park on the W. side of the second butte and walk to the summit 100 ft. (Boots should be worn for protection from rattlesnakes). The only known SAND CRYSTAL BED in North America is atop the western butte. The unusual cylindrical, pipe-like crystals occur only on this butte. Exposed banks of the crystals jut out of the hill and extend several yards; the crystals, varying in size from ¼ inch to 15 inches, are hard, whether lying singly on the ground or in large masses. Six or eight inches under the surface, the sand becomes wet—like the beach of a seashore—although in a semiarid region and at the highest elevation of that area. In the wet sand are lumps which, when delicately excavated, assume the appearance of a group of ill-proportioned fingers. Although easily broken while damp, the crystals harden quickly on exposure to the air. They are 60 per cent sand and 40 per cent calcium carbonate, the former occurring as an inclusion and the latter as a mineralizing and crystallizing agent. In this bed of sand, less than 3 ft. thick, the sand crystals occur in numbers measured in tons. Every form, from solitary hexagonal crystals to crowded bunches of multiplets, can be obtained. The formation discloses evidence of internal molecular or crystalline arrangement, and weathered specimens show a radiate or rosetted structure, owing to the tendency of lime salts to crystalize according to the laws governing calcite.

The main side road continues straight ahead at the windmill to the BUFFALO PASTURE along Potato Creek, at 32.4 **m.** The pasture covers 36 sq. m. and work on it was begun in 1936; its purpose is to conserve herds of the fast-diminishing buffalo in a habitat natural to them—a region of creeks, trees, and hills. A new dirt road borders the pasture for 5.3 m.

CONATA, 13.8 *m.* (35 pop.), is in a picturesque ranching area.

SCENIC, 31.8 *m.* (2,812 alt., 349 pop.), was so named because of its situation in the shadow of Sheep Mountain among Badlands formations. The place was founded in 1907 as a station of the C. M. St. P. & P. R. R., with a boxcar for a depot and a cluster of tar paper shacks for residences. For 26 years water was hauled a distance of 10 m.; since 1933 it has been piped 2 m. from springs. The town has a fossil and rock MUSEUM (*free*). Nearby scenic attractions are Castle Rock and "Hell's Ten Thousand Acres."

At Scenic is a junction with a dirt road.

Left from Scenic on this road, at 1.5 m. is the foot of SHEEP MOUNTAIN. An extremely steep hill leads to the plateau above and cars should be put in low gear before attempting it. At the top is a gate (adm. $1 per car). After passing through the gate a trail completely encircles the rim of the plateau a mile in circumference, which comprises the top of Sheep Mountain. From every point along this road are splendid views of the Badlands. Their vast extent and varied character can perhaps be better determined here than from any other point. At the base of Sheep Mountain the State School of Mines (see RAPID CITY) maintains a permanent camp to which a party of students, in charge of a faculty member, comes every summer to excavate fossils, further to enrich the School of Mines Museum. This immediate territory is peculiarly rich in fossil remains, even for the Badlands. A roster of visitors to the Badlands reads like an international scientific "Who's Who," as scientists from every country have come here to inspect this rich storehouse of paleontological treasures and secrets. Even for the visiting layman, a scramble in the surrounding formations will be richly repaid.

North of Scenic the road winds through an almost deserted region to the junction with the Badlands Monument Highway, 61.8 *m.* (*see Tour 6*), 9 m. S. of Wall (*see Tour 5*).

TOUR 7

(Inwood, Iowa)—Canton—Lake Andes—Winner—Hot Springs—Edgemont— (Lusk, Wyo.). US 18.

Iowa Line to Wyoming Line, 474.6 m.

C. & N. W. R.R. parallels US 18 between St. Charles and Winner; C. B. & Q., between Hot Springs and Edgemont.

Roadbed graveled, with occasional stretches of hard surface.

Good accommodations east of Missouri River; fair, west of river as far as Winner. Gas and oil available west of Winner, but few lodging accommodations.

After pursuing a level course for many miles in Iowa, US 18 crosses the Iowa Line 6 m. west of Inwood, Iowa (*see Iowa Tour 11*), and passes through the valley of the Big Sioux River. Rising in the Coteau des Prairies of northeastern South Dakota, the river drains an extensive territory. The Selkirk colonists en route from Winnipeg, Canada, to St. Louis, Mo. followed the valley, which was first explored by Nicollet and Fremont in 1838. The Sioux Indians named the river Can-ka-sda-ta (*where-they paddle-softly-by-the woods*).

Like the other east-west routes across the State, US 18 crosses varied sections of South Dakota—rich agricultural lands, ranch country, Indian reservations, mountain region. With the flat stretches of the eastern section covered, the road swings abruptly down into the broad, rugged valley of the Missouri River, spirals up over rolling plains of the West-river ranching area, and begins its long, weaving course across the stretches of Indian country. The monotony of the gently rolling prairie stretches is often interrupted by hills, capped with clusters of cedars, and by buttes and sand knolls, until the Black Hills afford the fresh touch of a vastly different region. The scenery in the Indian country is far from drab, its character constantly changing.

Section a. Iowa Line—Junction US 281, 137 m.

After crossing the Big Sioux River, US 18 traverses wooded flats, luxuriant with vegetation, rising again to resume a level prairie course.

At 0.5 *m.* the upper structure of the Sioux Valley Ski Slide is visible ahead (L).

At 1.2 *m.* is the junction with a graveled road.

Left on this road is the SIOUX VALLEY SKI SLIDE, 0.7 *m.*, where the State championship tournament is held yearly, and the national tournament about every 5 years. Attracting thousands of spectators and amateur ski jumpers, this meet is the major winter sporting event of South Dakota. Crowds of 10 to 25 thousand people have attended the tournaments, which are held during the latter part of January or in early February.

At one time it was the longest slide in the United States and it still compares favorably with slides at Lake Placid, N. Y., and Brattleboro, Vt. Among those who have competed here are Casper Oiman, George Kotlarek, Roy Mikkelson, and U. S. Olympic team members.

A tournament never was cancelled because of lack of snow, though in 1931 it was necessary to import a large amount for the slides. Three national tournaments have been held at Canton, the last one in 1935. The annual tournament is sponsored by the Sioux Valley Ski Club of Canton. At the first meets announcing was done by someone with a resonant, stentorian voice aided by a large megaphone; but sound equipment now is installed, the hill serving as a sounding-board for the loudspeaker. The slide measures 600 ft. from the top of the scaffold to the bottom of the hill. The scaffold is 125 ft. high and the distance from the top to the take-off is 360 ft. Riders at various times have been clocked for speed, and rates of from 60 to 100 m. per hour have been registered. During practice one year Alf Bakken jumped a distance of 194 ft., but the fact that the jump was not made in a regular tournament prohibited its standing as a record. The hill is steep, but has a long flat base running several hundred feet, an ideal arrangement for a neat jump and landing. A scaffold has been added to give extra impetus to the jumps.

At 1.7 m. is a road leading (R) through the entrance to the PENITENTIARY ANNEX, built in 1901 for the purpose of caring for insane Indians. At that time it was the only institution of its kind in the United States, but its inmates were recently moved to Washington following an investigation of charges of carelessness and neglect. The institution received its present name from the fact that it is now used by the State to house first term lawbreakers, who are sent there instead of to the State Penitentiary at Sioux Falls, to segregate them from the company of hardened criminals.

The CANTON LUTHERAN NORMAL SCHOOL, buildings and campus are near the highway (R). The buildings are striking examples of the use of native Sioux Falls quartzite in construction.

CANTON, 3.2 m. (1,244 alt., 2542 pop.), owes its name to the belief by early settlers that it is situated diametrically opposite Canton, China. Founded in 1860, the town has become the center of an extensive Scandinavian community, with productive farms and substantial buildings.

It was in this section that the settings of two books, O. E. Rolvaag's *Giants in the Earth* and Phil LeMar Anderson's *Courthouse Square,* were laid. Central characters in Rolvaag's widely read saga of pioneer life are six brothers, named Berdahl, whose combined ages total 488 years. The oldest is 88 and the youngest 68 years old. Rolvaag, who is a son-in-law of the eldest brother, vividly describes many of their adventures. The Berdahls and several other families came to Dakota Territory in early days to obtain free land.

Only after arriving in the town does the stranger discover that the tall, odd-looking cylindrical object, jutting above all other structures near it, is the city water tower, practical but unattractive.

At 10.4 m. is the junction with US 77 (*see Tour 9*) and the two highways are united for 5 m.

The early settlers in the State took up land in this southeastern section and during those pioneering years they were faced with many hardships. In 1881, following the ever-memorable blizzard of 1880, there was considerable snow; and when this melted the valleys throughout the region held sweeping torrents. Even the Vermillion River, normally a small stream, became a veritable Mississippi, as it swelled to cut a mile-wide swath along its course. Bridges were washed out, homes flooded, and settlers were forced to flee to higher ground.

In 1885 a prairie fire swept through the center of Turner Co. Fanned by a furious gale, the blaze licked up the long grass, catching occasional haystacks and hurling the burning straw high into the air, as it wiped out farm homes in a relentless holocaust.

The blizzard of 1888, while not as severe as that of 1880, took a great toll of life over a wide area. Jan. 12, 1888, broke dark and lowering; a light steady snow was added to the foot that had already fallen. By 10 o'clock the region was blanketed with fog. Suddenly, without warning, the wind changed and the temperature tobogganed nearly 70 degrees. The wind continued to rise and soon a 60-mile gale was howling mercilessly across the open expanses. Steel-like snow in blinding eddies was hurled with withering intensity at whatever object happened to be in its path. So thick was the snow, and so sudden was the onslaught of the storm, that there was little opportunity for preparation. The devastating blast continued with unabated fury, choking and blinding victims unfortunate enough to be caught away from shelter. When the storm had subsided, it had written a pitiful tale of suffering and death across its icy pages. About 200 persons perished in South Dakota and adjoining States; men, women, and children, singly and in groups, lay where they had first fallen, unable to combat the cruel elements. Some were found in a sitting posture; some lying as though in their last step they had fallen, exhausted; some were propped against haystacks.

At 11.6 m. is the junction with a graveled road.

> Right on this road is WORTHING, 0.6 m. (1,364 alt., 276 pop.), one of the early towns in this part of the State. Its proximity to Sioux Falls and Canton has retarded its growth and forced it to remain a small town. A fertile argicultural region surrounds it.

At 15.5 m. is the junction with US 77 (*see Tour 9*).

DAVIS, 29.8 m. (1,253 alt., 214 pop.), has a well-kept city park and a new municipal building. It is a prominent grain shipping point in a productive farming area.

At 52.7 m. is the junction with US 81 (*see Tour 10*).

MENNO, 60.9 m. (1,325 alt., 978 pop.), is a contraction of Mennonite, there being many members of this sect in the surrounding territory (*see Tour 5*). Although there is no exclusive Mennonite colony near Menno, there are many descendants of the original German-Russian families, principally E. of the James River Valley.

At 65.2 m. the James River is crossed. This lazy, meandering stream moves along so idly and indifferently that it appears to be absorbing the full value of the scenery along its muddy banks as it crawls listlessly to join the impetuous, cloudy waters of the Missouri. During 1934, the period when the drought was most severe, the water along most of its course receded to mere pot holes and finally dried up entirely. Fish were trapped in these holes, but most of them were rescued by the Game and Fish Department and transferred to other places until water again returned to the abandoned river bed.

OLIVET, 65.6 m. (1,221 alt., 222 pop.), though without railroad connections, is the seat of Hutchinson Co., a distinction it has had since 1871. Despite numerous efforts to move the seat of county government, Olivet hangs tenaciously to the prize it has held so long. In 1878 the Free Methodists built a sod church at the town site, while they were doing missionary work in this part of the State. In this crude building court was held until a courthouse was constructed.

The soil in this region is of clay origin, and the country gradually becomes more hilly as US 18 moves westward. There are many curves and dips, and fast driving is not advisable.

At 70 m. the highway rises over a divide which separates the flow of the small feeders of the Missouri and James Rivers, respectively. From the divide, the streams flow SW. to join the "Big Muddy" in its long pilgrimage to the Mississippi.

TRIPP, 84.9 m. (1,563 alt., 901 pop.), stands on the brow of a hill in the SW. corner of Hutchinson Co. The town is modern in every respect, and its $70,000 school building, with school busses covering the surrounding country, provides good educational facilities. The Hutchinson Co. Fair is held here annually, and its grounds cover 34 acres, with grandstand, pavilions, and exhibit buildings, comparing favorably with the leading fairs of the State.

The greater part of the city's population is of German-Russian ancestry.

Tripp is at the junction of State 37 (*see Tour 11A*).

West of Tripp US 18 gradually enters a more sparsely settled area, farms are less numerous, and groves of trees appear infrequently.

DELMONT, 94.2 *m.* (1,488 alt., 518 pop.), is a well-kept little village, and the only town in Douglas Co. touched by US 18. The county was named for Stephen A. Douglas, a prominent political figure in the pre-Civil War days. Of approximately 7,000 inhabitants in the county, more than 2,000 are of German descent, and 1,700 are of Dutch descent. Towns in the northwestern part of the county have populations of nearly 100 per cent Dutch descent.

At 117.9 *m.* (R) is LAKE ANDES, a slender, boot-shaped body of water extending approximately 14 m. in length, with a varying width of from one to two m. It was first called Handy's Lake, the "H" later being dropped and an "e" substituted for the "y." For nearly 4 m. the highway runs near the lake, passing on the way OWEN'S BAY, part of a 340-acre waterfowl refuge, purchased by the U. S. Bureau of Biological Survey. The tract is separated from Lake Andes by means of a dike, and has two artesian wells to assure an independent water supply. Within the bay are three sets of islands, planted with duck feed, while 6 m. of duck-nesting can be found along the shore-line; the whole area is enclosed by a wire fence. During the winter season the open water of Owen's Bay is literally covered with thousands of wild waterfowl. Only a short distance from the bay is a STATE FISH HATCHERY, where bass are propagated to restock South Dakota's many lakes.

Sustained drought caused the water of Lake Andes to evaporate until it almost entirely dried up; an effort is now being made to reclaim it by means of a three-mile canal which would drain 5,500 additional acres into the lake bed. The major portion of the labor for excavating this canal and building the waterfowl refuge was supplied by boys from a CCC camp near this point.

Normal years find sportsmen and recreation-seekers coming here by the hundreds each summer to enjoy the diversions offered; in a section where lakes are few, the spot is a popular center for a wide area.

At 115.8 *m.* is the junction with State 50 (*see Tour 8*).

LAKE ANDES, 121.8 *m.* (1,441 alt., 845 pop.), became the seat of Charles Mix Co. in 1916, following a struggle of more than 40 years (*see WHEELER below*).

The town is picturesquely situated on a slope near the toe of the lake's boot, and has a neat, well-improved park. The open Yankton Reservation is near Lake Andes, and the town is a trading point for many Indians. Nearly every day they can be seen about the streets, some in modern garb, but many of the squaws retaining their style of dress of 50 years ago. They still carry their papooses on their backs, where the infants are held securely with bright colored shawls, an indispensable adjunct to the women's apparel.

Beginning at Lake Andes the road crosses a moderately hilly country which continues until the rougher, sharply broken slopes of the Missouri River valley are reached. Along the road, jutting from the hillsides, are many yucca plants, clustered growths with pointed green shafts surrounding a single large stem that protrudes above its protective palisade. The stem is capped by an oblong yellow pod containing seeds of the plant. As the Missouri River is approached, many cedar-lined draws and jagged hills offer the first hint of proximity to a new and different region of the State.

WHEELER, 137 *m.*, consisting of a store and filling station, in reality should be called New Wheeler, because the original town was located 1.5 m. up the river from this site. The original town was a trading point for river steamers.

Wheeler became the county seat in 1879 and retained it until 1916, when Lake Andes mustered enough votes to win the victory in a spirited contest. Although Wheeler has always been without railroad facilities and is far from the center of the county, the jealousy of the larger towns enabled it to hold the lucrative honor for 37 years. Whenever an effort was made to remove the county offices, rivalry flared up among the towns of Geddes, Platte, Wagner, and Lake Andes, and in the end Wheeler emerged victorious. After the seat of county government was removed to Lake Andes, old Wheeler experienced a sharp decline, many of its buildings falling into a state of desuetude, while the old frame courthouse was relegated to the less dignified role of a granary. Today the business section is deserted.

At Wheeler is the junction with US 281 (*see Tour 11*); at this point the two highways unite and follow one road for 10 *m.*

Section b. Junction with US 281—Hot Springs, 297.5 m.

At 0.4 *m.* the united routes cross the MISSOURI RIVER, the story of which, with its tributaries, is essentially a story of the State. River traffic began in the early 1830's and continued until late in the 19th century when the railroads displaced this mode of transportation. As many as 40 steamers plied up and down the Missouri River, sometimes 20 or more being tied up at a single landing point.

From the earliest days of settlement in South Dakota, the rivers of this valley have overflowed occasionally, causing suffering and damage. In March 1862 an ice gorge formed near the mouth of the James River, flooding the entire valley to a width as great as 12 m. in several places.

The flood causing the most damage came in the spring of 1881, the climax of a winter of unusual severity. Oct. 14, 1880, a slow drizzle began and soon turned to snow that sailed in on a strong wind. The storm lasted three days, blocking all communication with the outside world for weeks. Frequent snows followed, and held the valley in an ice-locked grip for five bitter months. On March 27, 1881, the ice began to move downstream, the melting snows soon swelling the river until it overflowed the banks and covered the bottom-land from bluff to bluff. An ice gorge formed near Yankton, and ice congested the stream as far as Springfield, more than 30 m. away. The following day the gorge suddenly broke, releasing millions of tons of ice that moved with slow, irresistible force down the river, sweeping everything in its path. Masses of ice were hurled against steamships, helplessly docked, crushing them like eggshells. The sudden rise of the water sent residents of the valley scurrying to higher ground to watch the roaring, impetuous flood swallow up their belongings—homes, livestock, machinery—and hurl them downstream. A village called Green Island was completely devoured by the swirling waters. Within two hours after the first masses of ice crashed into the village, every building was drifting with the current as it joined the growing procession of debris gathered along the river's course. Even the church was wrested from its foundation, and settlers 30 m. downstream told of seeing a building float by and of hearing bells tolling uncannily as the structure bobbed up and down in the surging river. The loss of human life was not high, but the loss of home and all other belongings wrought hardships that required years to overcome.

At 1 *m.* US 18 enters the eastern end of the ROSEBUD IN-
DIAN RESERVATION, named for the wild roses that still cover
large areas of this section. It was originally a part of the Sioux
Reservation, which was set aside under the treaty of 1868 (*see
INDIANS*). Modifications of this treaty subdivided the area, setting up the present boundaries. Although the reservation extends
E. to the Missouri River, the actual closed boundaries have been
reduced to Todd Co. only, the remaining area being open to white
settlement, with the laws governing the Indians applying to all
parts. With a total Indian population of about 6,400 the reservation
roll shows about one-half to be full-bloods; the native language is
used by nearly 90 per cent of the inhabitants.

The reservation section, like the western half of the State, has
many sharp draws and jutting buttes; the topography is not ironed
out like the land E. of the Missouri River. The tillable grazing
country has a very sandy soil which is subject to erosion by the
wind when native vegetation is disturbed by cultivation or over-
grazing.

In June 1934 the Wheeler-Howard Act, giving the Indians a
greater degree of self-government, became a law, and the Indians
voted to accept the act. Severe drought has caused critical conditions on this reservation as well as on others. While the average
Indian does not rate high as a farmer, the fertile soil of the region
usually produces crops that supplement the aid given by the Government through benefits accruing as a result of past treaties. Despite incomes from tribal sources, leases, and land sales, approximately half the families on the reservation depend almost entirely
upon some form of Government relief. Most farm plots consist of
a small patch of weedy corn, potatoes, and smaller vegetables.

Home conditions in a majority of cases are poor; the bulk of the
population lives in shacks and tents that have few sanitary
facilities.

Order is preserved on the reservation through a system of Indian police, aided by honorary law enforcement officers, who serve
without pay, and help maintain order at dances and other functions
where the most prevalent law violation—drunkenness—arises. It
is unlawful to sell or give an Indian liquor although it is sold to
whites on the open part of the reservation. It is unlawful to have
liquor in one's possession in the restricted area. Drunkenness and
adultery rank first and second, respectively, among the criminal
charges on the reservation.

Meandering up from the Missouri River bottom, US 18 enters a gently rolling region.

At 10.1 *m.* is the junction with US 281 (*see Tour 11*).

BONESTEEL, 13.2 *m.* (2,009 alt., 547 pop.), like other towns along US 18, sprang up when it was known that the C. & N. W. R.R. planned to extend W. of the Missouri River. With this in mind, Bonesteel, named for an early resident, gradually took on the semblance of a town and when the railroad actually came the population increased rapidly. However, it was never boomed to the extent that some of the other towns along the route were: the 1910 census shows a population only 16 greater than that of 1935. It has now settled down to the humdrum existence of the average small town, its tides of fortune ebbing and flowing with the current conditions of its surrounding territory.

ST. CHARLES, 20.2 *m.* (100 pop.), consists of a few scattered houses and a business district typical of a small hamlet. Never affected to any extent by the influx of homesteaders, the village was stifled in its infancy by the diversion of most of the business to Gregory and Dallas.

HERRICK, 25.8 *m.* (87 pop.), was named for Samuel Herrick, an attorney who was instrumental in opening the Rosebud Reservation to white settlement. This was effected in 1904 and a great wave of homeseekers flooded the new and promising territory. Gregory Co. suddenly became the mecca for families of all types. Some had lost all their worldly goods in the East, or perhaps never had any; some were college graduates, many of them adventurers, others were health-seekers; some were of substantial Scandinavian or German stock, looking for sites for homes.

BURKE, 34.6 *m.* (2,251 alt., 591 pop.), was named in honor of Charles Burke of Pierre, one-time Commissioner of Indian Affairs. Its beginning is traced to the pre-railroad days when the extension of the lines became a certainty. The 1910 census shows a population of 311, and the town has experienced a slow but steady growth since then. While many of the towns decreased in population, Burke was able to hold its own. It was settled largely by persons who planned to stay in the country, and was less affected by the influx of homesteaders than other towns of the semiarid region when the exceptionally dry years of 1911-12-13 ravaged the country. It still is a lively little center, deriving its business from farmers, ranchers, and Indians.

GREGORY, 44 m. (2,216 alt., 1,185 pop.), prior to 1904 was merely a town in the offing, but with the opening of the county for white settlement, houses were hastily built, and a busy village was an actuality in a few weeks. Today it vies with Winner as the chief trading center of the Rosebud country, the two towns eclipsing all others in the area in size. With a varied population, comprising a mixed Indian, ranching, and farming group, Gregory has the distinction of being a melting pot for different types of people. Western flavor is mixed with modern, Eastern customs. The frontier spirit of the West still dominates, and the people are noted for their liberal tendencies. When they have money, they are willing to spend it; when hard times come, they accept their plight without murmuring. Here, as well as in other western South Dakota towns, is a friendliness and hospitality that will evoke a glow of warmth in the most blase visitor.

DALLAS, 48.2 m. (2,238 alt., 308 pop.), was originally built about 10 m. distant from the present line of the railroad when the latter was extended W. of the Missouri River. To remedy this the citizens moved their little village to a location at the end of the proposed extension of the railroad. Their "hunch" proved correct and in 1907 the first train whistled into the infant town, gateway to the region that was next slated for opening.

Launching the new land boom with profuse and widespread advertising, Dallas became one of the most "heard-of" towns in the Middle West. Thousands of landseekers came to this section in the next few years, and the population of Dallas shot upward until it crowded the 2,000 figure. Seven churches, a library, water system, electric lights, and three blocks of business district marked this flourishing town. The cattleman saw his range divided and subdivided, saw with dismay the virgin prairie turned to brown as the branding iron was melted into the plowshare. The range days were gone; cowboys would live only in books and the movies; the old regime must succumb to the progressive spirit of the New West. Farm machinery was sold by the carloads, and soon rippling grainfields replaced endless stretches of dun prairie. Such was the setting of Dallas for a few years.

But the halcyon days of its prosperity were numbered. The meteoric rise that had wafted the little prairie town to heights of prosperity was quickly reversed and financial doldrums settled upon the community. Drought, crop failures, dust storms, low prices, and several disastrous fires wrought their havoc. Dallas today is but a fragment of its former self, although it still maintains many of the features that accompanied its early prosperity—churches, library, modern improvements.

At 58 m. is the junction with US 83 (*see Tour 12*); the two routes are united for 21.4 m.

COLOME, 58.9 m. (531 pop.), was named for the Colome brothers, of part Sioux Indian parentage. The founders of the town, looking into the future, located a town site on the railroad right-of-way and in 1909, following the opening of Tripp Co. for white settlement, the influx of settlers began. The county developed so quickly that the railroad was extended to Winner, in the heart of the new region, within three years after it reached Colome. Although successful farming is hampered by occasional dry periods, the productive soil of the area enables the people, through combination dirt-farming and stock-raising, to earn a comfortable livelihood during normal times.

WINNER, 70.6 m. (1,860 alt., 2,136 pop.), one of the newest towns in the State, is also one of the most typically Western in color. Founded following the rush of homesteaders, which began in 1908, Winner grew up mushroom-fashion, becoming the busiest trading point along the entire stretch of US 18 across South Dakota. Retarded somewhat by recent drought years and depression, the town has managed to retain much of its trade activity. Although the railroad did not reach Winner until 1911, its growth began three years previously.

Modern Winner has 48 blocks of paved streets, and in appearance its business district resembles a much larger city. Besides the usual types of business, Winner has an ice cream factory, a powdered soap and cleaner factory, and an awning factory. A few years ago one Winner business man bought more than 20,000 rabbit skins in one season, gathered from the surrounding country. The town is also a shipping point for turkeys and other poultry raised in the adjacent territory.

One block (L) from Main St. is the OUTLAW TRADING POST, a well known store of the West-river country. Started during the early days of Winner, the store was named by Ben Butts, the founder, who was called "the outlaw down the alley" by competitors, because of his large scale operations in buying goods in carload lots and selling them at cut prices. Unpretentious in appearance, the large interior is a scene of activity every day of the week. Little effort has been expended on appearance, the stock being arranged principally for convenience. The basement and several warehouses are filled with carloads of merchandise bought in large quantities.

JORDAN, 79.4 m. (60 pop.), is at the junction with US 83 (*see Tour 12*). Its nearness to Winner precludes the possibility of its becoming a town of appreciable size.

CARTER, 88.4 m. (61 pop.), with its present few inhabitants, represents a dream that never came true. With the opening of Tripp Co. for settlement, the Western Town Site Co. made arrangements with the C. & N. W. R.R. to extend its line W. of Dallas. Seven towns were slated to be on the extension of the line. After a delay of two years, the proposed extension was begun, but advanced only as far as Winner. Not until a few years ago was it built farther W. and then it missed Carter by taking a more northern route.

As originally planned, Carter would have been the gateway to the great undeveloped country to the W., a gateway through which all settlers moving into the new country would pass. As a result this region became known as the "jumping off place." A novel, *The Jumping Off Place,* by Marian Hurd McNeely, has as its setting this Rosebud country during homestead days, and the characters were drawn from life.

At 89.3 m. is the eastern edge of the Rosebud Reservation proper; this part of the reservation is not open to white settlement.

OKREEK, 97.5 m. (355 pop.), is typical of the many small communities that are scattered through the Indian reservations, towns that are centers of the social life of their districts.

Many of the houses in Okreek are typical of the social status of the Indian families on this reservation. The Superintendent's annual report of the Rosebud Reservation for 1935 tersely states: "The home conditions of the Indian families are for the majority very poor. Their homes are far from sanitary. Undoubtedly this contributes a great deal to the high rate of tuberculosis that is prevalent among the Indian population."

HAYSTACK BUTTE (R) is visible for several miles along the route. Long noted for its rattlesnake dens, the butte is visited each spring and fall by scores of persons either interested scientifically, or merely curious.

Rattlesnakes, while not prevalent and rarely seen unless looked for, hibernate and emerge in the spring when the temperature approaches the 80-degree mark. Then they scatter, but rarely venture more than four or five miles from their dens. Men who understand the habits of the reptiles visit the dens every day during the first balmy days of spring, and snare them as they crawl to the sunlight, or drag them from their holes with a specially devised hook. Often writhing balls of the reptiles, entwined around each other and comprising as many as 25 or 30 snakes, are dragged out. Rattlesnakes, authorities say, are one of the worst enemies of nesting birds, their ability to find nests and devour the fledglings, often the mother bird and the eggs, resulting in a huge loss every year.

At 111.5 m. is a large INDIAN BOARDING SCHOOL, maintained by the Government for the Indian children of the Rosebud Reservation. About 200 children are enrolled and classes range from the first to the tenth grades.

MISSION, 114.6 m. (2,150 alt., 275 pop.), is a trading point for Indians and white settlers of the neighborhood. A 12-grade public school is attended by both white and Indian children. The Episcopal church maintains a dormitory and school farm. The Lutheran church operates a day-school. There are Lutheran and Episcopal chapels in the town, and the Catholic chapel is on the highway near the boarding school.

An excellent CABIN CAMP and a small artificial lake, where swimming and fishing are available, are open to the public.

All through this part of the country Indian homes can be seen, each standing alone on its individual 160-acre allotment. There is little variety in the style of architecture of the homes of the Sioux. A one or two-room log house, plastered usually with mud, with a roof composed of poles, hay, and dirt, is the usual type; one or two small windows carry the burden of admitting light; the floors are often of dirt, while a small stove, frequently of sheet-iron, provides the heat that is generated from the burning of wrist-size sticks of wood. The Indians spend much time in tents, even during the bitterest winter weather.

The white men have attempted to eradicate Indian habits and practices of centuries. Superstitions, fetishes, and customs, however, defy the forces of change. Legends that have been handed down from one generation to another are still treasured by the Sioux. One that is told by wrinkled old squaws to their children and grandchildren, and which undoubtedly will continue to be handed down to future generations, describes the origin of the rainbow.

One bright summer day when all the flowers were nodding their heads in the breeze and proudly exhibiting their many beautiful colors, the Great Spirit, who watches over all the little earthlings, heard this conversation between two of the older flowers.

"I wonder where we will go when winter comes and we all have to die? It doesn't seem fair; we do our share to make the earth a beautiful place to live in. It would only be fair if we, too, should go to a happy hunting ground of our own."

The Great Spirit considered this idea and decided that they should not die when winter came. And so now, according to the legend, after a refreshing shower all the many-hued flowers are seen in the sky, making a beautiful arc across the heavens.

ROSEBUD AGENCY, 126.5 m. (120 pop.), is in a rough part of the country with some of the agency buildings on Rosebud Creek and some on the steep hills opposite. On the flat N. of the agency are old corrals and a fairground. About two m. N/W. of the corrals, Sugar Loaf Butte projects its cone-shaped top above the flat prairie. On this flat herds of issue cattle were turned loose every ten days in olden times. This was the beef issued to the Indians on the hoof; there was sport as well as food in shooting down one's own beef.

A celebration is sometimes held here on the Fourth of July, and the annual fair is held early in September. Riding, roping, Indian dancing and singing, baseball games, races, and often the old Indian game of shinny, give much local color. Beyond the flat is a sharp turn through a deep cut known to the Indians as the "Big Hole." At this point the whole agency comes into view. Below, on the hillside, is the Government hospital.

At the top of the hill (R) lies an old BURIAL GROUND. The white shaft in this cemetery marks the grave of Spotted Tail, the chief for whom this agency was first named. Spotted Tail was friendly to the whites and his own people mistrusted this friendship. A group of the headmen of the neighboring Indian bands drew lots to determine who should kill him. Crow Dog drew the fatal lot and killed Spotted Tail from ambush. Afterwards Crow Dog was ostracized by his own people and scorned by the white men.

The name, Spotted Tail Agency, was used until 1871. This place was heavily guarded during the Messiah War; and in 1890 the soldiers dug rifle pits on the hill for the protection of the agency. This hill overlooking the agency is still called Soldier Hill. The Government buildings are close together on the bench, in the form of a square.

The general office building is on the southwestern corner. Long established traders' stores carry candles, bright beads, gay calico, broad-brimmed Stetsons, and sheep-lined coats. Rows of canned goods give evidence of the derivation of the Indian word "mazopiye" (*the place where things are put away in tins*). The 25 members of the tribal council meet here for deliberations, and the Indian court of three men, appointed by the Superintendent, sits here to judge minor offenses. Below the hill the Indians live in cabins, or camp out, while transacting business for a few days.

West of Rosebud the topography is rough, with ravines and steep hillsides, spotted with dark jackpines. Beyond is the Little White River, one of the sources of the main river of the same name, fed by clear, copious springs.

PARMALEE, 139.5 m. (245 pop.), is a roadside town on the flat prairie. Ever since the days when He-Dog's band camped in this district, Parmalee has been a Government issue station and a trading post. The post office of Parmalee was named for Dave Parmalee, rancher, trader, and pioneer of this region. The old Indian name for the section was Cut-Meat, from the Indian word Wososo (*where they cut the buffalo meat into little strips*). The creek half a mile beyond Parmalee still bears the same name, Cut-Meat. There is an old story among the Indians that the Indian hunters used to drive the buffalo over the steep banks of this stream.

He-Dog and his followers camped on this creek and, when homes were built by the Government for the chiefs, He-Dog's house was erected on the flat, 9 m. beyond Parmalee, where it can be seen from the highway. A new consolidated school, called He-Dog School, is a half-mile off the highway, 8 m. W. of Parmalee. It is typical of the fine new day schools the Department of the Interior is now building as community centers in Indian country.

At 154.6 m. US 18 crosses the western boundary of the closed area of the Rosebud Reservation and continues through more Indian country—the open area of the Pine Ridge Reservation—ceded territory, containing isolated tracts of trust land.

VETAL, 161.7 m. (25 pop.), is another roadside trading center to which the scattered population of the sparsely settled neighboring area come to buy their "grub" and other necessities. At Vetal on busy days can be seen three types of vehicles—team and wagon, battered Fords of the Model T variety, and modern automobiles, with the first type most prevalent.

MARTIN, 182.2 *m*. (3,250 alt., 942 pop.), called the "metropolis of the Pine Ridge Reservation country" because of its surprisingly large population in such a thinly settled country, was founded in 1912 at the time Bennett Co. was organized, and has since remained the county seat. Indians, interspersed with cowboys, farmers, and white-collared men, make a composite picture that is truly Western and colorful. At fair time and on celebration days, the Indians appear in native dress and perform tribal dances, sing their songs, and go through other ceremonies.

Bennett Co., despite its lack of railroad facilities, has thousands of acres of good grazing and agricultural land with abundant water, good roads, and full-course schools.

> Left from Martin on State 73 is the LA CREEK TEAL AND MIGRATORY FOWL REFUGE, 12 *m*., a series of long dams impounding water in several artificial lakes.

BATESLAND, 201.1 *m*. (300 pop.), consists of a small residence and business district, the appearance of the town as a whole giving the impression of a group of buildings huddled together in the prairie hinterlands for mutual protection.

Here the Indian character of the country becomes more strongly pronounced, for US 18 is entering the PINE RIDGE RESERVA-TION. Living within its borders are more Indians than on any other reservation in South Dakota, a total of more than 8,000 having been recorded at the last census. Indian customs and characteristics are similar on all reservations W. of the Missouri River. (*See Tours 2, 3, and ROSEBUD RESERVATION, above*).

The extent of this reservation makes it difficult for the visitor with little time to see many parts of it. The old Indian life can best be studied in remote villages, where the Sioux pursue their old tribal customs, unchanged by white influence. The native language is used by 85 per cent of the population. A tribal council performs numerous duties including the management of tribal affairs, recommendations for positions, the settlement of domestic difficulties, the leasing of tribal lands, and the investigation of complaints against personnel or departments.

Few Indians on the Pine Ridge Reservation are successful farmers, virtually none of them producing enough from their tracts to support their families. Considerable handiwork is carried on, and, in 1937, the sale of articles was started. In wooded areas trees are often cut up and sold as fuel, although the Indians derive little income from this source. In gathering his own firewood, he usually seeks the smaller dead trees or branches of larger ones, full-grown timber being left until a scarcity of the other kind forces him to depart from his customary practice.

There are 33 separate Indian communities on the Pine Ridge Reservation, each designated by a tribal name.

At 210 m. (R) is seen PORCUPINE BUTTE, 7 m. away, so called because its shape resembles the humped-up back of a porcupine. Indians have long been familiar with the habits of these little animals, which have been of much economic value to them. The quills were used for decorative purposes by all the Sioux tribes. The porcupine is commonly used for food among the older tribesmen, who consider it a delicacy.

WOUNDED KNEE, 215.8 m., is a trading post on the highway; many kinds of Indian products made on the reservation are on sale.

At Wounded Knee is the junction with an improved dirt road.

Right on this road to the WOUNDED KNEE BATTLEFIELD, 0.4 m. where on Dec. 29, 1890, occurred the last important conflict between the whites and Indians. The battle marked the end of the Messiah craze, which for months had been deluding the Indians and terrifying white residents on and near South Dakota reservations. (see HISTORY).

Although today referred to as a battle, many insist the affair was nothing short of a massacre in which non-combatants—squaws with infants on their backs, boys and girls—were pursued and ruthlessly shot down by maddened soldiers long after resistance had ceased and nearly every warrior lay dead or dying on the field. Pictures taken on the battlefield two days after the encounter and before the Indians had been buried showed bodies scattered for 2 m. along the creek, mute testimony of the relentlessness of the pursuit.

Today, near the battlefield, is a monument and cement curbing, indicating a common grave, a rude trench, in which the bodies of the slain Indians—men, women, and children alike—were hastily buried.

The chief ritual of the Messiah delusion was a ghost dance, conceived and introduced to the tribes by a Nevada Paiute Indian named Wovoka, whose Christian upbringing had little effect on his Indian superstitions. He claimed to have seen a vision, following an eclipse of the sun in 1889, in which the buffalo were restored to the prairie and the whites driven from the earth. He declared he had seen the glory of the Indians returned to them as it was in the days before the white men came.

This vision Wovoka began to relate among the tribes near his home. Word of the supposed revelation spread like a prairie fire, and soon every tribe in North America had heard of it and many were practicing its teaching. It took deepest root among South Dakota tribes where two skilled exhorters, Kicking Bear and Short Bull, became imbued with the belief and began preaching it among their followers. Soon hundreds had flocked turbulently into camps to take part in the weird ceremonies.

During the ceremonial dance the Indian men wore a special garb, consisting principally of a calico garment, called a "ghost shirt." The ritual started with the participants joining hands and shuffling around in circles, slowly at first, and after careening crazily until one by one they fell exhausted. The medicine men pronounced them dead, but said that after a visit to the Great Spirit they would return to tell what they had seen. Needless to say, what they told was imaginary. "The buffalo are coming back!" they cried. They saw the whites at the mercy of the Indians; sickness had vanished from the earth; the red man's paradise was returning. They believed the bullets of the whites could no longer harm them.

Short Bull's band of dancers hurried away to the fastnesses of the Badlands to engage in further ceremonies (see Tour 2). In the meantime the implacable Sitting Bull had been killed, and his followers fled to join Big Foot's band of dancers on the Cheyenne River. Soldiers sent to arrest Big Foot found him willing to submit, but in the night he and his band escaped and reached the Badlands. He was overtaken at Wounded Knee Creek.

The soldiers were ordered to disarm the warriors, but found them wretchedly equipped with a few out-of-date rifles of little value. Dissatisfied with the results, the soldiers were ordered closer to the tipis, where a more thorough search was instituted. In the meantime Yellow Bird, a medicine man, was haranguing the Indians telling them the ghost shirts were impervious to the bullets of the enemy. As Yellow Bird spoke in the Sioux tongue, the soldiers did not realize the import of his talk. When one of the searchers began to examine the blankets of the Indians Black Fox jumped to his feet, drawing his gun as he rose, and fired at the soldiers. The rest of the warriors, as if waiting for a signal joined in so quickly that the attendant volley sounded almost like one report. The soldiers immediately returned the fire and for a few minutes the carnage was terrible. So close together were the combatants that many discharged rifles into the faces of their foes. When the firing started, a battery of Hotchkiss guns, firing two pounds at each charge and at the rate of nearly one a second, raked the camp, shattering and setting fire to the tipis and killing everyone within range.

The superior numbers of the soldiers, who were equipped with modern rifles and aided by artillery, soon routed the Indians; only a handful escaped through the lines of the whites and took refuge in ravines and depressions of a fringe of hills nearby.

Meanwhile the tipis were burning above the dead and dying within them, and the rest of the Indians—women mostly, carrying small infants on their backs—were fleeing in wild panic, as soldiers cut them down ruthlessly and left them scattered over the plain. Big Foot was killed, his son died beside him, while most of the warriors killed in the melee fell near the chief's tipi. The members of the burial party, who came with wagons three days later to bury the dead Indians, found several live babies wrapped in shawls close to the cold bodies of their lifeless mothers, though the temperature during the interval had been near zero. The bodies of the dead Indians were placed in wagons and hauled, several in each load, to a large grave where they were placed without ceremony.

PINE RIDGE AGENCY, 231.8 m. (618 pop.), was so named because of the abundance of dark pines that clothe the hills and line the ravines nearby. Until 1878 it was called Red Cloud Agency, for the chief of one of the leading bands in this territory. Of the 33 bands, identified by family relationships and living on this reservation today, one is listed as the Chief James H. Red Cloud Band. The outstanding indications of the new order are the Government buildings, the school, the hospital, and the administrative buildings. In the school, native arts and crafts are taught, and some of the older members of the tribe are called in to teach tribal history and native folkways; at the same time teachers, under Government employ, give the Indian children an education like that provided for white children. The hospital employs a staff of 8 nurses and, in addition, there are 4 field nurses and 5 doctors in the reservation.

Indian men with long hair and soft moccasins, and Indian women wearing full, bright-colored skirts, shawls, and head-scarfs, can always be seen near the Council Hall, at the Agency office, and on the steps of the traders' stores. There are also young Indian students neatly dressed in dark suits, light shirts, and polished shoes, and girls dressed in the latest fashion.

Indian dances take place often and an annual rodeo is staged in August. A small fee is sometimes charged for permission to use cameras.

At Pine Ridge Agency a business in Indian arts and crafts is being developed, and groups of Indians are often employed to travel with shows in the summer season; a number went to the Chicago Exposition in 1933, and it was reported that 30 families went to Paris on the same errand in 1936. Thus these people are turning their knowledge of old Indian customs into a means of earning a living.

From this agency W. to Oglala many Indian homes can be seen. There are still more than 1,500 log houses on this reservation. Many have dirt roofs and dirt floors. The 1880 report of the Indian agent says, "The people have taken to house building to a remarkable degree. In the past year they have erected by their own labor, or employed others to build them, between 300 and 400 log houses with dirt roofs." In the past 50 years little has been done to encourage these people in their house building. The primitive houses were, unfortunately, one of the causes of the high incidence of tuberculosis among the people who had been accustomed to outdoor living.

OGLALA, 248 m. (150 pop.), is known mainly for its large Indian boarding school, attended by children from many parts of the reservation. Oglala (Ind., *to scatter one's own*) is the name of one of the many tribes of the Sioux nation. In recent years Indian pupils at various schools, combining native athletic grace with sinewy litheness and speed, have threatened the accustomed supremacy of whites in modern sports. In 1936 the Oglala Indian school basketball team won the State Class B tournament, the first time in history that an Indian athletic squad has won a South Dakota title of such importance. Comfortable buildings, good playgrounds, gymnasium, and all modern equipment aid the school's program of diversified education.

At 235 m. the main fork of White River is crossed. Although a small stream, it often rises to surprising proportions during periods of hard and continued rains. Its source is in northern Nebraska.

At 263.8 m. US 18 crosses the Shannon-Fall River Co. line and winds snakelike over a high sloping ledge that tops a wasteland of rolling prairie, broken only by small humps or knolls that appear like scattered grass huts.

SMITHWICK, 277.2 m. (63 pop.), was at one time the center of a cattle-grazing country and a fair-sized cow town, but with the division of a part of the prairie to the S. into farms, its prosperity waned.

From Smithwick the road continues over a hilly section to the junction with State 79 (*see Tour 14*), which is reached at 282.6 *m.;* the two routes are united between this point and Hot Springs.

At 289.3 *m.* is the junction with a dirt road.

Left on this road is the HOT SPRINGS AIRPORT, 1.2 *m.* The hangar is an attractive building of native stone. It also has an excellent landing field, but the airport has been put to no commercial use as yet.

At 291 *m.* US 18 crosses the Cheyenne River and enters the Cheyenne breaks. From here to Hot Springs the road is oiled, a black ribbon of wide, well-guarded curves, rolling and weaving through the irregular country.

At 292 *m.* the highway skirts a ridge and drops down a steep hill. Gushing from a steep hillside (R) are artificial falls caused by discharge of water from the flume of the water and light plant at Hot Springs. At this point US 18 enters FALL RIVER CANYON, its breadth divided by the green Fall River. With forested slopes casting queer, dull shadows on the bare, sandstone cliffs below, and the thin blue ribbon of highway threading beyond, the Fall River valley drive is one of the most picturesque along the entire course of US 18 across the State.

At 292.3 *m.* (R) is FALL RIVER FALLS, a series of small cascades surging down over sandstone ledges; and (L) at 292.6 *m.* is the EVANS QUARRY, from which sandstone is taken and shipped for building and other purposes.

At 294.1 *m.* is the Eagle's Nest Curve, and high up on a ledge overlooking the road is an EAGLE'S NEST, discernible from the highway.

At 296.7 *m.* is the junction with a dirt road.

Left on this road; paralleling it (L) are seven peaks of sandstone, so similar in appearance as to height and slope from the N. that they were long ago named the SEVEN SISTERS by some of the earlier settlers.

Near the top of the Seven Sisters Range, are the SUNKEN WELLS—holes in the ground, ranging from 15 to 40 ft. deep. The wells are caused by underground water eroding the limestone layers, leaving an unsupported roof which in time drops. It is said that animals have occasionally been found at the bottoms of these wells, the ground supposedly having given away beneath their weight.

At 13 m. (R) CASCADE FALLS originates in a few large springs of warm water and tumbles over a 15-ft. cliff.

At 297.5 *m.* is the junction with US 85A (*see Tour 14*) in Hot Springs.

Section c. Hot Springs—Wyoming Line, 40.1 m. US18.

HOT SPRINGS, o m. (3,443 alt., 3,263 pop.), in the foothills of the southern Hills, has a mild, bracing climate. On the S. is the Saw-Tooth range, on the E., Battle Mountain, and on the W. and N., the southern end of the main Black Hills range, locally known as Evans Heights and College Hill, at the base of which flows warm Fall River. In the business section all stores are on one side of the main street and on the other side is the river.

Although the Indians had been making health pilgrimages to the springs for many years, it was not until 1879 that the first permanent white settler arrived. By 1881 a few more people had moved into the canyon and it was then proposed to divide the town, first named Minnekahta; into two parts, because of the narrowness of the canyon. Today, although each section has its residential and business blocks and they are called "upper town" and "lower town," Hot Springs is one unit. In 1891 the courthouse was built fixing the seat of Fall River Co. at Hot Springs.

The growth and development of Hot Springs has never been of the boom variety. The first settlers were interested in agriculture and cattle raising, but through the promotion of the Dakota Hot Springs Co., composed largely of professional men from other towns in the Hills, Hot Springs has developed into a health resort and tourist town. Badger Clark, in his book, *When Hot Springs Was a Pup,* relates that Dr. R. D. Jennings built a shed over a natural bathtub, and the spring, and in this place the first white patient took his treatments. This is the INDIAN BATHTUB, now in the Hot Springs Hotel bathhouse. The tub was supposedly used first by an old squaw, who was cured of rheumatism. It is the result of erosion and excavation of the solid rock over one spring.

Fall River, the warm stream famous for the water that never varies in temperature from season to season, is formed by the union of the spring-fed Hot and Cold Brooks on the northern border of Hot Springs and flows S. through the length of the town.

The largest spring in the Black Hills is MAMMOTH SPRING, 2 blocks N. of the Evans Plunge on Court St. Some years ago the city purchased this spring and later deeded certain water rights to the National Home for Disabled Veterans. The rest was put at the disposal of the Water, Light & Power Co. At its source this spring has a temperature between 95 and 100 degrees F. The EVANS PLUNGE SPRING, just outside the Evans Plunge building, furnishes the major part of the water for the plunge. Through the Evans Plunge pours 5000 gallons of crystal clear mineral water every hour at a temperature of 90 degrees. The plunge is open to the public summer and winter, and is subject to none of the disadvantages of open air pools.

The HYGEA SPRING, in the center of town, has long been visited by people who drink its sulphurous water for the alleviation of various disorders. The BRAUN SPRING, on Court St., was the incentive for the building of the Braun Hotel and bathhouse. Over the MINNEKAHTA SPRING has been built the Hot Springs Hotel, which not only provides bath treatments, but also recreation in the HOT SPRINGS PLUNGE, which, though smaller than that of the Evans, has both indoor and outdoor swimming.

The STATE SOLDIERS' HOME was established in 1889, and ten Civil War veterans were the first patients. Several additions have been made to the original building. The present (1937) population is 112 men and 95 women. Veterans of four wars—Civil, Indian, Spanish-American, and World—are now admitted, and the wives and widows of these men are taken, if they have only a limited amount of property and are 60 years old or more.

High on the slope of Battle Mountain is the BATTLE MOUNTAIN SANITARIUM (Veterans Administration Facility), home of disabled war veterans. The main buildings of Spanish-style architecture, constructed of native pink sandstone, form a wheel-like design, each building opening upon the beautifully kept acreage of the reservation. There are usually between 500 and 600 residents.

Others besides war veterans come to Hot Springs seeking health. For these two general hospitals are maintained, OUR LADY OF LOURDES (Catholic) and the LUTHERAN HOSPITAL AND SANITARIUM.

The quarrying of stone is one of the town's major industries. Begun before the year 1900, 5 m. SE of town, the quarry has been operated for many years for the purpose of obtaining pink sandstone, which is used in local and State-wide construction work. Other quarries in the vicinity have produced large quantities of buff Dakota sandstone and red Dakota sandstone, both used in many of the buildings in Hot Springs.

At 5 m. (R) is the JOHN ROBERTSON MEMORIAL, consisting of a suitably marked Black Hills boulder. It was dedicated July 18, 1935, by the South Dakota State Horticultural Association, in recognition of the work done by John Robertson since 1896 until his death in 1937, in the improvement of the hardier fruits. It has been proposed to set aside a 3-acre plot near the boulder as a park, for the purpose of planting native trees, flowers, and shrubs.

MINNEKAHTA (Ind., *hot water*), 6.8 *m.*, is a small railroad junction of the C. B. & Q.

At 11.8 *m.* (L) is PARKER PEAK (4,848 alt.), one of the oldest landmarks in the history of the Black Hills; when approached from the E., it looks small and unpretentious in comparison with other peaks in the Saw-Tooth range surrounding it. But from a greater distance, Parker Peak appears high above all others. This appearance is perhaps caused by the fact that the blunt-topped summit is shaped much like a loaf of bread and the surrounding peaks, which are much lower, are jagged.

At 14.8 *m.* is the junction with a dirt road.

Left on this road to the FOSSIL CYCAD NATIONAL MONU- MENT, 1 *m.*, an area containing large deposits of the fossil re- mains of fern-like plants of the Mesozoic period. It is said to be the best fossil cycad bed so far discovered, the specimens hav- ing been perfectly preserved. In 1937 this region consisted of a plowed field, the cycads having been removed to Yale Uni- versity. If any cycads remain, they lie buried beneath the sur- face in the cretaceous beds known locally as the Dakota forma- tion, a grayish-white sandstone, 30 ft. in thickness.

The fossil cycad is a member of the dacotensis family and the genus Cucadoidea. It has been proven that this species bore flowers millions of years ago when large egg-laying monsters such as the dinosaurs roamed the earth. The height to which the trunks of these plants grew depended upon the species and upon climatic conditions. The more intemperate and adverse the con- ditions were for this plant, the shorter the trunk. The fruit resembled a pineapple in appearance and became fossilized easily. Some specimens have been found in the Minnekahta fossil bed and have been removed to museums.

The beds were first discovered in 1892 when F. H. Cole of Hot Springs saw a resemblance between these fossils and certain plants growing in the tropics. He immediately sent photographs to the Smithsonian Institution in Washington. Prof. Henry New- ton, geologist, was put in charge of the investigation and found them to be the "fossil cycadean trunks." The area was set aside by Presidential proclamation in 1922.

At 17.7 *m.* is FLINT HILL (L), on which is an old Indian flint quarry.

At 25.8 *m.* is the junction with a dirt road.

Right on this road, which follows the course of Pleasant Valley Creek through Red Canyon, are the mysterious PAINTED

ROCKS, 7.1 m. The small parking space (L), from which the rocks are reached, is not marked, but a clump of cottonwood trees, a washout, high cutbank (R), and the 200-ft. cliff (L) are landmarks. Across the creek bed a steep path (L) leads up the face of the cliff to a pole with several crossboards. On the smooth face of the rock, at a height of 7 or 8 ft., are the faint outlines of crudely drawn figures cut into the rock. Deer, goats, beetles, crosses, and other figures can be distinguished. The animals have oval-shaped bodies and crude heads, with straight lines representing legs, tails, horns, and antlers. Some of the characters are simply a string of 00000, while others look like the family wash hanging on the line. Especially interesting are the crosses, used both as a symbol and an instrument of torture in ancient Mexico and far back into antiquity. The pictures are probably of Indian origin.

At 27 m. US 18 crosses the Cheyenne River again.

EDGEMONT, 28.4 m. (3,449 alt., 946 pop.), was given the name because of its proximity to the Black Hills. The town originated with the building of the railroad, and has been developed by railroad men and their families. It is the trading center for the surrounding area.

Edgemont boasts an excellent BAND HALL, a half-dome in shape, with a white interior, so that colored lights can be used as a background for the musicians. The walls are constructed of native stone from a quarry situated a few miles north of Edgemont.

At the EDGEMONT HOT WATER SULPHUR BATH SANITARIUM baths are given in water that comes directly from a well in town. The water that gushes from this well ranges in temperature from 116 to 120 degrees at all times. The sanitarium is a well-equipped building, with dining facilities and rooms for many patients.

Near Edgemont are large quantities of fossils and petrified wood.

At 28.9 m. US 18 passes the FALL RIVER FAIR GROUNDS (L). In the early fall every year, the Fall River Co. Fair is held at Edgemont, with a good racing program and exhibits from all parts of the county. The fair has been held annually for the last 24 years. Indians from the Pine Ridge Reservation lend a gay and colorful touch.

At 30.6 m. Parker Peak again stands out (L) in bold relief against the sky, high above the surrounding Edgemont Valley.

At 40.1 m. US 18 crosses the Wyoming Line, 50 m. E. of Lusk, Wyo.

TOUR 8

Junction US 77 (Elk Point)—Vermillion—Wagner—Junction US
18 (Lake Andes). State 50.
Junction with US 77 to Junction with US 18, 109.6 m.
The C. M. St. P. & P. R.R. parallels this route throughout.
Roadbed intermittently graveled or bituminous top.
Hotel and cabin accommodations in larger towns.

State 50, branching W. from US 77 10 miles north of Elk
Point, passes through the oldest and one of the richest agricultural
sections of South Dakota. With the Sioux, Vermillion, and James
River valleys, the southeastern section has become an intensive
livestock-feeding area, producing tall corn and forage crops for
fattening cattle and hogs. It is a virtual continuation of Iowa
farmland, with large modern houses, groves of trees, and big red
barns. Farther west a gradual transition takes place; the farmers
base their hopes on large wheat tracts, which one year may yield
thousands of dollars and the next give them no return for their
seed and labor. The farms and towns here are newer and less
numerous; the valleys give way to rugged, rolling hills. The
Yankton Indian Reservation is along the Missouri River toward
the western end of this route.

Between the junction with US 77 and Vermillion, State 50
passes through a flat country, where farmers haul their produce
and livestock to markets in large trucks two and three times a
week.

VERMILLION, 9 m. (1,131 alt., 2,906 pop.), the seat of the
University of South Dakota, is situated on the bluffs above the
peaceful Vermillion River, and also overlooks the turbulent Missouri. The town was so named because of the red clay obtained
from the banks of the river.

In 1835 a trading post called Fort Vermillion was built by the
American Fur Co. on the banks of the Missouri River, and in 1843
Audubon, the famous naturalist, visited the post and the trail now
known as the Ravine Road in the present city. A colony of Mor-
mons, enroute to the Rocky Mountains, spent the winter at the
fort in 1845-46, but the site of the fort has been washed away
by the bank-eroding Missouri.

When the Homestead Act went into effect Jan. 1, 1863, settlers
moved in to stake claims along the valley. A settlement was started

on the flat where the Vermillion and Missouri Rivers join, and the new town boomed. But in 1881 a flood roared down through the lowlands, sweeping away 150 buildings in the young city and leaving the rest in ruins. There was not a single life lost, however, as residents climbed to the high bluff and watched their belongings and five bridges float down the swirling river. The result of the flood was twofold: a new city was built high on the bluffs, and the Missouri cut a new channel four miles South, creating a large island.

The UNIVERSITY OF SOUTH DAKOTA, adjacent to State 50 on Dakota St., is an important factor in the development and growth of the State (*see EDUCATION*). Through the research work of its laboratories and the expert services of its staff, the University contributes widely to the development of wealth and culture in the State.

In 1862 the first Territorial Legislature established the University, but failed to provide any funds. Succeeding legislatures refused to make an appropriation, and 20 years later the citizens of Vermillion decided to take energetic action. The site was selected and the first 10 acres donated by Judge Jefferson Kidder. The county commissioners called an election to approve a $10,000 bond issue for the construction of one building. Although the building was not yet finished, the fall term opened in 1882 in the court house. The faculty consisted of one man, Dr. Ephriam N. Epstein, a Russian Jew who had become a Baptist clergyman; the student body numbered 39, but increased to 69 before the end of the first year. The next year the faculty was doubled, and the Territorial Legislature voted its support to the extent of $30,000.

Since 1882 the University of South Dakota has graduated more than 3,200 men and women and has trained thousands of others for service to the State. It comprises nine main divisions, more than 100 faculty members, and an average annual enrollment of 1,600 students. Through its various schools and colleges, it offers courses in nearly all of the accepted fields of modern university training.

The original plan for the campus was a semicircle, but the founders failed to realize the space needs of future growth. The buildings are now arranged on the 69-acre campus with more regard to convenience than symmetry. There is no uniform type of architecture. The LIBRARY and LAW BUILDING, of Colonial type, are built of Bedford limestone. English tendencies are noticeable in other buildings. OLD MAIN, EAST HALL, and the OLD ARMORY are constructed of Sioux Falls quartzite. All the others are brick.

The main public event of the year is Dakota Day (homecoming) in October.

AUDUBON PARK, S. Dakota St., borders the Ravine Road from the bluff to the flat, and is heavily wooded with natural timber. A monument to the first permanent schoolhouse in South Dakota (*see EDUCATION*), together with a miniature reproduction of the building, stands at the foot of the hill, across from which is a memorial to the first Masonic chapter in the State.

PRENTISS PARK, E. Main St., has a large municipal swimming pool (*open daily during summer*).

At the western end of Main St. is a junction with State 19.

> Right on State 19 to SPIRIT MOUND, 3 *m.*, a high hill rising from a level plain, and believed sacred by the Indians. Lewis and Clark stopped in 1804 to investigate the stories told by the Sioux of mysterious little people who inhabited the mound and shot arrows at anyone who approached. The explorers found neither inhabitants nor any evidence of their activities. There was nothing of unusual interest except the mound, which is approximately 300 ft. long, 70 ft. wide, and 65 ft. high.

At 10.4 *m.* the Vermillion River is crossed.

At 10.6 *m.* is a junction with a graded road leading to a ferry, 3 *m.*

A V-shaped valley between the Vermillion and Missouri Rivers, with high bluffs rising from the far sides of each, has productive and well-cultivated farms. To the S. the rugged bluffs form part of the Nebraska boundary.

MECKLING, 16.8 *m.* (1,156 alt., 148 pop.), has one of the largest consolidated schools in the State.

GAYVILLE, 22.7 *m.* (1,167 alt., 269 pop.), is the center of a large Scandinavian farming community. At 23.5 *m.* is the Gayville Cemetery, once featured in Ripley's *Believe It Or Not* series because of its name.

At 30.8 *m.* is the WNAX radio station transmitter.

At 31.3 *m.* the James River is crossed; along the river is WILD-WOOD, a pleasure resort.

YANKTON, 35.5 *m.* (1,157 alt., 6,759 pop.), was the capital of Dakota Territory before South Dakota and North Dakota were divided, and much of the State's early history had Yankton as its setting (*see HISTORY*).

In March 1858 George D. Fiske, representative of a fur company, pitched his tent near the Missouri River, becoming the city's first permanent white settler. Sixteen cedar rafts were floated down the river from Fort Pierre, out of which a trading post was built near the present Meridian Highway bridge. The Yankton Sioux Indians, led by Smutty Bear, gathered at Yankton in 1859 to protest being removed to reservations. A satisfactory argreement was

FIRST HOUSE IN YANKTON

reached, with the presentation of some trinkets by the U. S. Agent, and settlers moved into the region. The town was surveyed in August 1859, and construction of more buildings was begun to augment the two log cabins there. On Christmas Day, 1859, the first tavern was opened where the Merchants Hotel now stands; in fact, the original structure is part of the present building.

An unusual character of those days was James Witherspoon, a bachelor, locally known as Limber Jim; it is said that he walked to Washington, D. C., to procure the patent to his land, now known as the Witherspoon Addition.

Yankton was selected capital of Dakota Territory in 1861, and when the first Legislature met, nicknamed "The Pony Congress," the upper house convened in the William Tripp residence. The house has been removed to the city park, restored to its original condition, and is used as a museum. The lower house met in the Episcopal chapel. The first copy of the *Weekly Dakotan* was printed June 6, 1861.

An Indian uprising in 1862 resulted in the erection of a stockade, 450 ft. square, at Third and Broadway, and residents of Sioux Falls and Yankton gathered there for protection. After the excitement subsided, the prosperous city grew steadily.

The streets of Yankton are unusually wide, some 130 ft., with boulevards of flowers and shrubbery. A Negro community lies in the northwestern section of Yankton. The people own their homes and have two church buildings. Some of the young people are athletic stars in the city schools.

The SITE OF THE CAPITOL OF DAKOTA TERRITORY is marked by a bronze tablet on polished granite at Capital and Fourth Sts. The original two-story building was frame.

MERIDIAN HIGHWAY BRIDGE (*50c for car and driver; 10c for each passenger*), carrying US 81 (*see Tour 10*), crosses the Missouri River to Nebraska. It was built entirely by private capital raised in the vicinity. It is a double-deck, 7-span draw (or lift) bridge; the upper deck is used for highway traffic and the lower will be utilized for a railroad when a contemplated line is built. The 1937 State Legislature authorized the State Highway Commission to arrange for its purchase.

YANKTON COLLEGE (Congregational) is the oldest institution of high learning in the Dakotas, having been founded in 1881 by Dr. Joseph Ward. The Conservatory of Music is considered one of the best in the Midwest. The college has an attractive campus.

GARDEN TERRACE THEATRE, on Yankton College campus, is an out-of-doors amphitheatre used by the college and city, having a seating capacity of 5,000. Each season the Yankton College dramatic arts department presents one Shakespearean drama, a pageant, and other plays. Commencement exercises are usually held here also. The stage has a balcony and a pergola.

BANTON BAND AMPHITHEATRE, Forresters' Park, Locust and 8th Sts., is the scene of weekly summer band concerts. The bandstand is built of stone, entirely surrounded by pools containing goldfish and water lilies.

SUMMIT PARK, W. 5th St., is a tourist resort and has a large swimming pool. In spring it is especially pretty with its winding drives bordered by lilac hedges.

CARNEGIE LIBRARY, Capital and 4th Sts., has several valuable collections, among which is the Roane Memorial Collection of

1,000 volumes; a South Dakota Collection of 900 volumes; and a genealogical department consisting of 300 books.

> Right from the center of Yankton on a graveled road to the STATE INSANE HOSPITAL, 1 *m.* This is a $1,500,000 institution, taking care of about 900 patients. Until 1878 the insane persons of Dakota Territory were cared for, by special arrangements, in Nebraska and Minnesota institutions. When Gov. William A. Howard found the institutions in the other States overcrowded, and insane persons numerous within the State, he used his own funds to secure land and provide shelter at Yankton. The institution was almost immediately overcrowded. With 57 women packed in a cottage originally built for a laundry, fire broke out and 17 patients perished, the others escaping with only their night apparel.
>
> The hospital owns 1,700 acres of land, 1,400 of which are under cultivation. Fine, new buildings have been constructed to make it one of the outstanding institutions in the State.
>
> A collection of pictures, including 273 water colors, 27 oil paintings and 35 etchings, is on exhibition at the hospital.

At 35.6 *m.* is the junction with US 81 (*see Tour 10*).

At 42.5 *m.* is a junction with a graded road known as Postman's Road.

> Left on this road to the CHALK ROCK CLIFFS, 3 *m.*, bordering the Missouri River. This chalk rock has been quarried and used for building purposes. When first excavated it is soft enough to be cut with a knife, but hardens soon after exposure to air, and when weathered makes a satisfactory building material. It may also be crushed and burned in a kiln to make a good quality of lime.

TABOR, 50.9 *m.*, (391 pop.), is the center of a rural Bohemian settlement. The entire population of the town and of much of the surrounding country is of the one nationality, and all business transactions are carried on in the Bohemian language. Tabor has a Bohemian newspaper and the only all-Bohemian American Legion post in the State. Noted for fun-loving tendencies, they hold their "Sokols" several times each year. A Sokol is the performance of setting-up exercises similar to those practiced in the army; the Bohemians enter into them with great zest, every summer holding a contest in a spirit of keen competition. They also have the old folk dances, the best known and most difficult of which is the Beseda. This requires 20 couples and the participants are always dressed in native costumes.

The town has an all-Bohemian baseball team. Each year the inhabitants of the town present several stage shows at Tabor and in other Bohemian towns.

A Bohemian wedding is a festive occasion. The entire neighborhood is invited; there is plenty to eat and drink, and the air is filled with music and laughter. A dance always follows the wedding.

Housewives here are noted for the quality and quantity of food they prepare. Their best known food is kolacher, a small biscuit filled with fruit or with poppy seed. Bohemians are heavy meat eaters, with pork heading the list. Potato dumplings and sauerkraut, with pitchers of beer, are often included in their menus.

At 60 m. is a log cabin, one of the few remaining in the eastern part of South Dakota.

At 72 m. is the junction with a graveled road.

> Left on this road is SPRINGFIELD, 11 m. (1,234 alt., 661 pop.), seat of the SOUTHERN STATE NORMAL SCHOOL. This institution was established by act of the Territorial Legislature in 1881; but it did not come into actual existence until Oct. 11, 1897, when it opened with an enrollment of 21 students and a faculty of four, under Pres. J. S. Frazee. The school had a four-year normal course until 1931 and has had a two-year course since then. On a campus of 40 acres are a main building, containing the administrative offices and classrooms, a science hall, with laboratories and a gymnasium on the upper floor, and a dormitory for girls. A library of 15,000 volumes is in the main building. The school has a faculty of about 25 and a student body of 400.

TYNDALL, 72.5 m. (1,418 alt., 1,303 pop.), is the seat of Bon Homme Co. and the center of a prosperous farming community, largely of Bohemian and German origin. There is an excellent public swimming pool at the western edge of the town.

At 77.5 m. is the junction with State 37 (see Tour 11A).

AVON, 82.4 m. (661 pop.), was named by early settlers for Avon,, N. Y., the town from which they had migrated. It has a fine, shady park and unusually good drinking water.

At 88.6 m. is a deep gully, lined with oak trees, which virtually marks the dividing line between the rich farming region and an area of larger grain farms in which weather conditions determine the wealth of the people. The country beyond is more rolling, and the view far reaching.

DANTE, 89.1 m. (109 pop.), was first called Mayo, in honor of E. O. Mayo, owner of the town site, but when it was learned that there was a post office in the Black Hills by the same name, Mayo renamed the town for his favorite author, Dante. The town

was founded in 1908, when the railroad put in a siding to accommodate farmers who shipped large quantities of livestock. For a
town of its size, it has one of the largest Catholic parishes in the
State.

WAGNER, 98.1 *m.* (1,442 alt., 1,350 pop.), is a picturesque
trading center for the Indians who live on the Yankton Reservation, and is a live Western town. Indians are seen every day loiter-
ing on the streets, the women dressed in shawls and blankets and
the men in overalls. An annual Labor Day celebration is held,
featuring Indian dances.

A Government INDIAN HOSPITAL, costing $85,000, was opened
in 1937 to take care of Indians on the Yankton Reservation need-
ing hospitalization. The hospital is a one-story building, with wards
in the wings, so that all rooms receive sunshine. Indian labor was
used in constructing the building.

At Wagner is a junction with a graveled road.

Left on this road, which goes through Indian country; along this
route are improved and well-kept Indian homes, as well as
shacks with "squaw coolers," four posts in a square with a roof
of branches and leaves.

At 14 *m.* is a small graveyard where a group of Sioux members
of the Peyote cult have been buried.

Old Indians like to recall an incident that happened along this
road when it was only a foot trail. An Indian had gone about
5 m. to Greenwood Agency for supplies. While there he also
purchased a new hat which he put on immediately, and with
his sack of groceries thrown over his shoulder he started for
home. Night was coming on so he walked rapidly. After traveling some distance he noticed an object directly in front of him,
and finally became alarmed when he noticed it popping up before
him, no matter where he looked. Speeding up his pace, he
started across country; but still the bobbing object continued to
make its appearance. Frightened by the evil-appearing demon,
he tried vainly to go around it. So he set out at full speed,
zigzagging and stumbling as he sped through brush and undergrowth. Finally he saw a light glimmering through the dusk and
breathlessly made a last desperate effort to elude his pursuer
which, strangely, was behind him whenever he looked back. He
dashed on, falling exhausted against the door, battered and
bruised by his swinging sack of supplies. After being taken in
and revived, he was relieved to discover the demon was no
longer before him. When he put on his hat, there it was again.
Then he saw that the demon had been the heavy hat cord
hanging over the brim of his hat in front.

At 18 *m.* is GREENWOOD (200 pop.), which until recently was the Yankton Indian Agency. A boss farmer now has charge of the Indians there, under the direction of the Agent at Rosebud Agency (see Tour 7). Greenwood is on the banks of the Missouri River and has several large frame buildings no longer in use. Most families of the agency haul their water from the river in barrels. An incident of 1889 illustrates the difficulties confronted by the United States Government during the territorial period. At that time the Government took steps to allot the lands, but the measure was resisted by an Indian, Big Tobacco, and his band. Troops were called out and bloodshed almost ensued before the band consented to the allotment. Bobona, another Indian, opposed the act but surrendered after a 15-m. chase by soldiers with bayonets.

A legend Greenwood Indians tell concerns the origin of the sunflower. A certain boy early in life developed a deep affection for the sun. For hours each day he would sit and gaze at the flaming disc on its journey across the heavens. He would sing weird songs praising the object of his affections. And because of his strange communion with the sun he was named Sun Gazer. In time he became blind, and because he ate very sparingly his body wasted away. One evening when he did not return from his favorite spot on a nearby hill, a party was sent out after sundown to find him. They came upon him facing W, though blind, he had by force of habit followed the sun on its course as he did when he still had his eyesight. When they came close to him they found that the last spark of life had left along with the last ray of light. They buried him on that very spot. The next morning when they returned to the grave, they found that a flower had grown from the mound; as they watched it, they saw that it, too, followed the course of the sun.

At 104.1 *m.* is a junction with a graded road.

Left on this road is the WAGNER OIL WELL, 1.5 *m.* which has been worked on for years with little success but considerable optimism.

RAVINIA, 108.4 *m.* (153 pop.), was named for an Indian girl on whose property the town was started in 1909.

At 109.6 *m.* is the junction with US 18, 6 m. E. of Lake Andes (*see Tour 7*).

TOUR 9

Milbank—Brookings—Sioux Falls—Elk Point—(Sioux City, Iowa) US 77.

Milbank to Iowa Line, 215.1 m.

Except at intervals, US 77 is not paralleled by railroads.

All-weather roads, gravel and hard-surface alternating.

Good hotel and tourist accommodations.

US 77 passes through South Dakota's richest farming region— a region of ample rainfall, characterized by diversified argiculture. Bisecting the heart of the State's dairy section at the start, the road first crosses an area where small grains lead other crops, then touches a region of moderate livestock production, and finally passes through the portion where intensive livestock-feeding dominates. Incidentally, Deuel County on this route is the only County in the State where oats form the leading crop.

While the general character of the country is level, numerous hills and occasional tree-fringed lakes interrupt the monotony of the landscape. The northern half of US 77 touches the section known as the Lake Region, and the southern half the Sioux Valley region. Much of the soil is of a rich black loam quality, capable of producing abundant crops and able to withstand considerable drought.

The eastern section of the State was the first to be occupied, earliest settlers coming from Minnesota. The region is quite typically eastern, the descendants of the first settlers remaining on the farms during succeeding generations. There are pretentious farm homes, surrounded by large substantial buildings, in groves of trees.

MILBANK, o. m. (1,148 alt., 2,549 pop.), (*see Tour 2*), is at the junction with US 12.

LA BOLT, 14.3 m. (1,362 alt., 109 pop.), was named for Alfred La Bolt, early landowner, who is buried under a large oak tree near the town.

South of La Bolt the level country gradually changes to a series of low hills, the beginning of a rougher area which extends for many miles.

At 19.9 m. the Grant Co. line is crossed; significant because the semi-hilly land now becomes definitely hilly, with a multitude of grass tufted knolls forming irregular humps in the contour of the country, the region is more sparsely settled than farther N.

At 25.4 m. is the junction with US 212 (see Tour 3).

At 28.9 m. is the junction with a graveled road.

> Right on this road is ALTAMONT, 0.5 m. (1,834 alt., 144 pop.) so named because of the hilly country surrounding it. Situated picturesquely among the hills, the town has one of the highest altitudes of any town in this part of the State.

From Altamont the road winds with numerous abrupt climbs around and among the blunt-nosed hills, the land generally becoming more broken and creased by many steep-walled gullies.

CLEAR LAKE, 35.5 m. (1,800 alt., 929 pop.), was named for a lake with transparent, sparkling water and a clean sandy bottom, a half-mile E. of town. During recent droughts the waters of the lake gradually receded until its bed became entirely dry.

Erected here at a cost of $75,000, the county's new COURTHOUSE, built of Bedford limestone is one of the outstanding structures in Deuel Co. This handsome building is a far cry from the first courthouse that figured in a prolonged and bitter county seat war, settled finally in 1890. Gary, where the State School for the Blind is located, and Clear Lake were the principals in the contest. Clear Lake was situated in the approximate center of the county; but Gary was the older town, and in addition, had been presented with a new courthouse by the Chicago & North Western R.R. When the battle ended, Clear Lake had won, and Gary's new courthouse slowly began to fall into a state of desuetude. Today it is used as a chicken house at the State School for the Blind.

Despite the fact that US 77 traverses a rich farming section between Clear Lake and Brookings, there is not a single town on the highway along the 37-m. stretch.

At 70.1 m. is the Brookings GOLF COURSE, and a short distance beyond is the ATHLETIC FIELD of South Dakota State College.

BROOKINGS, 71.9 m. (1,636 alt., 4,723 pop.) (see Tour 4), is at the junction with US 14.

At 79.1 m., a few feet from the road (R), is the MEDARY MONUMENT, erected to commemorate the first townsite in Dakota Territory in 1857. Nothing is left of this little settlement of three-quarters of a century ago, but this rather unostentatious pillar of cobblestone on a base of gray stone and concrete.

At 79.6 *m.* US 77 begins to spiral slowly down into the valley of the Big Sioux River. Here are visible comfortable-looking homes, and almost every animal and fowl that falls under the category of diversified farming. The grass is rich, and groves of trees add to the attractiveness of this picture of rural life.

At 98.4 *m.* is the LONE TREE, a tall, well-proportioned cotton-wood. This stately tree, of little commercial value, was the cause of a controversy several years ago. It was planted by a pioneer in 1876 and for years remained a well-known landmark in its vicinity. When the highway was built, it was discovered that the tree was directly in the path of the road. For years traffic was diverted on either side of it. But the motor age called for improvement of this busy thoroughfare, and a paving contract was let. "The tree must go," said the Highway Department. That order caused a flood of protest that poured into the highway office and into the offices of leading newspapers. Nature lovers from all over the United States were aroused. So decided was the popular demand for the preservation of the tree that authorities decided to spare the well-known landmark.

Left from Lone Tree on State 34, a graveled road, is FLAN-DREAU, 14 *m.* (1,565 alt., 2,474 pop.), which was first settled in 1857 but destroyed the following year when Indians frightened the settlers away. In 1859 a band of Santee Sioux disregarded the dictates of the Government and settled "like white men" on homesteads in the Big Sioux River valley. In 1874 both Episcopal and Presbyterian churches were built, and in 1878 Flandreau was again settled by white people. Flandreau is the seat of Moody Co., and the home of the FLANDREAU INDIAN VOCATIONAL HIGH SCHOOL, (open; student guides). The school is situated in an Indian community at the western edge of the city. Its campus comprises 481 acres and 54 buildings. Here 420 Indian students receive both academic and vocational training. Native arts and crafts are given a prominent place in the curriculum—weaving, carving, and beadwork; articles made from native pipestone are featured. The craft work is for sale. The vocational department offers courses in auto mechanics, welding, millwork, cabinet making, engineering, book making, library work, nursing, sewing and commercial work. In the community surrounding the school, 75 per cent of the people use the Dakota, or Sioux language. Few traces of Indian habits of life and customs of dress remain, however. The Indian women operate a garment factory where they manufacture about 15,000 dresses annually for the Indian service.

At 109.5 *m.* (R) is the ODD FELLOWS HOME, a short distance from the road. At this institution old and indigent members of the lodge are taken care of.

DELL RAPIDS, 111.8 m. (1,489 alt., 1,636 pop.), first settled in 1864 is one of the most picturesque towns in south-eastern South Dakota. It was so named because of the dells and rapids of the Big Sioux River that flows through the town.

At the southeastern edge of town are the striking and picturesque DELLS, formed when the river cut a narrow gorge through the quartzite rock underlying the section. The Dells are about 0.8 m. long with several unusual formations in the distance. A well-maintained road makes it possible to drive the entire length of the Dells, but to appreciate them fully a walk along the cliff tops is necessary. Sunlight, evening shades, and moonlight all produce different and striking effects.

The rock in the Dells juts to the surface through a thin layer of earth for many feet from the edge of the chasm. Below is the swift-flowing Big Sioux River, which divides into two channels above the Dells to join again below. About halfway along the Dells is PULPIT ROCK, a small amphitheatre with a smooth floor of red stone at the top of the cliffs. This queer natural formation actually served as a place of worship in early days before churches were built, the congregation occasionally being subjected to a drenching because of the lack of a roof.

The road passes a spot where iron rails guard a deep crevice that joins the main gorge. From natural platforms of rock S. and N. of this point are impressive views; toward the S., visible for a long distance, is the river valley, its walls red and purple in the sunlight. Through the gorge is a view of pastures and small groves and a glimpse of the vast prairie country.

These gorges were formed by torrents which came down the Big Sioux Valley when the glaciers melted thousands of years ago. Coming from the N., the waters forced themselves over the barrier of Sioux Falls quartzite at Dell Rapids. The channel here was narrow and the rock more resistant than the drift through which the stream cut the wider part of the valley. The steep walls of the gorge are due to the method by which the stream cut its valley.

When a strong current crosses a formation like the Sioux quartzite which is broken by many cracks and fissures, a process known as "plucking" takes place. Instead of being worked off bit by bit, the blocks of rock are lifted out bodily and carried away by the force of the water. The strong current of the Big Sioux River carried everything before it, including any rock projections that may have been formed, and thus left the walls smooth.

The Dells are city-owned and no admission is charged.

The Dell Rapids POST OFFICE, established in 1871, began operations in a rude shanty with an old trunk for equipment. The town
then was called "Dell" and the postmaster, Albion Thorne, played
an aggressive part in its development. The post office was established on Dec. 11, and on Christmas the first mail arrived from
Sioux Falls. Celebrating the two events, the entire population, 13
in number, gathered at Thorne's shanty for Christmas dinner. The
mail carrier often made the trip on foot, sometimes on horseback,
and during times of deep snow used a cutter or light sled with
tall, narrow runners. A grain sack served as a mail bag during
the first trips. For his first 18 months service as postmaster Thorne
was paid $18. The salary of the office today is $2,000 per year.

At 117 m. is the junction with a graveled road.

Left on this road is BALTIC, 2 m. (1,471 alt., 276 pop.), a town
in which nearly every resident is of Norwegian descent. In "Little
Norway," as the community is often called, many customs of
the mother country are still observed by the residents. The Norwegian Lutheran church is the only place of worship in town.
The village was first named St. Olaf; later the name Keyes was
adopted; and this in turn was changed to the present name.
May 17, the Norwegians' Independence Day, is celebrated each
year. The town claims to have the oldest grain elevator in the
State, erected in 1887. Two dams built across the Sioux River
have created two lakes where fish abound. A Government nursery
here raises many varieties of shrubs and trees used in the
shelterbelt. Baltic has a cooperative funeral home and a cooperative telephone company.

In Baltic, as in many typical Norwegian communities, there is
a branch of the Hardanger Lag, a national organization composed of Scandinavians throughout the United States who have
emigrated from the community of Hardanger in Norway. Each
year they hold a 2-day wedding festival for the purpose of
perpetuating the customs of rural Norway. The first Hardanger
wedding in this part of the country took place in Sioux Falls
in 1911. Since that time these weddings have taken place in
different parts of the State, including Garretson, Colton, and
Canton.

Beginning the ceremony the toastmaster enters with a violin
player. The latter makes a very striking picture dressed in
knee breeches and white silk coat, elaborately trimmed in bright
colors. Tassels and buttons decorate the costume. The violin
player is followed closely by the bridesmaid, best man, and
maid of honor. A company of 50 girls follows, dressed in silk
costumes with red waists, black shirts, and white aprons. The
girls march in front of the stage and form an entrance for the

bride and groom. The bride wears a high silver crown upon her head and a black skirt trimmed elaborately with beads and beautiful lace. The bodice of her waist is covered with minute decorations in contrasting colors. Over the skirt she wears a white apron heavily trimmed with several panels of lace. In her hand she carries a beautiful corsage of roses. As the bride and groom stand upon the stage, a song is usually sung by a "mandskor."

Following the ceremony a huge banquet is served. The tables are decorated with American and Norwegian flags and banners, and a huge basket of apples is always present as a centerpiece. Apples are used because of the great abundance of especially delicious varieties in this region. The menu served usually consists of "krootakoka," flat-bread, "blodpotse" (blood bologna), mutton, rutabagas, potatoes, cream mush, "primost," and several other kinds of cheese.

While the guests are seated at the table entertainment is produced. All first rise and sing the Norwegian national anthem, "Yes We Love This Land." The toastmaster then welcomes them with an address. An outstanding feature of the entertainment is a pantomime by a young girl, dressed in peasant style. She walks upon the stage carrying a milk pail on one arm. Grouped around her are several men, who sing to her as she stands in a listening attitude.

SIOUX FALLS, 130.8 *m.* (1,422 alt., 33,644 pop.) (*see SIOUX FALLS*).

State's industrial center and largest city, State Penitentiary, Morrell Packing Plant, Manchester Biscuit Company, Pettigrew Museum, Terrace Park, Sherman Indian Mounds, Big Sioux River, Coliseum.

At Sioux Falls is the junction with US 16 (*see Tour 5*).

At 139.5 *m.* is a junction with a graveled road.

Left on this road is HARRISBURG, 1 *m.* (1,426 alt., 217 pop.), a town that spent many years in deciding on its present name. Harrisburg was the first name, but when the site of the post office was changed with the advent of the railroad, Salina became the new name. Then came another change and Salina gave way to Springdale. Finally in 1890, the present site was decided upon and "Harrisburg" returned to stay.

At 151.8 *m.* is the junction with US 18 (*see Tour 7*); US 77 and US 18 follow the same route for 5 m. (*see Tour 7*).

At 156.8 *m.* is the junction with US 18 (*see Tour 7*).

BERESFORD, 166 *m.* (1,505 alt., 1,618 pop.), was named for Admiral Lord Charles Beresford of England. The town has a shady, well-equipped tourist camp and a 10-acre park. The Bethseda Home, for aged and infirm members of the Lutheran faith, and a Children's Home are here.

It was in the fertile region in this section of the State that early settlers first made their homes. Beresford is in the heart of the corn-raising section of South Dakota, approximately 50 per cent of the acreage under cultivation being devoted to this crop. With so many natural advantages, there is little wonder that prosperous farms have grown up in this section.

Wild fruit is plentiful along the streams. There are several kinds of game-birds, including pheasants, prairie-chickens, quail, Hungarian partridges, ducks, and geese, while more than 50 varieties of little winged songsters make this area their habitat.

At 188 *m.* is the junction with State 50 (*see Tour 8*).

ELK POINT, 198.5 m. (1,126 alt., 1,524 pop.), was given that name because of the large number of elk seen near the original townsite, and it was in this vicinity that Lewis and Clark shot their first deer.

Beginning in 1889, an old settlers' picnic has been held every year. Most of these reunions are featured by inspirational programs, and, until the last few years, a field mass was held in commemoration of the ceremonies in 1877 to rid the country of the grasshopper scourge. (See JEFFERSON below).

While the population of Elk Point, like that of other towns in this part of the State, has fluctuated little in the last 20 years, the town has lost considerable trade because of paved roads over which residents in the vicinity can, in less than half an hour, reach Sioux City for a shopping tour.

JEFFERSON, 208 *m.* (1,114 alt., 493 pop.), claims a prominent place in the early settlement of Union Co. This beautiful and level tract, covered with lush grass and many trees, attracted pioneer homeseekers as early as 1859. The town was first started at the 14-MILE HOUSE, 2.5 m. NW., which was a stopping place for settlers as they pushed farther into Dakota Territory. An old post office building of early days is now used as a residence at the former townsite.

A large BLACK CROSS in the cemetery dates back to 1877 when grasshoppers ravaged the State. A few old-timers in the community still remember this devastating plague that swept the territory, leaving in its wake stark desolation, blighted hopes, and starvation. There were few inhabitants, then, but this part of the Territory was more thickly settled than other sections. Coming in hordes so dense that the sky was darkened and the sun nearly obscured, the grasshoppers devoured the scanty crops, already stunted by drought.

Frenzied with grief, the settlers, after exhausting all human efforts to rid themselves of the grasshoppers, decided to ask Divine aid. The pastor of the Catholic Church announced at mass that a retreat was to take place the next day. Messages were dispatched as quickly as possible to all the people of the county and community. Protestants and Catholics alike came to the church next morning. Many of them were barefoot.

The priest carried a cross and led the procession that formed 2 m. S. of town. From here the group marched N. 6 m., then proceeded from E. to W. in the form of a cross. At each of the four points they placed a simple cross and, in the cemetery at Jefferson, a larger one. The ceremonies connected with the procession were solemn, men, women, and children joining in prayer. Not long after the event great heaps of dead grasshoppers were found along the Sioux and Missouri Rivers.

Homes, filling stations, and stores are more numerous near Sioux City, and at 215 *m.* is STEVENS, consisting of a garage and a few scattered houses.

At 215.1 *m.* the Iowa line is crossed at the Big Sioux River 1 m. N. of Sioux City, Iowa.

TOUR 10

(Fairmount, N. Dak.)—Sisseton—Watertown—Madison—Yankton —(Crofton, Nebr.). US 81.

North Dakota Line to Nebraska Line, 249 m.

All-weather roadbed, intermittently gravel and hard surfaced.

Suitable hotel and tourist accommodations at above towns.

US 81, known as the Meridian Highway, crosses eastern South Dakota through a country long popular with the hunting Sioux Indian tribes because of its lakes, creeks, and grassy hills; but now, less than a century later, it is mostly an area of intensive farming. Indians still reside in the northern region, which is part of the Sisseton Indian Reservation (*see INDIANS and Tour 1*), and along US 81 are occasional Indian farm homes, squat, frame buildings, and barns, with a few horses nearby. This hilly country, known as the Coteau des Prairies, was once the habitat of buffalo herds, and the Sioux lived many happy years in the ravines and along the lakes. Few towns have sprung up and most of the country has been untouched by the plow. Farther S. the country is a rolling prairie with occasional shallow lakes, and frequent groves of trees. These were planted by homesteaders around what are now modern farm homes, built up, despite years of cold, snow-bound winters, hot, dry summers, drought, and depression. When railroads were built, towns sprang up along the sidings; in recent years new highways have been built to shorten routes and these towns no longer are on the main routes of travel. US 81 passes through few towns, but is bordered by filling stations that have sprung up to take care of increasing traffic.

Nine m. S. of Fairmount, N. Dak., in the Red River Valley (*see N. Dak Tour 1*), US 81 crosses the North Dakota Line, and enters the SISSETON INDIAN RESERVATION (agency at Sisseton). The reservation has been opened to white settlement since 1892 (*see INDIANS and Tour 1*). (*Visitors are cautioned against giving or selling liquor to Indians; this is a Federal offense.*)

At 1 *m.* is a junction with a graveled road.

> Left on the road is WHITE ROCK, 1.8 *m.* (253 pop.), a village in the extreme northeast corner of the State, bordering North Dakota and Minnesota. The Red River, also called the Bois De Sioux, flows through the edge of the village, on its way from Lake Traverse northward to Hudson Bay.

US 81 parallels a neck of LAKE TRAVERSE at 2.2 *m.*, the northern end of this narrow lake, which is over 30 m. long.

At 5.3 *m.* is the TRAVERSE-BOIS DE SIOUX GOVERNMENT DAM which controls the flow of water from Lake Traverse into the Red River.

ROSHOLT, 10 *m.* (369 pop.), was not founded until 1913 when the rich farming area needed a trade and market center. Julius Rosholt was constructing a short-line railroad with which to transport farm commodities to Fairmount, when the Soo Line purchased his enterprise, and the town was named for him. The train which serves the town is known as a mixed train, carrying freight cars and a passenger coach. Blacksmith shops are fast becoming extinct elsewhere, but Rosholt still has two.

At 14.3 m. is a marsh-banked lake called COTTONWOOD LAKE, one of several in the State by that name. The popularity and prevalence of the fast-growing cottonwood trees account for the repetition.

NEW EFFINGTON, 25 m. (1,305 alt., 335 pop.), was founded in 1913. The surrounding community is made up of Scandinavians, Germans, and a few Indians.

Between New Effington and Sisseton is an intensive farming region.

SISSETON, 39 m. (1,202 alt., 1,840 pop.), (see Tour 1), is at the junction with State 10.

At 45 m. is the break from the level Red River Valley to the Coteau des Prairies (see Tours 1 and 2). The road climbs 500 ft. in 4 m., past wooded gulches and steep clay banks. At the crest of the "hills of the prairies," 49 m., the road follows the ridge, known as the HOGBACK because the rounded ridge is not unlike the back of a large hog. From the highway there is a view over the plains region on each side of the Hogback. To the E. is Lake Traverse in the distance.

At 51 m. is a junction with a graveled road.

Left on this unnumbered road to the RENVILLE MONUMENT, 4 m., which was erected in memory of Gabriel Renville, treaty chief of the Sisseton tribe from 1862 to 1892, during which time the whites and Indians were often at odds. Renville, a half-breed, was one of the noted personalities of early Territorial days. The first Renville came from France to the Great Lakes in 1775, later marrying the daughter of Captain Crawford, who served the British at Prairie du Chien. An uncle, Joseph, who married an Indian, was guide and interpreter for the Zebulon Pike expedition and fought in the War of 1812 with the British. Gabriel Renville joined General Sibley's troops during the Minnesota Massacre, and because of his bravery and loyalty he was made chief of scouts in 1864. With other Indians, Renville began an attempt to secure a permanent closed reservation for his tribe. He traveled to Washington several times to plead with officials, but in the year of his death, 1892, the Sisseton Reservation was opened for settlement. He had three wives and 20 children, so that many Renvilles are found living today in the Lake Region.

At 5.2 m. is the abandoned SISSETON AGENCY, a few white frame buildings, that once served as the headquarters for the reservation; the agency was moved to Sisseton. Along the road are chokecherry and wild plum thickets.

PEEVER, 8.1 m. (262 pop.), is a small village of whites, half-breeds, and Indians.

Left from Peever on a graveled road to the THUNDER BIRD ROCK, 12.3 m., the scene of a Sioux legend. When the lightning flashes and thunder rolls, the Sioux say that the mysterious power is revealing itself to them. Just before rain falls, two white birds are said to fly across the darkened sky. These are the signs of a mysterious power. On this high rock the Thunder Bird left his track—a clear, deep imprint of a bird's foot.

At 56 m. is a spring of cool, clear water beside the road.

At 56.2 m. is a junction with a graded road.

Left on this winding road, which was built by Indians as a part of the Federal Emergency Relief program, to the ASCENSION CHURCH, 2.3 m., first Indian church on the Sisseton Reservation. It was built of logs in 1862 in BIG COULEE, and a frame structure has since replaced it. Services are held here Sundays.

At 59.3 m. is HURRICANE LAKE. According to an Indian legend, a hunter was riding his pony along the lake shore when he saw a lone buffalo feeding on the thick grass on the lowland. The hunter took good aim with his bow and arrow, wounding the buffalo above the front leg. In pain, the buffalo turned and pursued the hunter's horse, which became excited by the sudden charge, stumbled and broke his leg. The hunter jumped from the back of the horse to the buffalo and rode him, holding on by the tail. The buffalo ran in circles until he became exhausted and bled to death from the wound.

At 67 m. is the junction with US 12 (*see Tour 2*); from this point US 81 and US 12 are one route for 2 m.

At 69 m. is the junction with US 12 (*see Tour 2*).

Between the junction with US 12 and Watertown, US 81 passes through a level farming country, which was developed in the 1880's by farmers from other midwestern States who followed the farming frontier.

At 81 m. is the junction with a graveled road.

Left on this unnumbered road is PUNISHED WOMAN'S LAKE, 6 m. At this point is the junction with a graveled road. Right on this road is SOUTH SHORE, 6.2 m., a country hamlet. At 8.3 m. is the PUNISHED WOMAN EFFIGY. The two huge rocks are supposed to represent the legendary figures of Wewake, a Sioux maiden, and Wapskasimucwah, a young brave. The girl had spurned the favors of Chemoki, a 60-year old chieftain, for the young lover. The chief, enraged by her resistance, killed Wapskasimucwah and bound the woman to a tree on the north shore of the lake, now known as the Punished Woman's Lake. The bodies were placed on a nearby knoll and the chief, while making an angry speech exhorting his people to fear the example of his erstwhile love and her slain lover, was struck by a bolt of lightning out of a clear sky. The effigy of Chemoki in repentance was placed at the feet of the two lovers.

WATERTOWN, 94 m. (1,750 alt., 10,246 pop.) (see WATERTOWN).

Lake Kampeska, Fish Hatchery.

Watertown is at the junction with US 212 (see Tour 3).

At 96.9 m. is CHAPMAN HILL, the only hill in the region, which was used to test automobiles years ago. A car that could make this slight hill on high was considered good, and many a sale was made on its summit.

At 102.5 m. (L.) is a large lake bed. This region has scores of lakes— sometimes brimming full, and then completely dry a year or two later. This phenomenon is the result of the pressure and weight of glaciers that caused depressions and deposited waste around the edges, as they melted. There are no springs, creeks, or rivers flowing into the lakes to maintain a water level against evaporation, local rains being the only water supply.

At 103.4 m. is CLEAR LAKE (R), one of three lakes by that name in the NE. corner of the State.

At 111 m. is a junction with a graveled road.

Right on this road is HAYTI, 3.8 m. (332 pop.), a village that was named in 1880 when twisted hay, known as "haytie," was used as a fuel during the winter. At 4.1 m. is MARSH LAKE, a popular hunting region.

At 116 m. is the junction with a graveled road.

1. Right on this road is LAKE NORDEN, 1 m., a good duck and pheasant hunting region.

2. Left on this road is LAKE POINSETT, 1.4 m., a public resort.

US 81 skirts the shore of Lake Poinsett at 117.9 m., a lake with good perch and bullhead fishing.

At 119.1 m. is a junction with a graded road.

Left on this road is ARLINGTON BEACH, a resort on Lake Poinsett.

At 119.3 m. LAKE ALBERT is visible (R).

At 123.8 m. is a junction with a graded road.

Left on this road to TETONKAHA LAKE, 4.1 m., a large shallow lake which normally covers 8 sq. m. A band of Sioux Indians, on a hunting trip, lingered here late one fall because the buffalo were numerous. A sudden blizzard set in while they were camping on the shores of this lake, holding them there for the winter. Dry wood was scarce; so they all put their tents together, making one in which they all lived. The buffalo hides used for the tent were taken away in the spring but the poles remained, and Indians who came there later called the place Tetonkaha Bde (the standing of the big lodging house).

ARLINGTON, 133 m. (1,846 alt., 1,060 pop.) (see Tour 4), is at a junction with US 14.

At 148 m. is a junction with a graded road.

Right on this road is LAKE BADUS, 1 m., and around the small lake are families of the LEGIA GREISCHA COLONY. In 1875, 30 families came from Switzerland to America because they wanted more land and better opportunities for their children. They settled first near Stillwater, Minn., and then sent out representatives to locate suitable land for a colony. A lake, about one sq. m. in size, was found and promptly named Lake Badus for a mountain lake in their home country. In 1879 the group moved to Lake Badus and each man over 21 years old filed two claims— a homestead and tree claim. In order to provide shore-lines for as many homesteads as possible, each homestead was only 80 rods wide and a mile long. A cooperative system was followed, and a community store was operated. A schoolhouse built by the original colonists is still in use. While some of the men built houses, others plowed the fields. Joseph Muggli, leader of the group, and his descendants have remained on the original homestead, and the Tuors, Derungs, and Cajacobs are prominent names in the farming region of Lake Badus, although it has lost its old-world atmosphere.

The cooperative principle was discontinued as soon as each of the group became self-supporting, and many of the younger men have entered private businesses in surrounding towns. The only old custom still observed in the community is that at funerals the pall-bearers carry the casket from the church to the cemetery instead of conveying it in a hearse. A few years ago each family made Swiss cheese expertly; but that too is almost a thing of the past.

MADISON, 157 m. (1,669 alt., 5,024 pop.), founded in 1875, attracted early settlers because of its proximity to lakes and the abundance of game and fish within easy reach. Its environs reminded the pioneers so much of the capital of Wisconsin that they gave the embryonic town the same name. Soon it became a trading post, although at that time it was situated 4½ m. E. of the present site. Madison and Herman competed for the county seat, but a compromise was effected and both villages moved to a half-way point, merging and taking the name of Madison.

Noted chiefly for its Eastern State Normal School, its proximity to two lakes, where summer resorts attract many persons seeking recreational facilities, and as the center of a well-developed farming section, Madison has experienced a slow, steady growth ever since its beginning. Never considered a city of great commercial possibilities, it has enjoyed a large trade in flour, dairy products, and thoroughbred livestock.

Its pioneers endured the hardships attendant on life on the prairie—drought, grasshoppers, fuel shortage, severe winters—although Madison, like many other eastern South Dakota cities lacks the glamorous, romantic history common to cities and towns in the western section. It began as an agricultural area, agriculture developed it, and agriculture supports it today.

Before the advent of the white man, this region was a favorite camping ground of Indians. It was near the site of the present city that Wamdesapa (Black Eagle), renegade Indian chief, lived after being ostracized by his people in Minnesota for killing his brother, who was much loved by the tribe.

Established in 1881, EASTERN STATE NORMAL SCHOOL is the oldest institution of its kind in South Dakota. The first structure was destroyed by fire in 1885, but the campus now has six buildings. For nearly 10 years a four-year course was offered, but in 1931, the school became a two-year institution. There is a high school in connection with the normal school, which uses it for practice teaching; the institution has a 15,000-volume library, one of the largest in the State. The GYMNASIUM is near the athletic field. The GARDEN THEATER, with a seating capacity of 2,000, has an orchestra pit and wings on a stage shut in by clever landscaping. At the school is an extensive COLLECTION of stuffed birds (*open to public*).

Other large buildings and institutions in the city include the POST OFFICE, the new county COURTHOUSE, erected at a cost of $128,000, the COMMUNITY HOSPITAL, the ARMORY-AUDITORIUM, and the CARNEGIE LIBRARY. Industries include a packing plant and a creamery.

At the south end of Main St. is the junction with State 19.

Left on this road to LAKE MADISON, 2 *m*. In normal years it is one of eastern South Dakota's most popular resorts. A dancing pavilion, large hotel auditorium, and facilities for all kinds of water sports have contributed to its popularity. On the N. side are about 125 cottages. On the western side is IDLEWOOD PARK near the site of old Madison. WENTWORTH PARK with its small group of cottages is on the eastern shore.

At 161.5 m. is a junction with a graded road.

Left on this road to LAKE HERMAN, 1 m., another popular resort, with cabins and water sports—fishing, swimming, boating—
available during the summer months. Near the N. outlet of the
lake a clump of trees has been identified as the site of the ran-
soming of two white women, taken captive by Inkpaduta and his
band of renegades at the Spirit Lake Massacre in 1857. Inkpaduta's band raided the white settlement at Spirit Lake, Iowa,
killed all the men and carried four women into captivity. One
of the women was killed soon after by Inkpaduta's son. The
other three were taken by the band to a hide-out in the vicinity.
Certain Christian Indians were then sent by the whites to nego-
tiate with Inkpaduta's band for the release of the captives. They
met the outlaw chief under this grove of trees and were successful in their mission. Later a band of Indians, under pressure of
the Government, attacked Inkpaduta's band and killed his two
sons. The story of the rescue of a young girl who was among the
four is told elsewhere (see Tour 11).

JUNIUS, 163 m. (75 pop.), is a small farming community, the
few houses appearing to have been set in their present places in
order that the occupants might have a closer social contact than if
they remained on their farms.

WINFRED, 169 m. (1,500 alt., 251 pop.), exemplified the growing cooperative movement in South Dakota communities; its telephone exchange, the Winfred Telephone Co., is an unusual type of
the mutual association, the majority of which control elevators,
creameries, general stores, and lumber yards.

SALEM, 188 m. (1,520 alt., 1,171 pop.), during the years 1880-
1881, became known as the most important railroad point between
Sioux Falls and Mitchell. It was a flourishing town in early days,
although much of its original prosperity has been lost because of
its location between large cities. Crop failures, acute financial pains
from the over-inflation period, and depression have reduced Salem
to the condition of hundreds of other small towns.

The town has a large, well-equipped school, with the classrooms,
as someone once remarked, "built around the gymnasium." The
gymnasium has helped to develop the interest in athletics that has
carried Salem basketball teams to an enviable record over a long
period of years. Playing games for many years in a frame building
which competitors dubbed a "sheep shed," Salem won the State
basketball championship in 1914 and came within one point of
winning it the next year. The team finished third in championship
tournaments in 1912, 1913, 1923, and 1927. As runner-up in 1925,

it was invited to the National Tournament in Chicago, and lost to Clarkston, Wash. In 1926 it won the State championship, and lost the National Tournament to Fitchburg, Mass., the ultimate national winner, 17 to 16, in an overtime period. Besides the public schools, Salem has a Catholic boarding grade school and high school.

STANLEY CORNERS, 201 m. (sometimes called the Four Corners), consisting of two filling stations, is at the junction with US 16 (*see Tour 5*).

At 215 m. is the junction with a graveled road.

> Right on this road is FREEMAN, 1.5 m. (1,511 alt., 942 pop.), the center of a German-Russian community. Although coming to the United States from Russia, they are of German descent. Most confusing is the fact that so many families bear the same name. It has been said that around Freeman and Bridgewater the "woods are full of Tschetters and Hofers, with several Glanzers and Kleinsassers among them." More than 40 families of Tschetters are recorded, so many in fact, that they are distinguished from each other by numbers. Freeman is a flourishing town in the center of a rich farming section. The farmers in the community are hard-working, thrifty, and competent, and use the best farming methods. An annual grain and poultry show is the climax to the season's agricultural efforts. Here are FREEMAN JUNIOR COLLEGE and two parochial schools.

At 223 m. is the junction with US 18 (*see Tour 7*).

At 236 m. the James River is crossed. The valley, as at other points along its course, is gently sloping and the roads dip down into it with little previous warning. The river meanders lazily across the State, unlike the Missouri River and all streams W. of it, which are swift, restless, and with roughly-broken valleys.

YANKTON, 248.7 m. (1,157 alt., 6,579 pop.) (*see Tour 8*), is at the junction with State 50.

At 249 m. US 81 crosses the Nebraska Line over the MERIDIAN HIGHWAY BRIDGE (*50c for car and driver; 10c for each additional passenger*), 16 m NE. of Crofton, Nebr. (*see Nebr. Tour 3*).

TOUR 11

(Ellendale, N. Dak.)—Aberdeen—Redfield—Platte—(Butte, Nebr.) US 281.

North Dakota Line—Nebraska Line, 238.3 m.

C. M. St. P. & P. R.R. parallels the route between Aberdeen and Tulare.

Graveled roadbed greater part of distance, hard-surfaced at intervals.

Usual accommodations; most towns small.

Following the almost level basin of the James River valley south to Wolsey, midway on the route, US 281 crosses a level plain with little timber. Along this almost straight highway there are few hills north of the valley of the Missouri River.

The James (commonly called "Jim") River has been referred to as the "longest unnavigable river in the world"; its lethargic fingers reach into North Dakota for the source of its waters. So gentle is the valley of the river that it appears to be merely an irregular crease bisecting a flat surface. There is very little current, and in flood times the stream looks more like a long serpentine lake than a river, so imperceptible is its flow. The river drains most of east-central South Dakota, where large, diversified farms predominate and yields of small grain are normally high.

The North Dakota Line is crossed 5 m. S. of Ellendale, N. Dak. (*see N. Dak. Tour 2*).

FREDERICK, 6.8 m. (1,371 alt., 458 pop.), was named for the son of a railroad official when the branch line and town site were established in 1881. Although the town was settled by families from Illinois and Wisconsin, the rural population is largely Finnish. At Savo Hall each May Day there are labor celebrations, often resulting in serious disorder. Among the business enterprises in Frederick is a COOPERATIVE STORE, owned and operated by farmers of the community.

SIMMONS PARK is a recreational and scenic point having an arch built of unusual stones from the Black Hills, Badlands, and other parts of the State. Of special interest are two meteorites about 20 in. in diameter, one at each end of the park. There are also a bathing beach, bathhouse, and picnic grounds. It was near Frederick that Waanata, noted Indian chief, lived at one time during his career (*see Tour 1*).

BARNARD, 14.2 m. (60 pop.), though consisting of only a few business houses and residences, has an elaborate consolidated school, attended by pupils from a wide neighboring territory. In a neat row near the school are several cottages where teachers live during the school year.

At Barnard is the junction with State 10 (*see Tour 1*).

WESTPORT, 19.7 m. (200 pop.), is one of several towns in the Aberdeen territory that have been stifled by proximity to the larger city. Despite the variation in the sizes of the towns, all the upper James River Valley region is quite similar, there being little difference in the soil texture, land contour, and industries. The country has known its fat and lean years, the latter coming with periodic dry seasons.

It was during the summer of 1893, after a period of relentless drought, that this country was invaded by the "rainmakers,'" a small group of shrewd promoters who attempted to exploit the misfortunes of the farmers. Ridden by despair as they watched their green fields wither and brown under the blistering glare of the sun, farmers of the early 1890's were ready to welcome any scheme, no matter how impractical, that might bring precious moisture from cloudless skies. Descending like a welcome Moses upon a thirsty land, a Kansas man named Morris promised to bring water from the heavens instead of coaxing it from a rock, as the Israelitish leader did. He guaranteed to bring water to any community within five days, provided suitable remunerations were forthcoming from the inhabitants.

His first engagement was by the farmers on the eastern slope of the James River valley, where he guaranteed to produce a half-inch of rain over an area of 300 sq. m. within five days, or receive nothing; if successful, he was to be paid $500. Soon after he began operations, dark clouds hovered overhead and the farmers were jubilant. But on the second day a brisk wind sprang up, sweeping the clouds eastward. That evening Watertown, 50 m. distant, received a drenching downpour. The rainmaker said this was his rain and that the wind had carried it away. Undismayed by his first defeat, Morris persisted in his efforts, and on the evening of the last day the promised area had received a full half-inch of rain, and the rainmaker his $500.

Flushed with victory, Morris was besieged with offers from all over the State. He next moved into Aberdeen but found entrenched there a rival named Capt. Hauser, who had begun operations in the top story of a business building, erecting on the roof a long pipe that emitted a stream of evil-smelling gases day and night. With both rainmakers working desperately, Brown Co. residents fully expected a cloudburst. But three days wore away and no rain fell. Capt. Hauser's time was up, but Morris still had two days left. On the last day Morris once more brought rain, dampening the Fourth of July picnics. The thirsty soil received more than .5 in., and Morris again collected $500.

There were three general schools of rainmaking. One group used the artificial explosion method, such as artillery or dynamite. This was supposed to cause condensation and the falling of water. Many communities in North and South Dakota tried to bring rain through their own efforts, and instead of paying the rainmakers $500, bought dynamite and ammunition with which they bombarded the upper air.

Most reputed rainmakers favored the hydrogen method, which consisted of the emission of this light gas in large quantities. A combination of the two methods was used in the most desperate cases. Even a school for rainmakers was started, but history fails to reveal that the school had sufficient graduates to form an alumni association.

Later experiments of rainmakers were not so successful and they lost the confidence of the public. When drought struck the following year, the mayor of Aberdeen set aside a day of prayer for rain, and the rainmakers were forgotten.

At 24.5 *m.* is a junction with a graded road.

Left on this road is the HAMLIN GARLAND HOMESTEAD SITE, 4.6 *m.*, where the author began his writing career as a young man, and where he lived, intermittently, from 1881 to 1884. It was while stacking wheat in a field adjacent to the homestead that his ambition for a literary career was born. Writing in "A Son of the Middle Border" concerning this incident, he says, "Every detail of the daily life on the farm now assumed literary significance in my mind." Garland's poem, "The Color in the Wheat," had the homestead as its setting. "Mrs. Ripley's Trip," his first short story, was followed by "Main Traveled Roads," his first book, the characters of which were his neighbors. After this first book, other works followed, among them numerous short stories. "I began writing when there was no special market," he said. His favorite short story from his own pen is "The Return of a Private," which was based on the return of his father to the Wisconsin farm after the Civil War

"Under the Lion's Paw," another short story, was the outgrowth of a prairie incident. "Ideas for stories come in various ways," he says. Always imbued with a strict sense of right and wrong, he has said, "To spread the reign of justice everywhere should be the aim of the artist."

Biographical studies reveal the deep and lasting influence that Garland's residence in Brown Co. had upon his subsequent career as a man of letters. References to Ordway, Columbia, and Aberdeen abound in his writings. (see ABERDEEN)

For his work "A Daughter of the Middle Border," he received the Pulitzer prize for the best biography in 1921. His last trip to the old homestead was in 1915. In recent years he has been dividing his time between New York and Hollywood. The site of the homestead is marked by a 12-ton boulder which was placed there in July, 1936, at a ceremony sponsored by the South Dakota Writers' League and the Ordway Community Club. A biography, "Hamlin Garland," has been written by the South Dakota Writers' League.

Southwest of the Hamlin Garland Homestead Site is ORDWAY, 6.1 m., so small in population that it is not recorded in census records. Founded in 1881, Ordway enjoyed a meteoric growth, its citizens firm in the belief that Gov. Ordway of Dakota Territory would influence the choosing of the town as the capital. With this stimulus a Chicago syndicate bought land and platted it near Ordway in preparation for the boom. The town flourished for a time until Bismarck was chosen as the capital. The result was a sudden bursting of the bubble and today Ordway is one of the State's many "wide places in the road."

ABERDEEN, 33.2 m. (1,300 alt., 16,725 pop.) (See ABERDEEN).

Northern State Teachers' College, Baseball Park, Stockyards, Melgaard Park, Wylie Park.

Aberdeen is at the junction with US 12 (see Tour 2).

At 44.3 m. is a junction with a graded road.

Left on this road is WARNER, 1 m. (151 pop.), formerly somewhat larger, its decline being due to its proximity to Aberdeen. Despite its small size, the town has an unusually large and well-equipped school, and has developed amateur sports rather extensively during recent years. Warner today is called a town of retired farmers.

At 49.9 m. is a junction with a graveled road.

1. Left on this unnumbered road is DUXBURY, 1 m., a grain elevator; at 8 m. is RONDELL PARK and the OAKWOOD TRADING POST. The park, owned by the John Firey family, pioneer residents, is on the James River and consists of a grove of large oak trees, one of the few groves of natural oak in the

State. The willows and oaks along the river are usually covered with wild grape vines, and in the fall with grapes. It is a popular picnicking place. To the left of the road, across the bridge, is a large prairie boulder with a bronze tablet, marking the site of a trading post established by Major Joseph R. Brown in 1835. The Indian trading post was first occupied by Pierre LeBlanc, but he had trouble with an Indian customer and was murdered. Francis Rondell, a young Frenchman, took charge of the post in 1842 and lived there for nine years, marrying an Indian woman. Rondell named his first son Felix. The latter, in his old age, recalled that as a youth he was taken in a buckboard to St. Paul to enter a boarding school, but the restricted life there did not appeal to him and he actually ran home, about 300 m., returning ahead of his father. Francis Rondell established other trading posts later (see Tours 1 and 2B). Left of the marker, erected by the Aberdeen chapter of the D.A.R., is the scuffed and worn doorsill, the only relic of the trading post. Along the river was a prison camp in which Omaha or Pawnee Indians were held as hostages by the Sioux. These Indians who had come from the Mississippi River, built mud huts, known as dirt lodges, and occasionally artifacts are found along the river banks. The enemy Indians were held for ransom, sold as slaves, and made to work in the gardens by the Sioux, according to stories told by old Indians to Francis Rondell.

Right of the marker, 100 yards, is a buffalo wallow, where buffalo scratched themselves against the walls of the hole that is about 20 ft. long, 16 ft. wide and 5 ft. deep.

Some of the turtles in the river had shells 18 to 24 in. in diameter. In 1933 the James River dried up, leaving scores of mud turtles high, dry, and dead in the river bottom of the park.

2. Right on this road is MANSFIELD, 1.5 m. (194 pop.), a town of retired German farmers each of whom still keeps a cow or two and a flock of chickens.

At 9.4 m. is SCATTERWOOD LAKE, which in wet years is a large body of water with bathing beaches, and game fish; in recent dry years it has been used as a wheat and hay field. There are a few scattered cottonwood trees around the banks, with closed resorts and roller-skating rinks that function on week ends.

At 54 m. is a junction with a graded dirt road.

Left on this road is the James River, 4.4 m.; at this point in 1856 Major Abercrombie built a bridge, which was used on the route from Fort Ridgely, Minn., to Fort Pierre. It was never again used for military purposes, however. At 4.9 m. is the SITE OF FOSTER CITY, no longer existent. A store and several log houses once stood by the Foster homestead. In 1879 the C. M. St. P. & P. R.R. surveyed a line through the town, but it was never built, as it was expected the land would become part of the proposed Drifting Goose Indian Reservation. A bridge has been built where the banks were cut down years ago for an Indian Ford, 5.1 m., and ARMADALE PARK is entered there. The park is in a horseshoe shape, having 120 heavily-timbered acres of cottonwood, willow, ash, elm, and boxelder trees.

The older cottonwoods are 2 and 3 ft. thick. The Upper Yankton-nais tribe of Sioux Indians camped on the island as late as 1879, caching food there for summer camps. In the center of the island is a PAVILION and RACING TRACK, 5.4 m., where Fourth of July celebrations are held each year, as are club and lodge picnics.

At 55.9 m. is the junction with State 20.

Left on this road is MELLETTE, 1 m., a town named for the last governor of Dakota Territory, who was also the first governor of the State. Years ago the region near here was a resting place for wild geese enroute S. along the James River.

At 65.8 m. is a junction with a graveled road.

Left on this road is ASHTON, 1 m. (1,296 alt., 275 pop.), which replaced Old Ashton, first town in Spink Co. and the first county seat. It was Old Ashton that figured in the county seat race with Redfield (see Tour 3).

At 2.8 m. is the junction with an unimproved dirt road. Right on this road is the ABIGAIL GARDNER RESCUE SITE, 3.8 m., at the confluence of the James River and Snake Creek. Here was effected the rescue of Abigail Gardner, a 13-year-old girl who was held captive by a band of Yankton Sioux Indians following the Spirit Lake Massacre of 1857. She and three women were captured and taken north by the Indian party. One of the four was tortured to death near Flandreau and another murdered by Roaring Cloud, son of the ruthless Inkpaduta, who figured in the Spirit Lake Massacre. A third was rescued by two Christian Indians, while Abigail Gardner's freedom was obtained through two missionaries, Riggs and Williamson, and three Christian Indians, after she had been subjected to long and severe torture.

REDFIELD, 76.9 m. (1,295 alt., 2,573 pop.) (see Tour 3), is at the junction with US 212.

TULARE, 87.4 m. (1,317 alt., 257 pop.), accounts for its name in two different ways. According to one version, it was named for an Indian chief. The other version, more interesting but probably less authentic, is that the name was the outgrowth of a series of "tall" stories told by two brothers to passengers on trains that halted on an uphill grade near the present town. So persistent were they in their gross exaggerations, that after a few trips over the route it became customary for the passengers to refer to the brothers as the "two liars." From this, the story says, the two words were contracted into "Tulare."

BONILLA, 98.4 m. (100 pop.), has for many years been a feeding ground for pheasants. A few years ago William Hale Thompson, while mayor of Chicago, came here with a group of sportsmen to hunt.

At 107.4 m. is the junction with US 14 (see Tour 4), the two highways following the same route for 4 m.

WOLSEY, 111.4 m. (1,353 alt., 445 pop.) (see Tour 4).

At 114.4 m. is the junction with US 14 (see Tours 4 and 11A). US 281 continues through generally level country, with much of the broken ground showing the effects of erosion by dust storms. In this vicinity the Federal Government is carrying on soil conservation work, as much as 6 in. of top-soil having been blown away by persistent winds during the drought period. With this top soil has also gone the nitrogen so essential to crop nourishment.

This region also lies in the shelterbelt area. In the spring of 1936 approximately one million trees were planted. Those adapted to this particular soil were chosen.

At 120.4 m., is a junction with a graveled road.

Left on this road is VIRGIL, 1 m. (1,341 alt., 131 pop.), a hamlet on the C. M. St. P. & P. R.R. The village was founded in 1882, but was wiped out by a tornado shortly afterward. It was rebuilt in 1883 when the railroad arrived.

At 134.4 m. is the junction with State 34.

1. Left on this road is LANE, 2 m. (220 pop.), a town of retired farmers. A large consolidated school is here. Once the center of a prosperous farming community, the town has been stripped of most of its business, with the advent of improved roads to larger trading points.

At 10.2 m. is WOONSOCKET (Ind., City of mists) (1,308 alt., 1,128 pop.), named for Woonsocket, R. I. The most noteworthy feature of the town is picturesque LAKE PRIOR, an artificial body of water covering several acres in the center of the town. The lake was made many years ago by flooding a natural depression, and has been several times improved. A Government aid project made possible the facing of the shores with multicolored rock, improvement of swimming facilities, and restocking with fish. An island in the center of the lake is reached by an arched bridge.

Woonsocket at one time boasted the world's most powerful artesian well, from which a stream of water rocketed 96 ft. into the air. Because the water could not be controlled on account of the enormous pressure, and after numerous villagers had been drenched when the wind suddenly veered, the well was closed. Woonsocket is in one of the best artesian basins in the State, and many farms obtain their water supply by such wells. The town is noted for its excellent water, both hard and soft, depending on the depth to which a well is dug.

The town missed an opportunity in early days to have an important cereal factory—that of Post—when the governing body became skeptical of the intentions of a stranger who wanted the town to give him land on which to build his factory. Post considered Woonsocket a good site—in "the heart of the grain belt," as he said,—but because he was refused, he took his proposal to Battle Creek, Mich., where he opened business.

Woonsocket is the center of an area peopled by Scandinavians, Irish, and Germans. It has one of the largest Catholic churches in the State, and a parochial school.

2. Right on State 34 is WESSINGTON SPRINGS, 5 m. (1,410 alt., 1,418 pop.), set picturesquely in the recesses of the Wessington Hills. The town took its name from the hills and from the copious springs that are here. It was founded in 1880 by a small group of settlers under the Rev. A. B. Smart, who conceived the idea of starting the town on a "strong, pure basis of temperance, education, and Christianity." WESSINGTON SPRINGS JUNIOR COLLEGE, belonging to the Free Methodists, was founded here in 1887.

People from several counties gathered at Wessington Springs during the summer of 1893 to see a balloon ascension. The balloonist sat on a trapeze below the gas bag. He sought to improve his act by tying a hard slipknot to release the parachute instead of using a knife. As the band played the balloonist ascended. He first hung by his toes, then by one hand, and finally by his toes. When he prepared to come back to earth he discovered to his dismay that the knot would not slip. Up and up he went until he became a mere speck against the blue. Eventually the gases cooled and he landed only a few hundred yards from his starting point.

The WESSINGTON HILLS—a long, narrow range extending approximately 50 m.—were named for a man who was tortured to death by the Indians in 1863. These hills in early days were a hide-out of bands of horse rustlers and other renegades, the timber-lined draws affording excellent concealment for their movements, and the summits enabling them to discern approaching parties. Three m. N. of Wessington Springs is TURTLE PEAK, a long, high hill rising 500 ft. above the surrounding lowlands. It was named for an Indian chief. From this point distant towns—Woonsocket, Alpena, Huron—can be seen on clear days. Upon the highest portion of the hill (the whole range is a glacial moraine) is a low, broad mound of earth, 50 ft. in diameter and about 3 ft. high. Upon its southern slope is the gigantic figure of a turtle. The figure is constructed of stone 4 to 6 in. in diameter. There are many picnic and camping spots in the fastnesses of the hills, used by school classes and other groups for summer outings.

US 281 continues S. through a diversified farming section, not a single town being passed in 28 m.

PLANKINTON, 162.4 m. (1,528 alt., 715 pop.) (*See Tour 5*), is at the junction with US 16.

West of Plankinton US 281 and US 16 are united for 19 m. (*see Tour 5*).

At 181.3 m. US 281 again turns (L); US 16 continues W. (R). The nature of the country has been gradually, almost imperceptibly, changing. In this section farms are less numerous than farther N. and E., and rainfall is normally lighter. It is between the eastern farming section and the western ranching country.

PLATTE, 205.4 m. (1,139 pop.), was first settled in 1882 by a colony of Hollanders, and many descendants of the original immigrants still live in the vicinity. Situated at the end of a railroad line and in the center of a wide trade territory, Platte has many business houses, including a large creamery and flour mill. Its paved Main St. is a long landscaped boulevard. There are many attractive homes here, and a large, well-equipped school provides excellent educational facilities. The annual county fair held in Platte each fall is one of the outstanding fairs in the State. Northwest of town is LAKE PLATTE, where both swimming and fishing are available.

South of Platte the country becomes more hilly as the breaks of the Missouri River valley are reached. There are many dips and turns as the highway weaves its course down to the river bottom. From the heights above the river is a scenic view of the winding, indomitable Big Muddy, its green, tree-fringed shores standing out in sharp contrast with the light-colored sand bars between which the stream winds its restless way.

WHEELER, 221.4 m. (*see Tour 7*), is the junction with US 18 (*see Tour 7*) the two highways following the same course SW. for 10 m. Just S. of Wheeler the Missouri River is crossed.

At 231.4 m. the two highways separate, US 281 continuing S.; US 18 branches R. (*see Tour 7*).

FAIRFAX, 235.4 m. (393 pop.), was settled following the opening of the Rosebud Indian Reservation in 1890. Formerly this region was all Indian country but the closed area of the reservation has been reduced, now covering only Todd Co.; within its former boundaries, however, are many Indians, living under approximately the same regulations as those in the restricted part (see IN-DIANS). The country S. and E. of Fairfax is quite sandy, and soil erosion is prevalent during drought years when the grass has been grazed short or the crops are poor.

In normal years the light, sandy soil grows good crops, especially of corn and potatoes.

At 238.3 m. US 281 crosses the Nebraska Line, 10 m. N. of Butte, Nebr. (see Nebr. Tour 4).

TOUR 11A

Junction with US 281—Huron—Mitchell—Junction with State 50. US 14 and State 37.

Junction with US 281 to Junction with State 50, 114.3 m.

Paralleled roughly by C. M. St. P. & P. R.R.

About one-half of route with hard-surfaced roadbed, rest graveled.

Accommodations at all towns.

This route runs through the center of the east-central section of South Dakota, following roughly the fertile James River valley. The country is alternatingly level and slightly rolling, and is crossed or touched by four east-west highways. There are few curves in the road, which is featured by many miles of well-improved, "plumb line" stretches.

From the junction with US 281 (see Tour 11), 3 m. south of Wolsey this route is united with US 14 (see Tour 4) to Huron.

HURON, 11 m. (1,288 alt., 11,733 pop.) (see HURON).

State Fair Grounds, Huron College, Municipal Airport.

At Huron is the junction with State 37; this route leaves US 14 (see Tour 4) and turns S. (R) on State 37.

South of Huron the road crosses a level country, glimpses of distant hills breaking the otherwise unvarying prairie expanse.

At 39 m. is the junction with a graded road.

Right on this dirt road to the SAND HILLS, 4 m. These hills, topped with trees, are a popular goal of picnickers and hikers during the spring and fall. There is a story that the hills were once a rendezvous for horse thieves, the elevation making them a vantage point for rustlers who could see approaching parties for considerable distances. Residents of the vicinity tell of Horse Thief Cave, supposedly in the fastnesses of these hills, but no one has ever been able to find it.

FORESTBURG, 39.2 m. (200 pop.), was so named because of the number of trees near the town site.

The soil along the James River in this vicinity is noted for its fertility and its adaptability to the raising of watermelons and muskmelons. Every fall roadside stands are built along the highway and rarely a mile is passed without seing one. Here the melons are dispensed to customers without the necessity of a "middleman." Besides local sales, tons are shipped each year to other regions.

The brush and trees fringing the course of the James River harbor many pheasants and rabbits, the latter often becoming so numerous that concerted drives are staged and hundreds of the little animals are killed in an afternoon. When too numerous, they become destructive to small trees and other vegetation. The rabbits are usually shipped East, where the pelts are made into coats and other garments for women, the original name of rabbit being discarded for a trade name—lapin—upon the appearance of the coats in shop windows.

At 41.1 m. is a junction with a graded but winding road.

Right on this road is RUSKIN PARK, 0.8 m., in a large wooded horseshoe bend of the James River. With 50 cottages of from one to four rooms, with fishing, camping, and other recreational facilities, Ruskin Park is a popular spot during summer months. Dancing, roller-skating, golf, tennis, baseball, boating, horse-racing, and automobile racing constitute the diversified amusements available to the public. The mile racetrack is known to racing drivers from Indianapolis to Denver as being one of the fastest dirt tracks in the world. A recent survey showed some of the trees in the park to be 150 years old; there is one elm with a trunk so large that it cannot be encircled by three men joining hands. A large dance pavilion, the sides constructed of prism glass doors, 12 ft. high, is at the northern edge of the park. The material employed was used in some of the buildings at the World's Fair in Chicago in 1893.

At 43.3 m. State 37 turns R. at the junction with State 34.

Left (straight ahead) on State 34, a graveled road, is ARTESIAN, 6 m. (528 pop.), so named because it is in the center of a large artesian water basin. Three villages, FEDORA, 13.2 m.; ROSWELL, 18.4 m.; and VILAS,, 23.5 m., are passed before

HOWARD, 26.6 m. (1,564 alt., 1,191 pop.), is reached. Howard is the seat of government for Miner Co., and has a municipal tourist park and artificial lake.

At 62.5 m. LAKE MITCHELL is passed, the highway describing an arc and crossing the wall of the dam that impounds this large artificially formed body of water (*see MITCHELL*).

MITCHELL, 64.1 m. (1,312 alt., 12,834 pop.), (*See MITCHELL.*)

Corn Palace, Lake Mitchell, Custer Battlefield Highway Building, Indian Village, Hackberry Trees.

Mitchell is at the junction with US 16 (*see Tour 5*).

ETHAN, 77.2 m. (1,345 alt., 301 pop.), was named for Ethan Allen of Revolutionary War fame. The village is typical of others whose future has been determined through their proximity to a city.

DIMOCK, 81.2 m. (200 pop.), is the center of a community of mixed nationalities, many of the residents being of German-Russian descent.

At the northern outskirts of Dimock is the junction with a graveled road.

Left on this road is the NEW ELM SPRINGS MENNONITE COLONY, 8 m., on the banks of the James River. Following the unsuccessful migration to Canada, more than a hundred Mennonites returned to South Dakota late in 1936 and resettled here, beginning an attempt to regain their once prosperous financial status through their thrifty methods of community living. (See Tour 5, ROCKPORT MENNONITE COLONY).

PARKSTON, 87.3 m. (1,400 alt., 1,272 pop.), the largest town in Hutchinson Co., is surrounded by well-improved farms. Many farmers of the section are of German and Bohemian ancestry, their thrift and industrious habits having created many substantial homes. Drought years have taken their toll here as elsewhere, but, as residents of neighboring communities say, many of the long-time farmers in the vicinity have considerable money "in the sock," sufficient to tide them over until good times return.

TRIPP, 99.3 m. (1,563 alt., 901 pop.) (*see Tour 7*), is at the junction with US 18.

At 114.3 m. is a junction with State 50 (*see Tour 8*), 5 m. W. of Tyndall.

TOUR 12

(Linton,   N.   Dak.)—Gettysburg—Pierre—Winner—(Springview, Neb.) US 83.

North Dakota Line to Nebraska Line, 254.8 m.

This route is not paralleled by any railroads, but crosses several. A bus line operates between Pierre and Winner.

Roadbed graveled.

Hotel and tourist accommodations at above towns.

US 83 passes southward over a rolling, almost treeless stretch of prairie, much of it virgin, bisecting South Dakota's transitional farming-grazing area and the eastern fringe of the cattle region. The highway roughly parallels the Missouri River between the North Dakota Line and Presho; but the river is actually viewed only where it is crossed at Pierre. Although the Missouri River is one of the largest in the world, its valley is very narrow—from two to three miles—and is bordered by steep bluffs and breaks. The present course of the river marks the western edge of the last ice sheet. Consequently the soil E. of the river is composed of glacial drift and studded with stones; to the W. is Pierre clay, or gumbo. (*See GEOLOGY*).

Most of the State's early history took place along the banks of the Missouri River, which was the thoroughfare traveled by explorer, trapper, and missionary. In the middle of the 18th century the Arikaras occupied the banks of the river and its tributaries. Then the Sioux waged a 75-year fight against them and finally drove them northward out of the State. The Verendrye brothers' expedition followed the river southward in 1743, leaving the first record of white men in the State at Ft. Pierre (*see HISTORY and Tour 4*). The Lewis and Clark expedition went up the Missouri in 1804 and returned in 1806; the Astorians traveled the course in 1811. The early history centered around the fur trade, and this in turn centered on the banks of the Missouri. The fur trade decreased with the growing scarcity of fur, and was finally disrupted by the Civil War.

US 83 was built for one mile on the North Dakota Line, 7 m. S. of Hull, N. Dak. (*see N. Dak. Tour 3*).

At 1.5 *m.* is a junction with a graveled road.

Right on this road is POLLOCK, 10 *m.*; at 13 *m.* is a ferry across the Missouri River, one of the few still in operation along the river. From there a dirt road, good only in dry weather, winds through the river breaks, inhabited almost exclusively by Indians of the Standing Rock Reservation (see Tour 2). The Indians attempt to farm the rugged land, most of them living in log cabins, with shade huts, tents, and meat-drying poles nearby.

HERREID, 7 m. (594 pop.), was named for the late Gov. Charles Herreid when the town was founded in 1901. There are German-Russian families in the community and their native tongues are used to a large extent in business places, as well as in the homes.

At 9 m. is the junction with State 10 (see Tour 1).

MOUND CITY, 12.2 m. (204 pop.), is one of the five inland county seats in South Dakota. When the Minneapolis, St. Paul & Sault Saint Marie R.R. was built to Herreid in 1901, most of the population of Mound City moved there. The first court was held in an old machine shop, while the second session was given quarters in a haymow. On the north edge of the town there is a draw in which insignia of soldiers and Indian relics have been found together, indicating an unrecorded pursuit, probably in 1863 or 1864.

At 28.3 m. is a junction with US 12 (see Tour 2); the two routes are united for 2 m.

SELBY, 30.3 m. (1,877 alt., 613 pop.) (see Tour 3), is at the junction with US 12.

Between the junction with US 12 and Pierre, the road passes through the Missouri River ranges, where undulating, treeless prairies are broken by sharp, irregular hills rising from deep river bottoms, and where only an occasional farm is seen. For miles not a house is visible, and only here and there a fence. At the summit of each ridge a panorama of the immediate sections suddenly unfolds, and at the top of the next the scene is surprisingly similar.

LOWRY, 47.2 m. (89 pop.), has two tall red elevators and a corral for cattle.

At Lowry is a junction with a graveled road, an unnumbered county highway.

Right on this road and past AKASKA (203 pop.) (unimproved road from Akaska), is old LE BEAU, 17 m., one of the many ghost towns on the South Dakota prairies that owe their deserted state to some cruel quirk of fate beyond the control of the people who lived there. In the case of Le Beau it was not one disaster, it was several—fires, disappearance of the open range, abandonment of the railroad. Once a flourishing and boisterous cattle-shipping point of 500 population, Le Beau, in 10 years, faded to a mere wraith. For years a ferryboat plied across the clay-colored waters of the Missouri River, bringing cattle from the western range for shipment East. When the river was low, ranchers "swam" the stock across. The town, too, was a distributing point for Indian cattle. Every fall when the big cattle shipments were made, the town was packed with Indians and cowboys. The cowboys were bent on a good time and were willing to pay for it.

Then in 1910 a fire wiped out most of the town and much of it was never rebuilt. This was the first of a series of disasters for the luckless village, for in 1911 a second fire destroyed most of the remaining buildings. By this time the range was disappearing, homesteaders were scarring the prairie with their plows, and large cattle outfits were folding up. Many of the buildings were torn down and moved elsewhere, although the railroad company continued sending trains quite regularly over the line until 1918 to pick up stock. After 1918 the trips became more and more infrequent and finally stopped. The rails were torn up, the trading post was moved away, and Le Beau was left with a lone building—a monument to the prosperity the town once enjoyed.

At 65.4 *m.* is the junction with US 212 (*see Tour 3*); US 212 and US 83 are united for 10 m.

GETTYSBURG, 70.5 *m.* (2,082 alt., 1,414 pop.) (*see Tour 3*).

At 75.4 *m.* is the junction with US 212 (*see Tour 3*).

At 87.5 *m.* is a junction with a graveled road.

Right on this road is AGAR, 0.7 *m.* (200 pop.), a cattle-shipping point with a general store and a few houses. West from Agar, 12 *m.*, is the junction with a dirt road leading (R) to the SUTTON RANCH, 6 *m.*, which has a private herd of about 100 buffalo. Starting with three head from the "Scotty" Philip herd several years ago, the group has increased by propagation and additional purchase to the present number. Among the group are two "cattalos" (a cross between buffaloes and native cattle), smooth-haired animals with the characteristic buffalo hump above the shoulders. The buffalo are allowed to run at will along the Missouri River breaks and bottom land, their "rustling" ability carrying them through the bitterest winters with only range grass to sustain them. These animals have largely forsaken the nomadic tendencies of their ancestors and are generally content to remain the year around on the home range. Only occasionally does one wander away. Such was the case in 1936 when an old buffalo appeared in a farmer's yard near Witten in the Rosebud country. The children screamed and climbed the windmill; the

GENERAL STORE

excited parents called the neighbors on the party telephone line
and soon all were there with automobiles. Using cars, the farmers chased the decrepit old buffalo until he fell exhausted and
died.

The Sutton Ranch, one of the largest in the State, comprises
more than 15 sections over which approximately 1,100 cattle
roam. Every year a rodeo is held at the ranch and a few of the
more skilled broncho "twisters" ride, or attempt to ride, some
of the buffaloes. A buffalo team drawing a wagon is another
feature of the celebration.

On the ranch was the largest tree in the State—a giant cottonwood, measuring nearly 40 ft. in circumference at the base. It
was blown down during a gale a few years ago.

ONIDA, 97.8 m. (1,878 alt., 605 pop.), was the center of a
homestead boom in the early 1880's during which settlers came by
ox trains into the new, rough country. Houses sprang up almost
overnight in 1883, and several former New York State residents
gave the town its name, a modification of Oneida. Small patches
of land were broken here and there by those who had horses or
mules, and the yield of garden and grain crops amounted to a
bumper harvest the first year. Mail arrived once a week by stage
from Sioux City, Iowa.

The Onida residents in 1883 began a movement to secure the
county seat, competing with Clifton. The citizens of the county
went to the polls, and the result was Onida 504 votes, Clifton 499.
However, nine men did not vote in the election but declared themselves in favor of Clifton, after which the case was taken to court.
On April 9, 1885, a group of Onida men appeared in Clifton at
noon and marched off with the safe and county records, depositing
them in the Onida Hotel. A few days later the county sheriff, a
Clifton supporter, and a group came for the records, which were
given up without resistance. Two weeks later the case was heard
in district court at Pierre, and the judge ruled in favor of Onida.
As it was too late in the day, attendants from each town retired
to the hotel. However, one Onida man slipped out, hired a team
and drove to Onida, spreading the word along in Paul Revere
fashion. Early the next morning a large party of Onida people
hitched up their teams and drove to Clifton, arriving before the
Clifton men returned from Pierre. In half an hour the safe and
records were loaded and carried back to Onida, where they have
since remained.

Right from Onida, on an unnumbered road, is a NEGRO COL-
ONY, 15 m., which was started in 1880 and still has a few negro

families. Negroes who live on these farms, where wintry blasts howl over the prairies, tell how Norval Blair "done come na'th" back in 1880 after the Negroes had been set free. Blair brought with him his six children, all of whom filed claims; at one time their combined holdings soared near the $75,000 mark, but drought and taxes, coupled with a drop in real estate values, brought a crash. Blair is remembered in sporting circles as the owner of an excellent string of racing horses, outstanding among them being Johnny Bee, recognized as the fastest horse in South Dakota from 1907 to 1909. Other Negroes followed the trek to Sully Co. until there was a settlement of 400 in this new country, far from their native haunts. Among the Negroes induced to come to the State was a man named McGruder, who began life as a slave on a Mississippi plantation and later owned the same farm. Following the World War, many of the Negroes packed up and moved, until today there are only about 100 left. A cemetery association is the only community enterprise; but they still get together for occasional wakes and sings.

At 111.3 m. is the junction with US 14 (*see Tour 4*); US 83 and US 14 are united between this point and Ft. Pierre (*see Tour 4*).

PIERRE, 129.9 m. (1,442 alt., 4,013 pop.) (*see PIERRE*).

State Capitol, Memorial Building and Museum, Farm Island, Indian School.

FT. PIERRE, 132.8 m. (1,437 alt., 777 pop.) (*see Tour 4*), is at the junction with US 14.

South of Ft. Pierre, US 83 crosses Bad River, so named because of its destructive activities in the spring season. The river drains part of the Badlands and large stretches of rolling prairie; but when it reaches the Missouri River during high water, it backs up, causing frequent floods. At other seasons, it is a small, sluggish stream.

At the S. end of the bridge is a graded street.

Left on this graded road is LEWIS AND CLARK PARK, 0.5 m., at the confluence of the Missouri and Bad Rivers. At this site the Lewis and Clark expedition stopped and visited an Indian village in 1804. So anxious were the Indians to have the explorers remain, that blood was nearly shed before they were allowed to proceed up the river. On the return trip the party slipped past the place without stopping. A recreational park, with outdoor fireplaces, has been laid out here by the Works Progress Administration.

At 133.2 m. GUMBO BUTTES rise abruptly along the E. side of US 83, exposing a black shale formation almost devoid of vegetation. Yucca plants, commonly known as Spanish bayonets, cling to the hillsides, and in spring have a wax-like pink and yellow blossom. Magpies, although native to more mountainous regions, are often seen along the road.

At 134.4 m. is a junction with a graveled road, known as the Bad River Road, a new, unnumbered State highway and a short cut to US 14 near Midland (*see Tour 4*).

At 159.1 m. is a junction with US 16; US 83 and US 16 are one route for 14.9 m. (*see Tour 5*).

VIVIAN, 161.5 m. (200 pop.) (*see Tour 5*).

PRESHO, 173.4 m. (1,764 alt., 517 pop.), (*see Tour 5*).

US 83 continues S. through a range country with scattered houses, crossing the White River at 187.6 m., its tree-lined banks breaking the prairie landscape.

JORDAN, 212.3 m. (60 pop.), is at the junction with US 18 (*see Tour 7*); US 83 and US 18 are united for 21.4 m. (*see Tour 7*).

WINNER, 221.1 m. (1,860 alt., 2,136 pop.), (*see Tour 7*).

COLOME, 233.2 m. (531 pop.), (*see Tour 7*).

At 233.7 m. is the junction with US 18 (*see Tour 7*).

The high butte W. of the highway, at 249.8 m., is TURTLE BUTTE. The Keyapaha River is crossed at 254 m.

WEWELA, 254.2 m. (49 pop.) is a trading post.

At 254.8 m. US 83 crosses the Nebraska Line 15 m. N. of Springview, Nebr. (*see Nebr. Tour 5*).

TOUR 13

(Bowman, N. Dak.)—Buffalo—Belle Fourche—Spearfish—Deadwood—Lead—(Newcastle, Wyo.) US 85.

North Dakota Line—Wyoming Line, 164.1 m.

Not paralleled by any R.R.

Roadbed is graveled and hard-surfaced alternately.

Between Buffalo and Belle Fourche, a distance of 74 m., there are
no towns and only two filling stations. Motorists should check their
gas and water carefully before entering upon this stretch.

Hotel and tourist accommodations available at above-named towns.

US 85 offers a wide variety of scenery from the North Dakota
line southward. It passes through the eastern edge of the Cave
Hills, and crosses numerous picturesquely named creeks, redolent
of sagebrush and prairie. Between Bowman and the Black Hills
are Spring Creek, Cold Turkey, Alkali, North Grand River,
Crooked Creek, Big Nasty, Bull Creek, Jones Creek, Box Elder,
Sheep Creek, South Grand, Buffalo Creek, Clark's Fork, North
Moreau, Sand Creek, South Moreau, Four Mile, Twelve Mile,
Antelope Creek, Indian Creek, Owl Creek, Crow Creek, and the
Belle Fourche River. The territory between the State Line and
Macy is primarily a ranching country, well-watered, well-grassed,
and with sufficient shelter for stock. North of Macy the road runs
through a sandy-loam region. Between Macy and Belle Fourche
US 85 crosses the desolate gumbo, 40 miles wide. South of Belle
Fourche it skirts the edge of the Black Hills, a pleasant region of
scattered groves and prosperous farms, and continues through the
wooded Hills to the Wyoming Line. The region between the North
Dakota Line and Belle Fourche is antelope country, and glimpses
of these beautiful animals are occasionally caught.

Section a. North Dakota Line to Junction with US 14, 133 m.

Eighteen miles S. of Bowman, N. Dak., US 85 crosses the North
Dakota Line and leaves the broad flats of North Grand River
behind (*see N. Dak. Tour 4*). Passing over the divide between
North Grand River and Crooked Creek, it climbs through the eastern edge of the Cave Hills.

At *6 m.* there is a junction with a dirt road.

Right on this road are the CAVE HILLS, 2 *m.* These take their
name from a cave in one of them, although the cave is small and

has no significance. These hills are a part of the Custer National Forest. They·are a little lower than the Slim Buttes and the Short Pines, having lost their limestone caps. They have rounded tops with a sprinkling of pines. There is one particularly beautiful spot, Riley Pass, named for a horse rancher of early days. At the top of one of the hills is a popular picnic ground. The road through the Cave Hills is not graveled, but is good in dry weather.

LUDLOW, 8 *m.*, consists of a store, post office, and school beside the road. Around the school yard is a high, metal-mesh fence, and the children are forbidden to go outside this fence during school hours. This is for protection against the cars that customarily go by in a cloud of dust and gravel.

South of Ludlow the road runs in a general southwesterly direction through a hilly, well-watered and well-grassed country.

BUFFALO, 30.5 *m.* (2,800 alt., 250 pop.), the seat of Harding Co., is the center of a large ranching region, divided about equally between cattle and sheep. (*see Tour 2A.*) It serves a very large trade territory for a town of its size

Buffalo, a typical prairie town, is a lineal descendant of homestead days. Almost every inhabitant of the town who was of age in 1909-10, including the professional men, proved up on a claim. But it is not only a prairie town; it is still a range town. Big hats are the rule and other cowboy accoutrements are not uncommon; although anyone appearing in full cowboy regalia, as exemplified in the movies, would either be laughed out of town or placed under observation.

In 1909 the town of Buffalo was laid out on the N. bank of Grand River, in the geographical center of the county, with the idea of its becoming the seat of the newly organized county. But its ambition did not go unchallenged. Camp Crook (*see Tour 2A*), on the western edge of the county, situated on the banks of the Little Missouri River, was already an old town and was not at all backward about asserting its prior claim to county seat honors. Parties from both towns toured the county to secure votes, and their arguments were reinforced by certain liquid inducements to enable the voters to think more clearly. While the battle was at its height, a widely known and well-liked ranch hand from the eastern edge of the county staged an individual celebration in Camp Crook and was locked in the town jail overnight. In the morning he was found dead; and the resentment of the eastern half of the county at the occurrence was sufficient to swing the victory to the rival town.

Buffalo, like other prairie towns, is a blending of the old and new. There are still small frame stores, with flamboyant high square fronts, and also substantial modern buildings—a new hotel, a surprisingly large garage and filling station, and good restaurants. The courthouse is wooden, as are the dwelling houses; a beginning of tree planting has been made. and the town is outgrowing its cruder stage.

Buffalo still retains the spirit of the pioneer days. Hospitality and friendliness are the rule. No one enters the town for the second time as a stranger. The fact that it is 50 m. from the nearest railroad has perhaps served to preserve the pioneer flavor.

Buffalo is at the junction with State 8 (*see Tour 2A*).

At 32.5 *m.* is the junction with State 8 (*see Tour 2A*).

REDIG, 52.8 *m.* (5 pop.), consists of a store and post office.

At 54.8 *m.* are the Crow Buttes, a group of lofty mud buttes where a fierce battle between the Sioux and Crow Indians was fought before the coming of the white men. This is an opportunity to study that curious phenomenon, a mud butte. Formed of gumbo and clay, rising abruptly from the plain without a spear of vegetation, every rain that washes off its sides is thick with gumbo detritus, and it seems strange that it is not thus made level with the surrounding plain. It is often possible to pick up fossils around its base, since the formation is somewhat similar to that of the Badlands (*see GEOLOGY*).

At 57.2 *m.* is the junction with State 79, a graveled road.

Left on State 79 is MASON, 5.6 *m.* (3 pop.), a general store and post office.

At 5.9 *m.* State 79 turns R. and follows the same section line for 30 m., those lines which checkerboard the country, one mile apart, according to the original U. S. survey. Within this distance there is a correction line, a jog to compensate for expanding meridians. The road occasionally swings R. or L. a little to keep to the wind-swept ridges; but it always returns to the same section line.

At 18.4 *m.* (R) there is an extremely high hill rising from the level plain. On Government maps it is marked HAYSTACK BUTTE, but every old-timer knows it as SQUARE TOP. It is shaped roughly like a ridge-poled tent.

At 21.7 *m.* (L) is a lofty ridge with a rocky crest which gives its name of CASTLE ROCK; a splendid view is obtained from its summit.

In the distance (L), are two conical hills, very appropriately named DEER'S EARS.

CASTLE ROCK, 23.6 *m.* (4 pop.), is a store and post office.

At 37.2 *m.* is a very good view of Newell and the Belle Fourche irrigation project.

NEWELL, 41.6 *m.* (2,820 alt., 580 pop.), is at the junction with US 212 (see Tour 3).

At 63.5 *m.* (L) is the old abandoned post office of MACY. This former post office dates back to the earliest days of the country's settlement. Macy was an Englishman who homesteaded on the South Moreau River, and was reported to have written back to England that he had an estate of 160 acres entirely planted to sage. People used to travel long distances to get their mail at Macy. Some of the Macy family still live there.

Between Buffalo and Macy the country is somewhat flatter than that farther N., but is well-grassed and a good sheep region. Macy, however, is on the northern edge of a gumbo belt 40 m. wide, which deserves special mention and description.

THE GUMBO, as it is universally called, is a desolate region looking like a sea with long rollers that have suddenly become petrified. Few people make their homes here the year round. It is too bleak, and the soil conditions are too obstinate. Gumbo, geologically known as Pierre clay, is a black soil of almost unbelievable viscosity when wet. In the days of freight wagons, the freighters were obliged to remove their brake blocks as soon as the gumbo began to "roll." It is characteristic of gumbo to "ball up," and the feet of unlucky humans or animals forced to travel in it seem to grow continually larger. It is practically impossible to move a bunch of stock across it when wet. Gen. Crook and his cavalry, coming from the Battle of Slim Buttes, tried to cross the gumbo in a ten-day rain. Before they reached the Belle Fourche river half of the horses were dead of exhaustion and they had had to kill and eat many others. Gen. Crook in his report said that he doubted whether in the annals of the American Army there had been a journey involving so much hardship and suffering.

The gumbo, when dry, is creased with innumerable wrinkles, like the face of a very old man. When rain comes, these wrinkles disappear and the soil flows together in a sea of mud. It is difficult to farm when it is too dry, and impossible to work when wet. Therefore, the farmer's activities are apt to be somewhat curtailed at inconvenient times.

On the gumbo there is no sod. Each spear of grass grows independently from its own root. Compared with sod grass, gumbo grass is sparse; but in content it is much richer. Gumbo lambs always outweigh the sand lambs in the fall. In the summer the gumbo is apt to be covered with herds of cattle and bunches of sheep from the surrounding regions. Lack of water is the chief difficulty, but dams are solving that problem where water holes are not available.

At 99 *m.* US 85 leads over a series of steep gumbo hills, from the last of which there is a splendid view of the fertile Belle Fourche Valley. The contrast between the greenness of the irrigated valley and the brown of the gumbo is most striking.

At 101.6 *m.* is the BELLE FOURCHE AIRPORT, an undeveloped flying field.

BELLE FOURCHE (Bell Foosh), 104.1 m. (3,013 alt., 2,314 pop.), takes its name (beautiful fork) from its site at the fork of the Belle Fourche River and Redwater Creek. It is the scene of the Black Hills Round-Up (*see below*), and has historical associations and a commercial importance out of all proportion to its size, husky young city though it is. Its selection as a town site by the Fremont, Elkhorn and Missouri Valley R.R. was the signal for the demise of its rival, old Minnesela 3½ m. away. (*see below*).

Belle Fourche was at one time the capital of a far-flung cattle empire, and for several years it was the greatest primary cattle-shipping point in the world. The young town served a really immense territory. The C. M. St. P. & P. R.R. had not yet built through to the coast and the nearest railroad to the N. was the Northern Pacific, running through the center of North Dakota. Later when sheep shared the range with cattle, Belle Fourche became a sheep and wool marketing point. Today it has two large wool warehouses, and sheep as well as cattle chutes are in its stockyards. In the shipping season many carloads of sheep and cattle go out daily.

Naturally, since Belle Fourche ships the products of a large territory, it applies to this territory with trade goods as well, and also ministers to the wants of sections of Montana and Wyoming. It is the seat of Butte Co. Belle Fourche is also, in a way, a manufacturing town. It has a flour mill whose products are widely distributed; on top of the mill is a beacon which flashes red and white at regular intervals and identifies the town to airmen. It also has a brickyard, two bentonite plants, and a creamery with several branches throughout the Hills region. The largest manufacturing interest here is the sugar refinery.

The BLACK HILLS SUGAR PLANT was built in 1927 by the Utah-Idaho Sugar Co. at a cost of 1½ million dollars. From 1912 until 1917 sugar beets were grown in the Belle Fourche valley in an experimental way, and from that date until the building of the factory they were grown on a commercial basis and shipped out of the State for processing. The plant covers an area of eight acres. The length of the main building, including the warehouse, is 587 ft. and the height is five stories. The plant has a capacity of 1,500 tons of beets every 24 hours, producing 3,600 hundred-pounds bags of sugar. Since it started operating it has produced more than 2¼ million bags of sugar.

About 500 farmers in the surrounding country participate in the beet-growing industry. Under a contract, the grower receives one-half of the total value of the sugar extracted from the beets, minus the cost of manufacturing his share. The present beet acreage in the Black Hills district is about 9,500 acres. The active sugar campaign usually lasts from about the middle of September to the middle of December. During this period 300 men are employed at the plant.

The beet pulp from which the sugar has been extracted and the beet tops and byproducts are valuable as feed for livestock. Since the opening of the factory 50,000 head of cattle and 300,000 head of sheep have been fattened for market on the byproducts of the sugar beet, many of them in the feed yards of the sugar factory.

One of the largest known deposits of bentonite in the world (*see NATURAL SETTING*) is found along the banks of Middle Creek, a small stream that flows past the Belle Fourche stockyards. Much of this ore is exposed. Two factories are now in operation, preparing the bentonite for commercial use in face powder, cleansing cream, and numerous other commodities.

The Black Hills Round-up, a three-day celebration, is held in Belle Fourche each year on July 3, 4 and 5. This annual celebration began in 1918, and was first planned as a benefit entertainment for war funds, the United States being then engaged in its second year of the World War. So overwhelming was the success of the first year's show that the board of directors decided to make an annual event of the rodeo. Its proceeds since then have been used for various community and regional enterprises, no private profit being taken from the sale of tickets. The program is considerably varied from year to year, the usual events being bucking contests, bull-dogging, steer-roping, and wild-horse racing. Women as well as men vie for elaborate prizes in these daring sports. One of the three days of festivities is usually set aside as Governor's Day.

In 1927 the round-up celebration was honored by the presence of President and Mrs. Calvin Coolidge, who were spending their vacation at the State Game Lodge or Summer White House (*see Tour 5*).

A cavalry troop of the Fourth U. S. Cavalry at Fort Meade is usually engaged for parades and performances. Indians from various reservations have for some years been invited to spend the three days of the celebration in Belle Fourche. Aerial events have taken a prominent place in recent years, with each season bringing something new.

> Left from Belle Fourche on St. Onge road; at 3.5 *m*. turn L on the E. side of the Redwater bridge; at 4 *m*. is OLD MINNESELA, one of the few ghost towns of this region. This was a flourishing town for some time before Belle Fourche was born. It had many stores, including a drug store, a blacksmith shop, a large hotel, dwelling houses, a schoolhouse, a church, and several saloons. When it was evident that the railroad company was going to select a town site at the fork of the Belle Fourche River and intended to hold a sale of lots on a certain day, the enterprising citizens of Minnesela got out a map of the region showing their town as the general railroad center of this part of the country; listed on the back of the map were 40 or 50 reasons why Minnesela was destined to be the metropolis of this region. The citizens of Minnesela met the train bearing the prospective buyers, distributed the map freely, and not a lot was sold on the Belle Fourche town site that day. But of course the railroad won in the end; and one by one the business houses accepted the inevitable and removed to the new location. Only one man clung to the old location to the last. He took over the old hotel, cut it down to one-third its size, and converted it into a farmhouse with plenty of spare bedrooms. He made a success of farming and created a beautiful yard and garden. And there he lived until 1936 when he was laid to rest.

At Belle Fourche is the junction with US 212 (*see Tour 3*).

South of Belle Fourche US 85 goes through the Belle Fourche, Redwater, and Spearfish valleys. Previously the road has been traversing the barren prairies, but now it crosses a series of wooded ridges interspersed with crop-covered valleys.

At 110.6 m. Red Water Creek is crossed.

At 112.4 m. Spearfish Creek is reached, and the road roughly parallels the creek through the rich LOWER SPEARFISH VALLEY, a region of prosperous farms and substantial buildings. Sugar beets and garden produce mingle with the small grains. But when the road swings into UPPER SPEARFISH VALLEY and heads directly toward Spearfish, a most unusual sight is encountered. Picture a long, straight tarvia road, shaded by large trees on either side; small, irrigated fruit and vegetable farms to the R. and L.; little stands in front of each, loaded with produce and attended by some member of the family—such is the entrance to Spearfish, a ROADSIDE MARKET PLACE that is known throughout all this region. The miners from Lead, the ranchers from the range country to the N., who do not have time to raise the vegetables they need, the housewives of surrounding towns, all come to Upper Spearfish Valley for fruits and vegetables which are replaced on the stand as fast as they are sold. There are apple trees on every farm, large orchards on some, and in the spring when the apple blossoms are out this lane is a pathway of beauty.

SPEARFISH, 118.7 m. (3,637 alt., 1,738 pop.) (*see Tour 4*). is at a junction with US 14; for 14.3 m. US 85 and US 14 are united to a junction at 133 m., 1 m. N. of Deadwood.

Section b. Junction with US 14 to Wyoming Line, 31.1 m.

Southwest of the junction with US 14, US 85 goes through the principal mining section of the Black Hills.

DEADWOOD, 1 m. (4,534 alt., 3,662 pop.) (*see DEAD-WOOD*).
> Roosevelt Monument. Graves of Wild Bill, Calamity Jane, Seth Bullock, and Preacher Smith. Adams Memorial Museum.

At PLUMA, 2.5 m. (12 pop.), are a group of tourist cabins, filling stations, a night club, and a unit of the Homestake Mining Company's plant.

Here is the junction with US 85A (*see Tour 14*).

LEAD, 4 m. (5,320 alt., 7,847 pop.) (*see LEAD*).
> Homestake Mine. Open Cut. Grier Park.

At 6.5 m. is FANTAIL, a small settlement at the end of a spur.

At 10.7 m., after a climb of almost 9 m., the highest point of the road is reached (6,702 alt.).

At 10.8 *m.* is a junction with a dirt road.

> Right on this road to the summit of TERRY PEAK (7,071 alt.). Named for Gen. Terry, it is the 4th highest peak in the Hills, and from its summit is a remarkable view.

At 10.9 *m.* the road enters ICE BOX CANYON, and descends steadily. The canyon was so named by early-day freighters, who found a welcome coolness in its tree-shaded depths.

At 14.3 *m.* is the CHEYENNE CROSSING, where the old Cheyenne Trail crossed Spearfish Creek; here is the junction with the Spearfish Canyon road (*see Tour 13A*).

The road follows the W. branch of Spearfish Creek for some distance, through scenes of unusual beauty. The undergrowth has been cleared out, and between the straight trunks of the pines are glimpses of the swift-flowing brook. The grass and moss make a carpet of green and the pine boughs a canopy overhead. It is a scene that lingers in the memory.

At 18.3 *m.* the Forest Service has made camping grounds (L) for the convenience of visitors.

At 22.5 *m.* the road enters a recently burned-over area where the devastating effect of forest fires is in evidence. The character of the country gradually changes—the hills are leveling out, more open space is encountered, and instead of pine only, there are more aspen, birch, and ironwood.

At 31.1 *m.* US 85 crosses the Wyoming Line, 30.5 *m.* N. of Newcastle, Wyo. (*see Wyo. Tour 1*).

TOUR 13A

Cheyenne Crossing—Savoy—Maurice—Spearfish. State 16.
Cheyenne Crossing—Spearfish, 20.5 m.
No railroad parallels this route.
Dirt roadbed, usually rough but passable even in wet weather.
Usual tourist accommodations, improved camp sites.

One of the most attractive routes in the Black Hills is that through Spearfish Canyon. This trip should be made down the canyon from south to north rather than in the reverse direction, since the fall of Spearfish Creek is pronounced and the road quite rough in places. The upper portion of the canyon is comparatively shallow and open, but, farther down, the rock walls on both sides are higher and steeper; in the very depths of the canyon, the sun strikes the road and the creek bed for only a brief interval each day. This region lies in the so-called Deadwood Formation, made up of gray to red sandstone, greenish shale, and both slab and pebble limestone. The canyon, lined on both sides with cliffs of this material or at least a rimrock, is filled with constantly changing color, which varies still further in different lights. Here also is green pine, interspersed with the slim white trunks of birch, poplar, and quaking-asp. Private cabins, in the woods on both sides of the road for most of the distance, often can be rented for extended periods at very reasonable terms. Fishing is good at many points throughout the canyon and, for those who are not deterred by the temperature of mountain streams, swimming is available.

State 16 branches N. from US 85 (*see Tour 13*) at CHEY-ENNE CROSSING (3,310 alt.)

At 0.25 m. is a rearing pond for young trout, operated as a part of the STATE FISH HATCHERY (*see SPEARFISH*). North of this point the road drops down the canyon beside the stream, with low rocky points on both sides.

At 2.5 m. (5,221 alt.) is a group of picturesque log cabins grouped around a central lodge. The cabins, moderately priced, are available for those who wish to spend several weeks in quiet and beautiful surroundings. Here is fishing, hiking, and swimming. Meals can be taken at the central lodge, or provisions can be bought at the store.

At 4 m. is a DIVERSION DAM and intake of the Homestake Mining Co. At this point the waters of Spearfish Creek enter a wooden stave pipe and are conveyed in it for 6 m. to the hydro-electric plant at Maurice; for a corresponding distance the bed of the creek is practically dry.

SAVOY, 5.5 m. (5,012 alt., 8 pop.), consists of a maintenance station of the Homestake Mining Co., and LATCHSTRING INN, a summer and hunting resort which has been in operation since 1907. There are inn and cabin accommodations for 70 persons, and a large dining room. On both sides of the canyon limestone (*paha sapa*) cliffs tower 1,000 feet.

Left from Savoy on a crushed stone road, paralleling Little Spearfish Creek, is ROUGHLOCK FALLS, 1 m. From a parking space beside the road (L) there is a short path with foot bridges over three branches of the creek above the falls. The water circles a tree and falls about 30 feet, below which there is a series of cascades. A footpath parallels the creek for 100 feet. Roughlock is perhaps the most beautiful falls in the Hills.

At 7.2 m. is the junction with a crushed rock road.

Left on this road, which parallels Deer Creek, is an unnamed LAKE, 4 m. The lake was formed by damming Iron Creek in 1937 and, when filled, covers about 5 acres. When the WPA began building the dam, the beavers that inhabited the creek watched the operations several days and then rebuilt their house a half-mile up the creek. When the lake filled, the beaver house was ideally situated in the shallow end of the lake.

MAURICE, 7.5 m. (4,472 alt., 10 pop.). Here is HYDROELECTRIC PLANT NO. 2 of the Homestake Mining Co. There is a flight of 800 wooden steps leading to the point at which the wooden stave pipe pitches downward to the plant. Just below the plant are the dwellings of those who man it. At this point the full flow of Spearfish Creek is returned to the creek bed and runs for a mile before being taken out at another diversion dam to be carried in pipes to Hydroelectric Plant No. 1 at Spearfish. This mile of stream is kept stocked with trout by the hatchery, and there is good fishing.

At 8.5 m. (R) is BRIDAL VEIL FALLS. Since the drought of recent years the falls are not so impressive as formerly, but the water comes down over a rock-face from a considerable height and it is a beautiful spot to stop for a picnic lunch or get a cool drink of pure water.

RIM ROCK, 9.5 m., is a combined tourist and children's vacation camp in a remarkable setting. The walls of the canyon are very high and at their foot, a little distance above the road, is the main lodge. It is decorated with skins and curios and here the guests gather for their meals. Higher up on the slope is a large community hall, and still higher, on a rocky point jutting out a hundred feet above the road and creek bed, are cabins, with a splendid view up and down the canyon. For a part of each summer it is used as a children's vacation camp.

At 11.5 m. is the junction with a footpath (R).

Right on the trail is WILDCAT CAVE, 0.3 m., reached by a scramble up the steep hillside; the deep cavern is underneath a shelving rock, with a trickle of water running down the face of it. It is worth the climb to rest under the deep recess and look out over the still woods.

At 19 m. Spearfish Canyon widens out into Spearfish Valley, and at the mouth is HYDROELECTRIC PLANT NO. 1 of the Homestake Mining Co. At this point the water is finally returned to Spearfish Creek. But the busy waters of this stream are not through with their work yet: all through Spearfish Canyon and just below it, laterals lead the water out to irrigate the thirsty soil and to make the Upper and Lower Spearfish Valley both a garden spot and a market produce center for the region (*see Tour 13*).

The Canyon road winds through beautiful woods and at 20 *m.* (R) is the MUNICIPAL CABIN CAMP of Spearfish.

At 20.2 *m.* (L) is a US FISH HATCHERY (*see Tour 13*).

SPEARFISH, 20.5 *m.* (3,637 alt., 1,738 pop.) (*see Tour 13*), is at the junction with US 85.

TOUR 14

Junction with US 85—Sheridan—Hill City—Custer—Hot Springs —Oelrichs—(Wayside, Neb.). US 85A and State 79.

Junction with US 85—Nebraska Line, 131.2 m.

The Chicago, Burlington & Quincy R.R. parallels this route between Junction with US 85 and Hot Springs, and the Chicago & North Western, between Hot Springs and the Nebraska Line.

Roadbed is graveled, except for short stretches of hard surface.

Accommodations between towns; hotels and cabin camps in towns.

This route offers some of the most beautiful and varied scenery in the Black Hills. Winding up three-mile Strawberry Hill, the road emerges onto the broad central plateau. Unlike the densely-wooded fringes of the Hills, this central region alternates forested ridges with open, park-like spaces, where the lonely settler ploughs a little patch and the shy deer emerges from the woods to graze at twilight. Here the beaver, nature's conservationist, checks the waters of the hurrying streams and startles the echoes with the pistol-crack of his broad tail. Here the angler wades the stream in hip boots or lazily casts from the highway bridge, while farther downstream the bearded prospector, still hopeful, searches the sands for their golden burden. Such is the land stretching for 50 miles S. of historic Deadwood and its neighbor, Lead; and in the distance there is only one straight mile of road.

But at Hill City the scene changes. The terrain becomes rougher and more broken, and no parks are seen; on every side granite crags and spires thrust themselves above the towering pines and etch their jagged peaks against the sky; the road begins its seven-mile climb to the shores of Sylvan Lake, attaining the final height in a sudden ladder of switch-backs. Having crossed the highest bony ridge of the Hills, the road drops down a canyon, seven winding miles, to Custer, "the cradle of Black Hills civilization," and the spot where white men first found that lodestone which sent a swirling flood of humanity into this region.

Below Custer the country flattens somewhat and the open spaces increase. The road passes through Wind Cave Park, skirting the buffalo pasture and passing the entrance of the cavern, and goes on to Hot Springs, where first the Indians and later the white men came and bathed in the health-giving water.

From this beautiful valley in which Hot Springs lies, the road follows the winding gorge of Fall River, out of the Hills to the broad plains beyond, angling SW. through ever flatter country to Oelrichs and the Nebraska Line beyond.

Section a. Junction with US 85—Hot Springs, 90 m. US 85A.

From the junction with US 85, US 85A goes S. up Strawberry Gulch.

At 3.4 *m.* the top of STRAWBERRY HILL is reached, a real test for car and engine.

At 5 *m.* is the junction with an unnumbered road (*see Tour 4C*).

At 5.9 *m.* the head of Bear Butte Creek is crossed.

At 6.9 *m.* (L) is the golf course of the DEADWOOD COUNTRY CLUB.

At 7.2 *m.* (L) is an artificial pond called TOMAHAWK LAKE, which in times of drought is apt to go completely dry.

At 7.9 *m.* the road crosses Elk Creek and for 2 m. winds upward through the forest.

At 9.8 *m.* is a junction with a dirt road.

Right on this road is CUSTER PEAK (6,794 alt.), 3 *m.* Although this is not the highest peak in the Black Hills, it affords a wider view than any other. It was named for Gen. George A. Custer, who stopped close to this peak while leading an exploration party through the Black Hills in 1874. A trail of the same name passes near the peak.

At 13.9 *m.* (R) is a marker to show where the highway crosses the trail made by Custer on his way to Fort Abraham Lincoln, N. Dak., from French Creek in 1874.

At 20.1 *m.* is the junction with a graded road.

Right on this road is ROCHFORD (5,307 alt., 75 pop.), 12 *m.* This is a sleepy old Black Hills mining town, now sunk into senile quiescence. Off the main tourist lanes, it lives in the past, since it has no significant present and no apparent future.

At 24 *m.* is the junction with the Rim Rock Road (*see Tour 4B*).

At 26.2 *m.* is the junction with a dirt road.

Right on this road, up Boarding House Gulch, is the METHO-DIST CAMP, 2 *m.*, a summer camp of the Methodist Church.

At 26.4 *m.* is Flavin's Corner, and the junction with a graded road.

Right on this road up Bear Gulch is CAMP JUDSON, 1 *m.*, a summer camp of the Baptist Church.

At 2 *m.* is a summer camp of the Presbyterian Church.

At 4 *m.* is SILVER CITY (4,594 alt.), one of the ghost towns of the Hills. The general store and neat, white-painted Catholic Church are in striking contrast with the rough, unpainted board shacks that still stand, eloquent of the days when mining was the chief industry, and the hope of wealth beat high in the heart of every miner and prospector in the Hills. Today, the only evidences of the old mining days are a huge hoisting drum and the dismantled engine that turned it, now lying beside the railroad track and not valuable enough to pay the freight for their removal. Silver City was founded in 1876, at the time of the gold rush along Rapid Creek. Jack, Tom, and Luke Gorman were the real founders of the town, although other prospectors had located ores in the hills and along the creek before their arrival. The Gorman brothers located the first mines on the hillsides, one called The Diana, and the other, The Lady of the Hills. These mines had a heavy yield of silver, combined with some gold and other metals. The camp was called Camp Gorman at first, but a company of seven men was organized and they platted a town site, had it patented, and named it Silver City. It grew to a community of several hundred inhabitants, and the hills and gulches surrounding it were thronged with searchers after precious metals. An Eastern syndicate sent representatives to try to buy the holdings of the Gorman brothers, offering them $300,000. The brothers were ignorant and uneducated men who could not figure whether the offer was more or less than a million dollars, which they insisted was their price. They delayed their decision till one night their cabin caught fire and the eldest brother was burned to death. The other two brothers disappeared. Their heirs in the East, still hold title to the property.

Left from Silver City is a trail leading into THE UNKNOWN LAND. This is only a foot trail, since in many places it is over-grown with brush, blocked by fallen trees, and gullied out. The

Unknown Land is a region bounded roughly on the N. by Rapid Creek, on the W. by the Burlington R.R., on the S. by Spring Creek and the National Forest Boundary, and on the E. by US 85A.

There is no public land within this territory. It is all United States Forest Reserve and staked mining claims that have been proved up and patented.

This whole region is practically inaccessible except to hikers and horseback rides, and in many places it is hard for a horse to find footing. High mountains, deep canyons, and tall timber are the principal features. The region abounds in game, being the home of most of the blacktail deer, outside the Game Preserve, in the Hills. Sometimes elk may be found hiding in some dark gulch. There are no streams of any size, so there is no fishing; but springs of pure sparkling water are found in all the gulches.

Little lumbering has been done except along the edges, as the rough nature of the country prevents the transportation of timber without expensive roads or railroads. The hiker or hunter who penetrates these hills and valleys to make his camp finds himself in woods and mountains much as they were in the days of '76.

In 1876-79, many prospectors located mining claims along the bars of Rapid Creek from Pactola westward. They found gold, but no very rich strikes were made, and they concluded that the "mother lode" must be somewhere in the hills to the S. and W., along the course of the stream. Some of the miners, more hardy than the rest, set out to prospect the hills, and penetrated into the wilderness seeking the source of the placer gold. They failed to find mines of any great value, although a number of quartz veins were discovered that yielded low grade ore. In the meantime the Homestake Mine was discovered at Lead, and most of the mining activity was transferred to that locality.

In 1879, however, O. F. Johnson located a mining claim in this territory and uncovered a vein of quartz 150 ft. wide and 3 m. long. Expecting to develop it, he succeeded in interesting a group of New York investors who gained control of the property, but never developed it. Ore from the vein assayed about $3 or $4 per ton, but various difficulties have so far prevented development.

About this time three brothers, named Scruton, built a cabin near the foot of the highest peak in this section which is still called Scruton Mountain. They had a mine somewhere in the vicinity and from time to time brought out gold, but they never told where the mine was located, nor did any one else ever discover it. They died without disclosing its location. It was this lost mine that gave the territory its name, The Unknown Land.

At 5 m. is CAMP WANZER, a Federal summer camp for tubercular and undernourished children. Here in the pine-scented air, where there is an abundance of clear cold water and good wholesome food, the less fortunate little ones of South Dakota come every summer. Under the supervision of doctors and trained nurses, they are given a chance to gather strength and health.

PACTOLA, 27.3 m. (4,461 alt., 30 pop.), one of the oldest settlements in Pennington Co., is a center of recreational activity. Soon after the discovery of gold in the creek beds, prospectors and miners began to flock into this pleasant valley until it became a populous, thriving community. Owing to its isolation in the heart of the Hills, there was little law enforcement and the valley became the hiding place for many who, for various reasons, did not wish their whereabouts known. The miners made and administered their own law, but the two things they would not tolerate were claim-jumping and horse-stealing.

At first the valley was called "O" Valley, because of its round shape. In 1876 General Crook with his United States Cavalry, on their way to fight the Indians, made his headquarters here and called it Camp Crook. The development of placer mines, together with the establishment of the first post office in Pennington Co., and a tri-weekly stage service, made things boom; so the populace decided that the camp should have a more appropriate name. A mass meeting was called, and a lawyer who had recently moved into the community was asked to make the nominating speech. Having had a number of drinks and feeling fanciful he recited the legend of Midas, whose touch turned everything to gold; and he proposed, in view of the gold being taken from the sands of Rapid Creek, that the place should be called Pactola, for the Lydian river Pactolus, whose golden sands were believed to be the source of the wealth of Croesus.

At 27.4 m. (L) is a public camp ground maintained by the Forest Service.

At 27.6 m. (R) is the PACTOLA RANGER STATION, with well-kept grounds and buildings.

At 30.4 m. are visible (L) the BALD HILLS, so called because there are no trees growing upon them. They extend SE. to within a few miles of Sheridan (*see below*).

At 33.5 m. the road leaves the Black Hills National Forest and enters the Harney National Forest Reserve.

At 35.4 m. is the junction with a graded road.

Left on this road, at 2 m. is BURNT RANCH (4,555 alt.).
In the earliest years of the Black Hills gold rush, while the placer mines along Rapid Creek were at the height of their production, General Crook and his troopers of the 5th Cavalry

made trips between Custer, S. Dak., and Fort Buford, N. Dak., passing through the valley of Rapid Creek and camping regularly on the present site of Pactola. The regular camp sites were situated about 12 m. apart, as nearly as they could be spaced, in spots where water and forage for the horses were available.

Another of the camps was at Sheridan on Spring Creek in Pennington County. Sheridan at that time was a wide awake town. Temporary county offices had been established, and the first term of United States Court W. of the Missouri River had been held here. The usual miners supply store, a saloon, dance hall and a gambling establishment were all thriving. The soldiers' visits were times of unusual hilarity. There was much dancing, gambling, and drinking.

One morning, when the troop was ready to mount and start on the march, one of the soldiers was missing. A detail was dispatched into the town to find him, but had no success. He was marked A.W.O.L. and the troop moved on without him. Some time after noon a man came staggering out of an empty shack, where he had been sleeping. He looked about for the encampment and, discovering that his comrades had gone, started on foot to overtake the troop at the next stopping place, O Valley. The next day the dead body of a miner, Norman McCully, was found near Burnt Ranch by freighters. Inquiries disclosed that he had been on his way from his claim in O Valley to Rapid City, where he intended to deposit about $3,000 worth of gold dust that he was carrying in his pack. It was thought at first that he had been killed by hostile Indians, but the tracks of cavalry boots in the soft earth seemed to be evidence that the crime had been committed by a soldier. Officers were dispatched to overtake the troop; when they submitted the evidence to the commanding officer, he admitted that it looked unfavorable for the soldier who had been left behind, but said that the man was already under arrest for being absent without leave and that he was responsible only to Federal authority. He promised to take the charge of murder under consideration, and to have the evidence presented to the next session of the Military Court of Inquiry.

The troop proceeded on its way to Fort Benton, and the soldier was put to work with a sawmill crew at the fort. One day a fellow worker made a remark about the miner who had been murdered, and the soldier, in a frenzy of anger, seized him and threw him against a circular saw. The man was horribly mutilated and died instantly. The mill crew then seized the soldier and, without delay, hanged him to a tree.

Although the soldier never confessed that he murdered the miner, it was believed that he committed the deed and then buried the gold dust somewhere on Burnt Ranch, intending to come back for it. The ranch has been visited by many treasure hunters, and the ground has been thoroughly searched; but, so far as is known, no one has found the buried gold.

SHERIDAN, 35.7 *m.* (4,603 alt., 10 pop.), started as a mining camp called Golden City when, in 1875, prospectors locating claims along Spring Creek found rich placer deposits of gold in the meadows. The bars of the creek proved unexpectedly rich. "If a man's claim yielded less than $20 per day in gold dust, he abandoned it and moved to a new location." Golden City was the usual type of mining camp of that day. Saloons, dance halls, and gambling places flourished, with all the accompanying excitement of a prosperous mining community. A general store, which carried all the usual miners' supplies, food, and clothing, did a thriving business.

In 1876 a feeling of civic pride began to manifest itself. The citizens felt that some kind of permanent social responsibility ought to take the place of the irresponsible recklessness and excitement of gold rush days. A meeting was called and it was decided to rename the place Sheridan. Pennington Co. had just been organized and the county seat was established here. The Federal Government established the first Federal Court W. of the Missouri River, and a log courthouse was built. A monument of native rock marks the spot where the first courthouse stood, just N. of the town site and E. of the highway.

The first term of Federal Court was held here in 1878. Judge Granville G. Bennett presided. The judge, lawyers, jurymen, and all the court attendants came in by stage, horseback, oxcarts, and on foot, until every place that could accommodate an extra person was filled to overflowing. Eating places were swamped, and men walked the one street seeking a place to eat and sleep. It turned cold and there was much discomfort because of the lack of blankets and bedding.

Sheridan became an important station on the Deadwood-Denver stage line. It was a regular stopping place for General Crook and his troops on their patrols through the Black Hills and the NW. It seemed destined to become one of the leading cities of the Hills, and a permanent community. But in 1878 the county seat was moved to Rapid City. With the coming of the railroads, the stage line gradually lost its patronage and was discontinued. The productiveness of placer mines began to lessen. The troops were withdrawn from the Hills. So Sheridan, which depended on all these things for its prosperity, gradually became an almost deserted village. In 1937 plans were started to create a 400-acre lake that would cover Sheridan to a depth of 20 ft.

At 36.7 *m.* Spring Creek is crossed and an area entered in which the speed limit is 35 m. per hour.

At 37 *m.* (R) is an outcrop of serrated slate rock, towering up to the cliff heights.

At 37.4 *m.,* on both sides of the road, lie the buildings of an old ranch. Above the gate of the corral hangs an old ox yoke.

At 40.5 *m.* is a camp ground provided by the Forest Service for the convenience of those who wish to camp and build fires. It should be noted that there are very strict rules against the building of fires on the forest reserve in any but designated places (*see BLACK HILLS RECREATIONAL AREA*).

At 41.6 *m.* (R) is a RANGER STATION.

At 42 *m.* (R) is a large dam built by the Civilian Conservation Corps. It is called MAJOR DAM and the water covers about 9 acres.

HILL CITY, 42.6 *m.* (4,945 alt., 450 pop.), lies in a small valley completely surrounded by pine-clad mountains. Discovery of tin, gold, and copper brought Hill City's first settlers in 1876. The city today is the center of a recreational area. The lake formed by Major Dam, is devoted to recreational purposes (*see above*). Spring Creek, which runs directly through Hill City furnishes good trout fishing. Wild flowers and wild strawberries, raspberries, and sarvice berries grow in abundance during the spring and summer months.

Today the main industry of the region is mining for gold and tungsten; many mines, such as the Empire, Ceko, Eldorado, and Tungsten are within a 5-m. radius.

At 46.8 *m.* (R) is a typical small Black Hills sawmill.

Custer State Park Game Sanctuary is entered at 47.2 *m.*

At 47.9 *m.* is the junction with the Rushmore Memorial Highway (*see Tour 5B*).

At 48.9 *m.* there is an excellent view of the surrounding hills and the granite rock formation of the region.

At 49.4 *m.* the road crosses the Custer Co. line, and the Needles' formation of granite spires is seen in the distance.

At 50.3 *m.* (R) is a mountain spring of clear cold water, running into a trough for the convenience of motorists.

At 50.7 *m.* the road passes through a tunnel cut in solid granite.

At 51 *m.* (R) is the entrance to SKI HILL, where a long ski slide leads out onto a meadow. Here and at nearby Sylvan Lake (*see below*) a program of winter sports is held with growing enthusiasm every year.

The NEW SYLVAN LAKE HOTEL, 51.4 *m.* (L), overlooks a placid mountain lake and faces Harney Peak (*see Tour 14A*). The hotel was built by the Custer State Park Board and Public Works Administration in 1936-37, replacing a wooden structure which formerly stood on the lake shore and was destroyed by fire in 1936. The new hotel is considered an excellent example of modern park-hotel architecture. The architect was Harold Spitznagel of Sioux Falls. The hotel appears a continuation of the timbered granite-crested cliff on which it stands, at an altitude of 6,300 ft. Slabs of rough, moss-covered pegmatite, above which is siding of native pine, make up the exterior of the rambling building. A wide flagstone terrace overlooks Sylvan Lake and the Harney Peak range to the E., and extends around the north wall of the building. Brown, with harmonizing blue and coral, predominate in the color scheme of the furnishings. The diamond motif is used extensively in design, as shown in huge columns that support the porte cochere. The fireplace in the dining room is faced with Hot Springs calico sandstone. On the walls of the dining room above the red cedar wainscoting are Indian murals, painted by Erika Lohmann, New York artist. In the lounge, only wooden pegs have been employed in the construction of knotty pine walls and exposed beams and rafters. Into the grayish-tan monks cloth draperies have been woven Indian designs by women of the Flandreau Indian school. The eight walls of the octagonal shaped lobby are of panelled California redwood, and Indian thunder birds are molded in relief against the ceiling. Excellent views of the lake, Harney Peak, Terry Peak, and the ski jump can be obtained from the windows in various rooms.

At 51.8 *m.* is the junction with the Needles' Highway (*see Tour 14A*).

At 51.9 *m.* the road begins its 7-mile descent to Custer, the first 3 *m.* being rather steep. Black Hills spruce lines the highway for short distances.

At 54.4 *m.* the highway passes out of the Game Sanctuary.

At 58.5 *m.* is the junction with US 16 (*see Tour 5*).

CUSTER, 59 *m.* (5,303 alt., 1,239 pop.) (*see Tour 5*), is at the junction with US 16.

At 59.4 *m.* (L) is a FELDSPAR MILL, where rock is ground finer than flour for use in making enamel, glass, and polishes.

At 60.4 *m.* is the GRAY ROCKS resort, at which mineral specimens and souvenirs are exhibited.

At 63.6 *m.* (L) is the STATE SANATORIUM (5,340 alt.). This institution is set back a short distance from the road in a grove of pines. It is in the Harney National Forest Reserve and its grounds comprise 171 acres. Founded in 1909 by Dr. Batti of Custer, for the treatment of tuberculosis, it was later taken over by the State. Construction of the present buildings was begun in 1910. At present they consist of wards for patients, a nurses' home, schoolhouse, and auditorium, dairy barns, silo, power-house, laundry, sewage disposal plant, residence of the superintendent, and garages.

PRINGLE, 70.7 *m.* (4,879 alt., 250 pop.), was originally called Point of Rocks, because of outstanding rocks nearby. The first post office, in 1886, was called Rocks. In the autumn of 1890 the Burlington R.R. reached the town and the station was called Pringle in honor of the owners of the water rights.

At 77.2 *m.* the road leaves Harney National Forest Reserve.

At 77.4 *m.* Wind Cave National Park is entered.

At 78.1 *m.* the road crosses a dam which impounds the waters of Cold Spring Creek. The resultant lake (R) is named in honor of the late Sen. Peter Norbeck, who did so much to conserve the beauties of the Black Hills. From this point the road proceeds over small hills, around wide curves, and through an open buffalo pasture where buffalo can be seen grazing.

At 79.9 *m.* (L) is the headquarters building of WIND CAVE NATIONAL PARK (*trips every hour from 7 a.m. to 7 p.m. during summer; once a day the remainder of the year, adm. 50c*). It is a long rambling building, containing a combined souvenir room and lunch counter; across the open arcade, which divides the building, is the general office and waiting room. From the arcade a series of steps leads down the slopes of the canyon to the entrance of the cave.

Wind Cave Park, with its game sanctuary, its beautifully landscaped hillsides, its rustic-looking residences for the officers and rangers, its attractive administration building, and especially its subterranean cavern, has become, in spite of its modest size of

18½ sq. m., one of the more attractive of our national parks. It was officially made a national park January 9, 1903.

The question of the discoverer of Wind Cave is a controversial one, inasmuch as the event dates back to a period in the history of the Black Hills region when few records were kept. But the credit is given to Tom Bingham, a pioneer, who, while hunting deer over the rolling hills in 1881, was attracted by a singular hissing sound issuing from some undergrowth and, upon investigation, he found a small hole in the rocks. This hole, not more than 10 inches in diameter, is the only natural opening to the cave so far discovered. It is just a few steps behind the present cave entrance building.

Another story is that a cowboy, riding the range on a calm day, suddenly had his hat blown off, and on investigating found the natural opening.

The present cavern entrance leads into corridors and galleries, appropriately named for their similarity to such subjects as the Bridal Chamber, Post Office, Opera Hall, Queen's Drawing Room, Monte Cristo Palace, and Garden of Eden. These natural hallways and chambers show a variety of crystal formations, called boxwork or frost work, which is composed of delicately colored crystal fins arranged in honeycomb pattern—tiny white crystals on a pink background, hanging in clusters from ceilings and ledges. The formations here differ from those in most caverns, stalactites and stalagmites being almost nonexistent. This peculiar boxwork formation is said to have been caused by rain water seeping down from the surface through decaying vegetation and absorbing carbon dioxide. This carbon-dioxide-bearing water first took some of the limestone into solution, then deposited it in cracks or crevices below and, upon evaporation, formed the boxlike fins. Later the more soluble limestone between the fins of the boxwork was dissolved and carried away, leaving the boxwork as it is seen today.

Wind Cave is a limestone cavern, and the limestone layer in which the cave is formed is known as the Pahasapa formation, a local variety of Mississippian, which was deposited in a great inland sea perhaps 300 million years ago. Following the deposit of this limestone, there occurred several periods of elevation and subsidence. During these periods of submergence the Pahasapa limestone was overlaid several hundred feet by other sediment. The final upthrust of the land occurred about 60 million years ago, and the beginning of Wind Cave probably dated from that time.

The principal routes in the cave are lighted by indirect illumination, producing a soft glow which sets off the different formations to advantage. A large elevator lowers visitors to the floor of the cave. The temperature of the cave is 47 degrees and does not vary with the different seasons.

All trips through the cave are under the guidance of competent park rangers. The shorter route through the cave requires approximately two hours and the longer one about three hours.

The game preserve, formerly under the U. S. Biological Survey, is now under the supervision of the National Park Service. Big game in this park is estimated as follows: 225 buffalo, 70 elk, 60 deer, and 30 antelope. Since June 1936 these animals have been free to roam at large throughout the park instead of being confined to certain areas, and each seeks his own natural habitat.

No hotels or tourist cabins are located in the park; however, there is a public camp ground, with free wood and water, near headquarters.

At 80.1 *m.* the road winds above the Wind Cave CCC Camp (L), which appears to have sprung from the floor of the canyon. From this point, for 3 m. it passes through an open buffalo pasture, where the shaggy, cumbersome beasts can be seen grazing on either hand.

At 83.1 *m.* is the southern entrance to Wind Cave Park.

At 83.5 *m.* is GOBBLER'S KNOB (4,233 alt.), and just ahead is BUFFALO GAP, through which buffaloes formerly came in droves.

At 85 *m.* is the junction with State 79, and the route continues on this highway to the Nebraska Line.

HOT SPRINGS, 90 *m.* (3,433 alt., 3,263 pop.) (*see Tour 7*), is at the junction with US 18.

Section b. Hot Springs—Nebraska Line, 41.2 m. State 79.

Southeast of Hot Springs, State 79 and US 18 are united for 15 m. (*see Tour 7*). At this point State 79 continues S. through a gently rolling country.

At 16.5 *m.* the road crosses Horse Head Creek, and at 27.2 *m.* Lonewell Creek.

OELRICHS, 28.3 *m.* (209 pop.), was named for a prominent rancher living nearby.

At 33.9 *m.* the road again crosses Horse Head Creek.

At 41.2 *m.* State 79 crosses the Nebraska Line 1 m. N. of Wayside, Nebr. (*see Nebr. Tour 6*).

TOUR 14A

Junction with US 85A—Sylvan Lake—Needles—Junction with US 16. Needles Highway.

Junction with US 85A—Junction with US 16, 14.3 m.

Roadbed is graveled and oiled alternately.

Accommodations limited.

Although this route is short, it presents unusual views of the Black Hills. Skirting the shores of Sylvan Lake, it affords a distant view of Harney Peak. It winds for a short distance through the forest, plunges into a tunnel cut through the solid granite, and emerges among some of the most picturesque country in the State —granite spires shooting skyward, weird forms such as the Needle's Eye, Balanced Rock, and the Traffic Cop, deep wooded valleys lying hundreds of feet below, with a downward slope so steep as to be in effect a precipice; and not a sign of human occupation is seen, with the exception of the road traveled. Then for 11 miles the trail winds steadily downhill through a dense forest, with ever-changing vistas and an occasional glimpse of other valleys to the right or left, until with a final steep pitch it drops to US 16 (*see Tour 5*).

The Needles formation is unique in the State. Composed of the original granite core of the Hills, which thrust up from somewhere in the interior of the earth and pushed aside all the sedimentary formations above (*see GEOLOGY*), it has been eroded by the action of countless centuries of wind and weather. According to Gutzon Borglum, the granite face of Rushmore weathers less than an inch in 40,000 years. It has taken ages to weather away the granite that left only graceful spires where solid rock must once have been. Countless centuries went into the making of the Needle's Eye in which a thousand pine trees could be threaded with room to spare.

While this fine scenic highway was being built, the late Sen. Peter Norbeck tramped on foot over every mile of this rough country and wherever he found a particularly striking view, he would say to the engineers, "Run the road here." They would assure him that it was impossible, to which he would reply, "Put it there anyway." And they did. This man did more than any other to make the natural beauties of the Black Hills region available and accessible to all.

The Needles Highway branches SE. from US 85A *9.2 m.* S. of Hill City.

At *0.2 m.* (L) is SYLVAN LAKE. No one viewing this beautiful body of water would imagine that it was anything but a work of nature. It is only after going through a natural chasm in the rock and emerging below the lake that the inconspicuous wall holding back the waters of a mountain brook is seen. But there is no surface indication to mar the beauty of this little lake, reflecting in its quiet mirror the rock walls that rise abruptly from its depths and those other rocks that jut from its placid surface to form picturesque islets. Overlooking it is the new State-owned hotel (*see Tour 14*), seeming like a continuation of the rock itself. At a broad wharf are boats in which one may idle away a summer's afternoon, fishing from the rocky islands or from the boat itself. For those who like the cold mountain waters, swimming suits are available. In winter when deep ice covers the lake, winter sports enthusiasts from all through the Hills convene here for skiing, skating, and tobogganing. Perhaps no investment made in Black Hills scenic improvements has yielded richer returns than Sylvan Lake.

At *0.3 m.* is the junction with a dirt road.

> Left on this road, skirting the southern edge of the lake, 0.1 *m.* is a campground with a store, tables, and fireplaces. At 0.2 *m.* is a stable where burros for the climb to HARNEY PEAK (7,242 alt.) may be obtained. At 0.5 *m.* the road comes to an end and cars must be parked. From this point a footpath leads three *m.* through the woods on a gradual upward slope to the base of Harney Peak. It is a beautiful, winding, shaded path, sometimes buried deep in the woods, sometimes skirting the edge of a precipice, with views of distant peaks and of pine-covered slopes and the granite spires of the Needles thrusting upward through the foliage. Halfway to the peak there is a wayside spring. The remainder of the path is a little steeper; the final pitches lead out of the trees to the foot of a ladder in a granite crevice, at the top of which a final short scramble over the rocks leads to the lookout station on the bare granite crag that forms Harney's summit. And here is unfolded a view that repays any weariness the climb may have occasioned.
>
> Far down, over the trail just traveled, are ridge after ridge with wooded hollows between, with stretches of granite cliff-face and jagged granite peaks. To the E., three *m.* away, a granite wall rises abruptly. It is on the other face of this wall that the great stone carving of Rushmore is taking form. Beyond, the ridges become ever lower until they flatten out into the plain, which in turn reaches out to the blue horizon line. To the S. is Mt.

Coolidge with its tower, and to the N. the peaks of Terry and Custer. All about is what seems to be primeval wilderness.

Harney Peak is not only the highest point in the Black Hills and South Dakota, but it is the highest point in the United States east of the Rocky Mountains. It was named for an army officer, General Harney, who in 1857 led a small force of men from Laramie to Ft. Pierre, passing through this territory. In the glass-walled lookout station on Harney's summit sits a fire guard during most of the summer season. With a swivel telescope swinging over a map, he can instantly and accurately locate the first wisp of smoke that curls upward from a fire. A telephone keeps him in constant communication with the ranger stations throughout the Hills. And of the 10,000 people who climb the peak annually, almost every one asks the fire guard, "Don't you get awfully lonesome up here, all by yourself."

At 1.5 m. (R) the road passes the TRAFFIC COP, a huge boulder that Nature has carved in the likeness of a hard-boiled Irish policeman.

At 1.6 m. the Needles Highway widens for a parking space. To the R. is that curious natural formation, the Needle's Eye, a huge upright fissure in a granite cliff, closed at the top as well as bottom. To the L. the road pierces a jutting promontory of granite and comes out upon one of the best views to be had in the Needles. Pinnacles and spires, strange and uncanny, reach into the blue of the sky hundreds of feet above their forested base, and multitudes of fanciful shapes lend to the whole a marvelous harmony. They are overtowered by massive Mt. Harney on the N., but their craggy heights, silhouetted against the sky, show for long distances from the E. and SE., even from far out on the prairie 50 m. away. This maze of sculptured granite, with its magic shapes of needles, organ pipes, cathedral spires, and castellated rocks, is impressive when viewed from Mt. Harney; but the peculiar individuality and sheer splendor of each formation appear to best advantage when viewed from the midst of the peaks; precipice and height alternate as granite formations spring with startling suddenness from the clinging forest of spruce and pine.

At 1.8 m. is another parking place where there is a wide view to the S., with Custer and Mt. Coolidge in the distance.

At 2.3 m. is a view to the N. of close-set pinnacles like organ pipes.

At 2.5 m. are two hairpin turns, with Skyscraper Rock just below (8).

At 5.4 *m.* (L) is a campground, equipped by the Forest Service.

At 5.7 *m.* (L) in the distance is BALANCED ROCK, pointed out by means of a wooden arrow.

At 6.8 *m.* the road passes through a second granite tunnel in its descent from the Needles.

At 8.3 *m.* is a series of beaver dams (R), of particular interest perhaps to those who have never seen one. It is probable, however, that the animals will not be visible, on account of their shyness. These dams are found near quaking-asp or birch groves, as a rule. Above and below these dams are a great many aspen and Black Hills spruce, as well as pine.

At 8.5 *m.* is the entrance to the fenced section of CUSTER STATE PARK (*see BLACK HILLS RECREATIONAL AREA*).

At 11.5 *m.* is the junction with a graveled road.

> **Left on this road, 1 *m.*, is CAMP LODGE. Right from Camp Lodge, 2.2 *m.*, is CENTER LAKE, an artificial lake created by CCC forces, when filled it is stocked with trout.**

At 14.3 *m.* is the junction with US 16 (*see Tour 5*), 8 m. E. of Custer.

TOUR 15

(Railway Tour)

Rapid City—Pactola—Mystic. Rapid City, Black Hills & Western R. R. (Crouch Line).

Rapid City—Mystic, 35 m.

Only one train a day, leaving Rapid City in the morning and returning in the afternoon.

Usual accommodations in Rapid City; cabins in the canyon.

The distance between the two ends of Rapid Canyon is 19.5 m. by airline, but owing to the winding course of the canyon bed the distance traversed by the railroad is 35 m. The river is spanned 105 times and the elevation at the highest point on the road is about 5000 ft.

This little railroad has had a colorful history. In 1896 C. D. Crouch and a partner raised funds in Maine and Pennsylvania to build a railroad up the canyon to Mystic, hoping later to extend it to Wyoming on the W. and the Missouri River on the E. It was called the Dakota, Wyoming and Missouri River R. R. The grade was built as far as Dark Canyon, but difficulties developed and the line went into receivership for eight years. In 1904 the company was reorganized as the Missouri River and Northwestern R. R., and Crouch was elected president. The road was completed to Mystic in 1906. Business was fairly good until, in 1907, there came a cloudburst. Seven inches of water fell in 12 hours. In some places in the canyon, the water rose to a height of 20 ft. After the flood subsided, much of the track was off the grade; and of 113 bridges, only two were strong enough to carry the engine. This disaster was too much for the finances of the small company, and it went into receivership a second time. In 1909 it was reorganized under its present name. In 1920, when old iron was commanding unheard-of prices, the creditors of the road wished to junk it. But the pride of Rapid City businessmen was touched, and they organized a company to purchase a controlling interest in the outstanding indebtedness, and so preserved the life of the railroad. The route, apart from its scenic interest, is important chiefly as a link between the North Western, Milwaukee, and Burlington systems. It is one of two railroads in South Dakota that are entirely within the State.

For the greater part of the distance the railroad follows the narrow winding course of Rapid Canyon, where the creek of that name has carved its way down from the central plateau of the Hills. At every turn of the road is a new vista with distinctive charm. Occasionally a startled deer climbs the steep canyon wall as easily as it would bound over a level plain. The echoes of the train whistle are tossed back and forth from the rocky canyon sides. The transparent waters of the rushing mountain stream are seen on one side or the other at frequent intervals.

This trip is interesting from a geologic standpoint, even to a layman. According to Dr. C. C. O'Harra, late president of the South Dakota School of Mines, Rapid City, S. Dak., more interesting geologic formations are to be seen on this route than on any other of similar length in the entire Black Hills region; one example is a cliff face with the strata running in several different directions within the same solid mass of rock, betokening some former violent convulsion of nature.

Dotted here and there are the cabins and summer homes of those who come yearly to the cool canyon depths to find relief from the blistering heat of the plains. Frequent stations, often only uncovered platforms, serve these summer residents. In warm weather the passenger coach is replaced by an open and roofless observation car, thus affording a more comprehensive view of the scenery.

The train heads W. from the Rapid City terminal and turns S. around the shoulder of HANGMAN'S HILL (*see RAPID CITY*).

At 3 *m.* is DEADMAN GULCH (R)' and CANYON LAKE (L). (*see RAPID CITY.*)

At 3.2 *m.* (L) is a STATE FISH HATCHERY (*see Tour 4B*).

At 3.4 *m.* the railroad enters RAPID CANYON proper.

At 4 *m.* (L) is the mouth of DARK CANYON. This is a deep, winding rent in the earth, where a stream has widened a crevice into a narrow canyon. The sun can penetrate it only for a few minutes at midday.

Between Dark Canyon and Mystic there is excellent trout fishing. Many visitors go up on the train in the morning, watch for a likely looking spot and get off the train to try their luck. The same train picks them up on its return trip in the afternoon. It is whispered that even the train crew have been known to indulge their fondness for this sport when the passenger business was dull. It is not reported, however, that they boasted of their catch on their return to town.

At 5.5 *m.* (R) is the mouth of Wild Irishman Gulch.

At 8 *m.* the waters of the creek issue from a 7-ft. hole in a rocky wall. In 1878, when prospectors first sought the canyon, someone conceived the idea of draining the creek bed above the hole to obtain gold. So a tunnel was driven through a rocky wall in a bend, and the entire stream diverted through it. That the experiment was by no means in vain is evidenced by the fact that no less than $2,000,000 was paid by a Rapid City bank for gold taken from the stream at this point.

At 10 *m.* is HISEGA and the Triangle I Lodge and Ranch (*see Tour 4B*).

At 14 *m.* is BIG BEND. Here there is a power plant operated by the creek waters, which are carried in a flume for 6 m.

At 16.8 *m.* is JOHNSON SIDING, a covered platform like a station stop on an interurban electric line.

At 19.5 *m.* (L) is the mouth of FRANCES GULCH.

PACTOLA, 20 *m.* (4,461 alt., 30 pop.) (*see Tour 14*).

At *22 m.* (L) is the mouth of Bear Gulch; and at *23.5 m.* (L), Ethel Gulch.

At *25 m.* is SILVER CITY, a ghost town (*see Tour 14*). To the R. is the mouth of Sunnyside Gulch and to the L. that of Nugget Gulch.

At *28 m.* (L) is the mouth of Stewart Gulch; Kelly Gulch is at *28.8 m.* (R)

CANYON CITY, *29 m.,* is merely a station stop where hardly a trace of the ghost town is visible.

At *30.5 m.* the railroad leaves Rapid Canyon and begins to climb the canyon of Castle Creek.

MYSTIC, *35 m.* (4,868 alt., 30 pop.), marks the junction of the R. C. B. H. & W. R.R. with the Deadwood branch of the Chicago, Burlington & Quincy R. R., and is the terminus of the former line.

BIBLIOGRAPHY

(Prepared under the direction of Lawrence K. Fox, Secretary of the South Dakota Historical Society.)

GENERAL INFORMATION

Greater South Dakota Association. *Facts about South Dakota.* Huron, Greater South Dakota Association, 1937. 15 p. il.

South Dakota. Game and Fish Department. *Game and Fish Laws of the State of South Dakota.* Pierre, Game and Fish Commission, 1935-1936. 38 p.

South Dakota. *South Dakota Legislative Manual.* Pierre, State Publishing Co., 1935. (Issued biennially)

SOUTH DAKOTA TODAY AND YESTERDAY

Atherton, Loren G. and Atherton, Nora M. *South Dakota Geography.* Sioux Falls, Will A. Beach, 1936. 150 p. il.

Faris, John Thompson. *Roaming the Rockies.* New York, Farrar & Rinehart, 1930. 333 p. il.

Peterson, Purl D. *Through the Black Hills and Bad Lands of South Dakota.* Pierre, Olander, 1929. 189 p. il.

South Dakota. State Planning Board. *State Finance in South Dakota.* Brookings, 1937. 65 p.

South Dakota. State Planning Board. *The People of South Dakota, A Preliminary Study of Population.* Brookings, 1936. 46 p.

South Dakota State School of Mines. *Black Hills Engineer, Badlands Number.* Rapid City, South Dakota State School of Mines, 1926. 65 p. il.

Visher, S. S. *Geography of South Dakota.* Vermillion, University of South Dakota, 1918. 189 p. il.

Warren, Lieut. G. K. *Preliminary Report of Exploration in Nebraska and Dakota in the Years 1855-56-57.* Washington, Government Printing Office, 1875. 125 p. maps. (U. S. Army. Topographical Engineers)

White, John M. *The Newer Northwest.* St. Louis, Self-Culture Publishing Co., 1894. 205 p. il.

NATURAL SETTING

a. Mineral

O'Harra, Cleophas C. and Connolly, Joseph P. *Mineral Wealth of the Black Hills.* Rapid City, South Dakota State School of Mines, 1929. 482 p. il.

O'Harra, Cleophas C. *Mineral Resources of South Dakota*. Rapid City, South Dakota State School of Mines. 88 p. il.

O'Harra, Cleophas C. *The White River Badlands*. Rapid City, South Dakota State School of Mines, 1920. 277 p. il.

South Dakota. State Planning Board. *Portland Cement, Gypsum, and Lime Industries in South Dakota*. Brookings, 1936. 71 p.

South Dakota. State Planning Board. *Tin Deposits in South Dakota*. Brookings, 1936. 35 p.

South Dakota. State Planning Board. *Tungsten Mining in South Dakota*. Brookings, 1936. 32 p.

b. Water

South Dakota. State Planning Board. *Artesian Well Flow in South Dakota*. Brookings, 1937. 138 p.

South Dakota. State Planning Board. *Dams in South Dakota*. Brookings, 1937. 179 p.

South Dakota. State Planning Board. *Water Resources of South Dakota*. 14 bulletins. Brookings, 1937.

c. Flora and Fauna

Atherton, Loren G. and Atherton, Nora M. *Dakota Birds*. Pierre. Olander, 1926. 238 p. il.

Audubon, Maria R. *Audubon and His Journals*. New York, Scribner, 1897. 2 vols. il.

Churchill, Edward and Over, W. H. *Fishes of South Dakota*. Pierre, South Dakota Game and Fish Commission, 1935. 87 p. il.

Hornaday, William T. *The American Natural History*. New York, Scribner, 1904.

Johnson, Floyd A. *4-H Club Guide in Wild Life Conservation*. Pierre, South Dakota Game and Fish Commission, 1935. 52 p. il.

Over, William H. *Amphibians and Reptiles of South Dakota*. Vermillion, University of South Dakota, 1932. 51 p. il.

Over, William H. and Thomas, Craig. *Birds of South Dakota*. Vermillion, University of South Dakota, 1921. 142 p. il.

Over, William H. *Flora of South Dakota, An Illustrated Checklist of Flowering Plants, Shrubs and Trees of South Dakota*. Vermillion, University of South Dakota, 1932. 161 p. il.

South Dakota State School of Mines. *Black Hills Engineer, Black Hills Plants. Description of Black Hills Flora*. Rapid City, South Dakota State School of Mines, May 1931. 123 p. il.

Terrell, Claude B. *Wild Fowl and Fish Attractions*. Pierre, South Dakota Game and Fish Commission, 1932. 72 p. il.

INDIANS AND INDIAN LIFE

Barton, Winifred (Williamson). *John P. Williamson.* New York, Revell, 1919. 269 p. il.

Byrne, Patrick Edward. *Soldiers of the Plains.* New York, Minton, Balch, 1926. 260 p.

Catlin, George. *The North American Indians.* Philadelphia, Leary, 1913. 2 vols. il.

DeLand, Charles Edmund. *The Aborigines of South Dakota.* S. Dak. Historical Collections, Vol. III, 267-586; Vol. IV, 275-730.

DeLand, Charles Edmund. *The Sioux Wars.* S. Dak. Historical Collections, Vol. XV, 9-730; Vol. XVI, 175-552.

Drift, Ivan (Iktomi Licala). *America Needs Indians.* Denver, Bradford-Robinson, 1937. 424 p. il. A young Indian, educated by the white man, attempts to solve the "Indian Problem."

Eastman, Charles Alexander. *From the Deep Woods to Civilization.* Boston, Little, Brown, 1916. 206 p. il.

Eastman, Charles Alexander. *Indian Boyhood.* New York, Mc-Clure, 1920. 289 p. il.

Eastman, Charles Alexander. *Red Hunters and the Animal People.* New York, Harper, 1904. 249 p. front.

Eastman, Charles Alexander. *Wigwam Evenings.* Animal Tales. Boston, Little Brown, 1930. 250 p. il.

Ellis, Edward S. *Indian Wars of the United States.* Chicago, Kenyon, 1902. 484 p. il.

Gessner, Robert. *Broken Arrow.* New York, Farrar & Rinehart, 1933. 280 p.

Gessner, Robert. *Massacre, A Survey of Today's American Indian.* New York, Cape and Smith, 1931. 418 p. il.

Gilmore, Melvin Randolph. *Prairie Smoke.* New York, Columbia University Press, 1919. 80 p. front.

Hans, Fred M. *The Great Sioux Nation.* Chicago, Donohue, 1907. 575 p. il.

Holley, F. C. *Once Their Home: or, Our Legacy from the Dahkotahs.* Historical, biographical and incidental material. Chicago, Donohue, 1890. 423 p. il.

Hyde, George E. *Red Cloud's Folk.* Norman, University of Oklahoma Press, 1937. 331 p. front.

Lange, Dietrich. *The Threat of Sitting Bull.* Boston, Lothrop, 1920. 370 p. front.

McLaughlin, James. *My Friend the Indian.* Boston, Houghton Mifflin, 1926. 417 p. il.

Neihardt, John G. *Black Elk Speaks, Being the Life Story of an Holy Man of the Ogalala Sioux.* New York, Morrow, 1932. 280 p. il.

Olden, Sarah Emilia. *The People of Tipi Sapa (The Dakotas).* Milwaukee, Morehouse, 1918. 158 p. il.

Riggs, Stephen Return. *Mary and I. Forty Years with the Sioux.* Chicago, W. G. Holmes, 1880. 388 p. il.

Schultz, James Willard. *Bird Woman (Sacajawea), The Guide of Lewis and Clark.* Boston, Houghton Mifflin, 1918. 235 p. il.

Shetrone, Henry Clyde. *The Mound Builders.* New York, Appleton, 1930. 508 p. il.

South Dakota. State Planning Board. *Indians of South Dakota.* Brookings, 1937. 97 p.

Vestal, Stanley. *New Sources of Indian History, 1850-91.* Norman, University of Oklahoma Press, 1934. 351 p. il.

Vestal, Stanley. *Sitting Bull, Champion of the Sioux.* Boston, Houghton Mifflin, 1932. 350 p. front.

Vestal, Stanley. *Warpath.* Boston, Houghton Mifflin, 1934. 291 p. il.

Will, George F. *Archaeology of the Missouri Valley.* New York, American Museum Press, 1924. 59 p. (Anthropological Papers of the American Museum of Natural History, Vol. 22, Part 6.)

Wellman, Paul I. *Death on the Prairie. The Thirty Years' Struggle for the Western Plains.* New York, Macmillan, 1934. 298 p. il.

Zitkala-sa. *Old Indian Legends.* New York, Ginn, 1901. 165 p. il.

HISTORY

a. General

Andreas, A. T. *Andreas' Historical Atlas of Dakota.* Chicago, Donnelley, 1884. 246 p. il.

Armstrong, M. K. *Early Empire Builders of the Great West.* St. Paul, Porter, 1901. 446 p. il.

Dunham, N. J. *History of Mitchell Corn Palace.* Mitchell, Mitchell Gazette, 1914. 48 p. il.

Gering, John J. *After Fifty Years.* Marion, Pine Hill Printery, 1924. 60 p. il.

Hebert, Frank. *Forty Years Prospecting in the Black Hills of South Dakota.* Rapid City, Rapid City Daily Journal, 1921. 199 p. il.

Humphrey, Seth K. *Following the Prairie Frontier.* Minneapolis, University Press, 1931. 265 p. front.

Hunkins, Ralph V. and Lindsey, John. *South Dakota; Its Past, Present, and Future.* A school history. New York, Macmillan, 1932. 312 p. il.

Hunt, Frazier. *Custer; the Last of the Cavaliers.* New York, Cosmopolitan, 1928. 209 p. il.

Lowe, Barrett. *Heroes and Hero Tales of South Dakota.* Minneapolis, Hale, 1931. 196 p. il.

Lowe, Barrett. *Twenty Million Acres; The Story of America's First Conservationist, William Henry Harrison Beadle.* Mitchell, Educator Supply Co., 1937. 465 p. il.

Putney, E. F. *In the South Dakota Country.* Mitchell, Educator Supply Co., 1922. 2 vols. il.

Ransom, Frank L. *The Sunshine State.* Mitchell, Educator Supply Co., 1922. 159 p. il.

Robinson, Doane. *Brief History of South Dakota.* A school history. New York, American Book Co., 1926. 232 p. il.

Robinson, Doane. *History of South Dakota.* Chicago, Bowen, 1904. 2 vols. il.

Robinson, Doane. *History of South Dakota.* Chicago, American Historical Society, Inc., 1930. 3 vols. il.

Rosen, Peter. *Pa-ha-sa-pa,* or *The Black Hills of South Dakota.* St. Louis, Nixon, 1895. 645 p. il.

South Dakota. Department of History. *South Dakota Historical Collections, compiled by the State Historical Society.* Historical documents, and articles pertaining to South Dakota history. Vol. 1-18. A valuable series; a volume is issued every two years.

South Dakota Historical Society. *South Dakota Historical Review.* A quarterly magazine. Oct., 1935.

South Dakota State School of Mines. *Black Hills Engineer, Semi-Centennial Number.* Rapid City, South Dakota State School of Mines, 1924. 82 p. il.

Sutley, Zack T. *Last Frontier.* New York, Macmillan, 1930. 350 p.

Taber, Clarence Wilbur. *Breaking Sod on the Prairie.* Yonkers-on-Hudson, World Book Company, 1924. 292 p. il.

Tallent, Annie D. *The Black Hills, The Last Hunting Ground of the Dakotahs.* St. Louis, Nixon, 1899. 713 p. il.

Van de Water, Frederic F. *Glory-Hunter; a Life of General Custer.* Indianapolis, Bobbs-Merrill, 1934. 394 p. il.

b. Early Settlement

Aikman, Duncan. *Calamity Jane and the Other Lady Wildcats.* New York, Holt, 1927. 347 p. il.

Aken, David. *Pioneers of the Black Hills, or Gordon's Stockade Party of 1874.* 151 p. il.

Bennett, Estelline. *Old Deadwood Days.* New York, Scribner, 1928. 300 p. il.

Brown, Jesse and Willard, A.M. *The Black Hills Trails.* A history of the Black Hills region. Rapid City. Rapid City Journal, 1924. 572 p. il.

Chittenden, Capt. Hiram Martin. *History of the American Fur Trade of the Far West.* New York, Press of the Pioneers, 1935. 2 vols.

Chittenden, Capt. Hiram Martin. *History of Early Steamboat Navigation on the Missouri River.* New York, Francis P. Harper, 1903. 2 vols.

Connelly, William Elsey. *Wild Bill and His Era.* A standard work dealing with the life and times of James Butler "Wild Bill" Hickok. New York, Press of the Pioneers, 1933. 229 p. il.

Coursey, O. W. *A Complete Biographical Sketch of General William Henry Harrison Beadle.* Mitchell, Educator Supply Co., 1916. 99 p. il.

Coursey, O. W. *Biography of Senator Alfred Beard Kittredge, His Complete Life Work.* Mitchell, Educator Supply Co., 1915. 224 p. il.

Coursey, O. W. (compiler and editor). *The First Woman in the Black Hills. As Told by Herself, Mrs. Annie D. Tallent.* Mitchell, Educator Supply Co., 1923. 181 p. front.

Coursey, O. W. *Wild Bill (James Butler Hickok).* Mitchell, Educator Supply Co., 1924. 80 p. il.

Custer, Mrs. Elizabeth Bacon. *"Boots and Saddles"; or, Life in Dakota with General Custer.* New York, Harper, 1885. 312 p. il.

Dye, Eva Emery. *The Conquest. The True Story of Lewis and Clark.* Chicago, McClurg, 1903. 443 p. front.

Finerty, John F. *War-Path and Bivouac, or the Conquest of the Sioux.* Chicago, Donohue, 1890. 460 p. il.

Hanson, Joseph Mills. *Conquest of the Missouri, Being the Story of the Life and Exploits of Captain Grant Marsh.* Chicago, McClurg, 1909. 458 p. il.

Irving, Washington. *Astoria.* New York, Putnam, 1902. 519 p. il.

King, Capt. Charles. *Campaigning with Crook; and Stories of Army Life*. New York, Harper, 1890. 295 p. il.

Kingsbury, G. W. *History of Dakota Territory*. Chicago, Clarke Publishing Co., 1915. 5 vols. il.

Rapid City Journal. *Holiday Greeting from Rapid City*. Rapid City, Rapid City Journal, 1915. 148 p. il.

Reese, John B. *Some Pioneers and Pilgrims on the Prairies of Dakota, or From the Ox Team to the Aeroplane*. Mitchell, Author, 1920. 94 p. il.

Rhoads, William. *Recollections of Dakota Territory*. Pierre, State Publishing Co., 1931. 52 p.

Stokes, George W. *Deadwood Gold*. History of early gold mining in the northern Black Hills. Yonkers-on-Hudson, World Book Co., 1926. 163 p. il.

Torrey, E. C. *Early Days in Dakota*. Minneapolis, Farnham Printing and Stationery Co., 1925.

Vestal, Stanley. *Mountain Men*. Boston, Houghton Mifflin, 1937. 296 p. il.

Waldo, Edna LaMoore, *Dakota. Scenes from Pioneer Days in the Dakotas*. Caldwell, Ida., Caxton Printers, 1936. 459 p.

Wilstach, Frank J. *Wild Bill Hickok; the Prince of Pistoleers*. Garden City, Doubleday, 1928. 304 p. il.

c. Statehood and Government

Atherton, Loren G. *The Government of South Dakota, State and Local*. Pierre, Olander, 1927. 328 p.

Johnson, Willis E. *South Dakota, A Republic of Friends*. Mitchell, Educator Supply Co., 1923. 334 p. il.

Johnson, Willis E. *The State and Nation*. Mitchell, Educator Supply Co., 1922. 273 p. il.

Smith, G. M. and Young, C. M. *History and Government of South Dakota*. New York, American Book Co., 1913. 339 p.

AGRICULTURE

South Dakota. State Planning Board. *Agricultural Resources: a Preliminary Report*. Brooking, 1935-1936.

South Dakota. State Planning Board. *Land Ownership in South Dakota*. Brookings, 1937. 176 p.

South Dakota. State Planning Board. *Noxious Weeds in South Dakota*. Brookings, 1937. 38 p.

South Dakota. State Planning Board. *Selenium Problems in South Dakota.* Brookings, 1937. 30 p.

Byers, Horace G. *Selenium Occurrence in Certain Soils in the United States with a Discussion of Related Topics.* U. S. Dept. of Agriculture. Technical Bulletin No. 482. August, 1935.

TRANSPORTATION

South Dakota. State Planning Board. *Transportation in South Dakota.* Brookings, 1937. 2 vols.

RACIAL ELEMENTS AND FOLKLORE

Shephard, Esther. *Paul Bunyan.* Collection of Paul Bunyan folk tales. New York, Harcourt, 1924.

EDUCATION AND RELIGION

Coursey, O. W. *A History of Dakota Wesleyan University for Fifty Years* (1885-1935). Mitchell, Dakota Wesleyan University, 1935. il.

Durand, George Harrison. *Joseph Ward of Dakota.* A biography. Boston, Pilgrim Press, 1913. 252 p. il.

Howe, M.A. De Wolfe. *Life and Labors of Bishop Hare, Apostle to the Sioux.* New York, Sturgis & Walton, 1911. 417 p. il.

Kraushaar, R. W. and others. *Studies in South Dakota Education.* South Dakota Historical Collections, Vol. XVIII, 638 p. il.

McMurtry, William John. *Yankton College, A Historical Sketch.* Yankton, 1907. 160 p.

Powers, W. H. *History of South Dakota State College.* Brookings, South Dakota State College, 1931. 146 p. il.

South Dakota. State Planning Board. *Elementary and Secondary Education in South Dakota.* Brookings, 1937. 165 p.

Stewart, Edgar I. *Yankton College, The Second Twenty-five Years.* Yankton, 1932. 220 p.

LITERATURE

Boyles, Kate and Virgil D. *Langford of the Three Bars.* Chicago, McClurg, 1907. 278 p. il.

Boyles, Kate and Virgil D. *The Homesteaders.* Chicago, McClurg, 1909. 346 p. il.

Burleigh, B. W. and Wenzlaff, G. G. *A Book of Dakota Rhymes.* Yankton, Yankton Printing Co., 1907. 168 p.

Carr, Robert V. *Black Hills Ballads.* Denver, Reed Publishing Co., 1902. 175 p. front.

Clark, Anna Morris. *Sylvia of the Hills.* Custer, Chronicle Shop, 1936. 140 p. il.

Clark, Badger. *Skylines and Wood Smoke.* Custer, Chronicle Shop, 1935. 73 p.

Clark, Badger. *Spike.* Boston, Badger, 1925. 215 p. il.

Clark, Badger. *Sun and Saddle Leather including "Grass Grown Trails" and new Poems.* Boston, Richard G. Badger, 1922. 221 p. il.

Coursey, O. W. *Literature of South Dakota.* Mitchell, Educator Supply Co., 1916. 201 p. il.

Fargo, Lucile F. *Prairie Girl.* New York, Dodd, Mead, 1937.

Federal Writers' Project. *Hamlin Garland, Memorial Dedication.* Pierre, Federal Writers' Project, 1936. 12 p.

Federal Writers' Project. *MSS (Manuscripts).* Pierre and Custer, South Dakota Writers' League, 1936-37. 8 issues. il.

Garland, Hamlin. *A Daughter of the Middle Border.* New York, Macmillan, 1921. 405 p.

Garland, Hamlin. *Afternoon Neighbors. Further Excerpts from a Literary Log.* New York, Macmillan, 1934. 589 p. front.

Garland, Hamlin. *Back-trailers from the Middle Border.* New York, Macmillan, 1928. 379 p. il.

Garland, Hamlin. *Main Traveled Roads.* New York, Harper, 1930. 377 p.

Garland, Hamlin. *Prairie Folks.* New York, Macmillan, 1899. 283 p.

Garland, Hamlin. *A Son of the Middle Border.* New York, Macmillan, 1928. 467 p. front.

Gates, Mary. *Out of This Nettle.* New York, Crowell, 1936.

Gilfillan, Archer B. *A Shepherd's Holiday.* Collection of humorous sketches. Custer, Chronicle Shop, 1936. 39 p. il.

Gilfillan, Archer B. *Sheep.* A modern treatment of an ancient industry. Boston, Little, Brown, 1929. 276 p. il.

Harris, Kennett. *Meet Mr. Stegg.* Black Hills stories. New York, Holt, 1920. 320 p. front.

Hueston, Ethel. *Blithe Baldwin.* Indianapolis, Bobbs-Merrill, 1933. 320 p.

Hueston, Ethel. *Good Times.* Indianapolis, Bobbs-Merrill Co., 1932. 315 p.

Hueston, Ethel. *Calamity Jane.* Indianapolis, Bobbs-Merrill, 1937.

Kirk, Murray Ketcham. *The Beacon Light and Other Poems.* New York, Vinal, 1927. 66 p.

Lane, Rose Wilder. *Let the Hurricane Roar.* New York, Longmans, 1933. 152 p. front.

Lillibridge, Will. *The Dissolving Circle.* New York, Dodd, Mead, 1907. 314 p. front.

Lillibridge, Will. *Where the Trail Divides.* Chicago, Burt, 1907. 302 p. front.

Lindberg, J. C. (editor). *Fifteen South Dakota Poets.* New York, Harrison, 1930. 96 p.

Lindberg, J. C. & Gunderson, Gertrude B. *An Anthology of South Dakota Poetry.* Mitchell, Educator Supply Co., 1928. Second Anthology, 1935.

McNeely, Marian Hurd. *The Jumping-Off Place.* New York, Longmans, 1930. 308 p. il.

Neihardt, John G. *Song of Hugh Glass.* New York, Macmillan, 1915.

Neihardt, John G. *The Splendid Wayfaring.* A trip down the Missouri River. New York, Macmillan, 1920. 290 p. il.

Palmer, Roy. *Marie of Circle A.* Boston, Meader, 1928.

Patton, Don. *The Bunch Quitter.* Philadelphia, Macrae, 1935.

Pendexter, Hugh. *Pay Gravel.* Indianapolis, Bobbs-Merrill, 1923. 353 p. front.

Richardson, Mabel K. *Killdeer.* Philadelphia, Dorrance, 1936. 97 p.

Rolvaag, O. E. *Giants in the Earth.* New York, Harper, 1927. 465 p.

Rolvaag, O. E. *Peder Victorious.* New York, Harper, 1929. 350 p.

Rolvaag, O. E. *Their Fathers' God.* New York, Harper, 1931. 338 p.

White, Stewart Edward. *Gold.* Garden City, Doubleday, 1913. 449 p.

White, Stewart Edward. *The Claim Jumpers.* New York, McClure, 1901. 284 p.

White, Stewart Edward. *The Westerners.* New York, Doubleday, 1917. 344 p. front.

SPORTS AND RECREATION

South Dakota. State Planning Board. *Recreation in South Dakota.* Brookings, 1936. 184 p.

CITIES

Case, Francis, et al. *Black Hills Engineer. Hot Springs Number.* Rapid City, South Dakota State School of Mines, 1928. 97 p. il.

Clark, Badger. *When Hot Springs Was a Pup.* Hot Springs, Kiwanis Club, 1927. 53 p. il.

Federal Writers' Project. *Guide to Pierre, The Capital City and Vicinity.* Pierre, City of Pierre and Chamber of Commerce, 1937. 24 p. il.

Federal Writers' Project. *Pioneer Mitchell.* Mitchell, Parent-Teachers Association of Mitchell, 1937. 16 p. il.

BLACK HILLS RECREATIONAL AREA

Anonymous. *Black Hills, South Dakota.* Casper, Wyo., Prairie Publishing Co., 1937. 32 p. il.

Baldwin, George P. (editor). *Black Hills Illustrated.* (Edited for Black Hills Mining Men's Association). 207 p. il.

Coursey, O. W. *Beautiful Black Hills.* Mitchell, Educator Supply Co., 1926. 265 p. il.

Federal Writers' Project. *Vacation Guide to Custer State Park.* Custer State Park Board, 1937. 36 p. il.

Lange, Dietrich. *The Lure of the Black Hills.* Boston, Lothrop, 1916.

O'Harra, Cleophas C. and Connolly, Joseph P. *The Geology, Mineralogy, and Scenic Features of Custer State Park, South Dakota.* Rapid City, South Dakota State School of Mines, 1926. 242 p. il.

Price, Sam Goodale. *Black Hills, the Land of Legend.* Los Angeles, DeVoras, 1935.

Sanford, Rev. John I. (compiler). *The Black Hills Souvenir, A Pictorial and Historic Description of the Black Hills.* Denver, Williamson-Hafner, 1902. 222 p. il.

U. S. Department of Agriculture, Forest Service. *National Forests of the Black Hills of South Dakota and Wyoming.* Washington, Governmetn Printing Office, 1935. 48 p. il.

General Reference

Coursey, O. W. *Who's Who in South Dakota.* Mitchell, Educator Supply Co., 1916.

Fox, Lawrence K. *Fox's Who's Who Among South Dakotans.* Pierre, Statewide Service Co., 1924-28. 2 vols.

Robinson, Doane. *Doane Robinson's Encyclopedia of South Dakota.* Pierre, Robinson, 1925. 1003 p.

INDEX